ECONOMIC THEORY
AND METHOD

ECONOMIC THEORY AND METHOD

by

F. ZEUTHEN

HARVARD UNIVERSITY PRESS
CAMBRIDGE MASSACHUSETTS
1965

Published throughout the world except the United States
by Longmans, Green & Co. Ltd.

First published 1955
Second impression (with minor corrections) 1957
Third impression 1965

Printed in Great Britain by
Lowe and Brydone (Printers) Limited, London, N.W.10

PREFACE

THIS book is a translation of my Danish book *Økonomisk Teori og Metode* (Nyt Nordisk Forlag, Copenhagen, 1942) thoroughly revised and considerably enlarged.

I once more thank Professor Carl Iversen, University of Copenhagen Professor Erik Lindahl, University of Uppsala, and Professor Erich Schneider, formerly University of Aarhus and now University of Kiel, for their kind revision of the manuscript of the original Danish edition. Further, I thank Mr. Bjarke Fog, Copenhagen Graduate School of Business Administration, and Mr. T. W. Hutchison, of the London School of Economics, for reading parts of the manuscript, Dr. Hans Brems, now of the University of California, Berkeley, for assistance in revision of the manuscript, Mr. Nørregaard Rasmussen, University of Copenhagen for writing the last part of Chapter 39, Mr. Alan T. Peacock, Reader of Public Finance, London School of Economics, for some valuable suggestions and not least Mr. Peacock, Professor Edward H. Chamberlin, Harvard University, and Professor Machlup, Johns Hopkins University, for their friendly cooperation in arranging for the publication of the book. I also thank Mr. Maitland for his assistance in proof-reading and in compiling the index.

The translation has been performed by my wife, Else Zeuthen, to whom I also am very thankful, and it was at an early stage revised by Professor Harold M. Somers of the University of Buffalo, U.S.A., to whom I am very grateful for his able corrections and valuable suggestions. I also gratefully acknowledge the financial assistance of the Rask-Ørsted Foundation, which has made a grant covering a part of the expenses of the translation. The author alone is responsible for the form and substance of the contents of this book.

January 1954   F. ZEUTHEN

CONTENTS

PART ONE

METHOD AND THEORIES

PART TWO

ECONOMIC LIFE—A NETWORK OF PARTIAL INTERDEPENDENCES

vii

PART THREE

DYNAMICS

PART FOUR

FORMS OF MARKET AND STRUCTURE OF SOCIETY

B

FIGURES

PART ONE

METHOD AND THEORIES

CHAPTER 1

AIM OF THE BOOK

ECONOMICS is an unfinished science. It is, therefore, too early to confine one's self to one definite system of dogmas and one definite method. The practical problems are so manifold and are changing so fast that a collection of ready answers, however useful, would never suffice. Thus it becomes necessary to resort to the famous economic tool-box. To be sure, the standardized instruments in our tool-box are not always adequate to the complexities of the real world. But working with economic tools and models provides a training, an orientation, a marshalling of problems, which may be useful in the treatment of most actual cases, however complex. The trained economist must be able to make his own tools and must be willing to discard them without misgivings.

This book does not aim at providing a summary of the most important contributions that have been made by economics towards the solution of practical problems. Essentially, the purpose is only to treat one type of contributions: those of economic *theory*. By these are meant those deductions from practical experience which, as a rule, are of a comparatively general and easily accessible character. The other, and no less valuable, tools of economics are statistical data, the special experiences of history and real life, which vary greatly according to time and place, and the statistical methods which must be used for the analysis of the data. Since theorizing of the kind to be found in this book forms only part of the work and interests of economists, non-economists and, perhaps, philosophically minded readers should not be induced to believe that economics consists only of deductive abstractions.

Economic theory must be flexible and varied in order to satisfy different assumptions as to the structure of societies and markets. At the same time it must consist of a number of special branches relevant to different spheres of economic life, as, for example, the theory of production, the formation of price for individual commodities, money and credit, foreign trade, wages, and interest. When theory is specialized in this way, a host of special experiences, differentiated as to time and place, enter as components into the theoretical analysis.

An important subject, however, is the relation between theories having different alternative assumptions, and the relation between the special theories dealing with different spheres of problems. The common sphere, or connecting link, is what has, somewhat grandiosely, been called "central" or "general" theory. To avoid internal contradiction as well as loose eclecticism or vague compromise, it is necessary to have a central

3

theory, with clear and firm connections in all directions, and at the same time a theory which can stand up under the use of different real assumptions in larger or smaller segments of the system as a whole.

Parts II and III of this book may be characterized as central or general theory. Great importance is attached to a brief indication of how the special theories, which are not subjected to detailed treatment here, are connected with those parts of economic theory that are discussed at some length. The selection and relative emphasis on the various subjects included in this work are, perhaps, arbitrary and partly dependent on the special interests of the author. As an argument in favor of making Part IV, "Forms of Market and the Structure of Society," relatively comprehensive, the following statement from a book by the Danish economist, L. V. Birck, may be quoted: "The day may come when the theory of monopolistic price-determination dealing with the many possible types of exploitation will become so extensive as to fill a volume as thick as a Bible, particularly if distribution under monopoly and the finance of monopoly are also to be included in it. Then the condition of the free market will be regarded as a significant exception for purposes of propaedeutic study as a means to understanding the prevailing forms of monopolistic markets."[1]

The effects of state intervention, in spite of their overwhelming importance nowadays, have been dealt with quite briefly in this volume on economic theory. The economics of public policy would call for a more concrete treatment adjusted to profoundly changing conditions. Moreover, a narrowly economic treatment of problems of economic policy is likely to be less useful because of interaction between economic conditions and *political* action.

It is true that monetary theory and price and distribution theory should not be dealt with as two separate sciences. But unless one is interested mainly in short-run phenomena, it is misleading to place money in the center of a general theory. Contrary to the pattern of Keynes' *General Theory of Employment, Interest and Money*, these phenomena, which are elsewhere subjected to a comprehensive and excellent treatment, are here dealt with only briefly, mainly to emphasize their connection with the other parts of economic theory. As will appear from what follows, this does not mean a relapse to what Keynes calls "classical theory", in the sense of the theory of the traditional English school.

It seems practical to consider the economic world, like the physical world, as one big continuum, where each particle has a close connection with certain other particles, from which connections spread like a network or chain. This all-pervading interdependence in the economic world is not vague and uncertain, but consists of definite and demonstrable links such as demand and costs. If we begin with a simply constructed system, for example, a model like the equations of Walras, we may then extend

[1] L. V. Birck, *Den Økonomiske Virksomhed*, Gads Forlag, Copenhagen, 1918, p. 277. Cf. the English edition: *The Theory of the Marginal Value*, Routledge, London, 1922, p. 292.

or rebuild the system by including fresh assumptions, *e.g.*, dynamic or monopolistic assumptions, that is, by changing the form of some of the links in the interdependent network. Theories for the various special spheres of economics may in this way be linked up with the central theory. In analyzing economic interdependence, it is possible, just as in physics, either to deal with individual particles or, by summation, to consider larger groups.

Economics in its entirety comprises only one sphere or system of the universe which, necessarily, is connected with many other spheres or systems. Even if we only want an explanation with regard to a limited number of variables, such as prices, quantities of goods, and income, we are led in our search for an explanation to other magnitudes and conditions of quite different kinds when we get to the frontiers of economics: natural conditions, technology, the physical and mental qualities of human beings, social institutions and unique historical phenomena. Since coherence and agreement are aimed at in all scientific explanations, the delimitation of a science like economics can only be a practical form of division of labor where this can be done without detriment, as a preliminary orientation and in order to facilitate work. In some investigations it often appears wise to draw different boundaries, so that particular economic questions may be studied together with certain other problems.

The purpose of economics is, to a great extent, a practical one: to enable people to forecast or influence economic activity. To this must be added the purely intellectual satisfaction of understanding, *i.e.*, of seeing the connection between economic conditions and the connection between these and other conditions, such as technology, human institutions, etc. From another point of view we may say that it is very largely a question of solving practical and theoretical problems of a special nature. The aim may, moreover, be to attain a more or less comprehensive understanding of economic life as a whole. This may partly serve as an orientation in the solution of special problems; partly it satisfies idle curiosity. In our own time, however, the understanding of economic life as a whole is looked upon with great scepticism. It will be understood that fixed systems, giving a comparatively simple solution to all problems, cannot be expected to be applicable, especially under present conditions, where the structure of society and, consequently, the forms of economic life, *e.g.*, the degree of monopoly and competition or state interference, are subject to constant and great changes and are completely different as between the different parts of economic life in a single country. The understanding of economic life as a whole must, therefore, be of the above-mentioned elastic type, a framework or a method of putting together the separate frames so that different special pictures may be inserted.

In any case, one must be prepared for the necessity of later replacing the pictures, not only as a consequence of fresh facts and fresh assumptions, but also, as has very largely been the case earlier in the history of economics, because it becomes apparent that the previous work has been done in an unsatisfactory way. The theories are hypotheses, drafts useful for later work, but not infallible and unchangeable laws. Consequently, an essential part of economics is verification of hypotheses. Only a few examples, however, are given in this book.

There is reason for thinking that considerable parts of economic theory owe their existence to the fact that certain hypotheses by repetition have become venerable dogmas. Gunnar Myrdal finds that teaching probably does more harm to professors than to students, "because the professor teaches year after year and often in the end believes what he himself preaches, after which he is, of course, lost to science". In the case of students, who are not inoculated by wide and varied economic reading, there seems nevertheless to be a considerable danger of their accepting the abstract points of view and the imaginary constructions without the necessary reservations and believing in their direct applicability to real life. We may in this connection recall the statement of Epictetus, the Stoic philosopher: "Sheep do not bring back grass to the shepherds to show them how much they have eaten, but assimilate it and yield wool and milk as a result. You must do the same. Show the layman not philosophical theorems but action springing from their assimilation." What is aimed at is, in other words, a useful preparatory mental exercise, giving a training enabling the economist to create the method required by concrete cases rather than supplying ready answers or finished methods applicable to concrete cases. To these warnings against a too direct and dogmatic application of theory, we may add, on the other hand, that a banning of systematic scientific thinking will unavoidably give room to unsystematic, personal, and often perhaps self-interested phantasies. It is self-delusion to think that common sense or experience alone can give a correct understanding of the complicated interdependence of economic life. Therefore, perhaps the most useful quality of professional and systematic economic theory is that it forms an antidote against all the wrong theories, which are passed off as practical understanding or personal interpretation of facts.

CHAPTER 2

THE ROAD TO KNOWLEDGE

At the end of the last century there was in Germany and in other countries a great deal of discussion concerning the method of political economy. The historical school criticized the large amount of space which deduction, based on simple assumptions, took up in classical economics. Even if most economists now agree that we need both methods: to procure a great many facts and a considerable amount of deduction, the controversy is renewed from time to time, when one-sided, or apparently one-sided, pleas excite the always combative economists or philosophers holding the opposite points of view. A certain brotherly rivalry will, moreover, always be present on account of the human inclination to emphasize the part of the common work for which one has one's self the greatest aptitude. It is, of course, wrong when youthful, enthusiastic, and kind-hearted people blindly admire what they are not able to do themselves and are not, as a rule, able to understand. But it is in no way better when people with the opposite characteristics automatically despise or show contempt for work that does not fall within the scope of their own faculties or special interests. The ideal arrangement is division of labor and cooperation without pride or prejudice.

The problem of method, however, is not a special problem for economists. The methods of acquiring knowledge and proofs of its truth must, on the contrary, be common to all science. Economists have also sought guidance in philosophy. But philosophy having developed at a rapid rate, older or modern philosophical tendencies, which were in vogue for a certain time, may have manifested themselves rather strongly among economists.

According to a certain philosophical school that cannot be said to be one-sided, as its very name, "logical empiricism", implies and which may be regarded as the continuation of many other schools of philosophy,[1] we have a sharp distinction between two kinds of statements: the analytical, following from the meaning of the words and the logic of the language; and the synthetic, saying something about reality.

The analytical sentences are in the nature of definitions or they are deductive conclusions arrived at by the treatment of other sentences, according to the rules of logic. Whether a deduction is true or not is decided according to purely formal rules and is independent of the truth of the sentences from which the conclusion has been drawn. For instance, if A as well as B is true, the possibility of *either* A *or* B being valid is excluded. Another example is the identity, $47^6 = 10779215329$. These are tautologies. They are true irrespective of the truth of A and B and irrespective of whether in the calculation we had had the meaningless denomination, "existing Utopias". The result contains nothing new, which is not to be found in the assumptions; but it may possibly give the same real content in a few form, which gives us a new and more satisfactory understanding. Formally, by logical operations of this kind, *i.e.*, by tautologies, we obtain sentences which are always and necessarily formally "true". Whether the result and the conclusions are *really* true, however, depends on the reality of the assumptions on which we have built. Similarly, it is a question of fact whether the chosen definitions are of practical value.

---

[1] Georg Henrik von Wright, *Den logiska Empirismen*, Natur och Kultur, Stockholm, 1943; Eino Kaila, *Den Mänskliga Kunskapen*, Söderström, Helsingfors, 1939; Jørgen Jørgensen, "Den logiske Empirismes Udvikling", Copenhagen, 1948— English translation, "The Development of Logical Empiricism" in *Encyclopedia of Unified Science*, Chicago University Press, 1949.

Statements with regard to reality are arrived at by concrete observation. Where there may be doubt as to actual conditions, great importance must be attached to an exact description, with an indication of time, place, and the person who has made the observation, and possibly such external or personal conditions concerning the observation as may have led to errors.

The condition for the scientific character of a statement is that it can be verified by others; it must be open to "intersubjective tests". "In general, truth cannot be scientific unless it is demonstrable, which means it must be alike for all observers and accurately communicable."[2]

From observation of individual cases, one derives general laws by induction. It is characteristic of statements about reality, as opposed to deductions which follow the rules of logic, that they can be imagined to be proved false. This is a consequence of their saying something beyond the rules of logic which we did not know in advance. Especially the induction from a series of individual cases to a general law may always be imagined to be falsified by new observations. The laws arrived at are consequently only hypotheses. Also the statistical laws saying that there is a definite probability of the occurrence of a definite event may be changed by new observations.

If statements about reality are to have a meaning, and if they are not direct statements as to individual observations, it must be possible, by means of logical transformations to translate them at least into possible observations. There must be a possibility of verifying their reality or the reality of their consequences. In a rationalized theory, as, for instance, in micro-physics, it is still not considered necessary to be able to translate each individual statement into the language of reality, if only verification of a certain complex of statements is possible. In this connection we may also quote Paul Samuelson: "By a meaningful theorem I mean simply a hypothesis about empirical data which could conceivably be refuted, if only under ideal conditions."[3]

Statements from which there does not follow anything that can be imagined to be observable in reality, but which nevertheless pretend to say something about it, must according to a positivistic terminology be conceived of as metaphysical misuse of the language. In economics, for instance, this applies to statements about utility, if one does not at the same time indicate a method of measurement. Nevertheless, even if the aim is to achieve objective measurability and establish definitions of concepts taken from the technique of observation (operational concepts), it may very well be necessary and practical to begin by speaking about things in the sometimes rather "mysterious" language of daily life, in order to signify what one is aiming at.

Direct or indirect measurability (or the possibility of other factual testing) is a necessary condition for the avoidance of mystery, where everyone

---

[2] Frank Knight, "Limitation of Scientific Method in Economics", in the collection, *The Trend of Economics*, edit. by R. G. Tugwell, 1924.
[3] *Foundations of Economic Analysis*, Harvard University Press, 1948, p. 4.

may have his own ideas as to the same words. Scientific statements about reality must be verifiable by others. As Hutchison[4] says, they must "conceivably be capable of empirical testing or be reducible to such propositions by logical or mathematical deductions". If there is no conceivable possibility of proving if an assertion is right, it is of a mystical character.

Understanding of phenomena depends on the finding of regularities, uniform qualities about the things or the relations between them. Then, on the basis of one's observations, one sets forth theories, giving systems with the simplest possible assumptions, from which the actual conditions within a certain sphere can be deduced. This means, in other words, that one gets a comprehensible knowledge about things.

In economics one will often attach importance to certain quantitative properties and relations, such as magnitudes and price. These are fully capable of description in formulae or figures, but without the multitude of other attributes to be found in real life. If we undertake such a formalization, we shall be better able to draw conclusions from the said quantitative properties, often in themselves very complicated. If one does not in this way facilitate the work for one's self, but tries to find the quantitative connection at the same time as one thinks about all the other properties of the things, such as all the individual characteristics of persons or subjects involved, it becomes difficult both for one's self and for others to control which conditions are included in the original and with what weight; it is also difficult to determine whether or not emotions have influenced the result. As an advantage of the strictly formal way of expression, Morgenstern emphasizes that it makes away with the obscurities and contradictions inherent in "the material mode of expression". "Only in the formal mode of expression is it possible to test whether a statement really is a consequence of another and what is meant hereby."[5] Formalization means, among other things, that one works with distinct and explicit assumptions.

The order of procedure in scientific investigations is, as a rule, the following: a preliminary orientation on the basis of the experiences and problems of daily life, a rationalization of concepts, by which preliminary investigations of reality are undertaken, new empirical investigations and the drawing of conclusions on the basis of these, and, finally, verification of the conclusions. On the whole, it is a question of interplay, a movement to and fro, by which a revision is undertaken of preliminarily formed concepts, according to the experiences encountered.[6] The quantity of work may be very unevenly distributed among the different forms of work,

[4] T. W. Hutchison, *The Significance and Basic Postulates of Economic Theory*, Macmillan, London, 1938, p. 9.
[5] Oskar Morgenstern, "Logistik und Sozialwissenschaften", *Zeitschrift für Nationalökonomie*, 1936.
[6] Milton Friedman in his *Essays in Positive Economics*, Chicago University Press, 1953, argues against being satisfied with realistic assumptions and prefers the final proof that predictions are not (too often) contradicted. See also his comment and Richard Ruggles' article in *Survey of Contemporary Economics*, vol. II, 1952.

according to the character of the material and the stage of the investigation. In trying to solve the urgent questions of daily life one must confine one's self to a rather indefinite mixture of references to diverse observations and conclusions. It is necessary in theoretical scientific work to make clear what propositions express observations and are consequently premises for the conclusions, and what are only conclusions, which can say nothing beyond the premises.

At any rate, within a science so practical as economics, it will surely be possible to be satisfied with the following preliminary definition, given by my countryman, Jørgen Jørgensen: "By the word 'science' I shall provisionally (*i.e.*, as a first—and in this connection sufficient—approximation) understand systems of sentences, which after application of generally recognized methods of control by well-trained scientists are considered to be true (or at least well founded) and which are arranged (or at least arrangeable) according to certain principles (generally called 'logical principles')." The somewhat vague expression, "well trained", if it is going to be further determined, must no doubt be understood in connection with the strict demands of the philosophers outlined at the beginning of this chapter. As may be seen, the definition refers to actual conditions, but it seems, however, worth while to discuss how it is possible to improve scientists themselves.

CHAPTER 3

MATERIAL AND METHOD IN ECONOMICS

As mentioned above, economists must make use of the ordinary scientific methods. However, the special conditions within the area under consideration must influence the extent to which collection of observations, deduction and verification are needed and possible. That perhaps 90 per cent of this book—just as the philosophical works of some keen empiricists are of a deductive-analytic character—cannot convey to people, knowing the actual distribution of work within economics, a false impression of the character of this science.

It would seem natural to ask whether economics should not follow the example of the successful natural sciences, and whether it is not due to incompetence that our science has not attained the same results. Should it not be possible within the economic sphere to find simple constants, corresponding to the specific gravity of metals and simple laws of reaction and formulae, corresponding to the law of gravity and other physical laws?

Even if it is clear that the economic problems are essentially of a quantitative nature, *i.e.*, concern quantities and the connections between them, conditions are still far less simple within economic theory and politics than within natural sciences and technology. The material with which we work is far less homogeneous. Reduction to some few elementary quantities and units of measurement is not possible, and, what is almost worst of all, the lack of homogeneity appears in the course of time as lack of constancy with regard to the properties of things and the behavior of people.

Whereas it is possible with great exactness to predict the physical and chemical reactions of 1 kilogram of iron or gold, it is far more difficult to predict the economic reactions of a producer, a consumer, or a commodity price. We do not find the same homogeneity and stability for given types. If we have observed certain properties, we cannot, as in the physical sciences, infer that a number of other properties must be present.[1] We cannot reckon with a standardized "economic man" with a constant behavior. We have rather to reckon with different types according to time and social position or a distribution within the groups, which possibly in certain periods may be represented by averages.

The number of commodity qualities is immense and, owing to gradual transition, indefinite. Moreover, localization and time are of importance for the valuation of commodities and services. Individuality is especially conspicuous with regard to aggregates as enterprises or real property. Particularly in the case of intellectual and entrepreneurial work, the different services have a strongly individual stamp.

A recalculation to a common unit of measurement, *e.g.*, physical units of energy, cannot be relevant, of course, since the same quantity of energy has a quite different economic importance, *e.g.*, in a waterfall in Greenland and in the fingers of a watchmaker. Neither is the value in money in all cases a constant and relevant standard of measurement. And finally, there is no possibility of applying the measure which is the essential thing in human economy: the satisfaction of wants, utility, or the like, as an objective unit. (Cf. Part II, Chapter 19.2.)

Another difficulty with regard to setting up laws applicable to economic factors is that not only are the qualitative aspects within the groups of things and services changing, but also the paths of reaction followed. Under a given technique of production we have constant physical and chemical regularities, but as soon as we get to the animals and plants used in production, changes and adjustments take place as a result of the changing conditions. The problem is considerably more difficult with regard to labor, where the result is dependent not only on nutrition, housing, and working hours, but also on the culture and educational level of the society as well as on political and other attitudes.

But worst of all there is the difficulty that also the functions which can be set down, *e.g.*, for the quantity demanded, as dependent on price,

---

[1] Frank Knight, "Limitation of Scientific Method in Economics", and F.C.Mills, "On Measurements in Economics", both in the volume, *The Trend of Economics*, 1924.

income, time of adaptation, etc., are shifted according to the condition of the whole of the surrounding society. If merely the salary of school-masters is changed or the importation of wine is prohibited, a change in the demand curve, *e.g.*, for shoes, may follow. Thus, the figures and rela-tions to be found from statistics do not indicate constant regularities but are only the result of historically and locally conditioned observations. Since so many great and small conditions simultaneously influence the quantity demanded, there can be no question of finding a simple and cor-rect formula for demand, but only of finding the most usable approxima-tions under specified conditions. It is we ourselves, moreover, who deter-mine to which formula or type or curve we will try to find the best possible approximation in our statistical work. A number of experiences from simi-lar previous cases may, of course, when used in a cautious way, give some guidance with regard to the probable behavior of demand in new cases.

Besides the abstract and displaceable time scale, which is applicable to a series of production processes, or to an abstract calculation of interest, where the starting-point may just as well be the year 1200 or 1900 or 1980, it is necessary in economics, as emphasized by Johan Åkerman, to reckon with the actual historic scale of time, where each period and each year has its special stamp, dependent on the total economic, political and cultural situation ("the calendar scale").

In consideration of this multiplicity, lack of homogeneity and constancy, and susceptibility to all kinds of immaterial forces which are relatively immeasurable and intangible, it might seem tempting to abandon the attempt at building up a theory of causation between economic quantities, and content one's self with an historical, descriptive science. This would mean an aggregation of a heterogeneous mass of facts without much possibility of generalization and without theories giving probable expres-sions of what will happen in the future.

The state of economics is, fortunately, not quite so gloomy as that. The great changing and heterogeneous mass of factual material must be collected, and economists must take it into account. But in addition there also exists a number of phenomena having a considerable degree of regu-larity, for which it would be worth while to find the laws. It is also worth while studying the connection between these laws of a less general nature. The laws are quantitative, because it is a question of connections between measurable, or potentially measurable, quantities, but the heterogeneous, highly mixed and unstable character of the factual material makes it impossible to find constants and simple functions.[2]

[2] Cf. Ewald Schams, "Die Determinierbarkeit des Wirtschaftsgeschehens", *Zeitschrift für Nationalökonomie*, 1934, p. 622. Schams speaks about the economic quantities as variable according to the situation and historically determined. "The economic laws can only be expressed in generally determined (algebraic) magnitudes, but never in actual figures. It is also possible to calculate some figures, *e.g.*, the coeffi-cient of elasticity. When these do not refer to a constant and stable state of economic conditions, they are never generally true and independent of time. They are economic history. Every special quantitative calculation therefore always applies to individual cases."

We cannot expect, for instance, to find a demand curve of the first, second or third degree for a market of a certain size, because the quantity demanded is the sum of the quantities for the individual parts of the market, each of which is determined by its special conditions. It should here be added that, contrary to some authors, I use the word "quantitative" whenever the mathematical nature of the connection between factors can be indicated, *i.e.*, when algebra is applicable, even if a numerical determination of the economic variables and the coefficients which are characteristic of the connections, is not possible. The transition between qualitative and quantitative analyses must here, as in other fields, be gradual. It should also be noted that pure mathematics does not necessarily deal with absolutely fixed quantities; it may deal with "quantities within limits", "sets", etc.

The number of relevant variables that must be taken into consideration in economics is very great, compared with planetary astronomy for instance where the investigation as a rule can be confined to two-body problems. Further, we have in economics a great number of less important variables which it is impossible, separately and accurately, to include in the investigation, and which make economics a stochastical science.

As the behavior of the individual person cannot be predicted, room must be allowed for individual deviations from the average. In so far as it is possible on the whole to reckon with unchanging conditions, one must be content with a statistical knowledge of the behavior of a greater number. This is quite analogous to the corresponding limitation in micro-physics. Where conditions are not unchanging, it is necessary, even where one has a greater number of individual cases, to confine one's self to uncertain expectations.

As a consequence of the nature of economic data, we cannot formulate exact laws applying to real life. Nor can we attain concrete and exact knowledge about economic conditions.[3] Since we do not know all causes, a knowledge of concrete conditions can only be a statistical or probability knowledge (stochastical). A simultaneous appearance of two phenomena gives only a symptomatic knowledge. Therefore, one feels the need of a causal knowledge of the nature of the interdependence. Consequently, among the numerous possible causes one examines those that are supposed to be the most important and considers their isolated effects. In real life this isolation can be realized experimentally in the economic sphere only to a very limited extent. In so far as experiments can be undertaken and the costs involved are not too heavy, the conditions of the experiment will as a rule be so special that the results will rarely be valid for broader spheres.

As in a number of other branches of learning we are faced with the difficulty that the object observed is influenced by the observation. This is true, for instance, in the case of income tax returns which, besides being

---

[3] Alexander Bilimovič, "Zur Verteidigung der Gleichgewichtsidee", *Zeitschrift für Nationalökonomie*, 1937.

C

of scientific interest, are also of importance for tax purposes; social inquiries, in which the persons examined imagine the possibility that the information will affect their individual condition or the social institutions which prevail; as well as investigations of individual firms, where the latter may be interested in concealing either favorable or unfavorable results. In all cases, the person being examined may, moreover, be eager personally to make a favorable impression on the examiner. Experiences must mainly be collected by historical and statistical treatment of the connection between events that have already occurred. This creates great difficulties on account of the great number of the relevant variables, the unstable conditions, etc.

These conditions necessitate partly a continuous collection and arrangement of empirical data and partly, owing to the many simultaneously relevant conditions, the formation of a great number of theories. The latter may be simple abstractions which alternately take small groups of phenomena into consideration or they may be more complicated theories aimed at finding the connection between a greater number of phenomena.

The theories, on one hand, are final results, the usefulness of which depends on the help they render in predicting and controlling the economic conditions. On the other hand, they serve as orientation, "questionnaires", for further empirical investigations. In other scientific spheres we are also forced to use deduction, in spite of the general preference for facts. The most revolutionary parts of modern science use, as is well known, the most complicated and to others entirely incomprehensible theories. But in order to take an illustration from a sphere which we all understand, let us repeat the following conversation from an English detective story:

"'Don't you make Theories as you go along, Pointer?' 'I like finding facts better,' Pointer thought. 'Of course, if you cannot find a fact lying around, you have to fish for it with a theory.' Both men were silent on that; both lost in thought."[4]

How the conception of economics as an empirical, *i.e.*, a logical-empirical, science is compatible with a considerable amount of deduction and theorizing will be apparent from the following statement by O. Lange: "Theoretical economics puts the pattern of uniformity in a coherent system. This is done by presenting the laws of economics as a deductive set of propositions derived by the rules of logic (and of mathematics) from a few basic propositions. The basic propositions are called assumptions or postulates, the derived propositions are called theorems. Theoretical economics thus appears (like all other theoretical sciences) as a deductive science. This, however, does not make it a branch of pure mathematics or logic. Like the rest of economics, economic theory is an empirical science. Its assumptions or postulates are approximative generalizations of empirical observations; *e.g.*, the assumption that business enterprises act so as to maximize their money profit. Some inaccuracy of approximation (*e.g.*, some considerations, like safety, may keep enterprises from

[4] A. Fielding, *The Craig Poisoning Mystery*, p. 65.

maximizing money profit) is accepted for the sake of greater simplicity. The theorems, in turn, are subjected to test by empirical observation. A deductive set of theorems to be subjected to empirical test is also called a theory, hypothesis, or a model. We can thus say that theoretical economics provides hypotheses or models based on generalization of observations and subject to empirical test. Since the assumptions (postulates) under-lying a model are only approximative, the theorems do not correspond directly to results of empirical observations."[5]

On the one hand there is the danger of one-sided theorizing on the basis of unreal premises derived from common-sense conceptions and popular or ideological arm-chair introspection. The accusation is made that one fills out holes in one's empirical knowledge by drawing conclusions from a self-created deductive system, the hypothetical character of which one will be inclined to forget.[6] On the other hand, there is the naïve empiricism which throws itself unsystematically into the mass of empirical material, making laws of, maybe, purely accidental correlations between time-series or inexplicable coincidences. Against such one-sidedness Mackenroth says: "(1) It can never be the aim of economic studies by means of 'theory' to deduce laws about prices and business cycles, etc. That is only possible on the basis of experience. (2) But before every study of facts a special kind of theoretic work is always necessary: to put down an instrumen-torium of conceptions, a system of logically coherent problems to be solved by empiric research." (*"Ableitung eines kategorialen Apparates als eines Systems logisch korrelierter Fragestellungen."*)[7]

Besides the process of deduction in a vacuum and the blind empiricism there is a third danger: that one does not make clear where one method of work ceases and the other begins, passing off theoretical arguments as factual generalizations or in a complicated chain of reasoning letting one's

[5] "The Scope and Method of Economics", *Review of Economic Studies*, Vol. XIII, 1945–46, pp. 20–21.
[6] Svend Ranulf, *Socialvidenskabelig Metodelaere*, Ejnar Munksgaard, Copenhagen, 1946, p. 165. Ranulf maintains that economics is a science the history of which is particularly characterized by hasty and uncritical axiomatizing and gives a detailed criticism of the traditional method of this science, which in his opinion has been described and defended in the Danish edition of my book. By further explanation on certain points and some few minor corrections, I think that I have paid sufficient regard to, and given sufficient answer to this, as far as I can see, mistaken criticism. The little Danish discussion on method may be considered as closed. Cf. the follow-ing statement by Theodor Geiger, which in "Socialvidenskabelig Metodedisku-tion", *Socialt Tidsskrift*, 1946, p. 257, is accepted by Jørgen Jørgensen: "Any scientific observation and investigation of facts assumes certain concepts. . . . A concept, however, does not stand isolated, by itself (for then it has no meaning), but it is a link in a conceptual system. The point, then, is to have a whole set of concepts, covering the sphere of a science, and with such an interrelationship that they form a theoretically coherent and non-contradictory system. The whole of this system, representing an abstract order, in which a field of events is being conceived, is eternally tentative in the sense that it may be overthrown by each step in the investigation of details. But since an investigation of details cannot be started without a set of concepts, it may be reasonable to devote to them a good deal of careful reasoning."
[7] Gerhard Mackenroth, *Theoretische Grundlagen der Preisbildungsforschung und Preispolitik*, Sozialwissenschaftlichen Studien, Berlin, 1933, p. V.

self unconsciously be influenced by facts that are not mentioned or do not concern the matter. In this connection we may refer to the above-mentioned advantage involved in a formalization of the work of reasoning (p. 9).

Whereas economic science must submit to the strict precepts described above and the complete answer with regard to the economic conditions of the present, therefore, can only be given several years later, when all experiences have been collected and tested, and when one has had time to deliberate on the hitherto adopted theories, it is at the same time a practical task for economists to help towards the solution of the acute problems of the present and the future. A quick, briefly stated and easily comprehensible answer, such as it is required in this case, cannot be truly scientific. However, it is presumably the most important task of economic science to enable the economist or others to give relatively rapid answers to concrete questions. Besides an extensive knowledge of the relevant facts, it is important at this point to have an acquired training and method in the treatment of models and abstractions and, if necessary, to be able to let analogies from theoretical models enter into the estimate of the concrete, more complicated cases; or to construct more special models as a modest guidance that may have to be modified according to an estimate of the special circumstances of the case. The convincing character of such an estimate will, however, partly be dependent on a confidence founded either on previously verified estimates or on convincing statements, where time and material allow a more detailed explanation.

Not least of all because it is very largely the same persons who in some cases set forth more loosely founded statements for preliminary guidance and in other cases perform work on a purely scientific basis, it is important to make it absolutely clear what degree of validity is to be attached to the different statements. Generally speaking, it is a fact that there are different kinds of language, each of which may be justified for its special use, but that it is disturbing for scientific work if statements which are merely intended as value judgments are taken as science. The scientist, like any other citizen, has a right to speak all these languages, if he only makes it clear what degree of validity he intends to attach to his various statements.

CHAPTER 4

USE OF STATISTICS AND MATHEMATICS

It is scarcely practical to draw a sharp line between economic statistics and economic theory. If we are not to carry on our search blindfolded, statistics must take its bearings from the theoretical explanation of the existing possibilities. And a theory which one should be able to test and apply to concrete conditions must, as mentioned above, choose its concepts in such a way that there is a possibility of direct or indirect measurement.

Econometrics,[1] besides stressing the close connection between theory and statistics, emphasizes mathematics as an important tool. Deduction takes place according to the rules of logic and, since in all essentials economics is concerned with the nature of the connection between quantities, this science must to a great extent apply quantitative logic, *i.e.*, mathematics. This does not require that formulae and figures are going to occupy very much space. Logical verbal reasoning about quantities (without any intermingling of irrelevant words) is also included in mathematics. Conditions are generally so complicated, owing to the large number of relevant and often heterogeneous quantities, that the choice of assumptions and concepts, *i.e.*, the choice of variables and quantities to be included, becomes a major problem. Moreover, one must not cherish exaggerated expectations of finding simple connections that might be expressed analytically in a definite formula, as for instance the formula on v. Thünen's gravestone $\sqrt{ap}$, indicating natural wage as the mean proportional between the minimum of subsistence and the quantity produced. In the frequent cases where we have a sum of magnitudes, products of price and quantity, or the calculation of interest, the rules of which are also applicable in case of a constant increase in population, we shall still have simple mathematical expressions. As a consequence of the heterogeneous nature of the economic goods, however, a very great and often changing number of quantities will generally be relevant and partly will act in different ways. If we apply simple formulae, it is essential to remember the limited number of relevant assumptions we have taken into consideration. In a number of cases it is possible to use blank formulae which only indicate that a quantity is dependent on a series of others without saying in which way. But in other cases where we have a heterogeneous or changing mass of conditions, one must confine one's self to a broad description in words, as, for example, in the concept, "historic dynamics", applied by Ragnar Frisch with regard to complicated tendencies of the development of institutions, etc. As to certain questions, it seems only possible to deal with them in a qualitative way, as for instance political and psychological conditions, or the effect of general education on technical progress.

The main utility of simple formulae, figures and models is in many cases to give a simple and exact idea of a kind of interdependence which must be assumed to have an approximate validity, but which must be corrected at discretion, according to one's knowledge or conjecture as to the deviations. A literal belief in and a direct application of the simple pictures as if they were real is foolhardy. The foolhardiness which practical people

---

[1] See the journal, *Econometrica*, issued by the Econometric Society, Wassily Leontief, "Econometrics", in *A Survey of Contemporary Economics*, vol. I, 1948; Tinbergen, *Econometrie*, 1941, Danish translation from the Dutch, 1948, American Edition, Blakiston Co., 1951.

sometimes ascribe to theorists is often due, however, to a disregard of the
limited importance which is tacitly attached to the models, even if it
happens that a theorist becomes so charmed by his own models that he
believes them to be alive.

Statistical observations, as a rule, do not give simple formulae, but
rather a discontinuous series of possible combinations of the variables
(*e.g.*, price and quantity). We can always choose a formula one degree
lower than the number of observations, which will be valid for the combinations observed. In reality, there is a great number of formulae which
fulfil the condition, and the choice of the most expedient formula to be
used for interpolation often depends on a theoretical assumption which is
outside the observed data. Where there may be supposed to be errors of
observation in the material or other, less essential, variables than those
investigated, one would not insist that the data should absolutely fulfil the
formula. In such cases, however, one tries a relatively simple formula of
a definite nature—if we have some basis for this from other sources—
giving the smallest total deviation from the observations. Where the
variations are small, one can generally confine one's self to equations of
the first degree without too great an error. The unknown is $x = a + by
+ cz + du \ldots$, where "a", "b", "c", and "d" are constants[2] and
"x", "y", "z", and "u" are variables.

As a simple example of the usefulness of applying a mathematical way
of thinking to economic problems, we may mention Frisch's criticism of
the older economists who dealt with the problem of distribution in special
chapters in which they discussed wages, rent, interest and entrepreneurial
profit, and each time actually said the same thing in different words: that
the payment for the individual factor is determined by the total product
minus the payment to the other factors. Thus, the same condition or
equation was used to find a whole series of unknowns, in so far as the
various authors chased the individual variables, one after another, over to
the left side of the equals sign as the unknown.[3] In this connection it is of
interest to emphasize that several equations are necessary, a complete
explanation requiring just as many equations as unknowns. Whereas it is
impossible, when it is a question of establishing numerical laws for the
real world, to apply mathematical methods to the same extent as in
natural sciences, such methods are often fruitful in revealing logical errors
and insufficiency in reasoning.

The mathematical treatment of the connection between the variables,
according to quite definite mathematical rules, offers a greater security
against logical errors. Human feelings and distracting impressions do not
run away with one. In a conversation, Leontief is said to have stated:
"It is the beauty of mathematics that you do not understand what you are

[2] Tinbergen's *Econometrics*, § 6. As to "stability conditions", see § 13.
[3] *Nationaløkonomisk Tidsskrift*, 1929, pp. 329–30, cf. a similar point of view
in Wicksell's article, "Matematisk Nationalekonomi", in *Ekonomisk Tidskrift*, 1925,
reprinted in *Archiv für Sozialwissenschaft und Sozialpolitik*, 1927.

doing." This must, of course, be so understood that one may mechanically apply the mathematical rules without caring about the meaning of the symbols. This way of working may, however, be felt inconvenient by economists who are not very familiar with carrying on calculations in terms of formulae: they want some support during the operation. That the application of formulae of a general character is a safer way in which to include all possibilities with their corresponding conditions, than treatment by means of numerical examples and concrete cases, has been illustrated by the highly different developments that may be the result of a sequence analysis with the same general assumptions, but with different values for the constants.[4]

Incomplete or wrong applications of mathematics, however, are also dangerous. It is not correct to consider the variables on the right side of a single equation as the causes which determine the unknown, for instance, the level of prices in the equation of the quantity theory. It is not even always safe to consider the changes which occur earlier as causes of those which follow chronologically. Where more than two variables are involved, the explanation of the interdependence, according to correct mathematical methods, requires a corresponding number of equations.

As an example of the danger of an inexact "verbal" treatment of quantities, we may mention the frequent arbitrary use of the words "proportion" and "difference", when one variable increases and another reduces a third one, seen as the result of the two former. It is here necessary to make clear whether one or the other kind of relation exists between the two quantities, or whether the relation is possibly of a more complicated or unknown nature. A naïve, primitive, and uncomprehending use of the mathematical way of expression, on the other hand, is dangerous if one is content with simple and exact deductions, whereas in actual life conditions are more complicated or even impossible to determine.

The right procedure will often be the use of simple models in conjunction with supplementary considerations of a non-exact character. The advantage of constructing very complicated models and especially of demonstrating them to other persons is doubtful. The necessity, alone, of remembering the meaning of a great number of symbols, makes it very difficult. Where a simple result is arrived at because a number of factors cancel each other out, there is an undoubted advantage; but the opposite seems to be the case where the result, for instance, is a fraction taking up more than a line of print. This is true all the more when we remember that we have only with difficulty been able to press a part of the determining factors into the formula. As my father, H. G. Zeuthen, the mathematician, said, "Mathematics is a science of laziness".

Just as with other types of specialization, the use of higher or more complicated mathematics makes cooperation among economists difficult.

[4] Cf. Chapter 35, and Bjarke Fog, "Matematik og Økonomi", *Nationaløkonomisk Tidsskrift*, 1948.

Thus a considerable need has gradually arisen for translation, so far as possible, of the most important contributions of the more mathematical economics, into ordinary language. On the other hand, a translation into mathematics and back again might often be a useful test of the logic of verbal economics.

CHAPTER 5

ECONOMICS AND POLITICS

JUST as technics comprise a group of applied sciences, corresponding to the pure sciences, physics, chemistry, etc., economic policy may be said to comprise a series of applications of pure economics. Before we are able to proceed to the applications, however, it is necessary for the pure sciences to add, as given assumptions, aims, determined by interest or moral attitude, and possibly also certain prejudices with regard to the effectuation, which will have to be respected.[1] Not till then is it possible to undertake a scientific determination of the means. There must always, however, be an opportunity for the representatives of science to criticize the said prejudices as lack of consistency in the political aiming. The economist may also of his own accord call attention to effects, *e.g.*, long run effects, not considered by political powers.

Besides finding means for the effectuation of given aims, economic policy has other tasks of a perfectly objective character: (1) a descriptive statement of past and present political measures, (2) historical and statistical investigations of the effects of the latter, (3) a systematical description of conceivable measures, (4) theoretical investigations of the probable effects of possible measures, and finally (5) analysis of political motives, wishes and opinions.

What has been said above concerns economic policy, which, however, is beyond the scope of this book. In Chapter 19, in connection with utility, something about welfare is added. The existence of economic policy, however, gives rise to serious problems for the theoretical economist. On one hand, there is a danger that theoretical work will suffer in objectivity through political influence and, on the other hand, there is the

---

[1] Max Weber: "Die Objektivität sozialwissenschaftlicher und sozial-politischer Erkenntniss", in *Archiv für Sozialwissenschaft und Sozialpolitik* 1904; Axel Nielsen: "Forholdet mellem Teori og Politik", Lübechers Forlag, Copenhagen, 1912. Gunnar Myrdal: *The Political Element in the Development of Economic Theory*, London, 1953 (Swedish edition, 1930, German edition, 1932), and: "Das Zweck-Mittel-Denken in der Nationalökonomie", *Zeitschrift für Nationalökonomie*, 1933. Myrdal says that political attitude does not only find expression in briefly defined aims, but in the whole situation of the social groups, which also comprises taboos regarding the choice of means; L. Robbins, *Nature and Significance of Economic Science*, London, 1932.

necessity of investigating political reactions as an important component in the explanation of economic interdependence.

Older economists have been inclined to believe in an *ordre naturel* and to regard economic laws as valid theoretically as well as constituting moral norms and positive descriptions of actual economic life.[2] As late as in Cassel, we come across the raised forefinger: do not sin against the economic laws—a warning directed against the interference of the state.

The motive for occupying one's self with socio-economic questions is no doubt very largely of a political nature, in the broadest sense of the word, *i.e.*, a wish to bring about better economic and social conditions, perhaps for certain parts of the population or for national or other local groups. With regard to the choice of tasks, one cannot expect or require complete impartiality. A consequence of the demand for objectivity is, among other things, that we deal with the more important aspects of economic life. But "important" must here be taken in the meaning of welfare of human beings. Therefore, some welfare valuations are implicitly required in the choice of questions dealt with, though welfare valuations of the economic phenomena are not given.

In the mixed, verbal, everyday kind of argumentation, personal sentiment and individual desires have great opportunity to influence the result. If the solutions are to have intersubjective applicability to people with any political ideology or any kind of interest, it will be necessary to proceed to a documentation of actual experience in all doubtful cases and to formal methods of deduction. An analysis of the author's emotional presuppositions may also contribute to the correction of errors. A certain defense against a pseudo-science is to be found in the fact that economists as state officials and part of the country's intelligentsia, *e.g.*, the statistical departments, in any case, in some countries, work at the same time for the benefit of all economic and political groups, in the same way as congressional or parliamentary printers and window cleaners. Other active factors are idle curiosity and the professional and sportsman-like interest in getting at the truth.

If the state did not interfere in economic conditions and, for instance, confined itself to maintaining the rights of private property and the freedom of contract, economic theory might be studied without taking economic policy into consideration. An understanding of economic problems might also be attained without knowledge of the political motives and deliberations, if the reactions of the state were entirely automatic and based on given laws or principles. Taxes would rise in a definite way during the boom and unemployment benefits during a depression. The same would apply to a certain extent with regard to the effects of an old-fashioned

---

[2] Ivar Sundbom, "Gesetz und Norm in der Nationalökonomischen Theorie", *Zeitschrift für Nationalökonomie*, 1937; the works by Gunnar Myrdal, quoted in previous note, and a third Swedish author, Johan Åkerman; Theodor Geiger, "Om Bureaukratisme", *Nationaløkonomisk Tidsskrift*, 1935, and *Intelligensen*, Wahlström & Widstrand, Stockholm, 1944; Thomas Sinding, "Some Remarks on Objectivity and Subjectivity", *Nordisk Tidsskrift for Teknisk Økonomi*, 1948.

central bank which automatically maintained the gold standard by means of discount policy.

Under modern conditions, however, one must take into account the fact that greater changes in prices, employment, etc., occasion non-automatic reactions on the part of the state, which are very much determined by changing political motives and doctrines. The state is more active in slumps than in booms. An interplay takes place between economic and political forces.[3] It is consequently impossible to give a complete explanation of economic interdependence without also including political factors. Since the latter, however, are highly variable in time and place, and there does not exist any usable generalization thus far, it seems practical in the first instance to keep policy outside general economic theory, in spite of its great importance for economic phenomena. In the last chapters of the book we do, however, give some examples of economic adaptation to political interference and mention briefly the connection between economics and policy. Further, readers are referred to the great and important partially economic spheres: fiscal policy, credit policy, agricultural policy, social policy, etc., where economics must be combined with history, law, psychology, sociology, etc.

CHAPTER 6

THE SCOPE OF ECONOMICS

WE are not going into greater detail here on questions of definition. Economic science deals with the interdependence between consumption and production. The study of consumption and of production themselves are of interest in so far as they concern this interdependence. The theories of exchange and distribution deal with essential aspects of the relationship between consumption and production. Like Cassel, one can set up a definition based on a single condition.[1]

It is also possible to assume as one's starting-point that real life forms an interdependent whole and that there should preferably be the greatest possible interrelationship and harmony between the different branches of science. If, nevertheless, we have a special economic science, it is because

---

[3] Cf. Johan Åkerman, *Ekonomiskt Skeende och politiska Förändringar*, Gleerup Lund, 1946, and "Political Economic Cycles", *Kyklos*, 1947.

[1] See *The Theory of Social Economy*, (Fisher Unwin, London), 1923. House-keeping (*i.e.*, economics) covers the whole of the activity that makes the satisfaction of wants possible, without coinciding with it. In order that an activity shall be economic, there must, according to Cassel, be scarcity, *i.e.*, a limitation with regard to the possibilities of attaining satisfaction of wants.

there exists a particularly intensive connection within the circle of phenomena which are generally termed economic, so that in a great part of the
work of investigation these can with advantage be considered as mutually
interdependent variables, whereas a series of other phenomena, as for
instance technical knowledge and the size of the population, are to a
lesser extent influenced by the economic phenomena and therefore with a
very good approximation may be taken as data.[2]

Commodity prices must at any rate be considered as economic phenomena. Other magnitudes that especially vary with prices and also are considered as economic are, *e.g.*, the volume of commodities produced and
consumed, wages, interest and other prices of productive services as well
as the quantities used of these services. Economic theory, then, comprises
the conditions determining these quantities and possibly other quantities
having a close connection with them, such as monetary conditions.

As will be apparent from what follows, it is not possible to make any
sharp distinction between the variables of economic science and its data.
When nevertheless we work with economics as a special branch of science,
it is because it pays to concentrate work and organize collaboration within
this branch. The cultivation of economics as a special branch of science
does not preclude, however, that the delimitation of one's investigation
may not also be made in a different way; and it may then appear that work
in the less cultivated marginal fields or combined fields is particularly
fruitful. In the following we shall in several places touch on the connection with engineering, psychology, and, as mentioned in the last section,
political conditions. We shall see how all these conditions, which are
generally taken as constants in economic theory may also be considered as
variables. Every explanation, however, must stop in some place or other.
We can never reach further than explaining some conditions by their
connection with certain others. Reality and science must both be conceived
of as units. The limits, therefore, are dependent on a preliminary division
of labor. Logically, there is nothing fundamental about the traditional
boundaries of economic science. If, for instance, for the understanding
of business cycles a theory of government policy is demanded, the economist can ill afford to neglect this need on the ground that such problems
are outside his province.[3]

---

[2] Joseph Schumpeter, *Wesen und Hauptinhalt der theoretischen Nationalökonomie*,
Duncker & Humblot, Wien, 1908.

[3] Samuelson, *Foundations of Economic Analysis*, Harvard University Press, 1948,
p. 9.

CHAPTER 7

DIFFERENT TYPES OF THEORIES

IN this chapter we are going to give a comparatively short survey of some of the most important points of view from which economic theories can be classified into different types. Through the simultaneous application of a series of these points of view, we obtain, of course, a very great number of more or less important combinations. However, as in most other cases, it is more fruitful to consider the distinctions than to attempt a mechanical and uniform elaboration of the many special cases that may be formed by combining them. An elaboration of those combinations which contain real problems is more profitable than an impressive system with many "empty boxes".

The distinctions essentially correspond to different types of tasks. It is not a question of designating some as right and others as wrong; on the contrary, the important thing is their applicability in different fields and the connections between them.

7.1, TOTAL VS. PARTIAL

Total economic theories are concerned with economic life as a whole or greater sections of it, which it is possible, in all essentials, to explain by phenomena within the field. To this category belong world trade and the economy of the individual countries. The term partial is mainly applied to the formation of price for a single commodity or kind of productive service. Thus, the question is here of a single quality of goods within a certain economic sector. In these cases we take as given the prices and quantities of other goods or services. In other words, the problem to be investigated is considered in isolation, *i.e.*, *ceteris paribus* is assumed with regard to other variables. The condition that is necessary for a statement to have a definite meaning, *i.e.*, permitting of empirical testing, is a clear indication as to which factors shall be taken as given; otherwise the statement will always be true, *i.e.*, tautological. More simple than this explanation is, of course, L. V. Birck's general warning, "*Ceteris* is never *paribus*!"

Where, as in the case of interrelated prices, there is a strong interplay between the formation of price for several commodities, it is important to extend the partial analysis to include them all at the same time. So it is scarcely appropriate to make any sharp distinction between total and partial, because a total investigation, if it is not to be completely abstract, must take certain givens as its starting-point. The partial character of the analysis may also be due to the fact that it is limited with regard to geographical area or time.

In partial analyses of price formation for a commodity, it is generally assumed that supply and demand are independent of each other; in so doing we especially disregard the fact that costs at the same time act as income to the persons demanding the commodity. This is reasonable so long as it is a question of a single commodity, which forms only a small part of the total budget, since the income due to its production is only of slight importance for the demand of the commodity as compared with the income resulting from the production of all other commodities. If we are to treat the effect of income, we must include all commodities, *i.e.*, make the investigation a total one. As an exceptional case, where it is possible to include the effect of income in a partial analysis with a substantial degree of accuracy, covering only a few variables in connection with a single commodity, *ceteris paribus* being assumed with regard to all other commodities, we may perhaps mention the relation between the wages of Ford workers and their demand for Ford cars.

7.2, HOMOGENEOUS VS. NON-HOMOGENEOUS QUANTITIES (AGGREGATES)

The conditions necessary in order that quantitative indicators (quantities of commodities, prices, etc.) shall have the same meaning in different situations are that they should concern units of commodities and services which are completely uniform from all economic points of view.

Certain differences with regard to physical properties of different commodities, for instance, between round and angular units or more or less finely divided quantities of a raw material, may sometimes be irrelevant as to any effect on production, sales and consumption. Consequently, it may be irrelevant in relation to all economic valuations. In other cases, certain properties are economically relevant, for instance, heating power per unit of weight of fuel. A recalculation in terms of tons of prime coal or calories or the calculation of an average price in a fixed proportion cannot be used as an exact economic expression when the relative importance of the different criteria are changed. This may be the consequence of a changed distribution of weight between the sub-types. A recalculation in terms of fodder units or nutrition units is inadequate for economic analysis owing to the special demands for the different types. This is still more the case when groups so great and heterogeneous as consumers' and producers' goods, or some few sub-categories of these, are summed up as categories with a single quantity and average price. A uniform price, such as price per unit or per working hour, means a varying price in relation to an economically more relevant index for the quantities.

In many cases, especially in the treatment of dynamic problems for society as a whole, it is practical, in spite of many limitations, to work with statistical expressions of the major categories, such as quantity indices and average prices. The lack of exactness may to a certain extent be corrected afterwards by discretionary comments on the calculations made on the basis of a more detailed knowledge of the individual qualities that have in the first instance been considered as one category. Discussions on the basis of "major categories", aggregates, may easily assume a mystical character if we do not make clear what they comprise and how they are measured. In Chapter 31 we shall return to "the problem of aggregation" or "summation" which has been alluded to several times in this chapter.

We assume homogeneous types of goods throughout the preponderantly deductive analysis in Part II. This is the older conception of economics: that there is a definite number of different, but essentially homogeneous, consumption and production goods, each consisting of a great number of units. But what is a "commodity"? This concept is actually a hypothetical one because an exact sorting according to economically relevant characteristics (including geographical location) will lead to a break-down into smaller groups of similar units and consequently, among other things, exclude free competition in many spheres. If, on the other hand, we use categories that are so comprehensive that we get large markets, the homogeneity in these will become very limited. However, in speaking of a "commodity", we assume homogeneity.

As opposed to commodities, money is homogeneous in quality. For individuals as well as for larger or smaller groups of individuals, we may establish an exact bookkeeping system, showing the distribution of the sums of money over different accounts and the transfers between these. Exact explanations within this system play the part of links in the explanation of real economic phenomena. The cash balance at the beginning of the year 1950, for instance, plus or minus changes in the course of the year, becomes exactly the cash balance at the end of the year. But the real economic importance of the individual sums of money is constantly varying with changing prices and, if we want to include this variable, with the incomes of the owners. A recalculation in terms of a real economic standard of measurement can only be made on the basis of more or less arbitrary hypotheses and by methods of calculation which cannot express simultaneously its relative importance from all points of view. As an expression of the real aspects of production, consumption and distribution, measurement in terms of money is consequently an inexact index which is subject to many qualifications. The heterogeneous quantities which we are often obliged to reckon with in economics require that the statistical problems of measurement, through such devices as averages, become of very great importance in the analysis of practical economic problems.

7.3, ECONOMICS OF SOCIETY AS A WHOLE OR OF THE MARKET VS. ECONOMICS OF THE FIRM, THE HOUSEHOLD OR THE INDIVIDUAL

In order to understand the economics of society as a whole, it will often be important to consider its smaller component parts, the economics of the individual firms and of individuals (or households) themselves. It is not only a question of the entrepreneurs, but also of individual persons, such as workers, owners of capital, consumers, savers, etc. An "internal" psychological understanding of the plans of the economic subjects is an important link in the explanation. The separate, objectively measurable, individual economic quantities may be summed up. The possibility of summing up of the plans, which cannot be realized simultaneously, is, however, open to serious question. The business-economic or individual-economic analysis may be looked upon as a special form of the partial analysis, even if by this expression we usually mean the formation of price for the individual commodity or service as a whole within a certain sphere.

Whereas the division total vs. partial concerned the extent of the sphere considered, and that of homogeneous vs. non-homogeneous the exactitude regarding the quality of the goods under consideration, it is here a question of the number of economic subjects. The highly varying use of the expressions "*macro*" and "*micro*" by different authors shows a mixing together of these three divisions. While in a great competitive society the partial approach naturally centers around the individual commodity, it will be more practical in a society with great firms, competing monopolistically, to operate with the firm as the decisive part of the totality. This will be so much more appropriate because very large firms normally produce several qualities of commodities.

7.4, STATIC VS. DYNAMIC;
7.5, STATIONARY VS. CHANGING

Following Ragnar Frisch,[1] we distinguish between the static and the dynamic approach, on the one hand, and between stationary conditions and developmental conditions, on the other. An investigation is static when it does not include anything about the connection between conditions at various points of time (about movements in time, increases, lags, uncertain expectations, etc.). A society where everything repeats itself from one year to another is stationary. A static investigation is then sufficient. A dynamic investigation is also possible in this case, but we shall obtain a velocity of increase of 0 throughout. Besides being fully applicable to a stationary condition where everything repeats itself, the static approach may also be applied with precision to an analysis of conditions at each given moment in an imaginary, changing society, in so far as adaptation to changes in data takes place with infinite speed in all directions. (These are called atomistic assumptions.) In other cases the static analysis gives an incomplete, but to a certain extent applicable, explanation of the main features of a changing society. The approximation is best when there are few impulses which induce change and when the adaptation is quick and frictionless. Various difficulties inherent in the static analysis of equilibrium will be mentioned in Chapters 24 and 25.

[1] "Statikk og Dynamikk i den økonomiske Teori", *Nationaløkonomisk Tidsskrift*, 1929, p. 321 ff.

7.6, SHORT RUN VS. LONG RUN

Following Marshall, we refer here to the equilibrium of, for instance, demand and supply that is achieved a shorter or longer time after a change in price or other variables. The neo-classical equilibria in the short and in the long run are static, but in the former case certain conditions are given (size of plants, habits, etc.). The movement from one equilibrium to another, on the contrary, requires a dynamic analysis. Not only is there a series of transitions between the short and the long run, but there are also different reactions depending on the duration, velocity, certainty, etc., of the changes in price.[2] Thus far, both approaches are of a partial sort. In the short-run approach we disregard adaptations which take place slowly; in the long-run approach we disregard speedy reactions which are not assumed to have any lasting effects of importance.

7.7, MODELS VS. DESCRIPTION

All the economic theories build on observations and aim at giving pictures of real life. The pictures, however, are of very different types: at the one extreme we have the greatly simplified models which are only intended to give a simple and clear statement of a few main properties, and at the other extreme we have pictures that resemble photographs and include many details, even to the point of obscuring the view.

7.8, CENTRAL THEORY VS. BRANCH THEORIES

Central Theory deals with those parts of economics which are suitable to be taken as the starting-point for the whole science, and on the foundation of which the other sections can be built up by the addition of further assumptions. There is, by the way, a possibility of choosing the starting-point in a different way, especially by including the monetary theory at once to a greater or lesser degree.

7.9, ALTERNATIVE THEORIES FOR DIFFERENT FORMS OF MARKET AND SOCIETY

The real conditions may vary so greatly that in dealing with important questions it becomes necessary to draw up entirely different sets of assumptions. If we make rough combinations according to the two criteria: statics vs. dynamics, and competition vs. monopoly, we obtain four combinations, of which—in accordance with tradition—we take the first one: statics and competition, as a starting-point. This combination gives the simplest explanation. We proceed to the others by including more conditions in our analysis.

[2] J. M. Clark: *Economics of Overhead Costs*, University of Chicago Press, 1923; as well as the treatment of this question in Business Economics.

7.10, GENERAL VS. SPECIAL THEORY

A theory may be special by being valid only under definitely stated assumptions. It may be so by reckoning with total indices for certain groups of goods, by confining itself to some few firms, by using static assumptions or, as in the case of the short-run theory, by assuming certain conditions to be given. The distinction between special and general theories only acquires a definite meaning when it is stated or implied in which respects.

It is, of course, of great importance not to have merely a number of separate and isolated approaches to economic problems, corresponding to the great number of types and sub-types of theories referred to above. If the unity of economic science is not to be lost, a close relation between the various approaches is necessary. In several cases it is possible to establish this relation, by means of a summation. The sum of the output of all firms is the output of a whole industry, and the sum of (homogeneous) amounts produced is the total amount of commodities produced. This would be measured, for instance, in tons or dollars, or according to some arbitrary index. As will be shown later, the problem is somewhat more complicated if one does not speak about *actual* production or consumption, but about the summation of the *plans* of several firms or individuals. So long as we confine ourselves, however, to the description of facts, or theoretically assumed facts, the problem of summation is easily solved by summation of the parts in accordance with the principles of double-entry bookkeeping.[3] Whether we consider the income and expenses or assets and liabilities accounts, or whether we sum up the corresponding real quantities, we shall get the accounts for any two or for all countries or firms as the sum of the individual accounts. In this case it does not matter how inadequately we choose our dividing lines. Similarly, we get the figures for a group of homogeneous types of commodities or services as the sum of the figures for the individual goods. The tendency in recent economic thinking to split up the accounts of the national income and the total categories (the "macro-economic" quantities) into their component parts, seems to indicate that the missing link between "macro" and "micro" economics will be established. In principle, at any rate, there is no gap.

According to the nature of the problem under consideration, either the commodity, the firm or the national income and its main components may be the most appropriate for our purpose. When analysing perfect

[3] Ivar Jantzen, "On the Basis of Planned Economy", *Nordisk Tidsskrift for Teknisk Økonomi*, 1939 (reprint in English from article in 1935); Ragnar Frisch, *Et generelt monetaert Begrebs-og Symbol-system*, Universitetets Studenterkontor, Oslo, 1935; Erich Schneider, "Uber einige Grundfragen einer Lehre vom Wirtschaftskreis", *Weltwirtschaftliches Archiv*, 1938. For problems of aggregation, see Chapters 7.2 and 31.

D

competition in a society under stable conditions, or as a starting-point for theoretical analysis generally, a homogeneous commodity or a number of assumedly homogeneous commodities seems to be appropriate (cf. Part II). By a closer study of market conditions, the firm, or the interplay between a limited number of neighboring firms, is the best basis (cf. Part IV). Finally, when studying dynamics, where income effects and other more comprehensive effects are of great importance, it often seems necessary to abandon the exactness of homogeneous groups and instead to reckon with total, very heterogeneous, categories and averages (cf. Part III). When doing this, or when resorting to partial analysis in terms of individual commodities or firms, it is of great importance, however, to have at the back of one's mind outlines of the whole and unretouched picture of the total economy as a network with an immense number of links between an immense number of homogeneous types. As this book presupposes some knowledge of economics, we shall start (at the beginning of Part II) with this rather abstract, theoretical background.

CHAPTER 8

SUCCESSIVE TREATMENT OF THE PROBLEMS

It is necessary to proceed one step at a time. The verbal exposition must proceed along a single line. Our line goes from the more simple to the more complex form. First we present a simplified picture of the economic network and its most important links, corresponding to certain very simple assumptions. Next, reconstruction and extension takes place, corresponding to assumptions of a usually more realistic character.

This procedure has been called the method of decreasing abstraction. A superficial knowledge of the working methods of economists may possibly lead philosophical critics to the misunderstanding that it is a question of an "axiomatic method", according to which it is thought possible, as in mathematics, to derive a great system of deduced statements from some few axioms or hypotheses. However, the expression "decreasing abstraction" means a gradually increasing degree of concreteness. Thus we build up new links or rebuild old ones by inclusion of fresh experiences. The simple models with which we start can only have some of the attributes of real life; but these ought to belong to the most important and most generally occurring ones. Owing to the very fact that we do not include some of the other attributes, the models get a certain special character, and the addition of new attributes must, therefore, at the same time involve the abandonment of some of the original ones. For instance, by the addition of monopoly, free competition disappears.

In this book we start by abstracting from factors which operate during changes in the economic conditions. These dynamic problems are later taken up for a detailed treatment in Part III. Similarly, to begin with, we abstract from monopoly, state interference and a number of related influences, which are dealt with further in Part IV.

What remains after the initial simplifications gives a picture of some main attributes of a static society with perfect competition. But this first abstract model has at the same time certain general economic attributes, which in dynamics and monopoly theory are to be found in a modified form combined with other attributes.

In the 19th century we have in real life had examples of societies with a comparatively high degree of competition and mobility, where dynamic phenomena were of smaller importance. What is essential in this connection is not competition, right of property or other institutional conditions, but easy adaptation to changed economic conditions. The economic process will have a similar course in a socialist society with free choice of consumption and employment.

Classical economic theory took it for granted that conditions of this kind prevailed to a great extent in real life and that the forces of nature worked in the same direction. Theories derived from such assumptions were, therefore, considered to be good approximations towards which real conditions were tending. It is, however, dangerous as a starting-point to refer to particular social conditions with an unspecified degree of more or less free competition and without any dynamic disturbances. Similarly, one must warn against taking an unspecified amount of classical tradition as our starting-point.

Instead of referring to types of societies that have actually existed, or of building on the foundation of the traditional classical conception of the "natural" economy, and instead of constructing a comprehensive system of verbal assumptions, we shall in the highly abstract sections at the beginning of Part II construct certain models and compare their attributes with various real situations. The discrepancies between the models and real life lead to reconstructions of the models at later points.

The static assumption is expressed exactly by the equations in Chapter 11 which only contain quantities of economic flows as variables within the same period. Assumptions of perfect competition are also expressed exactly in equations (2)–(4) in Chapter 11 by putting the prices of commodities equal to the sum of all costs and assuming either full utilization of the productive services or giving them the price of zero. Finally, since assumptions to the contrary are not made, all variables are treated as being continuous with infinite divisibility. The assumptions are expressed in the structure of the models. Therefore, by changing the structure of the models, it is possible to transform our picture of static free competition into a picture of an economy with dynamic and monopolistic elements.

The connection with real life is brought about in the usual way by making assumptions based on experience for the individual parts of the various models. As a result of the high degree of economic interdependence which exists, verification must very largely be piecemeal and incomplete. Verification of more than the main features cannot take place until a large number of special assumptions have been added corresponding to the complicated real cases. However, the models set forth in this book only constitute a beginning and must be used along with collection of facts and their statistical analysis. These models are dangerous only if one believes naïvely that they can be directly transferred to real life and can tell us everything we want to know about reality.

We insist that it is advantageous to illustrate the interdependence of the economy as a whole by a series of quantitative partial interdependences between groups of magnitudes, which together form the network of economic society. The rest will be questions concerning choice of details and the analysis of the extent to which the various models conform to reality. There is no thought of finding the only true system, but of choosing different links and combinations of links, suitable for elucidating various problems in different kinds of real life in greater or less detail. This work must proceed from the simpler to the more complicated forms.

Since it is impossible to study and still less to explain everything simultaneously, limitation and simplification are necessary. Therefore, even empirical description of economic history has to be abstract. The dangerous thing is, however, that unconscious and unregarded limiting assumptions and abstractions may become fixed data from the point of view of the economist, or dogmas for a school of economists. The limitation of the problems will then become more than a provisional arrangement of work, and each school of economists will live in a splendid isolation without troubling themselves about the unwelcome work of other schools.[1]

[1] George J. Schuller, "Isolationism in Economic Method", *The Quarterly Journal of Economics*, November, 1949. Schuller analyzes the limiting assumptions of the "maximizationalists", "the Marxists", and the historical school. About the latter he says, "But to the extent that these assumptions are made unconsciously (on the further assumption that they are making no assumptions), the extreme historicists increase their probability of error relatively to that of self-conscious theorists. In practice, then historical economists like any others attack their problems armed with assumptions, which tend to limit those problems themselves." (p. 462). The "maximizationalists" believe in the economic man, *i.e.*, rational maximization of profit and other advantages, and they take institutions and distribution of property as being outside the discussion. The Marxists, finally, beg the problem by defining value as labor value.

CHAPTER 9

MORE ABOUT THE STATIC ASSUMPTION

OUR aim in using static assumptions is to make it possible to start without all those conditions relating to the economic interdependence that are connected with the distance in time between the individual phenomena. As will be shown in Part III, this time factor is very important. But still it is possible to speak about an interdependence between certain quantities without including the time factor. Only where conditions are very stable, or where one is only interested in the enduring part of the phenomena (as, for instance, the reasons why, on the whole, prices, wages, etc., exist) is it possible to content one's self with the static assumptions. When the movements are faint, it may generally be taken for granted that they will not play any decisive part in the explanation of the situation. The static explanation is incomplete. The more the same processes are constantly repeated, the less is lost by simplification, however.

The interdependence of the economy as a whole may be described statically—and thus incompletely—through a series of partial interdependences, a system of simultaneous equations indicating a number of simultaneous conditions. In so far as the static explanation is sufficient, it indicates a set of prices and quantities, etc., *i.e.*, solutions with regard to the dependent variables of the system which, if once realized, has no tendency to disappear so long as the system is not influenced by changes in data.[1] This absence of any tendency to change is usually called "equilibrium". Besides this real equilibrium concept, we may also speak about a conceptual dynamic equilibrium when in investigating a system in movement we have a complete and consistent explanation, here including increases or other quantities connected with more than the actual moment. However, we cannot speak about static equilibrium as the stationary state which with certain data will be realized after a process of adaptation if no fresh impulses in the meantime are brought into the system from outside. For even with this assumption, the stationary state that may possibly be reached in the end will depend on the unequal speeds of adaptation in different parts of the economy and on uncertain expectations as to the reactions of the other parties, etc.; and moreover the result may be continued fluctuations. The static theory assumes as little dynamics as is necessary to explain why the state does not change. (Cf. Paul Samuelson's discussion of "stability conditions".)

There are two ways in which one might imagine static equilibrium to be realized after a change of data: (1) by an infinitely quick adaptation of

---

[1] Lindahl, *Studies in the Theory of Money and Capital*, Allen & Unwin, London, 1939, pp. 310–12; cf. Lundberg, *Studies in the Theory of Economic Expansion*, Norstedt, Stockholm, 1937, p. 27.

all dependent variables, (2) by allowing sufficient time for a complete adaptation before new changes of data occur. Also in the former of these cases the relation between the reactions of the different acting persons causes great difficulty. Mobility, at any rate, is necessary in order that the equilibrium may constantly be in accordance with a series of changing conditions. The unknown of the system must be really variable, and not confined by a frictional resistance which hinders adaptation. In order that there should here prevail a static equilibrium for the quantities regarded as dependent variables, these must not be confined by a resistance which does not itself enter into the equilibrium system to be explained. It has therefore been said that static equilibrium is characterized by free mobility, but no movement. There must, by the way, be a certain mutual agreement between the conditions which in economics are regarded as data, but which in reality cannot be quite independent of each other, as, for instance, technology and habits of consumption. So it is meaningless to ask which static equilibrium corresponds to any arbitrary series of "data".

The calculation of a possible tendency towards a definite stationary equilibrium or normal, consequently, is not applicable as a theoretical means of elucidating real conditions—owing to the constant flow of fresh impulses, the slowness of adaptation, and the unequal velocity on various points as well as the expectations of a non-stationary future—not at any rate when it is a question of the community as a whole or large and slowly adaptable spheres. Instead of constructing, by artificial means, a certain similarity between static equilibrium and real life, *i.e.*, further explaining the premises of a condition where static equilibrium has been realized, we shall prefer, as mentioned above, to confine ourselves to a static equilibrium concept, indicating a solution with regard to the variables which, when once it has been established, have no tendency to change so long as data are unchanged. The question of movement towards definite stationary conditions or in other directions is referred to Part III, which deals with economic dynamics, *i.e.*, the part of economics treating the relation between conditions at various points of time and, consequently, the economic movements.

The above-mentioned partial interdependences between the individual economic quantities do not connect various simultaneous quantities, either in real life or in an imaginary stationary community. The costs of production for a commodity, for instance, spread far back in time (sale, transport, production, transport and production of machinery and buildings, production of the means of production of the means of production, etc.). Since under stationary conditions everything is repeated, we shall here, however, during any short period find all economic quantities and processes represented in the same proportion as during the whole of the long period required for the production of a commodity. And the quantity of a productive service put in at the moment, but not yielding any result until, *e.g.*, one or ten years later, will be just as great as the services put in one or ten years before, and which now enter into the present consumption. We shall then be able to let the present conditions represent the corresponding earlier ones and confine ourselves to the connection between simultaneous quantities. Cassel very clearly explains the justification for this, saying that the condition for keeping up a stationary equilibrium is that the contributions of productive services, making the consumption of the future possible, should constantly take place in the same way. L. V. Birck in this connection speaks about the "simultaneously successive approach".

This way of considering the connection between simultaneous quantities instead of the actual, *e.g.*, technical, connections between quantities at different points of time may be illustrated by means of the dotted and thickly drawn lines respectively of Fig. 1 below.[2]

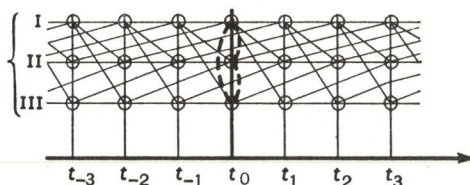

Fig. 1. Intertemporal and Simultaneous Connections

The simultaneous interdependence has in Fig. 1 been illustrated by the lines rectangular on the time axis. The time dimension is here eliminated in cases of constantly repeated phenomena. It is seen, for instance, how I (a price or quantity) at the point of time, t_0, is influenced by II at the point of time, t_{-3}, while II_{t_0} is influenced by $I_{t_{-1}}$. Further I_{t_0} influences II_{t+1} and II_{t_0} influences I_{t+3}. If we reckon with an instantaneous effect in both directions, or if a stationary equilibrium is present for the economic quantities, we obtain for any point of time the interplay between quantities I and II indicated by the broken line $I_{t_0}-II_{t_0}$.

While in static theory the direct links or indirect connections between economic magnitudes are generally considered as simultaneous interdependences, the links in dynamic analysis may often be considered as one-way dependences, causation, in which the first magnitude in time as a datum determines the later magnitudes. Cf. Chapter 35 and the end of Chapter 44 with different types of arrow schemes.

A stationary state does not imply complete stagnation, but constant repetition. There may very well be movement for the individuals. Men are born and die, enterprises are founded and disappear, production and consumption are constantly taking place. There must be stagnancy for the broad categories, *i.e.*, that the quantities within all types must be kept up.

[2] Cf. Tinbergen's "Arrow Scheme", *Review of Economic Studies*, 1940, p. 74, or his *Econometrics*, 1951, § 11.

Time enters into static theory in so far as production, consumption and income of any kind are measured per unit of time. But whether this unit is a second or a year is irrelevant because all quantities reckoned per unit of time are influenced proportionately with a change in the duration of the unit. Contrary to these economic quantities which are reckoned per unit of time (*i.e.*, period), namely, the economic flows, we have the economic quantities reckoned per point of time, the economic stocks, *e.g.*, the labor force, machinery, inventories, property and debts. The connection between these funded quantities and the flow quantities is of decisive importance for the dynamic approach of Part III. In the simultaneous, static approach generally applied in Part II we confine ourselves to the flows, the quantities per unit of time. Thus, we do not consider the quantity of means of production, but the productive services yielded by these. It is, moreover, a necessary condition for stationary equilibrium that the stocks be kept constant. Part of the production must, therefore, consist in maintaining real capital.

In spite of the fact that it is the state of equilibrium that is being considered in static theory, the consideration of changes is something of the greatest importance in this theory. It is not a question, however, of how the process of change takes place, but of the changes in the state of equilibrium when certain assumptions have been changed and equilibrium once more established; *i.e.*, questions about the connection between alternative assumptions and the states of equilibrium corresponding thereto.

PART TWO

ECONOMIC LIFE:
A NETWORK OF PARTIAL INTERDEPENDENCES

CHAPTER 10

THE ECONOMIC NETWORK

OBSERVATION of economic life shows a multitude of interdependences, repeating themselves with a certain regularity. Since the individual quantities, however, are dependent on many other quantities and conditions that constantly appear in changing combinations, it is impossible, without a thorough analysis, to get an adequate picture of the totality or of all direct or indirect interrelations of a particular factor. It seems necessary to start with what is most definite and tangible, the partial interdependences forming the links in the chain. If several links are joined, we shall also obtain the indirect combinations of the chain, or rather the multidimensional economic network. The aim must be to arrange the description of the economic interdependence in such a way that we get a consistent and complete explanation. There must be just as many links of connection or equations as unknowns. The condition necessary for obtaining an explanation is, however, that we assume as data certain things outside the range of variable economic quantities.

A great deal of numerical data is available in the accounts of firms and households and national accounts. The latter represent aggregates of the former. The interdependences are here expressed as groupings and summations and thus retain the character of equations of the first degree.

The denominator is money in the money accounts, which under money economy comprises all kinds of goods and relations between them. But at the same time it is possible, as another aspect of the same matter, to make at any rate partial accounts of commodities, services and goods of any kind. These, too, are groupings and summations, but it is only possible to make series of accounts for each quality of goods separately and calculated in its special units. These summations of accounts are based on definitions, and it is possible in concrete cases to express them in real figures.[1]

The book-keeping for money, commodities and services does not give a complete explanation, however. We further want a number of explanatory connecting links or equations for the determination of the dependent variables, the economic quantities. Where several flows in the economic network unite, or one flow continues in several separate flows, we have a summary equation, but since the number of flows is greater than the

---

[1] Erich Schneider begins his *Einführung in die Wirtschaftstheorie* with **Part I**, "Theorie des Wirtschaftskreislaufs", 1947 (Translation: *Pricing and Equilibrium*, William Hodge, London, 1951), which gives a book-keeping theory of the course of the economic process in time.

number of junction points, the system would have a certain number of degrees of freedom if we did not have other interdependences between the quantities.[2]

We do, however, have other kinds of interdependences[3] than the above-mentioned summations: the quantity of commodities demanded as dependent on price and other circumstances, the volume of commodities resulting from productions using different quantities of productive services, the quantity of labor which people are willing to yield at different rates of wages, and, as a special condition, the variation of saving in relation to income, the rate of interest, and other conditions.

It is not here a question of summation, but of a generally complicated and strongly varying functional interdependence which is observable in the individual cases. Decreasing return in the cultivation of the soil is a well-known and comparatively easily measurable example of these formulae. The quantities to be included in each case are not, as in the book-keeping summations, determined in advance by simple definitions, but they must be found, and the relation seems as a rule to be far more complicated than the summations which are equations of the first degree.

The economic questions are concerned with the interdependence between quantities: the quantity of commodities, productive services and money, and the proportions in which these goods are mutually equalized in exchange, production and consumption, the simplest expression of which is price in terms of money. The condition necessary for an exact and thorough treatment of all these kinds of goods is that one imagines a definite number of homogeneous qualities of commodities and services. The assumption of homogeneity as to quality is a simplification and thus a fiction, at least if one does not imagine millions of separate types of goods. If we go so far in the opposite direction as to imagine only very few aggregative economic categories, the quantity of which is measured by an index and its price by an average, an exact result can only be obtained if we arbitrarily lay down definite rules of calculation. As the simplest way we shall, however, preliminarily imagine a certain great number of homogeneous types of goods and services, *e.g.*, 10,000 or 1,000 of each.

Instead of an explanation in which the component parts are the different commodities and services, it is also possible to go into greater

[2] Cf. the end of Chapter 39.

[3] Tinbergen, in *Review of Economic Studies*, February, 1940, p. 75, (reprinted in *Readings in Business Cycles Theories*, 1944, p. 65), mentions the following kinds of economic equations:

(I) a definition, *e.g.*, value equals price times quantity;
(II) a balance equation, *e.g.*, production equals consumption plus increase in stocks;
(III) a technical, natural or institutional connection;
(IV) a reaction equation. In general, the more "interesting" equations belong to this class, such as supply and demand equations. They always represent the reaction of groups of individuals or firms on certain economic conditions (incomes, prices, costs, etc.).

detail, considering the individual persons and firms. By aggregating the consumption and production of all individuals and firms, we shall return to the first-mentioned explanation.

If we want to have a comparatively simple and complete model, it is preferable to confine one's self to a closed economy, corresponding to an isolated country or the total world economy. The system may then later be elaborated by consideration of the relation between several economies.

It is also desirable to begin with static assumptions, *i.e.*, considering the conditions for equilibrium between the quantity of commodities and services of a certain period and the corresponding prices. An illustration of the dynamic interrelationships which in reality exist between one period and another, requires that also, increases, acceleration, and stocks should be included. This is best done by a later elaboration or reconstruction of the static explanation.

Something similar is the case with regard to the existence of few or many monopolies or monopsonies, either for commodities or for services, and with regard to state interference. Some of the partial interdependences will then be different and more complicated than under the assumption of absolutely free competition. Finally, the assumption of continuity, *i.e.*, full divisibility, also entails a simplification. Complete mobility is one of the imaginary conditions that may lead to a realization of the above-mentioned static assumption.

The following chapters will first illustrate a simplified model by means of Walras' equations and next show how the explanation may be extended and transformed in such a way that it will also be valid under a series of other assumptions.

The consequence of considering the economic interdependence as a network of partial interdependences is that the investigation will comprise two parts: in the first place, the survey of the location in the network of the individual categories, *i.e.*, an investigation of what kinds of connections they have and with which other categories; and in the second place a more detailed analysis of the nature of the different kinds of links.

The relation between two quantities may be by way of intermediary links, *e.g.*, the connection of a commodity with its raw material, the competitive connection of the latter with another raw material at the production of another commodity, the connection of raw material number two with a third commodity, etc.

If great changes take place at a certain point, experience shows us that the effects are dispersed far and wide. The effects, by the way, are weakened for every link, being scattered over greater and greater numbers of quantities. With regard to time, the effects do not always follow the basic economic chain of interdependences. Possibly an expectation of effects may only make itself felt at later, more mobile links in the chain, letting several intermediary links remain untouched. Purchases of finished articles may for instance be made for fear of failure in the delivery of the raw material, while sales through the intermediary links continue to take place undisturbed. But these are dynamic complications in the inter-dependence, which we disregard at this stage.

The conception of economics as an explanation of many, but firmly connected, links is at variance with attempts at giving in a few sentences a single, brief and comprehensive explanation. Nor does it admit of an eclectical linking together of disconnected, more or less contradictory bits of theories. But the conception allows room for alternative explanations in different cases and for replacement of individual components that are found less satisfactory.

More or less consciously the aim of all modern quantitative economics, according to the above-mentioned conception, seems to be the finding of explanations which, at any rate in essentials, correspond to determinate systems of equations. Adherents of the conception agree in assuming the aim to be that of giving a determinate solution on the basis of a great number of data and interdependences. The way in which one tries to solve the problem, or rather to find an applicable approximation, may differ, however.

CHAPTER 11

WALRAS' SYSTEM OF EQUATIONS

THE main purpose of economics is to explain a number of quantities: the quantities of commodities produced and consumed, the input of productive services, and prices of commodities as well as services. The explanation must account for the nature of the quantitative interdependences between the quantities examined and other exogenous quantities, which are taken as data. An interdependence between several quantities is expressed by an equation. Thus, if one wants to understand economic conditions, one cannot do without equations or, if one shies at mathematical symbols, one cannot do without the corresponding longer and less perspicuous and controllable verbal explanations.

The quantities sought for cannot be found separately, because several of them enter into the same equation. The price of a commodity, for instance, is connected with the prices of all the services used. If we have as many independent connections or equations as there are unknown quantities, it is possible, however, by changing the forms of our know-ledge, *i.e.*, by elimination and substitution of unknown quantities in the separate equations (or sentences), to set up a special explanation for each of the unknown quantities, into which no other unknown quantity enters, that is, a real explanation, an explanation by means of given data.

The number of independent equations must be the same as the number of unknowns. Neither must there be more since this would entail disagree-ment—unless the additional equations, by some remarkable coincidence, should agree with the results found from the other equations. However, as we shall see later, the possibility of more than one solution is not excluded even if the number of equations and unknowns is equal.

This is a short and popular explanation of the theory of equations. If we want to deal with the interdependence between quantities, there is no getting around this kind of logic, which is only the more difficult to carry through the more it is wrapped up in long and complicated verbal explanations. That systems of equations are applied to describe real life, is due to our belief in the interdependence and agreement between the economic phenomena, in the economic quantities being determinate in some way or other, which it is our problem to find out. What we are going to say about equations here is, by the way, not very complicated, because it is still a question of summations or, where this is not the case, because we leave open the problem of the form of the equations at this stage.

Though Walras' theory[1] dates from the beginning of the 1870's, it lived for a long time in the shadow of the classical English theory, just as in the case with Cournot's theory of monopoly, which also resorted to mathematical exposition. The theory was not known to larger circles until the period between the two wars, when Cassel's textbook appeared, and then only in a special simplified form (and without Walras' name being mentioned). The following is based on what may be called the central system of equations in Walras, who also has a treatment of demand based on the marginal utility theory, deals with interest, etc.

In this Chapter we have m qualities of commodities and their quantities

$$x_1, x_2, x_3 \ldots x_m,$$

and prices

$$1, p_2, p_3 \ldots p_m,$$

the currency being included as standard of value. It has the price "1", corresponding to the costs of production, and x_1 is the quantity produced and consumed, *i.e.*, the quantity with which it enters is the annual wear and tear (cf. Chapters 16 and 18.3).

Further we reckon with n productive services in the quantities

$$y_1, y_2, y_3 \ldots y_n$$

and prices

$$\pi_1, \pi_2, \pi_3 \ldots \pi_n$$

There are, moreover, mn technical coefficients, which indicate for each commodity how much of each productive service is used for production:

$$a_{1,1}, a_{1,2}, a_{1,3} \ldots a_{1,n}$$
$$a_{2,1}, a_{2,2}, a_{2,3} \ldots a_{2,n}$$
$$\cdots\cdots\cdots\cdots\cdots\cdots\cdots\cdots\cdots$$

[1] Leon Walras, *Élement d'Économie politique pure ou Théorie de la Richesse sociale*, F. Rouge, Lausanne, 1879, Leçon 20–22, Third Edition, 1896; *Mathematische Theorie der Preisbestimmung der Wirtschaftlichen Güter*, Ferdinand Enke, Stuttgart, 1881, especially pp. 47–52. *The Elements of Pure Economics*, published by The American Economic Association and Royal Economic Society, London, 1954, lessons 20–22.

In the present exposition we add hereto the possible unutilized remainders of each productive service:

$$r_1, r_2, r_3 \ldots r_n$$

These are the unknowns of the system. Between these and the quantities given as data we have the following six groups of equations:

11.1, DEMAND EQUATIONS

We here put down the conditions determining the quantities of a commodity demanded. Since in this sphere we cannot lay down a definite rule for the extremely complicated ways in which the other variables influence the quantity, we only write that the quantity is a function of certain variables. The quantity demanded is especially dependent on the price of the commodity itself and normally varies inversely with it. Further it is dependent on other prices, rises when the prices of substitutes rise, and falls when the prices of complementary commodities rise. Through the spending of incomes there is, moreover, a stronger or weaker connection with the prices of most other commodities. And finally, the level of income exercises a strong influence on quantities demanded. Income is here expressed in terms of prices of the productive services π_1, π_2, etc., disregarding subsequent redistribution of income. More detailed investigation of the conditions of demand follows in Chapter 19. As a preliminary we may say that the object is only to indicate the place of demand in the interdependence of the whole. In addition to the unknown quantities mentioned above, the demand equations contain constants, expressing the condition of wants, which are taken as data. As regards the demand for the unit of measurement, commodity No. 1, which we assume is used as money, special conditions prevail with which we are going to deal further in Chapters 16 and 18. We may put down tentatively the demand equations for the other commodities:

(1)
$$x_2 = f_2(p_2, p_3 \ldots p_m, \pi_1, \pi_2, \pi_3 \ldots \pi_n)$$
$$x_m = f_m(p_m, p_2 \ldots p_{m-1}, \pi_1, \pi_2, \pi_3 \ldots \pi_n)$$

We have here a demand equation for any commodity (with the exception of No. 1) set down in such a form that the quantities are the dependent variables. From the propensity to consume for all commodities, we might also derive equations in which the prices of commodities were placed to the left as a function of all quantities, together with income. On the whole, it is not a question of an isolated function, or a separate interdependence for each commodity, but of a more complicated consumption–propensity interdependence, comprising all prices and quantities, from which the separate demand functions may be derived.

It is not necessary to assume any rational behavior on the part of consumers, if only a constant behavior exists for all consumers taken together.

11.2, COST EQUATIONS

It can generally be assumed that prices have a tendency to vary in the same direction as costs. We here apply the simple assumption, which is but rarely fully realized (though at a high degree of competition and mobility it is very nearly valid) that the price per unit of a commodity is equal to the payment for the productive services used, *i.e.*, the quantity multiplied by the price. Thus for each commodity we get a cost equation:

(2)
$$1 = a_{1,1} \cdot \pi_1 + a_{1,2} \cdot \pi_2 \ldots a_{1,n} \cdot \pi_n$$
$$p_2 = a_{2,1} \cdot \pi_1 + a_{2,2} \cdot \pi_2 \ldots a_{2,n} \cdot \pi_n$$
$$\ldots\ldots\ldots\ldots\ldots\ldots\ldots\ldots\ldots\ldots\ldots\ldots\ldots\ldots\ldots$$
$$p_m = a_{m,1} \cdot \pi_1 + a_{m,2} \cdot \pi_2 \ldots a_{m,n} \cdot \pi_m$$

Contrary to the demand equations, which may be presumed to be of a very complicated nature, the cost equations are simple sums, *i.e.*, linear equations.[2] If we are satisfied with the main items, they are also easy to fill out with figures. The quantities $a_{1,1}$ etc., are the technical coefficients, indicating for each unit of a commodity how many units of a productive service have been used (the first subscript thus indicating the number of the commodity). These coefficients, as appears from equations No. 5 are also variable. If nothing of a productive service is used for a commodity, the technical coefficient, and thus the corresponding term in the price sum, will be 0. If one of the productive services is a free piece of goods, *i.e.*, has the price of 0, the price, and thus the term, also becomes 0. Joint production, the manufacture of intermediary products and other technical complications are disregarded temporarily, but they will be dealt with in Chapter 15.

Since the commodity and the services employed are different in nature, there can be no question of an equation in the same technical units between the commodity and the services employed. A loaf of bread is not equal to x grams of wheat plus y minutes of agricultural work, etc. A measurement, *e.g.*, in quantity of material or quantity of energy is not economically relevant; nor does it give any equation without including the possible wastage. It is, however, a question of an equality in price, which is here postulated. In other words, it is this hypothesis which gives the equation. If we are to deal with cases where equality in price does not appear, the equations here mentioned must be modified by the addition to costs of profits or losses, which must then be explained by monopolies, dynamic phenomena, etc.

Whereas the demand equations have been put down as a blank "questionnaire to real life", the cost equation contains a definite meaning, but, as mentioned above, this rests on a postulate, an assumption which can only be expected to be approximately realized under definite, rarely occurring conditions.

[2] The price is the relation between two quantities, consequently of zero degree.

E

11.3 and 11.4, QUANTITY EQUATIONS OF PRODUCTIVE SERVICES, AND SUPPLEMENTARY CONDITIONS

The total quantity of a productive service must be equal to the quantity employed for each of the commodities plus a possible unemployed remainder. If there should be a remainder, it is here assumed that the productive service in question is a free good, *i.e.*, has the price of 0. It is not justified in advance to confine oneself to the scarce productive services, *i.e.*, those productive services that are not free, because we do not know in advance which will be free. An example might be the question of where the limit for no-rent land will be.[3] The quantity equations of productive services may be stated as follows:

$$(3) \qquad y_1 = a_{1,1} \cdot x_1 + a_{2,1} \cdot x_2 \ldots a_{m,1} \cdot x_m + r_1$$
$$y_2 = a_{1,2} \cdot x_1 + a_{2,2} \cdot x_2 \ldots a_{m,2} \cdot x_m + r_2$$
$$\cdots\cdots\cdots\cdots\cdots\cdots\cdots\cdots\cdots$$
$$y_n = a_{1,n} \cdot x_1 + a_{2,n} \cdot x_2 \ldots a_{m,n} \cdot x_m + r_n$$

where y_1, y_2, etc., indicate quantities, and r_1, r_2, etc., the unemployed remainders.

To this must be added, however, expressions (of which the following are illustrations) indicating that a productive service cannot at the same time have an unemployed remainder and a price different from 0:

$$(4) \qquad r_1 \cdot \pi_1 = 0$$
$$r_2 \cdot \pi_2 = 0$$
$$\cdots\cdots\cdots\cdots\cdots$$
$$r_n \cdot \pi_n = 0$$

The quantity equations of the productive services (3) represent a formal statement of the relationships. The supplementary condition (4) is dependent on a simple hypothesis, which will be realized when there is free competition for the services.

11.5, EQUATIONS FOR THE TECHNICAL SUBSTITUTION

As mentioned above, the technical coefficients indicate how much of each productive service is used for the production of one unit of each commodity. The coefficients enter into both the cost equations and the quantity equations of the productive services. They are not given in

---

[3] Zeuthen, *Den økonomiske Fordeling*, Copenhagen, Nyt Nordisk Forlag, 1928, pp. 23–24; Ohlin in *Nationaløkonomisk Tidsskrift*, 1929, p. 73, Zeuthen, *ibid.*, p. 151, and *Zeitschrift für Nationalökonomie*, 1932 and 1933; Stackelberg, *Zeitschrift für Nationalökonomie*, 1933; Wald: *Zeitschrift für Nationalökonomie*, 1936, and *Econometrica*, 1951. Kennet J. Arrow and Gerard Debreu, "Existence of an Equilibrium for a Competitive Economy", *Econometrica*, July 1954, particularly pp. 265–6 and 287 ff.

advance, but are dependent on the prices of the productive services. Thus we obtain the following m.n equations:

(5)
$$a_{1,1} = f(\pi_1, \pi_2 \ldots \pi_n)$$
$$a_{1,2} = f(\pi_1, \pi_2 \ldots \pi_n)$$
$$\ldots\ldots\ldots\ldots\ldots\ldots\ldots\ldots\ldots$$
$$a_{2,1} = f(\pi_1, \pi_2 \ldots \pi_n)$$
$$\ldots\ldots\ldots\ldots\ldots\ldots\ldots\ldots\ldots$$
$$a_{m,n} = f(\pi_1, \pi_2 \ldots \pi_n)$$

for all n.m technical coefficients. It is worth noticing that it is the prices of productive services, and not of the commodities, that determine which technical coefficient is most advantageous and that these equations assume that the cheapest combination is chosen (or at any rate that there is a definite reaction to the prices of productive services). There is considerably more probability of a rational behavior on the part of firms, especially in the choice of a technique of production in the long run, than on the part of the individuals as consumers, workers and savers. Therefore, the teaching of business economics as to what is most remunerative may, with great caution and under competitive conditions, be used as a theory concerning the actual behavior of firms. But the whole of this question is dealt with further in Part IV, Chapters 59–61. With regard to conditions of production and costs, readers may be referred to Chapter 20.

11.6, SUPPLY EQUATIONS OF PRODUCTIVE SERVICES

Finally, the inputs of productive services during a period are dependent on the price of the services, as well as on the commodity prices, since it generally is the "real" income which is compared with real cost.

(6)
$$y_1 = f(\pi_1, \pi_2 \ldots \pi_n \, p_2 \ldots p_m)$$
$$y_2 = f(\pi_1, \pi_2 \ldots \pi_n \, p_2 \ldots p_m)$$
$$\ldots\ldots\ldots\ldots\ldots\ldots\ldots\ldots\ldots\ldots\ldots\ldots\ldots$$
$$y_m = f(\pi_1, \pi_2 \ldots \pi_n, p_2 \ldots p_m)$$

What one wants to offer of a certain kind of service is also, of course, dependent on the income yielded by the other services. The quantity of a certain kind of service may be imagined to be constant, and the dependence on price may thus actually be equal to 0, but the question of a possible dependence may at any rate be asked. These equations, like the demand equations and the technical substitution equations, are blank equations, which have to be filled in empirically (cf. further Chapter 21), whereas the cost equations and the quantity equations of the productive services with the supplementary conditions are based on definite hypotheses, which with a certain inexactitude may be called static free competition assumptions.

11.7, EQUATIONS AND UNKNOWNS. THE POSITION OF MONEY

The system we have outlined above has the following unknowns (dependent variables):

> m quantities of commodities (inclusive of the deterioration of coins during the period)
> $m - 1$ commodity prices (the price of money being given $= 1$)
> n quantities of productive services
> n prices of productive services
> n unemployed remainders of productive services
> mn technical coefficients

in all $2m + 3n + mn - 1$ unknown.

At the same time we have the following equations:

> (1) $m - 1$ demand equations
> (2) m cost equations
> (3) n quantity equations for productive services
> (4) n remainder conditions for productive services
> (5) mn technical substitution equations
> (6) n supply equations for productive services

i.e., also $2m + 3n + mn - 1$ equations. In Walras' own exposition, which does not include the unemployed remainders, the number is $2n$ instead of here $3n$.

Money is considered to be one of the commodities demanded, but at the same time is used as a measure of value. Its demand equation may be derived by subtracting all expenses for the purchase of other commodities, *i.e.*, the products of price and quantity for all real commodities, from total income. The calculation is made by application of all cost equations (2) and all quantity equations for productive services (3), in the way that the former is multiplied by the quantity of the individual commodities, and the latter by the price of the productive service, after which the sums are taken separately for each group. We shall then in either case on the right side have the same sum of products of three quantities ($x_1 . a_{1,1} . \pi_1$, etc.), while for the first group of equations on the left side we have an expression of total expenses, and for the second group an expression of total income. The equation also includes the quantity of money demanded, multiplied by the price of money, which, as mentioned above, was put at 1. The equation stating that total income is equal to total expenses, and from which the demand for money is found by subtracting the demand for the other commodities ($x_2 p_2 + x_3 p_3 \ldots x_m p_m$) from total income, we have obtained here from the equations (2) and (3). It is written:

(1a) $$x_1 . 1 + x_2 p_2 \ldots x_m p_m = y_1 \pi_1 + y_2 \pi_2 \ldots y_n \pi_n$$

As equality between total income and total expenses already is given as a consequence of the static assumption, this demand equation for money is not a new independent equation. One may, however, at will[4] exclude either this derived demand equation, or another equation, *e.g.*, the cost equation for money. This was only a simplified beginning: other more realistic assumptions with regard to money are dealt with in Chapters 18.3 and 42.

11.8, SOME SMALLER MODIFICATIONS

Cassel, as mentioned above, has contributed very much towards making the description of economic equilibrium by means of a system of simultaneous equations known in wider circles, and he has given it a central position in his theoretical system. However, Cassel's equations are a simplification, which on several points deviates from the original Walrasian equations: (1) in the demand functions only the commodity prices have been included as determining the quantity of the individual commodity, (2) only one single method of production is assumed, *i.e.*, the technical coefficients are considered as constant, (3) the quantity of productive services is assumed to be constant, (4) national income is taken as given. In this way one circumvents the questions of money and absolute prices, which are postponed for later treatment. Since Cassel, moreover, only considers "scarce productive services", *i.e.*, services having no unemployed remainders, he succeeds in reducing the number of groups of equations to 3: demand equations, cost equations, and quantity equations of productive services, and all these equations are given a simpler form. The danger is, however, that Cassel in his popular and self-contained formulation presents his own strongly simplified system as if it includes everything essential. In this connection, he relegates the technical substitution equations to a less important position as a "supplementary principle". In a similar way he degrades the effect of the prices of productive services on supply—in both cases with a strong polemical front against the classical and neo-classical economists who attach a decisive and probably much exaggerated importance to these conditions. The correct standpoint, however, seems to be to include all possible methods of variation and, consequently, all groups of equations as equally important,

[4] Cf. Walras, *Mathematische Theorie*, p. 52 above; Lindahl, *Studies*, p. 283. Lindahl follows Walras' explanation of money as coins, but adds, "If the prices, however, are expressed in an arbitrary monetary unit, the problem is determined except for a certain 'multiplicative factor' (cf. Cassel, *Theory of Social Economy*, p. 151) which enters into all money prices and determines the absolute height of the general price level and the value of money." Arthur W. Marget in "Monetary Aspects of the Walrasian System", *Journal of Political Economy*, 1935, emphasizes that Walras does not, as some people think, build on the assumption of barter with money only as a standard of measurement (Cassel), but considers it as coins. Rosenstein-Rodan in "The Coordination of the General Theories of Money and Prices", *Economica*, 1936, describes the difficulty of including money in a static system of equilibrium. Don Patinkin, "Relative Price, Say's Law and the Demand for Money", *Econometrica*, April, 1948, and "The Indeterminacy of Absolute Prices in Classical Economic Theory", *Econometrica*, January, 1949. See p. 241 in *The Elements of Pure Economics*, 1954.

so long as it has not been empirically demonstrated that some of them are of small importance, which at any rate cannot be proved with regard to technical substitution.

On the other hand, one may agree with Cassel as to the possibility of giving a picture of economic life with the maximum of simplification by means of the three above-mentioned groups of equations, which together express the scarcity of means of production in relation to wants. (The corresponding simplification: one commodity that may be produced in different ways, is too unrealistic.) If in the end everything is included as it ought to be, it will be an expositional or didactic question if one wants to begin with Cassel and proceed to Walras. I shall here, contrary to what I have done previously, choose to start directly with Walras, the more so because the road further forward from Walras, by additions to and rebuildings of his system in view of real conditions, is of special importance. In Chapter 16 dealing with the relation between technical substitution in the production of the same commodity, and substitution of different commodities in consumption, as well as in the next chapter, dealing with a miniature model founded on the limited assumptions of Cassel, we continue the discussion of these problems.

A simple reformulation[5] of some of the equations may be made by multiplying both sides of the equation by the same quantity. In this manner we obtain, instead of price or quantity of commodities and services, price multiplied by quantity, *i.e.*, flows of income and expenses. Especially when we abandon the exact approach with homogeneous categories and aggregate series of related categories, we have sums of money, which are, like average prices and quantity indices, of a somewhat arbitrary character. This descriptive device has been employed with reference to the circular flow of the economy, Chapters 14 and 39.

Besides putting together several special categories so as to form total economic categories, which is of special importance in the more practical, dynamic investigations, it is possible, without leaving the static free competition assumptions, to proceed to an individualization both with regard to the demand of the population and its incomes from productive services and with regard to firms. This phenomenon has also been illustrated in the above-mentioned circular flow model with the in other directions somewhat simplified system of equations. The functions of reaction for demand and supply of productive services have here been put down for each household, and the quantities of these are summed up. In the same way the quantities are summed up for the individual firms.[6]

Ohlin[7] illustrates the effect of the distribution of income on demand by

[5] Cf. Lindahl, *Studies, inter alia* equation (4), p. 282, in accordance with Bowley, *Mathematical Groundwork of Economics*, The Clarendon Press, Oxford, 1924.

[6] A special case of an analysis going down to the individuals is the barter market with constant individual production (during the period). Economists have also spoken about the barter market without production, but the analysis must in this case be dynamic since it had to be a question of gradual consumption of given stocks.

[7] Bertil Ohlin, *International and Interregional Trade*, Harvard Press, 1933, p. 555.

substituting for the prices of the productive services, expressing the functional distribution, the total income of individuals. At the same time he adds some new equations in which the income of the individual is put equal to the sum of the products of quantity and price for the different productive services he delivers.

What has here been mentioned is only a few minor modifications of the Walrasian equations. Of considerably greater interest are the greater additions and rebuildings that must be made when from "static free competition assumptions" we proceed to dynamics, monopoly, state interference, etc., and when the theory of money and capital is to be built into the economic system. But with regard to these questions we refer to Chapter 18. As mentioned above, the essential thing is not a specific system of equations, but the understanding of economic life as a network of interdependences which can be illustrated in exact form by a system of equations.

CHAPTER 12

THEORETICAL REFLECTIONS AND PRACTICAL "SOLUTIONS" OF THE EQUATIONS

WALRAS' system of equations and the above-mentioned modified versions of it have as many equations as unknowns.[1] Consequently, they are determinate by the data of the system. The recording of this fact does not say much until we know something more about the contents of the equations, *i.e.*, about the interrelationships among the determining factors. An explanation of economic life which is to be significant must do more than name the determining factors. It must above all elucidate the causal relations in a practical way by telling us something of the manner in which different changes in assumptions will change the result, since the aim of economics is to predict and control.

We know something, however, about the different kinds of links in the chain, the different types of equations. From accounting and statistics we have a very comprehensive knowledge of the interdependences which are summations, *i.e.*, cost connections between the sum of prices for the productive services and the prices for the commodity produced thereby, and the distribution of the total quantity of productive services among different commodities. The nature of the other equations, which are expressing the more complicated reactions, *i.e.*, the demand functions,

---

[1] Not any system of equations filling this condition, however, is suitable to describe economic conditions where all prices and quantities must be either a positive figure or zero.

the production functions and the laws of supply for productive services, is to be dealt with further in Chapters 19–21. In those fields our knowledge is still limited.

As it must be presumed that there are non-linear demand curves and non-linear curves for the production function as well as for the relation between labor supply and wages, part of the equations must be presumed to be of a higher degree. Several solutions are therefore possible.[2]

If we reckon with a large number of homogeneous qualities and multi-dimensional functions, a very large number of solutions may be presumed to be consistent with the given conditions. Since nevertheless, the actual state of things is determinate in one way or other, there must be some further conditions which we have not included in our theory. The explanation of the actual solution must presumably be dynamic, and may be obtained by following the path towards it.

Even if we assume full determination with regard to real life, our theory must sometimes stop at several possible solutions. This will especially be the case when, as in the systems of equations dealt with above, we make strong abstractions. We then disregard a number of determining conditions—partly conditions which it is impossible to know anything about, *e.g.*, the intentions and caprices of leading persons.

An argument in favor of a single solution determined by economic forces (and therefore popular among economists) is the assumption of a behavior giving the individual firm an absolute maximum of profit and the individual person an absolute maximum of welfare. Making unrealistic assumptions about full knowledge, unlimited willingness to exchange goods, as long as the parties can obtain an advantage thereby, and absolute continuity, it should be possible *in abstracto* to construct a common absolute maximum as the only stable point of equilibrium. The said tendencies must be assumed, however, to have only a limited strength in real life.

A plurality of solutions does not mean lawlessness. On the contrary, a number of conditions will have to be fulfilled. The solutions found must still be considered as an infinitesimal part of all imaginable possibilities, *e.g.*, some million points in a multi-dimensional room. It is, of course, an extremely unrealistic idea that it should be possible to obtain the politically most desirable of the possible solutions by a small temporary shock, leading to a realization of another of the imaginable solutions. It is by changing data and not by manipulations with unchanged data that there are possibilities of attaining political aims. With otherwise unchanged data and frictionless adaptation, conditions after small disturbances will generally revert to the previous equilibrium, whereas it is in practise

---

[2] A. Wald: "Über einige Gleichgewichtssysteme der Mathematischen Ökonomie", *Zeitschrift für Nationalökonomie*, 1936; Stackelberg, *ibid.*, 1932, Zeuthen, *ibid.*, 1932 and 1933, as well as "*Den økonomiske Fordeling*", I, lo. In some cases other defects may appear even if the number of variables and equations is equal, cf. p. 4 in Don Patinkin's article in *Econometrica*, January 1949. See Chapter 11, n. 3, for Arrow and Debreu.

impossible by means of a vigorous temporary influence to reach one of the other solutions of the old system. Real conditions seem to be too complicated and too little known to permit a conscious manipulation which by a temporary change of data lead to another equilibrium under the original conditions. The possibility of an only temporary effect of that kind of small shock, is very limited since any influence, even a short one, *e.g.*, through changed saving and investment, will alter the data for the subsequent development.

A solution indicates a combination of the quantities for the dependent variables that are consistent with the data. The stability of the solution is another question. Will it reappear after a greater or smaller change of data? This as well as the question whether a tendency of movement, towards static equilibrium is likely to lead to the goal will be dealt with in Part III, Chapters 25 and 26, where we deal with dynamics.

Though it is impossible to construct a complete and absolutely correct system of determining conditions or equations, it is still possible in some ways to discuss how the equations are solved in real life, if by this we mean the way in which a system of several equations brings about a definite solution. It will then be seen, for instance, how a surplus or deficit arises if the cost condition is not fulfilled, and how, consequently, with the assumption of free competition, an adaptation is started in the direction of equality between price and costs.

For simplified models it is possible to solve systems of equations. The invention of large-scale electronic computing machines makes the solution even of a great number of equations possible, in any case in which linearity is assumed. How much error this simplification involves in different cases seems to be an essential problem. An important example is the use of fixed coefficients of production (cf. the end of Chapter 39).

The adaptation, *i.e.*, the tendency towards a solution in real life in accordance with all conditions applying to economic affairs, takes place by the individual units: consumers, firms and owners of labor and other means of production, adapt the quantity produced or consumed by themselves, or choose the way in which to apply their own productive services, taking prices and other conditions as given. In monopoly the individual also adapts his price. Thus, even if the individual persons take all conditions with the exception of a single one or some few ones as given, their influence is felt nevertheless. Commodity prices, for instance, are raised by greater consumption and are lowered by an increase in production. The quantities that are variable in the economy of the whole society are in a big market with free competition considered to be constant by the individual.

Only if we confine ourselves to a limited number of equations, will it be possible to attempt a solution by means of statistics. Especially when we use a dynamic approach, it is of advantage to have equations for comprehensive, total economic categories (average and index). In that case we shall first, by means of the "unknowns", *i.e.*, the dependent variables, which in fact are known for a number of periods, find the form and constants of the equations (the data), and next the unknowns, corresponding to new data, either by a prognosis, reckoning with continuation of certain tendencies of movement in the ensuing periods, or as guidance for political action by investigating the consequences of certain chosen changes in data. At the construction of national budgets, which partly use summations from ordinary statistics and partly—no doubt often extremely approximate—calculations by estimates of certain reaction functions with regard to changes in production, consumption and input of labor, an orientation is actually given by means of an incomplete system of equations for society as a whole. A numerical solution can in any case only be given if we confine ourselves either to some few total categories or to a small sector of the whole system.

The object in constructing an abstract and complete system of equations like that of Walras is not to solve the equations. Nor can anything really new issue from the construction of them, the equations being on one hand founded on hypothetical assumptions made by ourselves, and on the other hand being blank questionnaires to be filled in with real figures. But what we attain is a testing of the internal consistency of our conceptual apparatus. It is shown that by a series of sentences, giving simplified pictures of essential real conditions, we may arrive at a consistent explanation with regard to some of the most important economic conditions. In other words, a coordination takes place of a number of separately known partial explanations, by which we make sure that the total explanation within its frame becomes complete and consistent. Thus we obtain a systematic survey of the totality as well as an orientation, a questionnaire, a map to be used in partial investigations. The practical usefulness becomes considerably greater, however, when we proceed from the very limited assumptions of the first model and include dynamics, monopoly, state interference, money capital, etc. But the logical character of the explanation is not changed by these extensions.

CHAPTER 13

A MINIATURE MODEL

THE numerical example below and the adjoining figure are intended to give the simplest possible picture of the main lines in the economic interdependence which exists within a closed society. In accordance with the simplified equation system of Cassel, we here assume given quantities of productive services, a single method of production for each commodity, a given total income and demand functions independent of the distribution of income. As above, x indicates the quantity of commodities, p the price of the commodity, y the quantity of productive services, π the prices of these, and r possible unemployed remainders of the services.

Demand equations:

$$x_1 = \frac{24}{p_1} \quad (1) \qquad\qquad x_2 = \frac{48}{p_2} \quad (2)$$

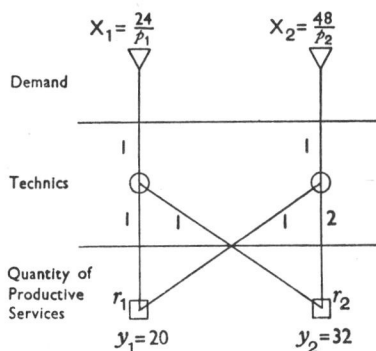

Fig. 2. A Miniature Model

With the special form we have chosen here we assume a constant total income of $24 + 48$ and, moreover, the elasticity 1 for each commodity. The use of absolute figures makes it possible to find the absolute height of prices.

Cost equations:

$$p_1 = \pi_1 + \pi_2 \quad (3) \qquad\qquad p_2 = \pi_1 + 2\pi_2 \quad (4)$$

For each of the productive services we reckon with the alternative: either no unemployed remainder or the price 0. Of the three possibilities: no remainder, remainder of the first productive service, and remainder of the second productive service, we shall try first possibility No. 1, and we have then the quantity equations of the productive services (5) and (6) not containing any r. The fourth possibility, a remainder of both productive services, is impossible with the insatiable demand assumed in the example.

$$y_1 = 20 = x_1 + x_2 \quad (5) \qquad\qquad y_2 = 32 = x_1 + 2x_2 \quad (6)$$

So long as full utilization of both productive services is assumed, the quantities of commodities can be found solely from the quantity equations of the productive services, (5) and (6):

$$x_1 = 8 \text{ and } x_2 = 12$$

By inserting these in the demand equations (1) and (2) we find:

$$p_1 = 3 \text{ and } p_2 = 4$$

and in the cost equations (3) and (4):

$$\pi_1 = 2 \text{ and } \pi_2 = 1$$

If the assumption of no unemployed remainder of any productive service had given a negative price for one productive service in the solution of the equations, we should have had to try the said second or third possibility and in the equations (5) or (6) have included a remainder as unknown, while the price of the service in question was put at 0. If, for instance, we had $y_2 = 16$, we should have had a remainder of y_1 and the altered equation (5) $20 = x_1 + x_2 + r_1$, as well as the new equation $\pi_1 = 0$ and equation (6) in the new form $16 = x_1 + 2x_2$.

If the quantity of the first productive service, y_1, is kept constant $= 20$, the quantity of the second productive service, y_2, if there are to be no unemployed remainders, solely for technical reasons cannot be smaller than 20 or larger than 40. If y_2 is below 20, we must have a remainder of y_1 (*i.e.*, $r_1 > 0$), even in case only the least y_2-consuming commodity, x_2, is produced. On the other hand, if y_2 is larger than 40, there must be a remainder of y_2 (*i.e.*, $r_2 > 0$), even in case only the most y_2-consuming commodity, x_2, is produced.

Since according to the demand equations (1) and (2) price and quantity vary inversely and a major curtailment of the quantity of one commodity involves a considerable price rise, production of only one commodity could not absorb the available quantities of the productive services, y_1 and y_2. Consequently, the economic margins for full employment of both productive services are more narrow, however, than the above-mentioned technical ones. The economic margins 30 and $33\frac{1}{3}$ are found by putting the price of a productive service and its remainder equal to 0 at the same time. The size of the above-mentioned margin for economic adaptation with full employment for both productive services is dependent on the nature of the demand functions. If the two commodities had been complete substitutes, the economic margins would have coincided with the technical ones.

The size of the dependent variables for different values of y_2, with the assumptions indicated in the above equations and in the figure, is given in the table below. The table shows how a change in one of the data of the system (y_2) involves changes in the dependent variables. Corresponding tables[1] and curves may be constructed for a change in one of the technical coefficients or one of the constants of the demand equations. As will be evident, there is a possibility, within certain limits, of a continuous adaptation when data are changed, but the adaptation changes its character at the points where one of the productive services becomes scarce. So long as a productive service is a free good, the other factors are not affected by

---

[1] F. Zeuthen, *Zeitschrift für Nationalökonomie*, 1932; cf. also the more detailed analysis concerning, among other things, the similarity between the effect of the increase of a factor in the production of a single commodity and, in the present example, with two commodities, in B. Gloerfelt-Tarp, "The Marginal Productive Function and the Walras Cassel System of Equations", *Nordisk Tidsskrift for Teknisk Økonomi*, 1948. With regard to the effect of income on demand and the application of one commodity as standard of measurement, cf. the Danish edition of this book, pp. 55–57.

changes in its quantity; only the unemployed remainder varies. If both productive services have a positive price, a change in quantity involves a change in all variable factors. Gradually as the quantity of the service decreases, its price is increased (from 0 at the margin), the price of the other service falls (towards 0), the quantities of at least some commodities fall, and the price rises. The reverse may be true, however (see Table 1 with regard to x_1). If, finally, the quantities of the variable service become so small that the other service becomes a free good, the commodity quantities fall and the commodity prices as well as the prices of the services themselves rise together with the unemployed remainder of the other service.

TABLE 1

	T	E						E	T
y_2	50	40	$33\frac{1}{3}$	33	32	31	30	20	16
x_1	$6\frac{2}{3}$	$6\frac{2}{3}$	$6\frac{2}{3}$	7	8	9	10	$6\frac{2}{3}$	$5\frac{1}{3}$
p_1	$3\frac{3}{5}$	$3\frac{3}{5}$	$3\frac{3}{5}$	$3\frac{3}{7}$	3	$2\frac{2}{3}$	$2\frac{2}{5}$	$3\frac{3}{5}$	$4\frac{1}{2}$
x_2	$13\frac{1}{3}$	$13\frac{1}{3}$	$13\frac{1}{3}$	13	12	11	10	$6\frac{2}{3}$	$5\frac{1}{3}$
p_2	$3\frac{3}{5}$	$3\frac{3}{5}$	$3\frac{3}{5}$	$3\frac{9}{13}$	4	$4\frac{4}{11}$	$4\frac{4}{5}$	$7\frac{1}{5}$	9
π_1	$3\frac{3}{5}$	$3\frac{3}{5}$	$3\frac{3}{5}$	$3\frac{15}{91}$	2	$\frac{32}{33}$	0	0	0
π_2	0	0	0	$\frac{24}{91}$	1	$1\frac{23}{33}$	$2\frac{2}{5}$	$3\frac{3}{5}$	$4\frac{1}{2}$
r_l	0	0	0	0	0	0	0	$6\frac{2}{3}$	$9\frac{1}{3}$
r_2	$16\frac{2}{3}$	$6\frac{2}{3}$	0	0	0	0	0	0	0

$$y_1 = 20$$

What is of interest here is that already in the little example given above, where each commodity can only be produced in one way, we have a certain elasticity of adaptation, so that there may appear a series of combinations with positive prices of commodities and productive services. This elasticity is essentially increased if we include a greater number of commodities and reckon with a higher degree of substitution between them. The elasticity of adaptation is further increased if we assume that the same commodity may be produced in several ways, *i.e.*, reckon with technical substitution. However, we are able to reproduce the most, essential features of a gradual economic adaptation also without including the type of variation just mentioned. The conditions which are expressed in the equations in this section and which always assert themselves, *viz.*, demand for the commodities, connection between commodity prices and price of the productive services as well as a limited quantity of the latter, are sufficient to explain a process of price formation in accordance with what Cassel calls the "scarcity principle". The result of the price formation is modified, however, if we include in our analysis other conditions, such as technical substitution or variation in the quantities of productive services as a result of the price offered. And it may be questionable which form of variation is of greatest importance. (Cf. Chapter 16.)

By means of the example it is also possible to illustrate the demand and supply of a commodity in partial equilibrium analysis. Equation (1) alone indicates demand for the first commodity. Its supply is determined by all the other equations (or the corresponding part of the figure), from which can be formed one equation between the price and the quantity of the commodity. (Cf. Chapter 17 and Figure 5C and D on p. 73.) It appears that supply depends on the technical conditions for production of the commodity, the supply of necessary productive services and their employment in the production of the other commodity, which, again, is dependent on the technical coefficients of this commodity, access to other necessary productive services, and demand. The more that must be taken from the other commodity, the more intensively the demand for the latter makes itself felt. This means that the reversed demand curve of the competing commodities enters into the supply curve of a commodity. Under real conditions, it is also necessary to add among other things the effect of the prices of the productive services on their quantity.

CHAPTER 14

THE ECONOMIC CIRCULATION

FROM the model just described we proceed to a circulation model by including the relation between the payment of the productive services and the demand for the commodities. We may imagine Figure 2 placed on a cylinder, and the supply function for services drawn on its back.[1] If we include the relation between incomes and demand, we may form a model with a network of connecting links or equations—in which we now also include the individual persons and firms and reckon with the possibility of choice between different techniques. This model illustrates the circulation of flows of payment from the incomes of consumers to the incomes of

[1] Phelps Brown, *The Framework of the Pricing System*, Chapman & Hall, London, 1936, pp. 12–13.

firms, and from firms in payment of the different kinds of services, which are gathered together again as the incomes of individual persons. At the same time there appears a circulation in the opposite direction for the real goods from productive services to the production result of the firms, from here to consumption, and finally, from the persons, who are both consumers and owners of the means of production, to the services.

For the flow of payments money may be used as a uniform standard of measurement, the equations of Chapter 11 being adapted to the "form of payment" by multiplication on both sides with either price or quantity, whereby the flows can be expressed as amounts in money per unit of time. The other flow of goods and services, for which payments are made, has no common standard. If we want to put up an account for it, we shall have to consider the way in which the quantity of materials and power is kept constant from link to link, also including wastage, the not-paid-for quantities. As an example of such a real account, we may mention the "water balance" of the country, its nitrogen economy, the circulation of nutrition, calories and power economy, as well as the budgets of the war and post-war periods concerning the use of iron, fuel, wood, and other scarce raw materials. This circulation for commodities and services or, from another point of view, for materials and power, is not investigated as a rule in the study of the economic interdependence.

Static equilibrium, to which we confine ourselves temporarily, assumes equally great payment from link to link. It can be shown how the circulating total flow of payments is transformed three times: (1) by the splitting up of the income flow of individual persons among the commodities and the collection of the payment of all individuals for each of these, (2) by the splitting up of the flow of payments for each commodity among the payment for each kind of productive service and the aggregation of the contributions of all commodities for each of the individual services, (3) by the splitting up of these income flows, of specific character, among the individuals as owners and the collection of the individual persons' flows from different sources into the total income of the individual. Whereas a collection and measurement of the flows of payment of the individuals (householding money) and of the firms is something actually taking place, the aggregation into a number of income categories is only a stage in national accounting, where a calculation is possible and of scientific interest, but not actually taking place. It is possible, therefore, to simplify the picture by excluding this only theoretical stage.

The static flow of payments has been illustrated on page 60 by the Fig. 3 and the adjoining Table 2, which also show the relation with the equations given in Chapter 11. In the figure we have taken account of 3 individuals or groups of persons, 4 commodities or groups of commodities, and 2 kinds of productive services or groups of services. The 6 lines marked "S" indicate the interdependences corresponding to summations. What takes place here is a joining or splitting up of the smaller flows. Each of the three transformations (S_1 to S_2, S_3 to S_4, S_5 to S_6) consists

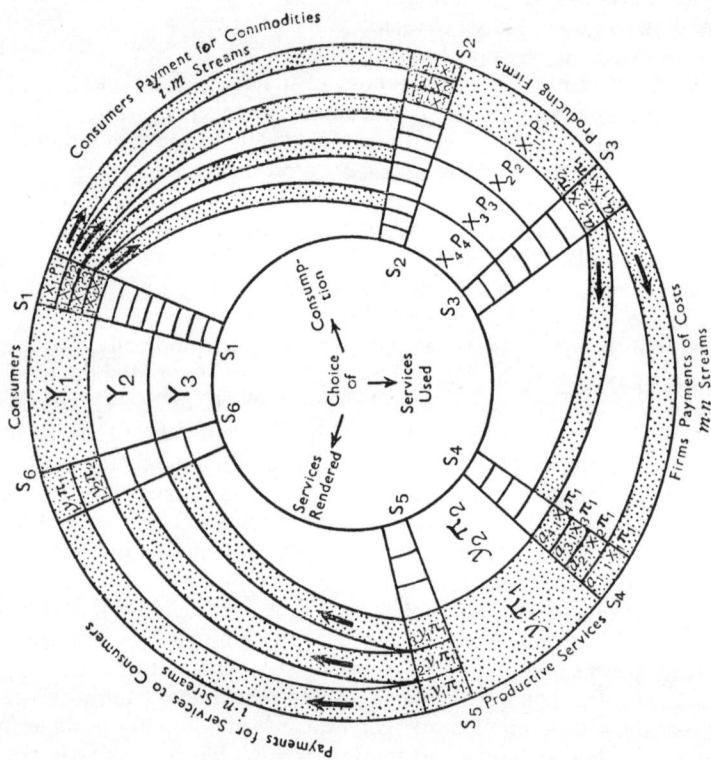

Fig. 3. The Circular Flow

TABLE 2

EQUATIONS:

F

Transformations		Forms of Payments	Form as in Chapter 11 (pp. 44-7)	Chapter 13	Number of Equations In General	In Figure
From individual incomes to value of commodities	S_1 Splitting of individual incomes on commodities Choice of commodities (Demand)	$Y_1 = {}_1x_1 \cdot p_1 + {}_1x_2 \cdot p_2 \ldots {}_1x_m \cdot p_m$ ${}_1x_1 \cdot p_1 = {}_1F(p_1, p_2 \ldots p_m, \pi_1, \pi_2 \ldots \pi_n)$	— $x_1 = f_1(p_1, p_2 \ldots \pi_1, \pi_2 \ldots)$	— 1	i i.m	3 3-4
	S_2 Summation of payments from individuals to firms	${}_1x_1 \cdot p_1 = {}_1x_1 p_1 + {}_2x_1 \cdot p_1 \ldots + {}_ix_1 \cdot p_1$	—	—	m	4
From value of commodities to value of services	S_3 Splitting of costs on services Choice of technique	$x_1 p_1 = a_{1,1} \cdot x_1 \pi_1 + a_{1,2} \cdot x_1 \cdot \pi_2 \ldots a_{1,n} \cdot x_1 \cdot \pi_n$ $a_{1,1} = F_1(\pi_1, \pi_2 \ldots \pi_n)$	$p_1 = a_{1,1} \cdot \pi_1 + a_{1,2} \cdot \pi_2 \ldots$ $a_{1,1} = F_1(\pi_1, \pi_2 \ldots \pi_n)$	2 5	m m.n	4 4-2
	S_4 Summation of payments from commodities to services	$y_1 \cdot \pi_1 = a_{1,1} x_1 \cdot \pi_1 + a_{2,1} x_2 \cdot \pi_1 \ldots a_{1,m} \cdot x_m \cdot \pi_1$	—	3 (& 4)	n	2
From value of services to individual incomes	S_5 Splitting of payments from services to individuals Choice of quantities of services	$y_1 \pi_1 = {}_1y_1 \cdot \pi_1 + {}_2y_1 \cdot \pi_1 \ldots {}_iy_1 \cdot \pi_1$ ${}_1y_1 \cdot \pi_1 = {}_1F_1(\pi_1, \pi_2 \ldots \pi_n, p_1, p_2 \ldots p_m)$	$y_1 = {}_1f(\pi_1, \pi_2 \ldots p_1, p_2 \ldots)$	— 6	n i.n	2 3-2
	S_6 Summation of payments to individuals	$Y_1 = {}_1y_1 \cdot \pi_1 + {}_1y_2 \cdot \pi_2 \ldots {}_1y_n \cdot \pi_n$	—	—	i	3

Total number of equations: $2m + 2n + 2i + m.n + i.m + i.n$ 44   3

Minus budget equations i

Remaining equations: $2m + 2n + i + m.n + i.m + i.n$ 41

DEPENDENT VARIABLES:

	Members in Equations of Payments	Unknown Quantities	Number of Unknowns In General	In Figure
Incomes = Outlays for individuals	$Y_1, Y_2 \ldots Y_1$	$Y_1, Y_2 \ldots Y_1$	i	3
Individuals' payment for separate commodities	${}_1x_1, p_1, {}_2x_1 p_1 \ldots x_1 p_1 \ldots {}_ix_m p_m$	${}_1x_1, {}_1x_2 \ldots {}_gx_1 \ldots {}_ix_m$	i.m	3-4
Total payment for each commodity	$x_1 p_1, x_2 p_2 \ldots x_m \cdot p_m$		m	—
Commodity quantities		$x_1, x_2, \ldots x_m$	m	4
Commodity prices		$p_1, p_2, \ldots p_m$	m	4
Cost elements in commodities	$a_{1,1} x_1 \pi_1, a_{1,2} \cdot x_1 \pi_2 \ldots x_1 \pi_n$	$a_{1,1}, a_{1,2} \ldots a_{g,1} \ldots a_{m,n}$	m.n	4-2
Total payment for each kind of service	$y_1 \cdot \pi_1, y_2 \cdot \pi_2 \ldots y_n \cdot \pi_n$		n	—
Quantity of services		$y_1, y_2 \ldots y_n$	n	2
Prices for services		$\pi_1, \pi_2 \ldots \pi_n$	n	2
Payment to each individual for each kind of service	${}_1y_1 \cdot \pi_1, {}_1y_2 \cdot \pi_2 \ldots y_1 \cdot \pi_1 \ldots {}_iy_n \cdot \pi_n$		i.n	3-2
Individual quantities of services		${}_1y_1, {}_1y_2 \ldots {}_gy_1 \ldots {}_iy_n$	i.n	3

Total number of dependent variables $2m + 2n + i + m.n + i.m + i.n$ 41

Money not among the variables. Level of prices not determined.
In the expressions ${}_1x_2, {}_1y_2$, etc., the first figure indicates the individual and the second the commodity or service.
In the technical coefficient $a_{1,1}$, etc., the first figure as usual indicates the commodity and the second the service.
F and f with different marks are functions with certain constants.

of (1), a summation by which the original flows (the total income of the individual, the total costs of the commodity, and the total income of a certain category of services) is put equal to the lesser flows into which they are split up; (2), another summation, by which the lesser flows which are joined, are put equal to the total flow thus produced; as well as (3), between (1) and (2), an equation determining the choice and thus the size of each of the lesser flows. The summation equations follow from the assumed static equilibrium. For instance, we have the transformation of the payment flows of the individuals to the payment flows of the firms (the commodities). It is determined by: (1) the income of each individual equal to the sum of his different applications of income; $Y_1 = {}_1x_1 \cdot p_1 + {}_1x_2 \cdot p_2 \ldots$ (where Y_i is the income of individual No. i, ${}_ix_j$ his consumption of commodity No. j, and p_j its price), (2) the total payment for each commodity equal to the sum of payments from all individuals, $x_1 \cdot p_1 = {}_1x_1 \cdot p_1 + {}_2x_1 \cdot p_1 \ldots$, and (3) for the determination of the chosen distribution of the incomes of the individual persons among the commodities: a demand equation for the demand of each individual for each commodity, *e.g.*, ${}_1x_1 \cdot p_1 = {}_1F_1(p_1p_2 \ldots \pi_1\pi_2 \ldots)$.

The choice of the quantities of different services to be used for each commodity is the previously mentioned choice of technical coefficients, which is dependent on the prices of the services. Finally, the choice of the quantities of the different services to be put in is dependent on the prices of services and commodities. The dependence, however, may here be imagined to be 0, *i.e.*, the quantities of the individual services, or rather the services for which the individuals receive the incomes, may be constant (independent of all prices).

As appears from the table, we have in all $2m + 2n + i + im + in + m.n$ unknown (i being the number of individuals, m of commodities and n of kinds of services), whereas the number of equations is i more, one equation for each individual. With static assumptions we have in the first place, for each individual, that the whole income is equal to the sum of the payments received for the different kinds of services, and, in the second place, that the whole income (equal to total expenditure) is equal to the sum of the expenditure of the individuals on each of the different commodities. One of these two systems of equations, however, is not contingent on independent conditions, but may be derived from all the other equations in the whole system, and therefore is cancelled from the list of independent conditions. Similarly, we have (as mentioned above on p. 48) one equation in the total system that is not independent of the others, since a new equation may be formed by putting the payment for all commodities equal to the payment for all services. This lack of one independent condition means that the system will be indeterminate with regard to prices if we do not have a further equation which binds the other prices to the price of money, 1. The number of dependent variables thus corresponds to the total number of independent conditions or equations. For each group of equations we have in the scheme indicated the first equation both in the "form of payment" and in the simpler form used in Chapter 11. The number of equations has been given, more generally as well as corresponding to the number of individuals, etc., in the figure.

The exposition also gives an analysis of the real economic phenomena underlying the flows of payments. At this stage, it is only a book-keeping system showing the payment obligations in connection with consumption and production, valued in terms of money. In order to attain an explanation of flows of money payments in a real society, the exposition must be supplemented in several ways. In the first place, part of the above-mentioned payments passes out, because it is here a question of barter without the use of money or services in one's own productive firm or for one's own household. In the second place, the actual payment in money takes the form of only two flows, from consumption to production, and the reverse. When we have in Table 2 inserted the functional distribution, the division into categories of income, it is, as said already, because the transformation here taking place is also of great importance in the total national account, as well as for economic theory. When we pass on to the actual payments in money, there is, by the way, a third essential modification, owing to transactions outside the circulation of commodities and services, *i.e.*, trade-in privileges and capitalized values.

The study of the circular flow of payments under static equilibrium is only a preparation for the more practical and more complicated phenomena under dynamic conditions. Here we find irregularities in circulation arising from, among other things, increases or decreases in payments ("purchasing power") on various points in the circle, from changes in the direction of consumption, in the quantity of products or employed productive services, as well as from changes in the velocity of the flows (cf. the more complicated pictures of circulation in Chapter 39).

CHAPTER 15

DIFFERENT TECHNICAL COMBINATIONS BETWEEN COMMODITIES AND PRODUCTIVE SERVICES

ABOVE we have preferably had the simplest form of technical combination between commodities and productive service in mind; this means that in each production there appears only a single kind of product, and the manufacture of finished articles takes place directly without passing through intermediate products. The theory, however, remains essentially the same even if the relation between finished products and productive services is more complicated.

Figure 4 on p. 65 illustrates a series of very elementary examples of connections between commodities and services. These technical connections are important both for the determination of the price of the commodity and for the distribution of the productive services between the different kinds of commodities. They are treated here under the assumption of full divisibility. The effects of the absence of full divisibility and, consequently, the effects of the size of the firms as well as the effects of several firms in one branch of production, requiring treatment beyond the "atomistic" theory here described, will be taken up for further investigation in Chapter 20. It is not only the connection through the production phase that is going to be dealt with here, however. The main purpose of this section is to give some example of details of the economic network.

Part 1 of the figure illustrates a performance by an artist or some other personal service. Practically speaking, the whole of the product consists of a single service without any supplement. There is here a given quantity of a service which is regarded as a commodity by the consumers; we have a demand equation, and price is the only unknown. The case is here treated as a partial adaptation, but enters as a link in the total adaptation when the quantity of service yielded is made a function not only of its own price, but also of the prices of other services; and demand is made dependent on other commodity prices.

No. 2 illustrates a joint demand, *e.g.*, for the production of a chemical product, requiring 3 raw materials in a definite proportion, say, $1:2:3$. If they cannot be utilized elsewhere, and if they are found in the quantities $10:25:35$, the first will obtain the whole share of the commodity price falling to the 3 raw materials, whereas the others become free goods. If, however, they can be used elsewhere in other combinations (cf. the dotted lines of the figure), they may all obtain positive prices.

No. 3 illustrates two methods of production for the same commodity, or two types of the commodity with the same demand, *e.g.*, grain produced by means of the country's own soil and labor, or by means of foreign soil and labor plus transportation. If we consider home-produced and foreign-produced grain as one commodity, we shall have 1 unknown price, 2 quantities and 5 prices of services. Besides we have 1 demand equation, 2 cost equations and 5 quantity equations for the productive services. In the figure we see the lines of connection for the effects in case of a change in one point (*e.g.*, a change of wages or the number of workers at home, costs of transportation or intensity of demand). If we consider home-grown and foreign grain as two different commodities, we obtain 2 demand equations, which may be quite or almost identical, and 2 commodity prices. We may then speak about competing supply. One of the two methods of production may sometimes only represent a potential supply with a possible price above the actual one.

No. 4 symbolizes two methods of production for the same commodity, *e.g.*, intensive and extensive grain production. We find a definite quantity of the commodity produced in each way. Where there is a limited number

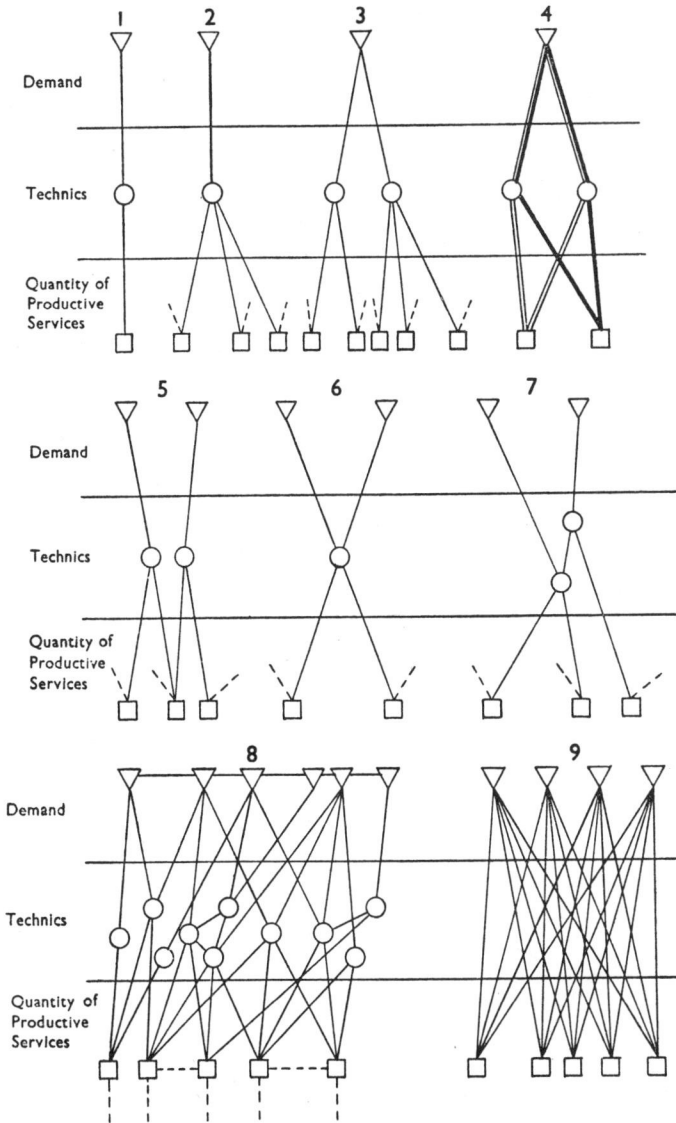

Fig. 4. Relations between Finished Products and Productive Services

of methods, one may sometimes apply more than one at the same time. If the technical coefficients with regard to two productive services in the case of the first is, *e.g.*, 1 and 2, and in the case of the second 2 and 1, both methods will be applied so long as the services are used in the industry in a proportion situated between the proportions corresponding to the methods of production.[1] (The two technical coefficients for one method of production make it possible to compare the quantity of the two services.) If we consider a continuous series of technical possibilities of substitution, the technical coefficients, as mentioned above, must be treated as variables. The substitution here mentioned is the most important of the technical variations and will be dealt with further in Chapter 20.

No. 5 illustrates the competing demand for a service at the production of two different commodities or groups of commodities which otherwise require different services, *e.g.*, the competition for labor on the part of manufacturing industry and agriculture. It is here seen how the effects of a change on one point spread through intermediary links, *e.g.*, how the effect of a diminished demand for agricultural products or greater efficiency for agriculture, through the labor market, which is common to several trades, spreads to manufacturing industry and, consequently, to prices and quantities of industrial products, as well as the income derived from industrial machinery, etc.

No. 6 is a case of joint production in a fixed proportion, and for the sake of simplification also with a fixed proportion between the productive services. We have here a special relationship, indicating the proportion between the products. The distribution of costs between the two products does not take place according to technical laws, but on the basis of the demand functions. If we assume that the quantity demanded is only dependent on the price of the commodity itself, we have joint supply (cf. p. 74). If the proportion between the products may vary, we must have a special equation for this variation.[2] The same is true if the proportion between the productive services may vary. If we reckon with fixed proportions, we have the following unknowns: 2 commodity quantities, 2 commodity prices, 2 prices of services, and 2 possible remainders of these; and the following equations: 2 demand equations, 1 equation indicating the proportion between the two commodity quantities, 1 cost equation, 2 quantity equations, and 2 equations for the remainders of services.

No. 7 illustrates a case with an intermediary product. This has a special price and quantity and a corresponding special cost equation, as well as a quantity equation in the same way as was the case with the productive services. Where there are several intermediary products or finished articles in a joint production, some of them may become free goods—and we shall then have a superfluous remainder as the unknown instead of price.

No. 8 gives a slight indication of the complexity of only a small section of the total interdependence and of the great importance of the indirect

---

[1] Gloerfelt-Tarp, "Den økonomisk definerede Produktionsfunktion og den heterogene Produktionsproces", *Nordisk Tidsskrift for Teknisk Økonomi*, 1937 (in Danish).
[2] Regarding conditions of joint production, see Børge Barfod, "Forenet Produktion og Kvalitetsændring", *Nordisk Tidsskrift for Teknisk Økonomi*, 1936.

relationships. If two quantities are only indirectly connected through many intermediary links, the connection will often be weak because a great part of the effect disappears to adjoining quantities.

Hitherto we have mainly confined ourselves to the technical connections through production. To this must be added the connection between the different types of commodities through demand (the horizontal line at the top of No. 8), the connection between qualities of productive services, which are only separate in the short run (workers with different training, different investments, the dotted horizontal lines), the possibilities of variation in the supply of productive services (the dotted perpendicular lines), and finally the connections between the prices of productive services and demand, as indicated in No. 9. Phelps Brown[3] places Nos. 8 and 9 on either side of a cylinder and thereby obtains a picture of the economic circular flow.

In all cases we find an agreement between the number of equations and unknowns. Though the equations concern several unknowns, it may be convenient to establish agreement between the number of equations and unknowns, *e.g.*, by matching them as follows:

commodity quantities matched by demand equations

commodity prices matched by cost equations

prices of productive services matched by their quantity equations

the possible unemployed remainders matched by supplementary conditions, saying that either the price or the remainder is zero

the quantity of productive services matched by their supply equations

the technical coefficients matched by technical equations with the
coefficients as unknowns

the prices of n commodities in joint production in a fixed proportion
matched by n − 1 relations between the quantities (besides the
common cost equation)

joint production with changing proportions between the products
matched by special technical equations

for the quantities when there is more than one method of production
of commodities with an identical demand, the common price may
be put *vis-à-vis* the demand equation, and the special quantities
vis-à-vis the special cost equations, and

the prices of intermediary products matched by their cost equations
and their quantities matched by quantity equations, as in the case
of productive services.

[3] *The Framework of the Pricing System*, Chapman & Hall, London, 1936.

CHAPTER 16

DETERMINING ELEMENTS UNDER STATIC FREE COMPETITION

IN what ways can the reflections and models of the previous sections contribute to the understanding of the economic conditions of real life? The connection with real life has partly consisted in references to some generally known, but not more closely analyzed facts (*e.g.*, the interdependence of demand), partly in the framing of some hypotheses (*e.g.*, the equilibrium between price and costs), giving highly simplified pictures of a definite type of life, which may be called static free competition. By the combination of a series of statements of this kind we obtain a comprehensive picture.

Though we cannot derive more information as to real life from a construction and treatment of equations or other deductive operations than we have ourselves put into the assumptions, there is still a possibility of attaining a better understanding by applying the assumptions in another logical combination. It appears to be possible to give an illustration of the whole economic system as a chain of partial interdependences of a limited number of types of a relatively clear sort. And when by including the essential assumptions we reach a logically connected system, with as many equations as unknowns, it appears that the picture corresponds to an important assumed attribute of real life (or rather, perhaps, our conception of the latter), namely, that it is determinate and self-consistent. By our construction we make sure that we have a sufficient system of independent conditions, and not only repetitions of the same conditions in varying forms which easily slip into a verbal explanation. An example of this is the older theory of distribution which, as already mentioned, "alternately chased the unknown over to the other side of the sign of equation".

If there is to be any question of really solving equations, we must confine ourselves to a smaller number of measurable quantities. This means that the concrete analysis must either be partial or apply to total economic categories with the arbitrariness attaching to adopted rules of index, average, symptomatic measurements, discretionary corrections, etc.

There is no possibility of constructing any fairly complete system of equations for the total interdependence, determining the constants and solving the equations so as to find the variables. Investigations in recent years have shown the difficulty of giving even an approximate picture of a single demand function. Besides, it is really the unknowns of the equations: prices and quantities of which we have a fairly good knowledge. The essential thing is to find the form and constants of the equations, in order possibly to be able to find the dependent variables when the data are changed somewhat. Add to this that the number of equations is overwhelmingly great, if we want to be exact and only indicate quantities for absolute homogeneous qualities. In reality there does not exist a definite number of equations and unknowns, for the number of them will depend on the exactness which is desired with regard to the homogeneity of the objects considered as the same commodity or service.

The result that can be achieved is far more modest. We obtain an abstract, schematic survey of the kinds of economic interdependences and their location in relation to each other, or a map of the interdependences within the spheres, which we want to subject to a closer investigation, and through the data of the system reference to the neighboring spheres which exercise some influence. As we see in the next section, this general survey is also of importance in partial analyses.

The fundamental hypothesis of all research: that it is worth while looking for an interdependence between phenomena, is not limited to the range of economic quantities which we have hitherto considered as unknown, the dependent variables of our systems of equations. An explanation of the economic network requires references to something outside the economic sphere. We have also tried to give an explanation by connecting our unknowns with other quantities: technical relations, certain constants in the behavior of human beings as consumers and workers, the scarcity of means of production, etc.

In our endeavor to explain economic interdependence, we always have to stop at a point where the explaining conditions, the quantities considered as data, are not in reality independent of the variables. It is not possible to have a definite and closed group of economic quantities which are interdependent and are determined by a series of data that are themselves entirely uninfluenced by the same economic quantities. Not only the technique employed, but also practical and theoretical technical science are influenced by our economic variables. The same is true of the size and taste of the population and the existing machinery, as well as of market forms and institutions generally. The definition of what in the individual case is considered as data, must always be a question of discretion, partly depending on what we want to know, partly on the relative independence of the possible data.

The phenomena which in our picture of economic interdependence are considered as data, we regard as determining factors for the closely connected prices and quantities of commodities and productive services. So long as we confine ourselves to a static free competition society, the form and constants of the demand functions, the technical production functions, the quantity of productive services and their functional dependence on the prices of services and of commodities become the determining elements.

The relative importance of the different elements cannot be determined in advance. The influence of the demand of commodities on the relation between the prices of productive services would disappear if all commodities required the same combination of productive services. The proportion between commodity prices would then be fixed. Not all the possibilities of variation dealt with in the equations are in any case effective. It is not possible to produce any commodity by means of different combinations of productive services. The technical coefficients are, in other words, constant in certain cases and consequently are not determined as functions of the prices of the services. The quantity of services may be constant and in other cases there may be only small possibilities of variation. In the last few chapters of this part of the book we shall touch upon the subject of the nature of the different reaction functions.

In the brief numerical example in Chapter 13, just as in the equilibrium system in which Cassel[1] expresses the essence of economic interdependence, we have assumed that each commodity could only be produced in one way and consequently that, if the quantity of a productive service or other data were changed, adaptation must take place by changing the proportion in which different commodities were produced. In the case of Walras' equations, a further possibility is an adaptation by changing the proportion between the quantities of productive services entering into the individual commodity. Cassel, however, considers the technical substitution a "supplementary principle", since it is not necessary in order that an economic adaptation may take place. An extreme application of the marginal productivity theory, on the other hand, attaches a dominant importance to it, treating all adaptation caused by changed proportions between the services as an adaptation of the technique of production.

The difference between the two forms of substitution: substitution in consumption and substitution in production, is not always very great. A plurality of commodities having approximately the same demand function, but each a fixed technical composition, have almost the same effect as the existence of several methods of production for the same commodity. It may be considered a question of definition whether the product of two different combinations of several productive services shall be considered as the same commodity, when they have an identical demand function. Do new types of commodities appear, for instance, in the transition from handicraft to factory industry, or are the same commodities produced in a different way?

Both different commodity types and different methods of producing the same type may form a continuous series or appear discontinuously, and we have correspondingly a continuous and discontinuous adaptation of quality and intensity (*i.e.*, adaptation of the method of production), when a change in the proportion between the productive services takes place.

Even when there is discontinuity between the commodity types or between the methods of production, the economic adaptation by continuous variation in data (*e.g.*, the quantity of a service) does not become discontinuous, however, because a gradual transfer takes place between different

[1] *The Theory of Social Economy*, Fisher Unwin, London, 1923, and *Fundamental Thoughts in Economics*, Ernest Benn, London, 1925.

commodity types or methods of production, appearing simultaneously side by side. The variation in the method of production, by the way, is not only a variation in intensity between a given number of kinds of productive service, but new types of services may be included (*e.g.*, less fertile soil cultivated) perhaps, at the same time as others are excluded.

All the different forms of adaptation enter into the total explanation. Their importance must depend on how great variations are involved, whether there are commodity types with strongly deviating compositions, and whether the composition of individual commodities may be varied greatly by changing the proportions between productive services used (*i.e.*, whether there is a great range of technical substitution).

If one uses a one-sided marginal productivity approach, and accordingly only takes account of technical substitution, an increase in the number of engineers in a country where adaptation is unrestricted should alone promote adaptation through the adoption of methods which require more labor. Part of the adaptation will take place, however, by means of a relative fall in the price and the consequent increase in the sales of such products of the industry as require most labor; another part by a fall in price and increased sales of the products of the industry in general as a result of the lower expenditures for wages. A numerical expression of the relative importance of the three forms of adaptation might be obtained if we imagined one or two of the possibilities to be acting individually. Such a hypothetical situation could only be realized in a very approximate way, however, and the analysis would be very unrealistic if carried on with static assumptions.

Economic life can be illustrated by the numerical example in Chapter 13 determining the prices of commodities and services as well as the quantities of commodities. This picture would provide for the possibility of variation in these quantities, even if we limit considerably the number of variable conditions, *i.e.*, if we assume a fixed technique and fixed quantities of productive services. This was what Cassel called price determination solely according to the "scarcity principle". The conditions which were here sufficient for the determination of prices and quantities of commodities—the demand relation between price and quantity, the relation between the commodity price and the price of the services used through the technique of production, as well as the limited quantities of productive services—will always assert themselves even when other conditions are included in the analysis. If, like Cassel, we maintain that the assumptions of this simplified system of equations, including the static free competition assumptions or something corresponding thereto, give a good approximation to real life, we have a simple and tangible, but much too one-sided a picture of what are really the determining elements of economics.

Even the picture of the economy which we have given in connection with the Walrasian system of equations includes other determining conditions. As we shall see in Chapter 18, however, there are still other elements which can and must be included if the picture is to be realistic.

But just as the few elements which Cassel includes in his very limited system remain valid in the broader system of Walras, together with several other determining elements, further extension beyond the Walrasian system also means that the Walrasian relationships between the quantities are still included, though in a somewhat changed form. The system may be supplemented in different ways according to (1) the degree of simplification we desire; (2) the aspects of economic life in which we are interested; (3) the kind of reality with which we are faced; and (4) information available.

What we attain is, in any case, only a tenuous model, which more or less arbitrarily includes a limited number of the many elements of real life. The decisive thing is the concept of total economic interdependence as made up of a chain of partial interdependences. This may very well be of a changing nature which will vary with time and the specific area of economic activity under consideration. It is out of the question, therefore, to say that one definite system of equations gives the correct picture. On the contrary, it may be said that the main principle of the system—total economic interdependence determined by a network of partial interdependences—is immensely elastic and holds out an invitation to include all possible rational explanations, if only they are inserted as coherent parts of the framework that is the essence of the system. It is a result of this attitude that theory becomes not rigid dogma but method.

CHAPTER 17

PARTIAL AND TOTAL ANALYSIS

A TOTAL analysis, *i.e.*, an analysis of the economy as a whole, is either only capable of dealing with economic interdependence in a general way, or, if it is to be made more concrete, it must be limited to large aggregates, comprising large numbers of heterogeneous variables in a single quantity.

Concrete results are obtained only by such necessarily inexact "macroeconomic" analyses, using aggregative categories, or by partial analyses, where the limitation in the number of variables investigated is attained by confining the scope of the analysis. This must necessarily make the analysis incomplete in view of the great degree of interdependence that exists. Our task must be to set up those models that comprise a limited and manageable number of variables, where the inexactness due to heterogeneity of variables or incompleteness of the model will involve a minimum degree of error.

The tragic circumstance is that concrete and exact results can only be arrived at by partial analysis, but that partial analysis must in advance be characterized as incomplete from the point of view of total theory.

The partial analysis takes into account a limited number of variables. The typical case is the analysis of the way in which demand and supply of a single commodity determine its price and quantity. In this investigation *ceteris paribus* is assumed. Among other things, constant prices are assumed for all other commodities and incomes are assumed to be unchanged. In real life, however, it is quite possible that a change in the price and quantity of a commodity will have a great effect on other commodities which, again, will react on the commodity itself so that the isolated relationship between the price and quantity of the commodity, *ceteris paribus*, is most inadequate. It is especially important that incomes derived from the production of a commodity may react on demand, which thus cannot be considered as independent of the supply conditions. The effect of income on demand is seen still more clearly when we consider the formation of price not for a commodity, but for a group of productive services, such as labor.

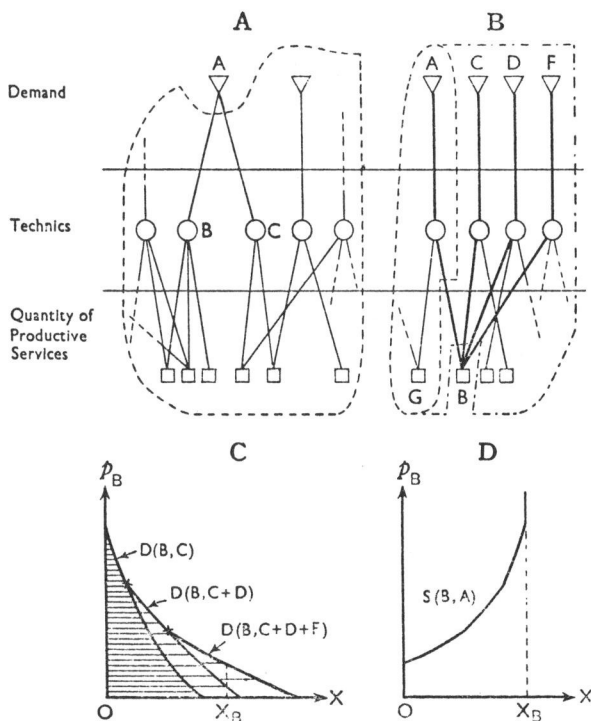

Fig. 5. Partial Analysis

Fig. 5A shows how, in a partial analysis, the supply of a commodity, A, which in the present instance may be produced in two ways, B and C, by means of quite different productive services, may be considered to be determined by, and at the same time acting on, all partial relationships in the economic system with the exception of the demand for A. In the figure this is indicated by the area within the enclosing dotted line. But in reality demand is not independent of supply, since both through the prices of the other commodities and through income it is related to factors of supply.

In Fig. 5B conditions within the dotted enclosure to the left in the figure determine the demand of the service B, used for production of commodity A, whereas all conditions outside this enclosure determine the supply of B for the production of A. The demand for the service, however, is not only determined by the demand for the commodity A and the quantity of B to be used in its production, but also by the supply of G and the use of the latter in the production of other commodities.

The demand of B for the production of commodities C, D and F, and all the conditions influencing this demand, will be decisive for the supply of B available for the production of A. Figs. C and D illustrate the way in which the demand of B for C, D and F forms a rising supply curve for B with regard to the production of A. The demand curves of C, D and F for B are added horizontally in Fig. 5C. A fixed quantity of B, X_B is assumed. The demand curve reckoned from X_B to 0 in Fig. 5C corresponds to the supply curve from 0 to X_B in Fig. 5D.

If we want to examine the total demand for the service B in Fig. 5B, we shall have to include all the conditions situated within both the dashed (- - - -) and the dot-dashed (.-.-.-) enclosure. Besides, the supply of B, if it can vary with price, is to some extent dependent both on the price of other services and the prices of the commodities. Consequently, it will not be independent of the conditions determining demand.

In these examples we have seen how the partial analysis is continued in the total analysis, and that only by taking a step in the direction of the latter can we decide to what extent we can rely on the *ceteris paribus* assumption, which is a necessary condition for an exact result in a partial analysis.

Here we shall only refer to the theory of joint prices. Thus by including more than one commodity in our analysis we shall take a first step in the direction of extending the partial one-commodity analysis to a multi-commodity analysis. Hereby special kinds of links in the chain of the total analysis are formed. The essence of this well-known theory may be expressed in a few words as a slight modification of the one-commodity analysis:

(1) Joint demand (*e.g.*, plaster and bricks): one demand curve, vertical addition of two supply curves.

(2) Joint supply (*e.g.*, first-grade bricks and lower-grade bricks): one supply curve, vertical addition of two demand curves.

(3) Competitive demand (*e.g.*, clay for bricks and for drain pipes): one supply curve, horizontal addition of two demand curves.

(4) Competitive supply (*e.g.*, bricks and concrete): one demand curve, horizontal addition of supply curves.

Complications arise when the jointly demanded commodities can be used in changing proportions or the jointly produced commodities appear together in changing proportions. Under conditions of competitive supply, preferences for the competing goods entail complications, and it is here necessary to distinguish between cases where all buyers prefer one commodity to the other (where demand for the principal article is formed by adding the demand for some special attributes to the demand for the attributes common to the principal article and the substitute) and cases where each of the commodities is preferred by one part of the demand (and where, if the price of one commodity is given, demand for the other may be deduced by means of a series of additions and subtractions).

As examples of more remote effects, the direction of which cannot be decided without further investigation, we may mention: (1) Increased demand of commodity No. 1 leaves less raw material for commodity No. 2, but the result may be, perhaps, a greater supply at the disposal of No. 3 of some raw materials which No. 3 has in common with No. 2. (2) Rationalization which reduces some technical coefficients for commodity No. 1, may, according to circumstances, lead to greater as well as smaller consumption of the productive service in question, thus increasing or reducing costs for commodity No. 2. (3) Meat and tanning materials, for instance, are economically connected through leather.

In agriculture we have complicated examples of the above-mentioned connections between goods and of the way in which, through such connection, indirect connections arise through a greater or smaller number of intermediary links.

Fig. 6, as an example of an intensive and complicated interrelation between different lines of production, gives a survey of the connections between some of the most important commodities and the means of production in Danish agriculture.[1] The nature of the connections (equations) has not been indicated in the figure, however. The lines of connection correspond to quantities per period. The arrows indicate the direction, in which the quantities of each good (measured by its own standard) move. Payments in money move in the opposite direction. Besides these two flows, we may regard the flow of material in pounds, and of energy, and here, too, find correspondence from link to link, if wastage is taken into consideration; but a comparison between these numerical values is not always relevant. The picture may, by the way, be considered as a part of the general economic circulation.

Instead of the method of partial equilibrium which we may call the "isolation" method based on the assumption of *ceteris paribus*, one may apply the "variation" method,[2] *i.e.*, examine the effect on the total interdependence of a change in an individual quantity; or conversely, how much an individual quantity is influenced by changes in the others. In an

---

[1] Calculations and graph made by Werner Rasmussen.
[2] Oskar Lange: "Die Allgemeine Interpendenz der Wirtschaftsgrössen und die Isolierungsmethode", *Zeitschrift für Nationalökonomie*, 1932–33.

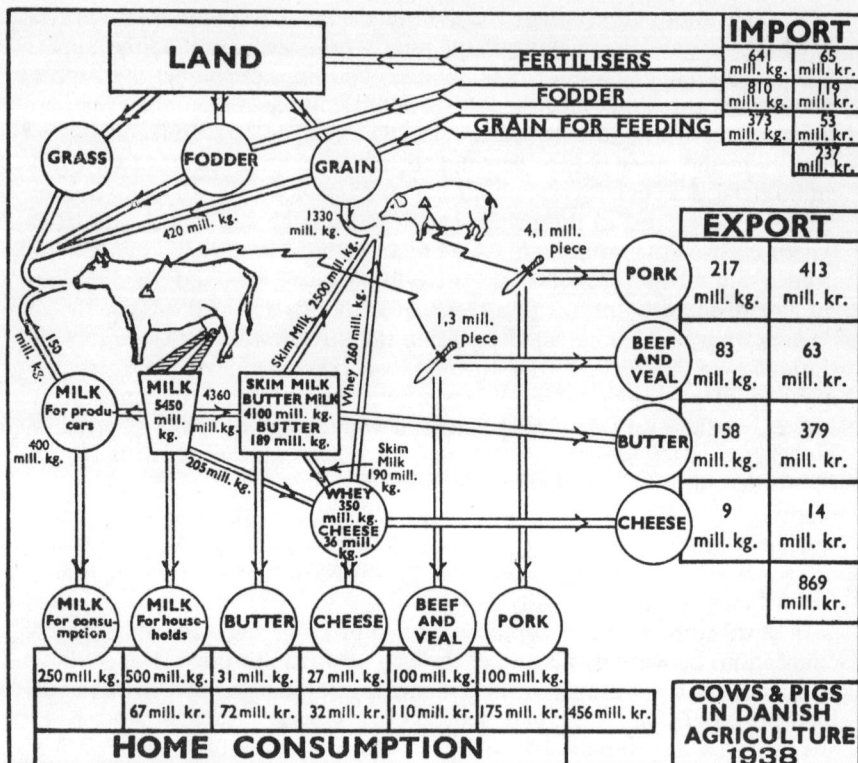

Fig. 6. Some Interdependences in Danish Agriculture

actual situation the distance between the methods, *i.e.*, between partial and total analysis, is not always so great as it may seem. In the investigation of the formation of price for a commodity, one may include a limited number of other commodities with connected prices, and on the other hand, any fairly concrete total analysis must in real life be limited to a few of the more important variables.

The problem is how far to go, which other variables to include into the analysis, and which effects to disregard as belonging to "the second order of smalls". It does not matter for the present purpose whether the connection is direct or whether it takes place only through a greater or smaller number of intermediate steps. Lange makes the partial elasticity between a quantity to be explained and other quantities the criterion of relevance. A change of 10 per cent in a number of other quantities for instance, may affect the one examined by 20, 10 or 1 per cent, and we then speak about a partial elasticity of 2, 1 and $\frac{1}{10}$. Lange now proposes that, according to the degree of exactness that is desired and can be obtained, we confine the analysis to variables in relation to which the one examined has a partial elasticity above a certain limit, say 5 per cent. This criterion of relevance cannot be applied mechanically, however, because the extent to which we consider closely related types of commodities or productive services as one or several variables is arbitrary. This lack of homogeneity in connection with lack of stability and measurability leads to the result that, in practical cases, we must very largely be content with an estimate instead of a definite result. The same criterion may also be applied with a reversed causal direction, *i.e.*, for determination of the variables that are influenced perceptibly by changes in a certain quantity.

Owing to discontinuities and frictions, the connection between two variables may in many cases be quite interrupted, at any rate so far as smaller influences are concerned. We might, for instance, have an elasticity of zero until the "quantum of action" is reached. A price, for instance, is generally only changed by whole numbers. One must be careful, however, in deciding that there is a lack of connection between price and small changes in costs in such cases. The reaction occurs seldom, but when it does take place, the amounts involved are so much the greater. If a price can only be changed by whole dollars, the increase of costs by 25 cents will perhaps lead to price being increased by one dollar in one quarter of the cases. If we have a limited knowledge of the situation in the individual case, it will often under such conditions be most correct to reckon with a chance of reaction (the magnitude of the reaction multiplied by its probability) smaller than the intervals by which the reaction may actually take place, or reckon with tensions (latent effects), *i.e.*, changes of other quantities than those observed, which in connection with further small changes may involve a visible change. Further it must be remembered that the relationships are not equally strong in all economic situations, *i.e.*, the partial elasticity between the quantities is not constant. These problems, however, are of a dynamic character and are not considered at this stage.

CHAPTER 18

EXTENSION OF ASSUMPTIONS

In order that the method previously applied—beginning with theories which disregard certain essential aspects of real life—shall be defensible, it is a necessary condition that the phenomena that have initially been disregarded in the description should be included later on. This has been done already to a limited extent in Chapter 15, where we included certain types of technical relations between commodities and productive services, which did not explicitly find a place in our Walrasian equations, as, for

G

instance, the existence of several kinds of commodities in the same production process, and the appearance of intermediary products. In this section we shall briefly mention some more important extensions of the original model.

It is mainly a question of proceeding further from what we have called "static free competition assumptions". The exact expression of these assumptions was given in the form of the equations, *i.e.*, in the two simplifications chosen: (1) that the price of the commodity was put equal to the price of the productive services used and (2) that we assumed productive services either to be fully employed or free goods. Further, (3) all magnitudes were simultaneous. As mentioned above, these assumptions might also be applicable to a socialist society with a free choice of employment and consumption and a price policy corresponding to our simplifications.

When real life is so little in accordance with the three simplifications mentioned, the explanation must preponderantly be sought in two kinds of conditions, partly a slow and incomplete adaptation to changes in data, *i.e.*, dynamic conditions, and partly deviations from free competition as a consequence of monopolistic price policy or state interference, etc. These conditions are briefly dealt with below, but are taken up for a more thorough discussion in Parts III and IV. They are mentioned in great detail here despite the repetition involved, partly in order not to support a naïve belief in the importance of static free competition assumptions in real life, and partly to warn against a hasty rejection of our initial abstractions as being unconnected with real life.

The position of money in the simplified picture has already been mentioned in Chapter 11.7. In 18.3 we shall say something more about this subject. The problem, however, can only be treated in a fairly realistic way under dynamic assumptions. The same is true of the problem of capital and interest, which is briefly mentioned under point 4, but treated a little more extensively in connection with employment and money in Part III, Chapter 42.

18.1, DYNAMICS

Since this subject is going to be dealt with in greater detail in Part III, we shall confine ourselves here to some indications of the direction in which the assumptions have to be changed in order to make the theory more applicable to real life and of the way in which, by a series of modifications, there seems to be a prospect of enlarging and reconstructing static theory.

The static approach as hitherto applied disregards the time factor. As mentioned above, we have a dynamic approach when differences in time are taken into consideration. This may, for instance, be done by considering the velocities with which changes take place. The words "static" and "dynamic", consequently, are used for different methods of approach, and not for different types of real conditions, but it is clear that the static approach can only be expected to give a tolerably complete explanation of real conditions, where changes in time are not of essential importance. We speak about stationary conditions, but the static method of analysis is also applicable to a community where changes take place, provided we imagine completely free mobility, *i.e.*, infinitely quick adaptation. Contrary to stationary conditions, we may speak about conditions in movement or in development. As examples we may mention societies with increasing population or economic fluctuations, or the period of adaptation after a single change of data, or the actual modern society with a great number of movements of a heterogeneous nature.

If we undertake a dynamic investigation, its object may either be to investigate the conditions of a single moment, where movement is going on, and we then speak of what Frisch[1] calls a momentary dynamic analysis, or the object may be the course of economic phenomena through a period of time.

The static system of simultaneous interdependences (or equations) can fairly easily be rebuilt so as to form a momentary (and thus simultaneous) dynamic equilibrium. If we apply a static approach to a society in movement, there is not equilibrium, *i.e.*, we do not obtain any agreement when trying to ascertain the interdependence between prices, quantities and other categories relevant within a short period of time. Price, for instance, is generally greater than costs in expanding industries. But if we pass on to a dynamic approach and take account of the rates of change of the dynamic factors, we shall be able to obtain equilibrium, *i.e.*, a complete and consistent explanation with regard to the size of all the variables considered, inclusive of the rates of change.

Scientific thinking assumes as a basic postulate that there is no indeterminateness or contradiction in real life, hindering a logical explanation. An explanation that is like reality in this respect must therefore be determinate. As we shall see later, the aim may often be attained only by including new conditions in the explanation, which perhaps would not be considered as "economic". We do not have a closed circle of economic phenomena which we establish in advance and out of which a determinate system can be built. We may find it necessary to obtain a more comprehensive explanation of reality by broadening our sphere of interest.

Only in static theory does equilibrium correspond to stagnation. The decisive attribute of the equilibrium concept is that it satisfies our desire to understand, *i.e.*, that a complete and consistent explanation is reached within the framework of the given assumptions. If there is movement, this, too, must be explained, *i.e.*, the equilibrium must be dynamic. If the result does not correspond to the expectations of a firm, there is a disequilibrium in its calculations. But if the disagreement is explained in

---

[1] "Statikk og Dynamikk", *Nationaløkonomisk Tidsskrift,* 1929.

a logically satisfactory way, equilibrium is present in the explanation itself. A correct account is in balance irrespective of the size of the deficit. As to the contrast between this "equilibrium" in our analysis and "real equilibrium", see Part III, Chapter 34.

In the momentary dynamic explanation the demand of artisans for repairs is added to the demand for new buildings, which is dependent on an increase going on. In a period of expansion, cost may be increased by a necessary cost of transfer. Changes in stocks and similar "fund quantities" must, in the dynamic analysis, be added to or subtracted from consumption, production and other "flow quantities". This means that the static interdependences or equations must in the dynamic analysis be supplemented by a series of velocities of change also with regard to the stocks. If these quantities are included, we may also here construct a system of simultaneous equations, stating the relationship among all variables.

When economic evolution is going on, the number of unknowns of the problem increases by the introduction of the time dimension. In other words, it is not any longer a question of the prices, quantities, etc., necessary to satisfy given conditions in a certain period, but rather a question of the development in time of a series of economic magnitudes, *i.e.*, the size of these at any given moment within the period investigated. Also in this case a determinate solution must be assumed. If we could carry through the momentary analysis for a short period, and if no further changes occurred, we should always have the necessary data for the analysis of the ensuing periods, and, consequently, for the movements in time. If we do not use highly simplified models, however, the work will soon be overwhelming. In the analysis of movements going on, one way causation between magnitudes belonging to different periods to a great extent substitutes simultaneous interdependences.

The applicability of static analysis is limited. This is true not only because we actually live in a society with numerous and violent changes in data and limited speed of adaptation. But it is true even if we only intend to examine the effect of a single new outside force in a previously stationary state, *e.g.*, the change of a price or a rate of wages dictated by the public authorities. It is not enough to find the new state of equilibrium which arises as a result of a sufficiently long or an infinitely quick adaptation to the new data. If the actual speed of adaptation is different in different spheres, we may in the end obtain a different result, since the more quickly adapted parts of the system will, after a certain time, have such a strong effect that the final result is changed. (Cf. Part III, Chapters 24 and 25.) Besides, the result may be fluctuations with decreasing, constant or increasing swings, and these fluctuations may themselves change the point round which the fluctuations are taking place. Measures to dampen business cycles, for instance, may change the political and economic structure.

What has been said above is an adaptation of physical dynamics to economics. Human nature, however, adds a number of complications. Uncertainty adds greatly to the difficulties involved in the transition to a dynamic analysis. For the purpose of explaining what takes place, we consider equilibrium conditions for the calculations of firms and other economic units. Their reactions to risk and expectations become important problems. It is here a question of an *ex ante* explanation on the basis of the assumption as to how the economic units would behave in order to achieve certain aims. By investigating the attitude of the economic units and other existing data, we may draw conclusions as to what will happen in society as a whole. An explanation of the changing expectations of the individuals—not least of all where the behavior of the individuals is mutually interdependent—is only possible to a very limited extent, however.

The transmission of effects through a number of links takes time, but in the course of this time many data have changed. In the initial stage, at any rate, it is impossible to say in what way. A concrete explanation of real events, therefore, must take the form of a subsequent causal analysis, into which also changes in data enter and possibly sporadic "shocks". The method of analyzing business cycles in development reaches its conclusions by constantly taking the most recently available information as revised data for a prognosis, which may only be valid for a very short time.

18.2, MONOPOLY, POWER, ETC.

If there is a seller's monopoly in a commodity market, and if the monopolist will and can maximize profit, the previously mentioned cost equation ceases to be valid. Instead we obtain a new cost or price equation:

$$p_i = a_{i,1} \cdot \pi_1 + a_{i,2} \cdot \pi_2 \ldots a_{i,n} \cdot \pi_n + g_i$$

where the last term indicates profit per unit. To this must be added the condition that total profit, $g_i \cdot x_i$, must be maximum.[2]

Now, let us imagine a fully realized monopoly policy of this sort, as applied to a single commodity or to several commodities. Some of our equations are then changed accordingly.

Monopoly for the owners of a productive service involves the abandonment of the condition that either price or the remainder shall be zero. Instead of that, we get a condition corresponding to the commodity monopoly, that the price of the service multiplied by quantity must be maximum.

In Part IV we shall deal further with cases of competition between a few firms (duopoly, monopolistic competition, etc.), as well as the cases where the firms do not desire or are not able to obtain a maximization of

---

[2] *I.e.*, the first derivative is zero and the second derivative negative. g_i is defined in the equation above as price minus cost.

profit, but pursue other ways of action. In all these cases it seems, however, to be a question of a transformation of one or more of the conditions (partial interdependences or equations), which we have discussed above. In so far as the number of unknowns is increased, by monopoly profits or some other new unknown, a corresponding number of new relations must be assumed to exist. It is another thing that the conditions (equations) often seem to be of a less stable and perceptible character than the equations of the theory of static free competition or that of simple monopoly, and that a more exact quantitative treatment, therefore, is often extremely difficult. If at the same time monopolistic price policy is carried on in a number of spheres, this will put its mark on the whole structure of society.

Aside from the monopolistic phenomena, it is necessary to consider interference by means of violence, authority, and other sorts of "power", *i.e.*, influences that are not exercised through the ordinary economic (monopolistic or competitive) channels. A number of interferences of this kind will not invalidate the whole of the economic interdependence, but only mean that the result must be modified to a greater or smaller extent. Where a commodity's price is fixed effectively by the state, then an unknown price is replaced by a known price. The other conditions must then adapt themselves thereto. Profit or loss will probably be influenced by the fixed price. If the price of a productive service is fixed, a similar problem arises. Corresponding to the fact that price is now known, the particular equation according to which either price or remainder must be zero disappears.

In this sphere, too, it is true that the interference of authority will often be of so changing and relatively indefinite a character (as where we have differently applied rules of price calculation), that a more exact quantitative treatment becomes very difficult and can only be used with great caution for purposes of preliminary orientation. And here, too, it is true that a number of drastic controls will change the whole structure of society and have important effects outside the sphere directly concerned.

18.3, THE PLACE OF MONEY IN THE THEORY OF STATIC EQUILIBRIUM

In Chapter 11.7 above, following Walras, we considered money as mint made of a monetary metal.[3] As the unit of measurement, it has the price 1. This price is put equal to the cost of production of money. The amount entering into the equations, since we are dealing with a liberalistic and static system of equilibrium, is the amount of coins worn out and replaced during the period. The relationship between the money produced (and "consumed") and the money given out in the period must be explained by monetary theory.

[3] Cf. also note 4 on page 49.

Under a system of paper money, the cost equation for money disappears and an unknown "multiplicative factor" enters, indicating the ratio of exchange between a unit of money and the level of value of commodities and services, the mutual value proportions of which are already determined.

The connecting link between paper money on one hand, and commodities and services on the other, may be of a very different nature. It is conceivable that the monetary norm or custom, which is followed more or less, requires that a certain level of prices or level of costs must be maintained. This means that we have, perhaps very approximately, an equation similar to the cost equation for coins: certain prices multiplied by quantities are put equal to the price of the unit of the money, *i.e.*, equal to 1. The aim of monetary policy may also be to fix the monetary value of the total amount of certain commodities or services, *e.g.*, total income or total expenditure, wages, or the cost of subsistence. Since price and the quantity relations are given in advance under equilibrium conditions, any tying up of the money value to a unit or a total quantity of real goods will determine the absolute height of all prices. In general, the actual fixing of the value of money is carried out, however, in a more complicated way, with many political and personal factors entering into the final decision. What has been indicated here, therefore, gives only a very rough approximation.

The quantity of money which is to be fitted into a static system of equilibrium, is money measured as a flow for a period. It may be the quantity of money produced during the period under a system of coinage, or the total sum of income or expenses, or a certain part thereof. The connection between this flow of money and the quantity of money existing at the moment and considered as a fund, is obtained through the velocity of circulation or a corresponding factor. Bitter disputes may arise in economic analysis when one writer measures—and defines—"money" as a flow and the other as a fund.

The utility of possessing money is an important problem in the discussion of the relation between flows of money (incomes and outlays) and existing funds of money. The proportion between them can be expressed as a velocity or as the reciprocal value of a velocity, *i.e.*, the length of time from payment to payment. Even in a stationary society, it is a convenience to possess some money for transactions during an income period. When individuals are exposed to risks and changes, it is further desirable to possess money for "precautionary" purposes. In an unstable society, cf. Part III, Chapter 42, the demand for this purpose increases and varies according to changing expectations, and finally speculation sets in. The demand for cash, on the other hand, is limited by loss of interest and in some cases by risk of theft.

The stock of cash in households and firms is equal to the sum of cash payments received or given out in a period, divided by the average number of transactions performed by a money unit in the period, *i.e.*, the velocity of money. We may therefore express the weighted sum of all payments from households and firms as:

$$M = \Sigma xp \cdot \frac{1}{v_1} + \Sigma y\pi \cdot \frac{1}{v_2} = \Sigma(xp + \pi y)\frac{1}{v}$$

M is the total fund of money, v the velocity of circulation, p and π the prices of commodities and services, and x and y the corresponding quantities. In order to distinguish between the effects of relative prices and the average level of prices of commodities and services, P, we may write

$$M = P \cdot \Sigma(\frac{p}{P} \cdot x + \frac{\pi}{P} \cdot y) \cdot \frac{1}{v}$$

The average distance between payments $\frac{1}{v}$ (like its reciprocal value, the velocity) is a function among other things of the rate of interest and with dynamic assumptions highly influenced by expectations. The rate of interest influences the amount of money people want to hold, when a certain level of prices is assumed. But changes in the amount of money do not in the long run, or with static assumptions, influence the rate of interest.[4]

We have a particularly simple expression in the equation of the quantity theory, $MV = TP$. This equation says that when we put the value of purchases and sales equal, we obtain the quantity of real goods sold (T) multiplied by their average price (P) equal to the quantity of circulating money, conceived of as a fund, (M) multiplied by its velocity of circulation (V). If the money is exclusively spent in purchasing consumption goods, and if we have only one kind of money, we have the simple form of equation of the quantity theory indicated above. Since V and T are not constants, the equation is only important when considered in connection with other equations. The conditions are more complicated if we reckon with other transactions than purchases of consumption goods, as, *e.g.*, purchases of productive services and intermediary products, as well as credit transactions, sale of existing real capital or land, payment of taxes, hoarding and dishoarding, etc. The velocity here involved is not income velocity, but transaction velocity.

Instead of total commodity purchases, we may also relate the turnover of money to total income, which under static assumptions corresponds to total purchases of consumption goods, but in a dynamic approach is influenced by the rate of saving. Lindahl[5] gives the formula $E(1 - s) =$

---

[4] Cf. p. 26 in Don Patinkin's article in *Econometrica*, January, 1949, cited in note 4, p. 49. The statement has here been modified. As to the distinction between the price level and relative prices, arrived at by division by P, cf. the formulae in the same article, p. 24. In these formulae the equilibrium condition for commodities and services (demand in excess of supply = 0) has been indicated by a function of all prices, the amounts of money and bonds, all divided by P, and further the rate of interest. As to the equation for money and bonds, there is no division by P.

[5] *Studies*, p. 142.

PQ, where E is income, s the saved part of the latter, P average prices of consumption goods, and Q an expression of their quantity.

It is only under dynamic assumptions that money plays any essential part in the formation of price. With respect to the complicated conditions which then arise, the reader is referred to the brief treatment in Chapter 42 and to the much more exhaustive treatment in books on the theory of money and business cycles. Here our intention has only been to discuss the relation between the quantity of money—the quantity of money produced and consumed, the quantity of payments, or the fund of money— and money value and the other parts of the economic system.

The use of money means that the economic quantities get a common standard of measurement, which, however, is only applicable to a limited extent due to the unstable value of money over time and its unequal distribution among different persons. The money values of groups of commodities, services, and means of production may, however, be added up. In terms of money, the calculation for the total economic categories will be exact. We may here consider relations or equations formed by summations, *e.g.*, equations for the sum of costs or value of commodities or the distribution of commodity values between wages and other shares of income. As was pointed out above, the sums of money are partly flows of payments during a period of time, and partly money values at a point of time.

18.4, CAPITAL AND INTEREST IN THE STATIC THEORY OF EQUILIBRIUM

Hitherto we have passed by the question of capital and interest in silence. In a short-run approach we may consider as given the quantities of real capital and the services these may yield during a certain period. But if we want to give a complete explanation, the existing quantities of real capital and, consequently, the corresponding quantities of services must also be explained. The explanation given hitherto would only be sufficient if production did not take time, *i.e.*, if all production was "momentary production". Then it would be possible to consider real capital only as an intermediary commodity and consider finished goods as produced exclusively by means of the original productive services, labor and use of land, that have gone into real capital. Production, however, takes time. Hence it is absolutely impossible to omit dynamic considerations, *i.e.*, considerations of the relations between quantities at different points of time. In order to include capital and interest in our theory, it is not necessary, however, to go further than to the margin between static and dynamic theory. We are here only going to examine the conditions necessary to maintain a stationary state for society as a whole. In this way we shall find a rate of interest and a quantity of capital which give us a static equilibrium. In the explanation of this equilibrium for society as a whole, it is necessary, however, to consider actual and potential processes of production extending over shorter or longer periods.

Whereas the quantities hitherto considered are flows: production, consumption and the performance of services per period (of indefinite length), the capital quantities are funds, *i.e.*, valuations per point of time. This is true both of the different kinds of real capital, each measured by its own standard, and capital measured in terms of money. These quantities cannot be immediately included in our equations, which are in the form of current accounts. Under static assumptions, the changes in the quantities mentioned will be equal to zero.

Since the different kinds of real capital, as investment yielding income and as a means of securing to one's self consumption goods now or later, in a community with free exchange, may replace each other, there will be an equalization of the ratio between the value of net output and the capital value, *i.e.*, of the rate of return. The same applies to land, bonds, and other saleable objects which yield an income. The possibilities of increasing output by time-consuming methods of production explains why it is possible to obtain income from investment in real capital.

If we pass on to dynamic assumptions, the relation between capital and money becomes important, since a change in the quantity of money in the short run acts as supply or demand for capital—in different ways, though, depending on the existence of idle means of production. These important relations between employment, interest and money will be dealt with in Chapter 42. Here we shall confine ourselves to the more abstract question of the conditions for static equilibrium in the long run with free mobility and free competition (or a corresponding form of economic adaptation).

We assume a uniform rate of interest, but we initially leave open the question whether it is zero, positive or negative. The experience of daily life in the most widely varied types of society, both with regard to the possibilities of production and the impulse to further saving, would make us expect a positive rate of interest with the stated assumptions.

Now it is possible to insert the rate of interest as one of the dependent variables in the equations[6] given above, while at the same time we distinguish between different generations of the services of original means of production, labor and natural forces used in the production of a commodity. In the demand equation, the rate of interest i is inserted as a co-determinant of income. In the cost equations, the quantity of each productive service employed is divided according to the length of time it has been taking part in the production, and a special technical coefficient for each period is included, at the same time as each item of cost is multiplied by the factor $(1 + i)$, to a power corresponding to the length of time from the input of the service to its consumption. If we sum up the equally

---

[6] Cf. Lindahl, *Studies*, p. 304 ff., and an earlier exposition in a somewhat different form in "Prisbildningsproblemets Upplägning från Kapitalteoretisk Synpunkt", *Ekonomisk Tidskrift*, 1929, p. 52.

long periods of using the different kinds of productive services, the cost equation for the second commodity, for instance, may be written:[7]

$$p_2 = (a^0{}_{2,1} \cdot \pi_1 + a^0{}_{2,2} \cdot \pi_2 \ldots) + (1 + i)(a^1{}_{2,1} \cdot \pi_1 + a^1{}_{2,2} \cdot \pi_2 \ldots)$$
$$+ (1 + i)^2(a^2{}_{2,1} \cdot \pi_1 \ldots) \text{ etc.}$$

In the quantity equations for the productive services delivered in the period, we now add the quantities employed in each of the production periods for each of the commodities. In the supply equations of the productive services, i is included as a codeterminant of service performed (labor) of different kinds. Since there is now a technical coefficient for each combination of commodity, service and period, we set up equations for each of these. (The unit of length of the periods is of course arbitrary.) By this reformulation the different kinds of real capital—the produced means of production—are resolved into the original means of production used for production and according to the periods between investment and consumption.

Beside the new unknown, the rate of interest, i, Lindahl uses an equation for total income,[8] into which the average period of investment enters. But it seems to the present writer that in doing so he only obtains a definition of this average period, weighted according to the addition of interest, which is a function of i, and that a decisive determining factor has not been taken into consideration.

Looking back at the so-called classical theory of interest, the idea occurs to one that something in the way of a supply function for total existing capital is lacking. Here, with static assumptions where net saving and net investment are zero, it is not a matter of the supply function of the market, but of the existence of a total capital of a certain magnitude without any propensity to increase or decrease, cf. Part III, Chapter 41. There is the previously mentioned difficulty, however, that the total existing capital value as a fund is not suitable for direct insertion into a static system of equations with flow quantities and relations between them (prices and technical coefficients) as dependent variables. But it is possible to get around this difficulty by expressing capital value in terms of total capital output capitalized at the rate of interest. Total capital output is the difference between total commodity value and payment for the productive services (apart from the service of capital value).

The supply equation for total capital value may then be written:[9]

$$(\Sigma xp - \Sigma y\pi) \; / \; i = f(i, \pi_1\pi_2 \ldots p_1, p_2 \ldots)$$

since with static assumptions, the propensity not to consume must be

---

[7] The same mode of expression is used as on p. 45, as indicated in footnote 8 below. The index above the technical coefficients indicates the period of production.

[8] *Ekonomisk Tidsskrift*, 1929, equation (6), p. 54; *Studies*, equation (7), p. 308, here with a slightly altered way of writing.

[9] x being quantities, p prices of commodities, i the rate of interest, y quantities and π prices of productive services.

dependent on the rate of interest, in connection with the payment for original services and commodity prices.

Since all the unknowns can now be found, it is possible to find the total value of real capital afterwards by insertion in the right or left side of this equation.

In a partial analysis, we have the following "supply equation" for existing capital: $C = f(i, \pi_1\pi_2 \ldots p_1p_2)$ and a "demand equation" formed by all other equations, including $C = (\Sigma xp - \Sigma y\pi) / i$.

The whole of this analysis may appear to be somewhat remote and abstract, but it seems to be necessary in view of the assertion frequently made that it is impossible to set up a static theory of interest on capital and that interest on capital, because it is claimed that it does not belong in a static system of equilibrium, must be a dynamic, monetary or institutional phenomenon. It is true that when we look at the way in which the rate of interest is determined, dynamic, monetary and institutional considerations play a decisive, practical, and, in the short run, a quite overwhelming, part. But the mechanism of the market, through which the rate of interest is determined, is one thing; the conditions that must be present in order that a certain rate of interest can be maintained without disturbances in equilibrium conditions, is quite another thing. The political valuation of the effects entailed by such special interference is a third question that must be dealt with.

The theory of the equilibrium rate of interest in a free, mobile and non-regulated market, may also be expressed in quite popular terms. The lower the rate of interest, the more capital it is profitable to tie up in production. This gives us a declining "demand curve" not for any momentary market, but for the magnitude of the quantity of capital giving equilibrium in the long run. If there exists a certain amount of capital, the willingness of the population to possess capital may be expected to react in a definite way to a change in the rate of interest. This corresponds to the existence of a "supply curve" suitable to be combined with the "demand curve" for segments near the point of equilibrium. Since the two curves must intersect at one or several points, the rate of interest and the total quantities of capital must be determinate. The demand curve being probably very elastic and not likely to reach zero with quantities at present imaginable, a positive rate of interest must be expected. The supply curve may be increasing or decreasing; but as it cannot be supposed to decrease as little as the demand curve within the decisive sphere, a single stable point of intersection must be expected.

What has been said above will seem to some readers of modern economics to be hopelessly orthodox, "classical" theory. This is, however, very largely due to the fact that we are here concerned with the conditions for a static long-run equilibrium, and not with the way in which the determination of the rate of interest and the variation in the quantity of capital are actually taking place. As we shall try to show in the Chapter 42 on

Employment, Interest, and Money, there is a possibility of bringing classical real capital theory and modern monetary short-run theory, with some Keynesian influence, into agreement with each other.

18.5, SEVERAL MARKETS

We have hitherto assumed a market that is internally homogeneous and outwardly closed. In the theory of interregional and international[10] trade, one assumes several internally homogeneous markets, separated by certain costs of transportation and other possible hindrances to movements across the frontiers. Special treatment is given to the case where commodities are freely mobile, but factors of production absolutely tied to the region. To each of these markets we may then apply the static equilibrium approach of the kind described above, supplemented by considerations of the mutual influences between the markets. The rate of exchange between the currency of the two regions is introduced as a new unknown, at the same time as a new equation puts the value of imports and other payments equal to the payment for exports and other credits.

In Chapter 50, we proceed from several internally homogeneous markets to heterogeneous markets. Actually, costs of transportation, as well as small differences in quality or in the preference of buyers for certain sellers, entail a series of very important gradual transitions in the conditions of the market. With regard to local differences this continuous approach, in so far as there is no question of national frontiers involved, seems to be more practical than the discontinuous, interregional one.

In Chapter 18.1 we have shortly indicated how it is possible to supplement the description of the economic network by adding the time dimension. In a similar way it is also possible to introduce spatial dimensions in our system of equations, which must become very complicated, however, when the heterogeneity of the surface of the earth is taken into consideration. From the beginning it will here be necessary to give up the assumption of competition. In Part IV, Chapter 51, we are going to deal separately with some of the problems of distance and costs of transportation, but of course the problems of location of production and consumption, local prices, interlocal trade and differences in local methods of production are closely connected and all interdependent with all other economic conditions.[11]

18.6, ALTERNATIVE MODELS

It seems to be futile, by means of a simultaneous extension in all imaginable directions of the Walras equations, to formulate *the* correct and

[10] Ohlin, *Interregional and International Trade*, Harvard University Press, 1933; Carl Iversen, *International Capital Movements*, Munksgaard & Oxford University Press, 1935.

[11] Walter Isard, "The General Theory of Location and Space-Economy", *Quarterly Journal of Economics*, November, 1949.

complete economic theory in the exact form of equations. Only models of some simplicity are workable and able to be built up from facts. What kinds of models are helpful varies with economic conditions, problems dealt with and material available. If for example we do not know anything about demand functions, given prices and quantities may be our starting point. As a consequence we limit ourselves to alternative incomplete models and abstain from the construction of *the* system of equations, correct and complete in all situations. The essential thing is the ability to construct the model suitable for the case discussed. With regard to Walras, the present book concentrates on the simplified form of equations (described in Chapter 11 above) and his central view on the economic network.[12]

CHAPTER 19

DEMAND AND UTILITY

IN the previous nine chapters of Part II we were mainly interested in placing the economic quantities in relation to each other within the economic network. The different types of links between the economic magnitudes were mentioned. Further, it was explained how a national account or an illustration of the economic circulation consists of a series of summations, arrived at by splitting up and gathering the flows. As a supplement to this study of the summations, we shall in the present chapter and the two chapters which follow deal with the more complicated functions of reaction: demand, techniques of production and supply of productive services, which determine the relation between the subflows and in some cases the width of the flows. Since we have already briefly mentioned the extension of the initial assumptions in the previous Chapter, a subject which will be dealt with in detail in Parts III and IV, we shall not here confine ourselves strictly to the assumptions of static free competition, even though here, too, they will generally form the starting-point.

19.1, THE DEMAND FUNCTION

It has already been mentioned in Chapter 11 that the quantity demanded of a commodity must be considered as a function not only of the commodity's own price, but also of the prices of all other commodities as well

---

[12] Much criticism of Walrasian details and reference to literature are to be found in Robert E. Kuenne: "Walras, Leontief, and the Interdependence of Economic Activities", *Quarterly Journal of Economics*, August 1954.

as of incomes. This function changes in the course of time. Where there is a tendency for regular development, it is still possible to simplify the analysis and take account of a demand function for a period with a certain trend factor included. The quantities demanded at points of time within the period must then be considered as dependent also on the point of time (year) as one of the independent variables. Further, the quantity demanded will at any time be dependent on all the previous changes.

The interdependence of demand demonstrates the regularity that asserts itself between the quantities purchased of various commodities. Since it is a question of choice, this interdependence (the consumption function) takes account of all commodities. It may, however, be expressed by an equation for each commodity, indicating quantity as a function, among other things, of the prices of this and of other commodities, but not of their quantities. But the consumption function might also be expressed by an equation for each price, stated, among other things, as a function of the quantities.

If the demand equations are to be applicable in a practical way, one must confine one's self to considering quantity as a function of a smaller number of factors that have the greatest influence on it. The most usual simplification used is the demand curve, which only considers the interdependence between the price and quantity of a commodity, and which is usually interpreted in such a way that one can choose either price or quantity as the dependent variable. The only really known point on the demand curve valid at the moment—and the same is true of the more comprehensive demand functions—is the actually prevailing price-quantity combination. The further we get away from this, the more difficult it is to know anything, and the greater is the necessity of taking many variables into consideration.

As an expression of conditions prevailing for small variations round the actual situation, the concept of *elasticity* is useful. If we have no better information, we may assume constant elasticity or, alternatively, a constant slope of those parts of the demand curve that are situated most closely to the actual price and quantity. The unequal distribution of income seems to indicate that the demand curve of the market, especially with regard to larger groups of commodities, curves inwards towards the origin, such as, for instance, curves with constantly negative elasticity. The opposite case, a curving outward in the diagram, is likely to appear if demand price for the first part of the curve is limited by competition with commodities that can roughly satisfy the same wants, whereas the curve ends with a comparatively steep decline, since a high degree of satisfaction prevails at that point.

Demand curves are static. They consequently deal with alternative states of equilibrium. Therefore they do not tell us "what will happen" the next day or month, when the price changes. For some time after a change in price, the propensity to buy will still be influenced by how much one has bought, and how much money one has spent previously when price was either lower or higher. Hence it is wrong to assume that adaptation takes place by moving up and down a fixed demand curve. It follows that time series of information about price and quantity taken in short intervals are not suitable for the construction of static demand curves.[1] Since some purchases take place only at very long intervals (the length of which, moreover, may vary with prices), one cannot assume any regularity when considering short periods. The purchases of the present, besides being influenced by those of the immediate past, are also influenced by expectations as to the future, which are also very largely dependent on preceding developments. When studying the effects of a change in price, one may get a useful simplified expression of demand by including the time elapsed since the change as one of the determining variables.

What we have dealt with here is the economist's conception of demand, the "real" or *ex post* demand curve (or function). Another very important thing is the entrepreneur's conception of future demand, the *ex ante* demand or sales function, determining his price policy. (Cf. Part IV.) Here the *ceteris paribus* assumption is realized. The entrepreneur estimates the effects of changes in price on quantity sold having no reason to expect changes on other points.

On the whole we may assume that any statistical or concrete theoretical expression of demand must be a simplification which disregards most of the immense number of determining conditions. Hence there is no question of finding exactly correct and complete demand functions nor demand functions independent of time and place.

The well-known great dispersion among individual budgets illustrates the strong influence which other factors than prices and income must have on consumption and demand. Due to differences in composition of population and differences in environment, aggregate market conditions also differ very much. A thorough-going explanation of demand must therefore necessarily investigate a number of circumstances belonging to the data of the central and pure economic theory. Cooperation with Psychology and Sociology is necessary, and literature about Business Economics is useful. A more precise treatment must be dynamic, taking into consideration past experiences, habits, standards of consumption and living, and time elapsed since changes in price or income. With regard to durable goods the distinction between purchase and consumption comes in. And saving must be dealt with as the alternative to purchasing of commodities. Age and family conditions are important as well as supply of free goods from state, employer or others. The influence of environment, income distribution, other people's consumption and the degree of contact or independence between individuals must also be considered. Finally all the kinds of economic and other trends, change in quality of

---

[1] Oskar Morgenstern, "Demand Theory Reconsidered", *Quarterly Journal of Economics*, February 1948.

goods or the appearance of new goods are important.[2] In spite of all that, economic statistics seem to have found fairly regular formulas for the variations in demand, with prices and income, within definite periods and geographic areas.

19.2, UTILITY AND WELFARE

In order to understand demand it is desirable to know something about its origin, *i.e.*, what is behind the demand function as it actually appears on the market. Above all it is clear that the demands of several persons are related to each other. In so far as the demands of these persons are independent of each other, the quantities demanded may be added up. A simple summation, on the other hand, cannot be used where the individuals either set a value on consuming the same as others, or desire to have something entirely for themselves. The demand of the individuals is dependent on income and wants. As to income conditions we have good statistical information, and it would be very desirable if we had corresponding direct and measurable information as to wants, so that one could build up an explanation in the individual cases and thus get a supplement to the very uncertain, direct statistical knowledge of demand.

However, here we are up against the decisive difficulty involved in an objective ascertainment of subjective phenomena like wants and utility.[3] Later psychological schools have attacked the assumptions of the marginal utility theory, inherited from utilitarians and hedonists, that the pleasure and pain of the individual are ascertainable quantities, which in a rational way may determine the behavior of the individual person.

Objections have been put forward from many sides. Modern psychology attaches much importance to the fact that human behavior is very largely dominated by habit, impulse, instinct, suggestion, and advertising. This means that conceptions which more or less casually dominate consciousness are decisive in so far as the activity is not completely unconscious.

[2] Ruth P. Mack: "Economics of Consumption", *A Survey of Contemporary Economics*, Vol. II, Richard D. Irwin, 1952; James S. Duesenberry: *Income, Saving and Consumers' Behavior*, Harvard Univ. Press, 1949; later Hugo E. Pipping, *Standard of Living*, Academic Bookstore, Helsingfors, 1953.

[3] Max Weber: "Die Grenznutzenlehre und das psykologische Grundgesetz", *Archiv für Sozialwissenschaft*, 1908, and *Gesammelte Aufsätze zur Wissenschaftlehre*, 1922 Gunnar Myrdal: *The Political Elements in Economic Theory*, 1953, Chapter 4. *Das politische Element in der Nationalökonomischen Doktrinbildung*, Duncker & Humblot, 1932; *in Handwörterbuch der Statswissenschaften*, 2. Auflager, Rosenstein-Rodan: Grenznutzen, and F. X. Weiss: Nachtrag, to the article "Wert"; Tugwell and others: *The Trend of Economics*, 1924; J. M. Clark: "Economics and Modern Psychology", *Journal of Political Economy*, 1918; Jacob Viner: "The Utility Concept in Value Theory and its Critics", *Journal of Political Economy*, 1925; O. Lange: "The Determinateness of the Utility Function", *Review of Economic Studies*, 1934. R. G. D. Allen, "A Note on the Determinateness of Utility", *ibid.*, 1935, and the discussion in the following issues; Frantz Alt: "Über die Messbarkeit des Nutzens", *Zeitschrift für Nationalökonomie*, 1936; Ragnar Frisch, "Kvantitativ formulering af den teoretiske økonomikks lover", *Statsøkonomisk Tidsskrift*, 1926; Erik Schmidt, "Graensenyttelaere eller Valghandlingsteori", and "Behovenes og Forbrugets Psykologi", both articles in *Nationaløkonomisk Tidsskrift*, 1941.

H

The wants of the moment depend on the prevailing recollections, expectations, and tensions of the individual. All this means that the decision is not made after a careful weighing of feelings, or, rather, a rational calculation of the sensations created by a possible act of consumption and a rational comparison of the possible quantities of pleasures and pains entailed by different combinations of consumption. Stronger than any weighing of the sentiments attending a definite pattern of consumption are the concrete impulses which initiate the action (stimulus-response). Wants and satisfaction are experienced as a wave movement in time. The question is to what extent memory and rationalization may bring about regularity and plan.

Instead of trying to understand the actions of people from within by finding the rational connection between the strength of the feelings of pleasure caused by the consumption on one hand, and the sacrifice of payment on the other, one may study the economic behavior of people from the outside. The different feelings of pleasure and pain are not homogeneous, and so cannot be summed up and subtracted from each other. It is asserted that the law of decreasing marginal utility has no general application, but that quite different laws apply for the satisfaction of the individual wants. Further, critics with historical interests emphasize the effects of social conditions, habits, class conceptions as to what is right and reasonable, etc. Finally, it may be mentioned that as a matter of fact we do not value the different kinds of commodities in utility units, but in money.

The question now is whether it can still be asserted that statements as to wants and utility supply us with information which can be used as the basis for objective determination, *i.e.*, measurement. In the first place, there is the possibility of deriving a kind of measurement deductively from certain premises founded on generally accessible, but not further analyzed observations. A second way is to give them a more solid, empirical foundation by reference to psychological and biological observations. Finally, there is a possibility of regarding them from the point of view of the "theory of choice".

Similarity or difference with regard to utility is in the latter case determined on the basis of the actual behavior of people in the market, or on the basis of statements as to how they would behave in definite situations. In this way we do not get any causal explanation in the individual case concerning the phenomena of the market since it is from these that the deductions are made. But in so far as we dare assume regularity, the concept of relative utility formed on the basis of choices made in certain cases may be a useful guide with regard to the choices to be expected in other cases.

In connection with the criticism of the marginal utility theory suggested above, the application of psychological experience, on the whole, has been criticized. It has been maintained that this was a case of introspection of a mystic character or the arm-chair theorizing of economists, which was often more influenced by theoretical presuppositions than by actual observation. No doubt it is true that the empirical foundation of the marginal utility theory has often been very weak and unreliable. On the other hand, there is reason to believe that information from people concerning their experience as consumers may be useful material, especially when it is collected from other people under controlled conditions. These controlled conditions must allow for the circumstances of the persons involved as well as for the total situation, *i.e.*, the "field" in which the wants arise and the consumption takes place. One must not, however, be so naïve as to believe that the permissible limit to introspection depends on the investigator's dressing himself up in a white coat and using the terminology of psychologists. External observations of behavior and physiological reactions may also show regularities that may be informative either in themselves, or as a supplement to controlled and carefully applied introspection.

Psychological investigations of wants and consumption show, among other things, that the wants are not constant, but are highly conditioned by the situation; and further, that the wants are especially characterized by a state of "tension", and that the feelings of pleasure and pain, accompanying the consumption, do not vary proportionately with needs felt and actions performed.

Since more exact empirical knowledge of demand is only available to a very limited extent, even an assumption whose validity is uncertain and cannot be demonstrated in any strict, scientific sense, being founded on casual introspection, may, for want of a better basis, be useful as a start. The statistical investigations of demand, moreover, are often so uncertain and give results that are so unrealistic that an estimate based on utility concepts may act as a first control on the statistics themselves. Compare in this respect the situation before exact physical measurements were accomplished, as well as our reactions when a thermometer, a watch, or other exact instrument of measurement, deviates too much from what we consider to be correct. Finally, it is worth while mentioning that many statements by economists concerning the utility curves for individual commodities, etc., are stated formally in terms of feelings and units of utility, but are actually based on observations of external market conditions, which may make them useful.

By studying the results of acts of choice in a larger number of cases, we may, as suggested above, arrive at inferences concerning other related cases. It is the actual choice, and not want or the utility that is observed. If we have observations with regard to choice in comparable cases, no consideration of wants nor utility in the ordinary subjective sense is necessary in order to form an idea of what will happen in the market in the individual cases. We may, in other words, confine ourselves to quantities that may be observed objectively.

If a person has a choice between two kinds of commodities, he has a possibility of indicating in action or words which of the two he prefers in different combinations of consumption. He may also indicate that two combinations are of equal value to him, *e.g.*, 1x + 3y and 2x + 2y. We may now, as in Fig. 7A, imagine a diagram with the quantities of com-

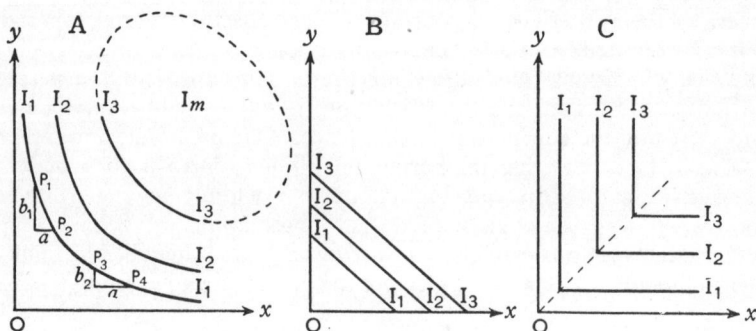

Fig. 7. A, B, C. Types of Indifference Curves

modities x and y plotted along the axes, and a person valuing equally combinations of commodities corresponding to the points on the indifference curve,[4] I_1, whereas he prefers all combinations on I_2, which also are valued equally, but that he prefers the combinations on I_3 to the latter. The whole of this attitude on the part of the individual person may be imagined to be objectively observed. In real life, however, comparatively little may actually be observed, and actual conditions are immensely complicated by the existence of not two, but a great number of commodities. As to most commodities, it will also be very difficult to imagine combinations corresponding to more than a small segment of the curves round the actually known exchange ratios. If, instead of the indifference curves, we consider multi-dimensional indifference surfaces, we shall be able to take the quantities of a great many commodities into consideration. A simpler method is to plot income or expenditures on all commodities other than x along the y-axis.

The indifference curves must be assumed generally to curve towards the origin, as in Fig. 7A. In accordance with the law of diminishing marginal utility, we can say that if a person gets more of one commodity, he is satisfied with less than before of the other, in exchange for an additional unit of the commodity. If one begins with the combination P_1, we are willing to go to the combination P_2, *i.e.*, exchange b_1 of y for a of x. The curve, consequently, is downward sloping. If we begin at P_3, we have more of x and less of y than at P_1 and P_2, we are only willing to give up b_2 of y in order to get a more of x; $b_1 > b_2$, *i.e.*, the bend of the curve is as indicated in Fig. 7A.

---

[4] As to this theory, formulated by Pareto, see J. R. Hicks, *Value and Capital*, (The Clarendon Press, Oxford,) 1939, Part I; J. R. Hicks and R. G. D. Allen, "A Reconsideration of the Theory of Value", *Economica*, May 1934; R. G. D. Allen, "The Nature of Indifference Curves", *Review of Economic Studies*, February 1934.

In the marginal case where the two commodities are fully substitutable for each other, the indifference curve becomes a straight line from one axis to the other, as in Fig. 7B. If, conversely, they complement each other to such an extent that they can only be used together in a fixed proportion, we get the indifference curves of Fig. 7C. In so far as very great quantities give negative satisfaction, the curves become ring-shaped, as indicated by the dotted continuation of I_3 in Fig. 7A, and the highest point may be I_m (maximum of utility).

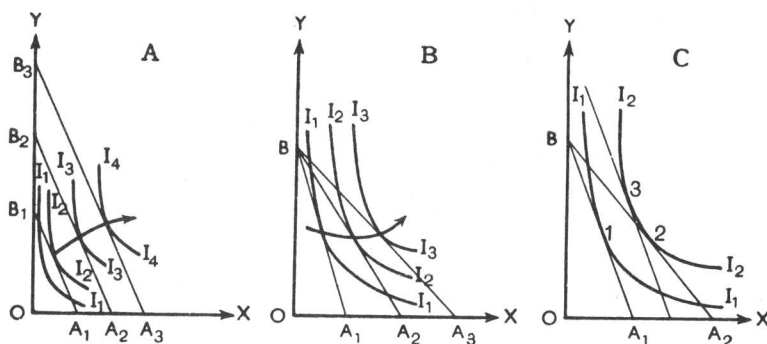

Fig. 8 A, B, C. Change in Income and Price

If a person has a system of indifference curves as in Fig. 8A and if A_1 of x or B_1 of y can be obtained for the amount the person wants to spend on the two commodities together, he may also buy for this amount all combinations situated on the straight line A_1B_1. As before, y may mean income or expenditure on all commodities other than x. Of these combinations he prefers the one situated on the "highest" indifference curve, here I_2, which is tangent to the line A_1B_1. If now there is a gradual increase in the amount at his disposal for the two commodities, and if the price relation between the commodities remains unchanged, the expansion of consumption follows the line through the points of tangency between the indifference curves and the price lines or expenditure lines, A_2B_2 and A_3B_3.

In Fig. 8B, the effect of a price reduction in x in relation to y is illustrated by new expenditure lines corresponding to different price relations. The effect of a reduction in price, however, may be divided into an income effect and a substitution effect.[5] If the price of x is reduced, as in Fig. 8C, by transition from the expenditure line BA_1 to BA_2, a shift takes place from consumption combination 1 to 2. The path from 1 to 2 may be divided into two stages by considering the two effects separately; first, as a consequence of increased income, we move from 1 to 3, the point where the indifference curve through 2 touches a straight line parallel to BA_1, and from there we move by substitution from 3 to 2. It would also be

[5] Cf. Hicks, *Value and Capital*, p. 31, and Schultz's book cited below, p. 44.

possible, however, to move in the opposite direction, *i.e.*, go from 1, as a result of the substitution effect, to the point not shown in the diagram, where I_1 is tangent to a line parallel to BA_2, and then, as a result of the income effect, to point 2. The above-mentioned effects on the consumption of x and y are measured on the axes. The greater the amount spent on commodity x, the price of which has been reduced, the greater the income effect. The substitution effect will always tend towards a greater consumption of the commodity which has become cheaper; but if inferior commodities are involved, the income effect may be so strong that the consumption of the commodity will be smaller instead of greater. We have the opposite situation in the classical case: the increased consumption of grain by poorer classes as a result of a great rise in the price of grain.

Since it is individual persons who make the choice, the indifference curves apply only to them, and not to society as a whole. In the case of changes in the total quantity demanded, there may be a possibility, however, of summing up the income effects and substitution effects for the individual persons.

From a system of indifference curves, it is possible to form a corresponding demand curve for the individual, where one of the two goods, which may then mean all other commodities (or money in relation to the commodities), is used as a measure of price.

If we want to consider indifference conditions for many kinds of commodities at the same time, it is necessary, as indicated above, to operate with multi-dimensional indifference surfaces. Indifference curves for two individual commodities are very unreal, apart from the segment near the actual terms of exchange, since they are based on the assumption of a constant consumption of all other commodities. Large parts of the indifference-curve theory, therefore, are of a very hypothetical character. Besides the whole indifference system is unstable.

The slope of the indifference curve, as indicated, for instance, in the ratio a/b_1 by movement from P_1 to P_2 in Fig. 7A, expresses—in the same way as the ratio between marginal utilities—the ratio in which one is willing to make an exchange. It may now be said that the ratio between the marginal utilities, *i.e.*, the relative marginal utilities, may be defined by reference to experience as to the person's willingness to exchange, or by actual acts of choice. It must be emphasized, however, in the first place that we only have a concept corresponding to the relative marginal utility and, in the second place, that no objective measure has been obtained for the amounts of the subjective feelings in question (neither those attaching to the choice nor to the consumption). The connection would be established if, in accordance with the subjective utility theory, we assumed that the visible effects of the acts corresponded exactly to the amounts of feelings experienced, *i.e.*, assumed that the subjective utility explanation of demand was correct. So we have not obtained an internal causal explanation of the market phenomena by means of utility experiences, but a concept of measurement, a rationalizing of the external observations, facilitating the transfer of experience from case to case and facilitating the drawing of conclusions. If one is afraid of using expressions reminiscent of the subjective theory, one may speak of marginal barter terms or a marginal rate of substitution instead of relative marginal utilities.

When indifference in exchange is assumed to signify equality of utility, it may be said that one has the same total utility on the same indifference curve; and correspondingly, we may speak about greater utility—in the sense of the theory of choice—on higher indifference curves or surfaces. How much greater this utility is, however, cannot be expressed in this way. There is always an endeavor to get on to a higher indifference curve, but the attitude of choice towards the different kinds of commodities cannot tell us whether the progress from I_1 to I_2 is greater than or equal to the progress from I_2 to I_3. Nor is this of any importance, so long as we are only concerned with explaining the actual behavior of people in the commodity market.

It would, however, be desirable, for the purpose of general economic policy, *e.g.*, in the distribution of taxes or in similar decisions, to be able to compare the importance of changes in income at different levels of income. In order to be able to use observations of the choices of individual persons in order to make comparisons of utility for different individuals, the further hypothesis is required: that the individuals are uniform to some extent. The importance to be attached to changes in income for the same individual at different possible levels of income, is also of interest, however, in theoretical investigations. This is the case, for instance, when in the determination of working hours and the extent of saving there may be a question of obtaining income at the cost of certain sacrifices. Similar considerations apply in the case of risk valuations.

The problem now is whether we may imagine situations of choice which make measurement possible as the ratio between the marginal utility of income at different levels of income, in the sense of the theory of choice. It may be said in advance that one cannot expect any simple formula for marginal utility as a function of income, like Bernoullis' formula, for instance (a constant divided by income, less the minimum of subsistence). Actual wants and possibilities of consumption, as well as current prices, must influence the shape of the curve.

That the problem has an objective meaning, since measurement is imaginable,[6] may be illustrated by Frisch's interview method. It is possible at least to put hypothetical choices before people. How great a part of his

[6] Frisch, *New Methods of Measuring Marginal Utility*, Tübingen, J. C. B. Mohr, 1932, and "Kvantitativ Formulering av den Teoretiske Ökonomiks Lover", *Statsøkonomisk Tidsskrift*, 1926, pp. 330–33; cf. also the above-mentioned discussion in *Review of Economic Studies*, including my article, "On the Determinateness of the Utility Function", 1937, vol. IV, No. 3, with solution by means of probability, p. 238; James N. Morgan, "Can we Measure the Marginal Utility of Money?", *Econometrica*, April 1945; William Vickrey, "Measuring Marginal Utility by Reaction to Risk", *Econometrica*, October 1945; W. E. Armstrong, "Uncertainty and the Utility Function", *Economic Journal*, March 1948.

income will a man relinquish, say, every second year or every second month, in order to have his income increased in the other periods by, *e.g.*, 50 per cent, and what is the variation of this proportion with the level of income? The carrying through of the experiment is full of practical and psychological pitfalls. (The possibility of putting off expenditure and pleasures to the "rich" periods, lacking ability to estimate remote eventualities, etc.) The best procedure will probably be to consider small changes in income. It might also be possible, by an investigation of the propensity to save, to try to isolate the effect of the desire for an equalization of income over time.

The willingness to run a risk or to pay an excess price for insurances may also be considered as a possible basis for measurement of the marginal utility of income, even if it is desirable to eliminate motives other than the increased marginal utility of income that is obtained by a more even distribution between periods. The question of how long the period is in which a non-insured loss reduced the possibilities of consumption, must also be taken into consideration.

Since indifference curves or surfaces correspond to different incomes, it may be said with reference to Fig. 7A that if a person is exactly indifferent to a 50 per cent chance of a position on either of the indifference curves I_1 and I_3, and a certain position on I_2, this may be taken as an expression of his valuing $I_2 - I_1 = I_3 - I_2$.

The same method may be applied in comparing different changes in income. Putting two changes of income equal means that Amount × Probability × Average Marginal Utility of Money in the two cases are equal; from this, the ratio between the marginal utilities may be found. If a man, for instance, is willing to pay $1,000 as insurance premium in case of 10 per cent probability of reduction of his income from $10,000 to $5,000, the method tells us that the average utility of his dollar between $10,000 and $5,000 is twice the average value of that between $10,000 and $9,000 ($1,000 \times 1 \times 1 = 5,000 \times \frac{1}{10} \times 2$). In order to get an absolute measurement of total utility, it is further necessary to have a zero point. However, the determination of it seems to lie outside the possibilities of economics.

Just as in Chapter 57, we obtain determinateness by means of probabilities. A more exact treatment is given by Neumann and Morgenstern.[7] Still a serious difficulty exists. It seems in some cases to be in striking contrast with the experience of common sense to define utility—as is done in the calculations above and also by Neumann and Morgenstern—in such a way as to exclude the specific utility or disutility of gambling. Many

[7] Neumann and Morgenstern (*Theory of Games and Economic Behavior*, Princeton University Press, pp. 8–9) say about the concepts, "utility", like the notions in physics such as "force" and "mass", that "while they are in their immediate form merely definitions, they become subject to empirical control through the theories which are built upon them". See further pp. 17–19 and 28, and Stone's article in *Economic Journal*, June, 1948, p. 197, concerning the valuation of risk, see also Chapters 32 and 33.

people are willing to pay a premium above mathematical expectation both for insurance and for gambling, though the gain in the latter case will be situated on a higher point on the income scale than the present income. It has been asserted that not only the position on the income scale, but also the relative size of two amounts involved are of importance. This is a postulate open to verification. However, the result will most probably be largely dependent on secondary aspects of the transactions. When people consider a choice as pure business and have a clear knowledge and understanding of what is involved, most people will demand something in order to take a risk. But if it is a game for them, the joy of taking part may lead to the opposite result. Further, it seems demonstrable that people's knowledge and understanding of the facts are quite often distorted. The newspapers tell much more about the winners in lotteries and games than about the losers and the relatively important goods they have to go without. A reliable analysis is, therefore, impossible without a psychological investigation of the secondary circumstances referred to and of their present knowledge and understanding. Comparisons between choices with different secondary aspects may also be informative. But here as well as in more elementary cases an apparently mechanistic analysis, based on the theory of choice, is really dependent on a preliminary psychological selection of "pure" material of a suitable sort. Without that we are still in the clouds: "pure" measuring without any "pure" material to measure.[8]

The above-mentioned methods aim directly at the essence of the problem: the marginal utility of income, which together with prices determines the marginal utility of the individual commodities. The most generally applied methods and those statistically most adaptable, however, use the utility of one or several commodities as a measure. In this connection we may mention Frisch's isoquant method, according to which a consumption surface is formed by composing and smoothing experiences as to the quantity consumed of a "commodity of comparison"—say, sugar or meat—in different income classes and under different price conditions. From the combinations of the consumption surface, of price, income and quantity, we may now, by alternatively keeping one of the three magnitudes constant, form Engels curves, demand curves, and "isoquants", respectively. The latter indicate the functional relationship between price and income for persons, consuming equally much of the "commodity of comparison". A well-to-do class uses as much of the "commodity of comparison" as a poorer class does at a lower price. If now it is assumed that the "commodity of comparison" has the same utility for all, the fact that some persons give p dollars for the "commodity of comparison" means that to one dollar is attributed 1/pth of the utility of the commodity assumed to be constant. Apart from the method's being statistically

[8] Experiments have actually been conducted giving not too significant results, cf. F. Mosteller and Philip Nogee: "An Experimental Measurement of Utility", *Journ. of Pol. Econ.*, October 1951, p. 371.

difficult and very uncertain, the assumption of the constant marginal utility of the "commodity of comparison" under changing conditions of life, seems very arbitrary from the point of view of the subjective-introspective valuation, which one unavoidably resorts to when it is a matter of estimating whether there is a rational basis for a complicated objective method of measurement.

If we adopt the point of view that the application of magnitudes is scientifically legitimate when it is possible in principle to measure them and to define them operationally, then the concept of marginal utility, which most economists have no doubt felt intuitively it was difficult to do without, will once more be reinstated in economics after having been definitely rejected a few years ago.

If only the marginal utility of income is constantly declining in some way or other, equality of income will give maximum of total utility in so far as all individuals are assumed to be similar. Since certain inequalities of income, however, may increase total income, the maximum of utility is reached at a distribution which means a compromise between full equality and a maximum of production.

Modern welfare theorists, however, are not so abstract and absolutely utilitarian.[9] A dominant branch of them follows Pareto in his disbelief in interpersonal comparisons. In more or less sophisticated form they only speak about increase in welfare, when some people's welfare is increased and no one's decreased. Others, like Bergson and Samuelson, formulate a welfare function comprising the welfare of all persons concerned. The formulation of a welfare function is hypothetical, instrumental model-building, and like all model-buildings intentionally simplified. The problem is to find forms that in a simple and effective way express what is intended. The same must apply to all welfare theories useful in practical life. Consequently I do not see any reason to stop at an order of aggregate preferences (ordinal utility) which is already a very strong

[9] Tibor Scitovsky, "The State of Welfare Economics", *Am. Econ. Rev.*, 1951; Kenneth E. Boulding, "Welfare Economics", *A Survey of Contemporary Economics*, Vol. II, 1952; Abram Bergson: "Socialist Economics". *A Survey of Contemporary Economics*, Vol. I. 1948, Paul Samuelson, *Economic Analysis*, 1948; D. H. Robertson, *Utility and all that*, Allen & Unwin, London, 1952; the discussion in *Econometrica*, Oct. 1952; Pipping's book mentioned in note; F. Zeuthen, *Vurderinger og Maalsætninger i Økonomien*, Copenhagen, 1952; "Recent Developments in Economics", Section III, *Quarterly Journal of Economics*, May 1954; Article in *Nationaløkonomisk Tidsskrift*, 1953; Myrdal's book and other works mentioned in Note 3; Charles Kennedy, "Concerning Utility", *Economica*, February 1954; H. Tyszynski, "Comparison between Increments of Utility", *Economic Journal*, June 1954; W. M. Gorman in *Econometrica*, January 1953, by means of very complicated mathematics proves "that a given system of indifference maps" only under certain very specific assumptions "yields a unique community indifference map"; a discussion about cardinal and ordinal utility is to be found in *Econometrica*, October 1952; Tinbergen in his book *On the Theory of Economic Planning*, 1952, as an introduction speaks about maximization of "some collective ophelimity function", but without giving any explicit formula. Actually he maximizes by trial with some chosen "target values". Finally, Paul Samuelson's short comment in *Survey of Contemporary Economics*, vol. II, to Boulding's article and his article in *Quarterly Journal of Economics*, February 1956 ought to be mentioned.

abstraction, extremely difficult to base on real observations and involving well-known paradoxes about aggregating individual preferences. A welfare function in any case goes far beyond what science can prove. Then why not make full use of the system of figures and arithmetic and quite openly speak about chosen weights making addition possible (cardinal utility)? Apart from extremely simple cases, models based on pure (ordinal) preference systems tend to become too complicated.

In reality we seem to be as far from a statistical determination of indifference surfaces as of marginal utility curves for purposes of practical guidance in political decisions.

A welfare function cannot be reached by pure scientific deliberation, but is a formulation of the economic purposes of some economic subject as an aggregate quantity to be maximized. This formulation is an instrument which, when combined with a system of equations about existing economic quantities and reactions, is able to give a definite plan, cf. Chapter 64. The economic subject making the choice (or in the name of whom it is made) may be a political party, a social group, an ethical or religious school, an individual or any other subject openly introduced and if necessary described to the reader. A principle for the compromise between the ideals of several subjects may also be defined. The extension of the political subjects' circles of sympathy or solidarity, and the way in which they decrease in intensity when moving away from the Ego as center, are essentially political and moral data.

In choosing the relative weights given to the marginal income of different persons some reasoning is, however, applicable. The rate at which a single individual's marginal utility of money decreases with increasing income is important but has to be combined with an essentially unscientific choice of the weight which the planner wants to give to the welfare of the different individuals. This choice may to a certain degree be influenced and motivated by facts as to the living conditions of the persons concerned. Further, facts and reasoning are to be considered with respect to their assumed sensibility. In any case, however, an essential part of the factors determining the weight which the planner chooses to give the marginal income of different persons depends on political or moral premises outside the field of science.

The conception of a welfare function may probably give only an unprecise starting point, a general orientation. It is scarcely possible to have an unbroken chain of deductions from the demand to maximize an explicitly formulated, aggregate magnitude down to a practical plan expressed in figures. The method must rather be to include as much as possible of logic and reliable experiences into the very mixed chain of political thinking and quite openly confess all the elements of political choice or guessing which it is necessary to include. Manageable, precise models may to a certain extent be useful as guides if we do not take them too seriously. The essential thing is that the ideal of a welfare function reminds us of the importance of consistency and unification between the various political ends and the generally strong interdependence between means. The formulation of aims must as far as possible be quantitative and explicit if the economic advisers are to be able to cooperate in the selection of rates of taxation, subsidies and other political measures.

The intensity of the discussion may probably be explained by the fact that two types of theories act ideologically in support of two opposite political aims: (1) indifference curves and the corresponding so-called "modern" (ordinal) welfare theory (Pareto) in favor of independence of the individual, and (2) measuring the marginal utility of income and the corresponding "old-fashioned" or rather revived and more radical (cardinal) welfare function theory in favor of economic equalization, simultaneously considering the effects on production. Pareto's theory was for a long time interpreted as a kind of tabu against moving any person from his present situation, or from a position with no state interference, to a lower indifference surface. Another interpretation recently given by Frisch[10] in collaboration with Pareto's old pupil Gustavo Del Vecchio reduces the Paretian principle to some kind of supplementary principle acceptable to any person: the principle that it would be an improvement of any actual or politically chosen order of things to make changes favorable to some one and not unfavorable to anybody. More important than the interpretation of Pareto is the application of his principle as a tabu or as a useful supplement to other principles.

The well-known and also very useful derived welfare principles about marginal equilibrium[11] in production and exchange are still applicable but not without exceptions. As in other fields, discontinuity in the possibilities of adaptation, for technical, institutional and psychological reasons, may make marginal equilibrium in all directions impossible. And further, chosen political aims may involve deviations from marginal equilibrium, *e.g.*, in the case of price control or redistributional taxation. Finally the Paretian principle with status quo as starting point does not determine a unique optimum, but a certain region, and consequently other principles may be of interest even to those bound by an ultra-Paretian tabu.

19.3, ELASTICITY

We now leave the study of the fundamental phenomena, the physiological and psychological causes of demand, the theory of choice, etc., in order to return to the direct study of demand as it appears on the market. In investigating the demand function the problem is to find how the quantity demanded of a certain commodity varies when other magnitudes, especially the price of the commodity itself, are changed. If we are only examining

[10] "Welfare Theory and the Pareto Regions", Appendix to *From National Accounts to Macro-Economic Decision Models*, Paper to International Association for Research in Income and Wealth, Rome, 1953. Also to be published in *Revue d'Economie Appliquée*.
[11] Reder, *Studies in the Theory of Welfare Economics*, 1942, Ch. 2, and Boulding in " Welfare Economics ", *Survey of Contemporary Economics*, vol. II.

the demand for the goods of a certain firm or in a given market, it is sufficient to ascertain the absolute changes in quantity and in the other factors. If we have a demand curve drawn to show price and quantity, we may consider the absolute variations or the proportion between them indicated by the slope of the curve. These methods of indicating variations cannot be applied, however, when we want to compare different real markets, other quantities, or data with different units of measurement. Here we apply the elasticity concept.

The price elasticity indicates the proportion between relative change in quantity and the relative change in price of the commodity with infinitely small variations:

$$e = \frac{dx}{x} \bigg/ \frac{dp}{p} = \frac{dx \cdot p}{dp \cdot x}$$

The reciprocal ratio expressing the sensitivity of price to changes in quantity is called *price flexibility*. In a similar way we have the elasticity of income, indicating the ratio between relative changes in quantity and in income with small variations in income, and the cross elasticity between two commodities, indicating the proportion between the relative variation in the quantity of one commodity and the relative variation in the price of the other.

The above-mentioned elasticities are partial elasticities and assume all other independent variables to be kept constant. The percentage by which the dependent variable is varied when the variable regarded as independent is changed by 1 per cent, gives a good approximation to the exact elasticity. If we consider variations that are not infinitely small, the calculation will be inexact, and the result will differ according as price and quantity at one end of the interval or at the other are used as the basis. By drawing on a piece of squared paper a rectilinear demand curve from axis to axis, and dividing it into, say, ten equally great parts, it may easily be seen how the approximate elasticity, calculated for an interval, varies down the curve from $-\infty$ to 0, being -1 in the middle of the curve; and how the approximate calculation gives a slightly different result according as the calculation is made for decreases or increases in price.

Instead of calculating elasticity by means of the four above-mentioned quantities, the elasticity at a point P of a declining demand curve may be found more easily as the ratio PA/PB where A and B are the points of intersection between the tangent in P, on the one hand, and the horizontal axis and the vertical axis, respectively on the other hand.[12]

Otherwise, it is easy to find, as in the Fig. 9, all possible positive and negative elasticities at an arbitrary point in a diagram, by drawing a

---

[12] Marshall, *Principles*, Mathematical Appendix, Note III; Lerner, "The Diagrammatical Representation of Elasticity of Demand", *Review of Economic Studies*, October, 1933; Carl Iversen, "Efterspørgslens Elasticitet", *Nationaløkonomisk Tidsskrift*, 1930, and the literature mentioned there. Further, the works mentioned in this section by Frisch, Schultz and Wold, as well as Frisch, *Forelesninger om statisk og dynamisk Verditeori*, 1931, and *Byttemarked* I, Oslo University, 1935.

straight line from the origin through the point. For this line we put the increase in quantity with a certain small increase in price as a unit, *i.e.*, we put it equal to +1, corresponding to an elasticity equal to +1. The variation in quantity for lines through the point with other slopes for the same variation in price then measure the elasticity in proportion to this unit. If we consider an infinitely small increase, we shall find that the elasticity thus calculated will agree with the formula given above. In the same way we may, of course, construct lines with any desired elasticity.

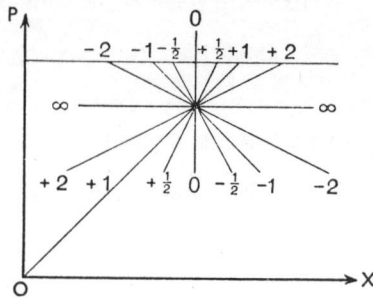

Fig. 9. Calculation of Elasticity

Elasticity on a declining demand curve is negative, the relative changes of price and quantity having the opposite sign. The negative sign, however, is often omitted as being obvious. The elasticity on a rising supply curve has a positive sign. Income elasticity is positive if one buys more and negative if one buys less of a commodity in the case of increased income. For a commodity only used by the middle class, the Engels curve is increasing from a point on the income axis and again decreasing to this, *i.e.*, income elasticity begins positive and ends negative.

With a price elasticity of −1, which is the limit between "elastic" and "inelastic" demand, the total outlay for the commodity is not changed as a result of variations in price and quantity. An equilateral hyperbola, converging towards the axes, has a constant elasticity of −1. Curves intersecting the hyperbola from below are elastic; curves intersecting from above are inelastic. Whereas steepness in a figure in itself does not say anything about elasticity, this is nevertheless indicated by the steepness at a definite point of a diagram, because we have here an expression of all four magnitudes in the above-mentioned formula. From the formula of elasticity, which may also be written $(dx \cdot p)/(dp \cdot x)$, it appears that we may in all cases measure the price elasticity by the ratio between changes in expenditure (or income) as a consequence of a change in quantity and as a consequence of change in price, cf. the areas $(B_1 + B_2)$ and A in Fig. 46 in Part IV, Chapter 64.

There is an important relation between the individual partial elasticities: elasticity of price, e, cross elasticities with regard to other commodities (saving included) e_1, e_2, etc., as well as income elasticity, E. The income elasticity is equal to the sum of the other elasticities with the opposite sign:

$$E = -(e + e_1 + e_2 \ldots e_n)$$

Thus a small increase in income has the same effect as a corresponding proportionate reduction of all prices, *i.e.*, as the sum of these effects. A 1 per cent increase in income has the same effect on the consumption of potatoes as the sum of the effects on the consumption of potatoes of a 1 per cent reduction in the price of potatoes and the prices of all other commodities. When the percentage is small, there is so small a change in the situation caused by the whole operation that the individual effects may be considered as independent changes in the original situation.[13]

It is obvious from the above-mentioned interdependence that income elasticity and price elasticity with the opposite sign are equal if all cross elasticities are equal to zero. The same applies if some are positive and others negative, and if the sum of them is equal to zero. If a commodity is easy to substitute, the cross elasticities are great and positive, and it may therefore be expected that the price elasticity of the commodity, being negative, will be essentially greater, numerically, than the income elasticity. Quantity, in other words, will then be subject to comparatively great changes when the price of the commodity is changed.

19.4, DEMAND STATISTICS

The theory of demand has developed in close correspondence with empirical investigations, which are very difficult in this sphere. The most obvious method is to compare observed prices and quantities at different points of time, and on this basis to try to construct demand curves directly (cf. Figure 14, p. 141). It soon appears, however, that such price-quantity relations, deduced from rough time series, do not correspond to the expected continuously declining demand curves. This is explained by the fact that other conditions have changed during the period. Hence it is necessary to determine a demand function which on the one hand includes some essential independent variables in addition to the price of the commodity, and on the other hand eliminates additional influences as, for instance, by using real price and quantity per capita.

Both demand and supply curves indicate relations between price and quantity. It is therefore obvious that combinations of price and quantity derived from time series need not correspond to demand curves alone. They can only be expected to correspond tolerably to a demand curve for the whole of the period in case the supply conditions—as for agricultural products—are changing substantially more than demand conditions. As for iron and similar raw materials, where demand fluctuates greatly with

---

[13] Herman Wold, "Efterfrågan på Jordbruksprodukter och dess Känslighet för Pris- och Inkomstförändringar", *Statens Offentliga Utredningar*, Stockholm, 1940, 16, p. 86.

business cycles, it must, on the contrary, be assumed that the curve found most likely corresponds to a rising supply curve, which is in this case comparatively stable.

If we make use of time series, it will, as pointed out above, be an advantage to find a demand function with several independent variables instead of a simple demand curve. In all practical cases where demand curves are useful in predicting the effects of a change in the price of the commodity itself, it is an easy thing to get back to the simple demand curve by inserting some average or estimated normal values for the other independent variables.

As a result of the many and changing conditions which act on demand, the right demand formula cannot be expected to be either simple or constantly valid. Since elasticity generally varies according to the level of price and income, etc., it is even more difficult to find, once and for all, general coefficients of elasticity, corresponding to the constants of physics. Statistical data only give a limited number of observations between price, quantity and other variables. Curves or formulae of a continuous nature must be added by ourselves, partly on the basis of theoretical assumptions as to the nature of demand, partly for the purpose of obtaining the simplest and most practical smoothing.

As an example of an empirical demand investigation by means of time series, we may mention Schultz' investigation of beef, pork and mutton in America during the years 1922–33.[14] In order to allow for the effects of an increasing population and a changing price level, the quantities were calculated per capita, and prices and incomes were adjusted for the general change in prices. The study then investigated how the quantities for each of the three commodities by themselves vary with the three prices and average income. Using the method of the least squares, constants were found for comparatively simple functions, ordinary equations of the first degree and logarithmic equations of the first degree, respectively, most nearly corresponding to the observed data. Two alternative methods are used. Quantity may be put equal to a constant plus price and the other independent variables, each multiplied by a constant coefficient. Another method which gives the same formula when logarithms of both sides are taken, may be used by putting the quantity equal to a constant multiplied by the independent variables, each brought to a constant power. The

---

[14] Henry Schultz, "Interrelations of Demand, Price and Income", *Journal of Political Economy*, 1935, Section V; further, Henry Schultz, *The Theory and Measurement of Demand*, Chicago University Press, 1938; see also the above-mentioned investigation by Wold and his *Demand Analysis*, Almqvist & Wiksell, Stockholm, and John Wiley, New York, 1952, I.6 and Part V; Trygve Haavelmo, "*Efterspørgslen efter Flaesk i København*," Studier fra Aarhus Universitets økonomiske Institut, 1939. A good short, and rather popular exposition of modern demand theory is to be found in A. R. Prest's article, "Some Experiments in Demand Analysis", *Review of Economics and Statistics*, February 1949. Later appeared: J. R. N. Stone, *The Measurement of Consumers' Expenditure and Behaviour in the United Kingdom, 1920–38*, Cambridge, 1954; Heinz Gollnick. *Die Nachfrage nach Nahrungsmitteln*, 1954. A discussion of important problems of methods is referred to at the end of Chapter 44.

constant coefficients thus found indicate the weight of the influence of the individual quantities. The exponents in the logarithmic formula correspond to the elasticities. Whereas the price of the commodity itself has a negative influence on quantity, prices of other commodities usually have a weaker positive effect, and income a comparatively strong positive effect.

It is very much easier to get information as to the dependence of consumption on income than its dependence on price. From information as to the former dependence the so-called Engels curves are drawn, which for the main categories of consumption goods are approximately rectilinear within limited intervals.[15] Income elasticity may be found directly from household accounts by comparing consumption in income classes which border on each other. Owing to the interdependence between income elasticity and price elasticity mentioned above, it is also possible to draw conclusions from the elasticities of income to those of price, or at any rate to control investigations of price elasticity on the basis of income elasticity and the differences which may be expected between them owing to assumptions of cross elasticity. Since it is difficult to find and describe the change in the proportions between the numerous subgroups of a commodity consumed when income or price is changed, it is useful to consider not only the variations in quantity, but also the variation in expenditures for the commodity.

In some cases, for instance, for electricity in economically similar localities, it seems to be safe to find elasticity by geographical comparisons of price for quantity per unit of potential consumption. Though the results of the elasticity investigations obviously cannot be directly transferred to other times and places, we shall, by way of illustration, mention a few of the results of Wold's Swedish investigation.[16] For workers and small employers, the following income elasticities were found with regard to the expenditures in 1933: for food, drink and tobacco, 0·51; for housing, 1·30; for fuel, lighting and cleaning, 0·65; and for intellectual pursuits, travelling and pleasures, 1·85. Among the income elasticities for separate kinds of commodities may be mentioned: meat, 0·39; skim milk, −1·17; margarine, −0·33 (and −0·37 when quantity and not expenditure is considered); flour, −0·50, tobacco, 0·94, meals in restaurants, etc., 2·14. The price elasticities were: for milk, −0·2 or −0·3; for meat and pork, −0·7; for eggs, about −1·0, and for the total quantity of butter and margarine taken together, −0·4 or −0·5; for butter alone, likewise in case of the same price movement in both commodities, −0·7 or −0·8; and for butter alone when the price of margarine is kept constant, −1·4 or −1·5.

[15] Tinbergen, *Econometrics*, §§. 26 and 32.
[16] Quoted in footnote 13, page 107, pp. 101, 105 and 136–37.

I

CHAPTER 20

PRODUCTION, COST AND SUPPLY

THROUGH the process of production, productive services are transformed into consumption goods. As we have seen, the technique of production is one of the determining factors in economic interdependence. The technical coefficients which indicate how much of each productive service must be used for each commodity, together with the prices of productive services, determine the cost of the commodity, which with static free competition assumptions is equal to price and, as we shall see in Parts III and IV, must also be taken as one of the starting-points for the formation of price under other market conditions. Moreover, the technical coefficients, in conjunction with the quantities of the individual commodities, determine how productive services are distributed. The same commodity may as a rule be produced in several ways, *i.e.*, by different combinations of the productive services, and thus by different combinations of the technical coefficients.

The laws for the possible combinations and the products produced by these means are dealt with in the theory of production. From this the theory of cost is derived. As mentioned above on p. 73, we derive a supply curve through a partial analysis of the formation of price for the individual commodities. In free competition this supply curve determines price and quantity by intersection with the demand curve.

20.1, THEORY OF PRODUCTION

The technical coefficients, as pointed out above, are variable, *i.e.*, there is a possibility of producing the same commodity with different combinations of the productive services.[1] If, as in Fig. 10, we have two kinds of productive services, x and y, we may imagine different quantity combinations of these in order to see how much is produced thereby. The problem is best elucidated by considering the effect of gradual variations in different directions. The movement along the line from O to A illustrates a proportionate increase of the services, the movements from B to C or from D to E, unilateral increases of one service, by which at the same time the ratio between them is shifted. The figure only indicates combinations; the

[1] Ragnar Frisch, *Innledning til Produksjonsteorien* I, 1 ed. Oslo, 1946, and II, Oslo, 1953; *Økonomisk Teori: Grundlinjer til Professor Lindahl's föreläsninger vid Handelshögskolan i Göteborg*, 1937; Erich Schneider's *Forelaesninger over Produktionsteori og Prispolitik*, Copenhagen, 1934. All the works here mentioned are only available in mimeographed form and in Scandinavian languages. Erich Schneider, *Theorie der Produktion*, Julius Springer, Wien, 1934; Jacob Viner, "Cost Curves and Supply Curves", *Zeitschrift für Nationalökonomie*, 1932; cf. further the textbooks of the last few years, including Erich Schneider, *Einführung in die Wirtschaftstheorie*, II Teil, J. C. B. Mohr, Tübingen, 1949 and English Translation: *Pricing and Equilibrium* (Hodge, London), 1952.

corresponding quantities of production may be imagined as the heights above the surface.

Now, let us first consider the effect of a unilateral increase of one ser-

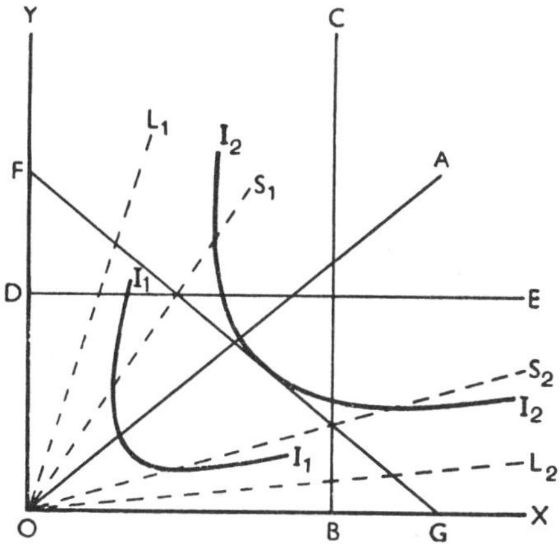

Fig. 10. Combination of Productive Services

vice by moving in Fig. 10 from D to E, *i.e.*, by combining a fixed quantity of y (*e.g.*, land) with increasing quantities of x (*e.g.*, labor). To provide a background for this question we turn to Fig. 11, with its corresponding table, where we have imagined how much production may be expected when an increasing quantity of one service is applied, *e.g.*, an increasing number of workers on a given piece of land. From the assumed series of figures for total product, the corresponding figures for marginal and average product have been derived. The curves indicate a corresponding smoothed movement. The somewhat elementary use of integers, or whole numbers, involves a certain lack of exactness, especially with regard to the beginning of the curves, which, on the whole, is problematic and of only little interest. The total curve must be assumed to begin by deviating more and more from the axis (possibly first following it for a certain distance). The marginal curve at first rises more steeply than the average curve. This is illustrated by the small figure inserted in the upper left-hand part of the figure and which does not correspond to the figures in the table.

The shape of the curves corresponds to what economists, on the basis of experience, usually assume to be valid for agriculture and other productions with a high degree of possibility for continuous variation. The construction of the two derived curves and a corresponding curve not indicated for the marginal product of the fixed factors are not to be dealt with here, any more than the connection between the decisive points on the curves —total maximum, marginal maximum, and average maximum—and the economic importance of these; with regard to the economic adjustment, readers are referred to p. 116. We shall, however, deal with the question of the basic assumptions for this line of approach and consider whether the curves really have the shape indicated.[2]

In reality, many types of productive services are used, and not only two. If we want our analysis to be complete, we must imagine a corresponding multi-dimensional illustration or a formula for total product as a function of all services. The two-dimensional illustration is of interest, however, because it elucidates the effects of a partial variation. The variation may comprise several variable services in a fixed mutual proportion, added to a fixed input consisting of definite quantities either of one or of several services. Beyond the expressly stated fixed and variable inputs, one may also assume one or more services as free, supplementary productive services. The fixed and variable inputs in the figure concern services which substitute for each other. Substitution, however, is not always possible; for instance, not in the case of chemical combinations. The services may be imagined to be "equivalent", *i.e.*, they completely replace each other in a constant proportion. We have the opposite extreme where one or more services are "limitational", that is, each of them sets an absolute limit to the amount of production. The three cases may be illustrated by Fig. 7 on p. 96, the I curves being here denoted isoquants, indicate the combinations of factors required for the production of a certain quantity of a commodity.

In order to obtain a definite curve for total product, we have to imagine a definite method of production. This may be imagined to be determined purely technically, so that for instance there is no possibility of any question as to what is most practical in order to save labor and raw materials. This kind of question, however, will play a part in any actual production, and it must then be said that the technique may be changed. No doubt it may also be difficult in real life to maintain that the quality of the product is quite unchanged in spite of a changed combination of the services. Instead of considering a method of production determined without any regard to economy, we may also regard the method of production which, with the quantities of productive services at the disposal of the enterprise, and with the given technical knowledge, gives the greatest quantity of production.

By an otherwise fixed method of production, there is a possibility that the product may in some cases be increased by reducing the quantity of a productive service used or by the simultaneous application of two methods

[2] Phelps Brown, "Report on Source Materials for Quantitative Production Studies", *Econometrica*, IV, 2–4; Hollis B. Chenery, "Engineering Production Functions", *Quarterly Journal of Economics*, November, 1949; Jens Warming, *Landbrugets Graense-Kalkulationer*, Copenhagen, 1933. A discussion of the problems is found in the following articles in *Nordisk Tidsskrift for Teknisk Økonomi*: B. Gloerfelt-Tarp, "Den økonomisk definerede Produktionsfunktion og den heterogene Fremstillingsprocess", 1937; Erik Schmidt, "Økonomisk definerede Produktionsfunktioner", 1939; and Rachel Plesner, "Proportionsloven contra Landbrugets Udbyttekurver", 1940. A provisional report was given by Knud Rasmussen at the European meeting of the Econometric Society in 1954—"Production Functions derived from Farm Accounting Data". Plessing articles in *Nordisk Tidsskrift for Teknisk Økonomi*, 1951 and 1953.

of production, one of which for instance uses much of the service x and the other much of the service y, instead of letting the whole of the production take place by an unfavorable intermediate form between the two methods. When at the same time we assume the law of proportionality mentioned below, the economically determined curve for the total product will begin as a tangent from the origin to the technically determined curve, and if the technical curve has concavities, the economic curve will follow the tangent across them. The fixed factor of Fig. 11 is here considered as variable.

The economies applied by technicians in real life, however, goes beyond this, in so far as they consider, more or less, the prices of the services and at any rate exclude methods of production that are unreasonably expensive under all imaginable price conditions.

In this way we do not get any technical (or scientific) law of production. In order to make the analysis as clear as possible, it is necessary first to consider the amounts of production resulting from definite, purely technically determined methods, or at least from methods that are quite neutral with regard to prices. Next one may go on to consider the economic choices between different combinations of services, taking in account their prices.

If a certain quantity of the variable service is necessary in order to produce any commodity at all (probably owing to lack of divisibility), the curve for the total product will begin by following the x axis. If now the curve is to be "smooth" (without leaps in the increases), and moreover is to end by converging towards a maximum, it must have the S shape usually represented by economists. That in agricultural experiments with variation in the quantities of fertilizers or fodder, several other shapes have been found, may, for instance, be due to the fact that the "constant" has already contained some of the same elements of service as the variable.

If we imagine that corresponding to all values of x with the corresponding variations of y, curves convex to the origin are plotted above Fig. 10, we obtain a surface rising from both axes, and at the same time rising when one moves along the line OA or other radiants from the origin. If a minimum of both factors is necessary in order to produce any commodity at all (*i.e.*, if they are limitational to a certain extent), no produce will appear outside of certain limits, *e.g.*, L_1 and L_2. By intersecting of the above-mentioned surface with planes perpendicular to the y axis, we obtain total production curves with y as a constant factor. If we connect points on the surface with the same quantity of production, we obtain indifference curves, or, as they are called here, isoquants, and corresponding projections on the xy plane as the curves I_1 and I_2, which may be considered as altitude contours on a map.

The movement along OA in the figure indicates a proportionate increase of x and y. If the total product is increased in the same proportion, we say that the law of proportionality applies.[3] The law which tells what

___

[3] Homogeneity of degree one.

happens when one factor is increased and the other kept constant (*i.e.*, the form of the total production curve in Fig. 11) may be called the law of proportion. The law of proportionality is not a law about real life, but a hypothesis, a simplification, which under certain conditions may be applicable to reality in an approximate way. The "law" of proportion raises

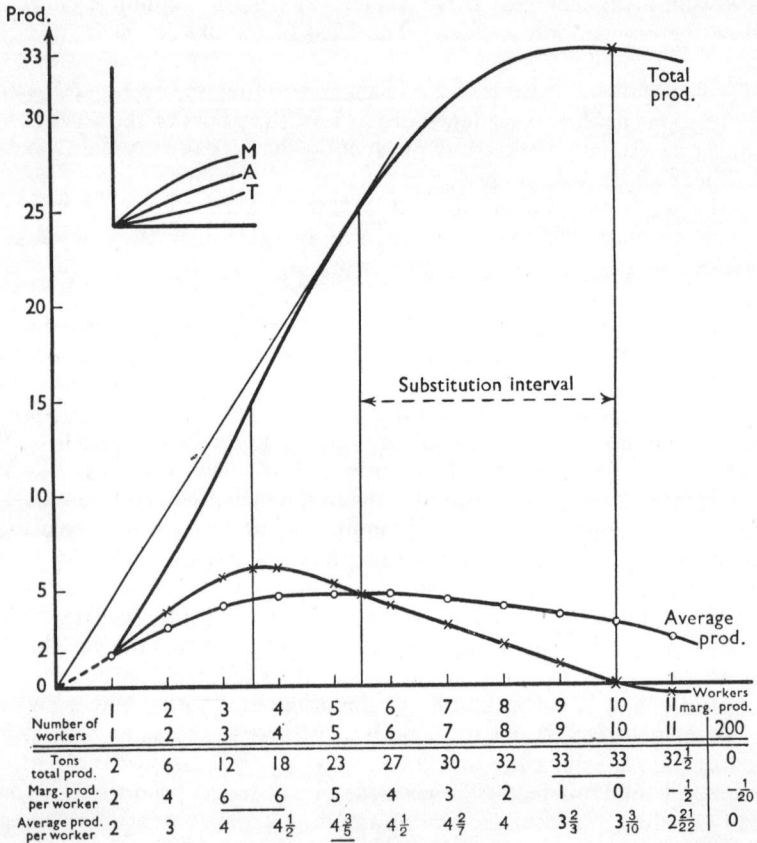

Number of workers	1	2	3	4	5	6	7	8	9	10	11	marg. prod.
Number of workers	1	2	3	4	5	6	7	8	9	10	11	200
Tons total prod.	2	6	12	18	23	27	30	32	33	33	$32\frac{1}{2}$	0
Marg. prod. per worker	2	4	6	6	5	4	3	2	1	0	$-\frac{1}{2}$	$-\frac{1}{20}$
Average prod. per worker	2	3	4	$4\frac{1}{2}$	$4\frac{3}{5}$	$4\frac{1}{2}$	$4\frac{2}{7}$	4	$3\frac{2}{3}$	$3\frac{3}{10}$	$2\frac{21}{22}$	0

Fig. 11. Law of Proportion

only a question to which an empirical answer may be found in every single case. The law of proportionality is valid if the productive services may be divided and composed without having any influence on their output. The latter statement requires a further explanation. The actual hindrances to the validity of the law do not only depend on the necessity of having indivisible workers, horses, machines, etc., and on having a sufficiently large number to obtain a satisfactory division of labor with full utilization of all resources; but they also depend on the economies which, owing to the relation between cubic content and area on one hand, and surface and length on the other, may be obtained with regard to containers, fences, pipes, etc., when they are carried out on a larger scale. Whereas, for instance, a field of 1 square mile requires a fence 4 miles in length, a field of 4 square miles only requires a fence of 8 miles. If conditions of this kind prevail, the quantity of production will rise more than proportionately when we move along the line OA in Fig. 10.[4]

20.2, COSTS

From engineering data we have information about possible combinations between quantities of productive services and quantities produced. Some of the technical possibilities are devoid of economic interest since the same quantity of production may be obtained by a smaller application of some productive services without a greater application of others. The cheapening of the product is here a purely technical question. In other cases the condition necessary in order to economize some productive service is that more of others is used in production. Both here and in the case where it is a question of deciding whether more of the commodity will be produced with the application of more productive services, prices are important. This means that the decision is no longer purely technical. Yet it is of a simple, technico-economic character so long as one may assume unchanged prices of commodities and services, which we do here, as opposed to the case in Part IV, where the influence on prices is considered.

When weighing the advantage of getting more commodities against the burden of applying more productive services, the cost concept enters into consideration. Costs represent the quantity of productive services used in production and measured in terms of money, *i.e.*, the quantity of services applied multiplied by their prices. Just as it is possible to speak about total, average and marginal product, it is possible to speak about total, marginal and average cost. As mentioned below in connection with Fig. 12A, the two kinds of concepts are closely connected. If we know the product per unit of service, we also know quantity of service and cost per unit of product, assuming given prices.

By measuring at times in terms of physical quantities and at times in money value, we get a number of different ways of expressing the relation between marginal and average quantities of commodities and services. The expressions: ton per worker, ton per dollar of wages (or per dollar of all services), dollar value product per worker, and dollar product per dollar of wages (or cost for all services), are all applicable. Especially where a common technical standard is lacking, we resort to the value in money. By reversing the relation indicating productivity or degree of output, we get expressions for the requirements and costs of production.

[4] Cf. Chamberlin's discussion of the question in the article, "Proportionality, Divisibility and Economies of Scale", *Quarterly Journal of Economics*, February, 1948.

It is possible in Fig. 10, p. 111, if G of x and F of y cost the same amount, to let the line FG denote combinations of x and y with the same cost. If one has at one's disposal an amount corresponding to this cost, the most advantageous combination of production is to be found where the cost line is tangent to one of the isoquants. If cost is increased, production will increase along a "path of expansion", which will be a straight line from the origin if the law of proportionality applies. If this is not the case, it must be expected that both this line and the lines L_1, L_2 and S_1 and S_2 will be curved. The lines S_1 and S_2 form the limits to the possibilities of substitution. Since the marginal contribution of production for either the fixed or the variable service becomes negative if we get beyond the range of substitution, we keep within the range where this is possible by allowing a certain quantity to be unutilized, if necessary. The curved path of expansion, where the law of proportionality does not apply—and it usually does not—indicates that different proportions between the productive services are optimal in different sizes of plants. Since infinitely small plants cannot be thought to exist in real life, the path of expansion does not begin at the origin, and it may also be misleading to imagine that its extension backwards goes through this point.[5] If x becomes cheaper in relation to y, the expenditure lines (FG) in Fig. 10, p. 111, become flatter and so relatively more of x will be used. In Fig. 11, p. 114, we may observe, by the way, what is the influence of prices on the quantities used of a service which is considered to be variable. If we assume that the prices of products and services are given from the outside, it is to the advantage of an enterprise to continue buying a service until the price of its marginal product corresponds to its own price. This applies simultaneously to all kinds of services. Correspondingly, we obtain as a condition of equilibrium in free competition the proposition that the price of a service is equal to the price of the marginal product of that service. The marginal equilibrium must thus apply to all services separately. Moreover, we see that with a small proportional increase of all services, the price of the product is equal to the sum of the marginal quantities of services employed, multiplied by their prices. (The marginal quantity of the individual service, of course, is smaller here than where it alone must produce the same increase in the output of the commodity.) Corresponding to the marginal product (or the marginal efficiency) we may also consider the productivity elasticity of the services, *i.e.*, the proportion between relative increase in the quantity of production and in the quantity of the service.

Now, it is interesting to note that it is possible to set up a technical equilibrium between the marginal unit of the commodity and the sum of the marginal contributions of the services with proportionate, partial variations. An infinitely small increase in the quantity of production—say, by α per cent—will be equal to the sum of a series of successive

---

[5] See Chamberlin, op. cit., p. 259.

increases in quantity with partial increases of all services, also by α per cent. The circumstance of α being infinitely small involves that each of the increases in the services has approximately the same effect when it is added to the original combination of factors as when it is added after all or some of the other services have been increased already. If the increase were not infinitely small, the order in which the services were added would play a part, since they would then be added to a different combination of other services.

When the law of proportionality applies, the proportion between productive services and product is the same for the marginal unit and for the total product. The essential consequence is that the total product is equal to the quantities of all services used, each multiplied by its marginal product. As a further consequence, a residual calculation of the contribution of any service must give the same result as the marginal one (cf. what is said about the theory of rent in Chapter 22).[6]

All kinds of services, in principle, have the same place in the production process; but their effects may be very different quantitatively. Besides considering the effects of different kinds of real capital, it is possible to consider the productive effect of a greater input of capital in the abstract, permitting a prolongation of a process of production. Factual curves in illustration of this have been calculated for forestry.[7]

However, neither continuous curves nor the law of proportionality apply to actual conditions of production. As already indicated, productive services often are not divisible and appear as a limited number of units of a fairly definite size. This circumstance may of course be modified, but only to a limited extent, by the use of machines of different size, apprentices or casual assistants instead of permanent, mature workers, or by letting the same tool or worker be employed in different ways during the week. It is often an advantage to have many specialized units of a certain size in an enterprise. Where units of different kinds are to work together, *e.g.*, machines in a series of successive processes, the question of harmonious coordination arises, *i.e.*, of the greatest possible degree of utilization for all units of all kinds. If, for instance, one unit of service A is necessary for the production of 2 commodity units per day, one unit of B for the production of 3 commodity units, and one unit of C for the production of 5 units, an enterprise only obtains full utilization of all three kinds of machines or other means of production, when by means of 15A, 10B and 6C it produces 30 units per day. The corresponding full harmony is again reached with the production of 60, 90 units, etc., but the average cost per unit is of course much greater with the production of 1 than with

[6] As to the economic conditions for the application of Euler's theorem, which we have used here, see, *e.g.*, the previously mentioned article by Chamberlin, p. 259.

[7] A. Howard Grøn, "Omdriftsberegning i Skovbruget", *Nordisk Tidsskrift for Teknisk Økonomi*, 1936, and *Skovbrugets Driftsøkonomi*, Munksgaard, Copenhagen, 1943. A theoretical treatment of the productivity of capital is to be found in Knut Wicksell, *Über Wert, Kapital und Rente*, Gustav Fisher, Jena, 1893; reprinted by London School of Economics, 1933.

the production of 61 and 91 units. This is the law of harmony.[8] The law applies to the short run as well as to the long run, *i.e.*, with full adaptation of firms which are not tied to existing buildings or other fixed plants, or to other means of production permanently connected with the firm.

A different question is the passing over to another technique in the sense that units of another kind are employed, or that the services—apart from changes in the degree of utilization—work together in a different way. In many cases, one technique will be cheaper with small-scale production, and another on a larger scale. Using given prices of services, we then obtain curves for the smallest total and average costs, which at small quantities of production are represented by the "lower" and at great quantities by the "higher" technique. Higher technique does not here mean a more comprehensive technical knowledge, greater personal ability, etc., but the methods giving lower costs at production on a large scale. It very often also means methods involving a large percentage of overhead costs, and the term "higher technique" is consequently used in a corresponding way. The "law of higher technique" may be illustrated by an envelope curve, indicating the costs which—with changing technique—become the smallest when the size of the firm is changed. This is a long-run law of costs. Total and consequently also average costs have therefore to be covered *ex ante*.

It is generally assumed that the effects in the direction of lower average costs with greater plants not only cease at a certain level of production, but that on the contrary costs also begin to rise again with very large output, owing to difficulties of organization and transportation. Where this is the case, we obtain the dashed U-shaped average and marginal cost curves illustrated in Fig. 12B; cf. Fig. 23A and B, p. 232. Since we are dealing here with curves describing full adaptation in the long run, we ought not to have exaggerated ideas as to the variation in the height of the curves, especially of the rising segment. Since there are possibilities of changing the size of the units and the composition of the tools and services, the decline owing to "higher technique" will also be essentially smaller than the one calculated for pure cases of the law of harmony. Further, it must be remembered that the experiences and some of the popular numerical examples one comes across in discussions of variation in costs, often do not at all deal with the adaptation of the whole of the production apparatus, but the utilization of capacity of given plants in

---

[8] With regard to the law of harmony, the law of higher technique, and the law of capacity, see Ivar Jantzen in "Report of the Washington Meeting", 1947, *Econometrica*, January, 1948, pp. 44–48; Jantzen, *Basic Principles of Business Economics and National Calculation*, Gad, Copenhagen, 1939, containing a translation of an article on "Increasing Return in Industrial Production", from 1923; Schneider's *Theorie der Produktion*, Julius Springer, Wien, 1934, including the résumé of Jantzen's theory in *Anhang*; Hans Brems: "A Discontinuous Cost Function", *American Economic Review*, Sept., 1952; Joel Dean, *Managerial Economics*, Prentice-Hall, 1951, P. Wiles, "Empirical Research and Marginal Analysis", *Econ. Journal*, Sept., 1950; and later discussion *ibid*.

the short run, which we are going to deal with below, and where variation at any rate is much greater.

A consideration of the relation between different production and cost curves is of interest. Whereas in cases where the law of proportionality applies, we obtain a proportionately rising quantity produced, *i.e.*, a curve rising rectilinearly in a vertical plane, if in Fig. 10 we move along the line OA, we shall obtain a curve of practically the same shape as the total curve in Fig. 11, when the above-mentioned effects of the size of the enterprise assert themselves.

If we assume a definite price relation between the services, we may let the horizontal distance in Fig. 12A[9] indicate total costs, and for three different combinations of services we then obtain total production curves I, II and III. From these, average and marginal productivity curves and cost per unit may be derived as in Fig. 11. More significant than the curves I, II

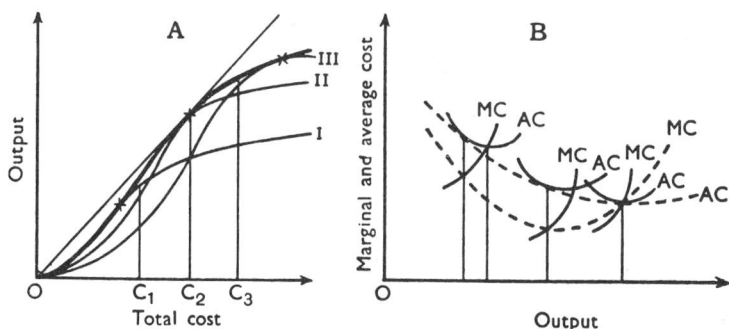

Fig. 12. Production and Cost Curves

and III, which apply to combinations of services in different fixed proportions, is the output of the most productive combination when a certain aggregate cost is given. This curve, which is drawn as a heavy line in the figure, is formed as an envelope to curves I, II and III. In correspondence with the law of higher technique, a changing series of combinations of factors will be most advantageous gradually as the output and total costs rise. This curve for the greatest total output at different total costs (with an assumed fixed price relation between the services) may also be regarded as a total cost curve, in which case the costs of different outputs are obtained. If we draw the curve and axes as heavy lines and look through the paper, we get exactly the form of total cost curve illustrated in Fig. 23A and B on p. 232. From this total cost curve the U-shaped marginal and average cost curves are derived, corresponding to the curves shown in dashes in Fig. 12B.

[9] Fig. 12 has, by permission of the author, been taken from Lindahl's mimeographed lectures, 1937, quoted in the note on page 110.

In Fig. 12B, the long-run average cost curve, AC (in dashes), is seen as an envelope curve of the corresponding short-run curves. Each short-run average cost curve touches the long-run curve at one point. If production is greater or smaller, fixed plants, etc., of a different size than the one corresponding to this short-run curve become cheaper. The short-run average curve is here also assumed to be U-shaped. The same is true of the marginal curves. Where the long-run average curve is decreasing, the short-run curve must also decrease at the point of tangency, *i.e.*, at the output with regard to which the given plant is cheaper than plants of other sizes. This circumstance is important in the discussion of unutilized capacity in the case of administered prices. A condition for the minimum of the short-run average curve being situated at a substantial distance to the right of the point of tangency, *i.e.*, for the appearance of idle capacity with administered prices is, however, that the curve has the shape indicated, and that the increase in costs does not take place suddenly and violently.

The special cost conditions in the short run are due to the fact that we must here reckon with the fact that greater or smaller parts of the means of production will be tied to the firm and be incapable of sudden expansion. It is here that the law of capacity applies, and that we have the concept of overhead costs. By way of illustration, we may draw the total, average and marginal cost curves for the simple case of a firm having some fixed costs, whereas the other costs vary proportionately with output. We have here constant marginal costs, *i.e.*, the direct costs which are at the same time the variable average costs. Average total costs follow a rectangular hyperbola, converging towards the y-axis and the line of the direct costs. In real life the picture is complicated, however, by the fact that marginal and average costs usually end by rising with increasing slope. The curves thereby reach a minimum, but are presumably as a rule so flat at the bottom that they cannot be called U-shaped.

The belief in a decided U-shape for short-run marginal and average variable costs was strong in the thirties, as may be seen in well-known books on monopolistic competition. In plants with a number of uniform machines and workers, the curves are almost horizontal, however, for capacities that are not extremely small or large. For the first units produced there might be a steep decline, but it depends very much on the definition of "short-run costs", *i.e.*, whether or not starting costs are included. The addition of average fixed costs (which by themselves form the well-known rectangular hyperbola) are of course able to create the left side of the U-shape. The right side of the U-shape, when capacity is reached, will probably often be very steep. Statistical investigations[10] seem to show that rather flat short-run curves are predominant.

[10] *A Survey of Contemporary Economics*, Vol. I, 1948, Haley, pp. 13–15, and Bain, p. 140; Ivar Jantzen's theory quoted in footnote 7, which is based on his own experiences in the Danish printing industry. Wilford Eitemann and Glenn Guthrie, in "The Average Cost Curve", *American Economic Review*, December 1952, give statistics, comprising 1068 commodities, about types of total average costs, criticised by Kaplan in *Amer. Econ. Rev.*, September 1953.

When speaking about utilization of capacity, one generally imagines that an increasing number of the variable services (workers, materials, etc.) cause an increasing part of the fixed services to be taken into employment (*e.g.*, more machines all working in the same way). We do not as above, under the law of proportion (which applies everywhere in the long run and which may moreover in the short run apply to agriculture) here assume that all the units of fixed services take part actively but in changing proportions (changing intensity) in accordance with the principle of substitution. An increased utilization of a fixed plant may take place in different ways, which have different effects on costs: either by employment of more workers, prolongation of time of utilization of the plant (longer seasons, working in shifts, longer hours) or increase in the tempo of work. Very often the number of machines employed is increased.[11]

By way of résumé we may say with regard to the shape of the cost curves:

(1) The marginal cost curves in the short run may be assumed to be more or less U-shaped, but they may also have a flat segment which may possibly extend from a very small production to nearly full capacity. When this point has been reached, the rise may be assumed to take place quite sharply as a result of the sudden impossibility of greater production; but it will presumably take place as a rule more gradually and at an increasing velocity.

(2) The average variable cost curve in the short run must have a shape derived from (1).

(3) The curve of average aggregate costs in the short run must be U-shaped in so far as it is formed by a vertical summation of a curve for fixed costs declining like a rectangular hyperbola converging towards the axes, and the curve mentioned under (2) which ends by rising infinitely. The shape may, however, differ greatly, depending especially on the importance of overhead costs and the conditions prevailing at the margin of capacity. If the fixed, or overhead, costs are small, there may be a large flat bottom as in (2).

(4) The marginal curve and the average curve in the long run must be assumed first to decrease and later to increase, but often with a comparatively slight percentage variation in height, apart from very small and possibly, in some cases, very large outputs. Where production with the lowest costs is large in proportion to the market, this will prevent equilibrium under free competition.

The generally used, deeply U-shaped and fairly symmetrical curves for average costs must, consequently be treated with considerable scepticism.

As will be seen, there are a number of different conditions which

[11] Besides the works mentioned above, see J. M. Clark, *The Economics of Overhead Costs*, University of Chicago Press, 1923; Thorkil Kristensen, *Faste og variable Omkostninger*, Munksgaard, Copenhagen, 1939; Winding Pedersen, "Omkring Kapacitetsudnyttelsesteorien", *Nationaløkonomisk Tidsskrift*, 1933; and Erich Schneider, "Kapacitetsudnyttelsesproblemets to Dimensioner", *Nordisk Tidsskrift for Teknisk Økonomi*, 1937.

determine the relation between output and cost. The old "laws" about rising costs in agriculture, constant costs in handicrafts and decreasing costs in industry, are not capable of being fitted into this scheme, because the question is about different kinds of variation, or, we may say, different combinations of the laws mentioned above. The effects of different proportions between productive services, different sizes of the firms, and different utilization of fixed means of production assert themselves everywhere, but are of different importance in the different industries. In agriculture the limited land area is of importance when the combination of land and other productive services is changed, as in the case of an increase in all crops. In industry the advantages of large-scale production are of relatively great importance when the production of the individual commodity is expanded by an increase in all services. The effect of the law of capacity or the increase in technical knowledge, which may also be of more importance in industry than in other spheres, is often mixed up with large-scale production. Finally, the old handicrafts may be mentioned as an example of cases where complete harmony is attained comparatively soon, and where increasing difficulties in procuring raw materials as well as variations in the composition of production as a result of price changes are of smaller importance.

20.3, SUPPLY

In free competition it is possible to construct supply curves or supply functions which are relatively independent of demand. On the other hand, where administered prices exist, demand is taken into consideration in determining the supply policy. Such cases are disregarded here, but will be dealt with in detail in Part IV. The addition of supply curves of individual firms can only be undertaken with great modification because the supply of productive services is not absolutely elastic when a whole industry demands them and because the actual realization of the curves indicated by the plans of the individual firms, especially in the long run, depends on what old and new competitors actually do.

As described in greater detail in textbooks and books on business economics, there are different supply curves, depending on the length of the adaptation which is being considered. What must be regarded as fixed and variable factors and corresponding costs, depends on the length of the period of adaptation. Questions concerning the course of the adaptation process, as well as the effect of existing stocks are of a dynamic character, and are not dealt with at this point. We confine ourselves here partly with a long-run static approach where there is full adaptation of all fixed plants, and partly to a short-run static approach, in which certain productive services are considered as being tied to the fixed plants while the others may be freely varied.

In a market which is very great in proportion to the optimum size of the individual firms, where there is free competition, and where everybody has the same technical knowledge, it may be expected that with full adaptation that all firms will attain the optimum size, as given by the price conditions, *i.e.*, that they have the lowest possible average costs. The technical coefficients will then be the same everywhere, and we shall everywhere have the simple cost equation for the commodity: price equal to the quantity of productive services employed, multiplied by their prices. The demand for the commodities, and thus the size of total output, will react, however, on the price of the productive services, and these again will influence the technique chosen and the size of the firms.

Each point of this ideal supply curve will correspond with marginal as well as with average costs of all firms. Seen through a microscope the long-run average cost curves in Fig. 12B will touch the horizontal demand curve of the market at the point where average and marginal curves intersect.

As just mentioned, the consequence of full adaptation in the very long run in markets with perfect competition is that all plants are in equilibrium, with average as well as marginal costs equal to price. This situation may be said to come into existence partly by elimination of high cost plants and partly by the adaptation of prices of productive services, including revaluation of scarce permanent means of production.

The ideal long-run supply curve which we here speak about is rising because of the increase in prices of productive services. Only in the case where the quantities of all the services used in the production of the commodity were of no account at all in the respective markets of services, the supply curve would be horizontal. Some counter-effects against the general rule of rise in the supply curves may, however, arise as a consequence of "external economies", *i.e.*, the advantages of size of auxiliary plants or cooperating systems of plants such as transportation or research. The advantages of external economies would disappear if we had optimum size in all fields. Actually external economies can only with difficulty be distinguished from institutional, historical and geographical differences and, consequently, they offer no suitable basis for the drawing of curves.

We are now going to use another approach starting with individual firms in a small market and provisionally assuming constant prices for productive services.

If we take the actual existing plants of different age and nature as given, and assume production to adapt itself thereto, we have a short-run static approach. The fixed means of production may now be considered as different qualities, of which there are fixed quantities, and we obtain different technical coefficients and, consequently, different variable costs, different capacity, and a different degree of utilization within each plant, all of them, however, adapting themselves to the same prices of commodities and productive services (and these prices, again, adapting themselves to output).

Fig. 13[12] illustrates the supply with alternative commodity prices in

---

[12] ATC indicates average total cost AVC the average of variable costs. MC marginal costs.

relation to fixed and variable costs. At p_1 even the cheapest plant, No. 1, will not be producing at all. At p_2 it suddenly gets started and then produces the quantity x_2, corresponding to the minimum of the variable costs; from there production is increased, the quantity being now determined by intersection between the price line and marginal costs. Quantity and price may, *e.g.*, be x_3 and p_3, or x_5 and p_5.

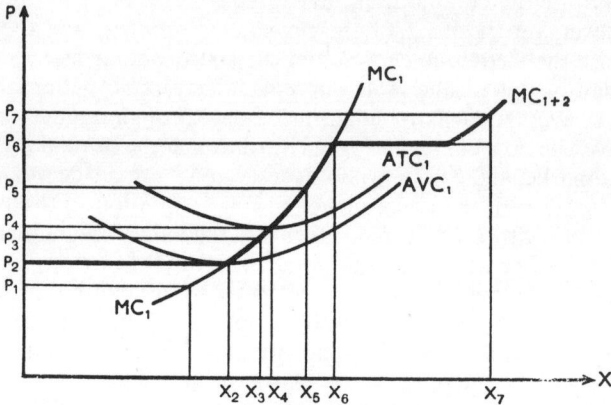

Fig. 13. Supply Curve

If we proceed to a somewhat longer run, the condition for the establishment of plant No. 1 is that price is p_4 where production is x_4; nor will it rise any higher when there is free access for new plants of the same type in a market that is very great in proportion to the size of the individual enterprise. So long as new plants are not being constructed, however, it is possible to attain, *e.g.*, p_5 and x_5.

In building up the supply curve for the market in the short run, the horizontal addition of the individual supply curves is made in such a way that the individual firms, when price rises above their individual minimum price for producing anything at all (p_2), suddenly leap in with the minimum quantity (x_2). In the long run we use long-run curves (cf. Fig. 12B, p. 119) and have correspondingly p_4 and x_4. Since the average variable costs usually may be presumed to vary only slightly within a large interval, thoroughgoing assumptions of competition between similar enterprises involve either no production or considerable production at minimum costs. Some limitation of competition gives a slightly declining demand curve and opens possibilities for sales corresponding to different capacities before x_2. Add to this the fact that considerations of future market position may make it profitable to keep production going, even though it does not pay in the short run.

In the case of rational maximization of profit, it may be said that only those factors that are variable or scarce at the time of decision have any influence as costs on price and quantity. Capital will be invested only if at the time of investment there is a prospect of a return on the outlay incurred. However, in this way there arises a scarcity of plants at a later date which, if the expectations of sales possibilities and costs are fulfilled, will yield exactly the expected return. If the fixed capital can be sold for use elsewhere, the profit thus obtainable must be put equal to direct costs. Otherwise, the investment costs of the past do not act as costs in the present. Pure gain or loss and the revenue from invested capital form a total surplus—gross revenue—comprising the whole of the income from sales in excess of direct costs.

By recapitalization of the possibilities of income from previous investments under changed conditions of the market, an appreciation or depreciation of value may be achieved. In this way it is possible, from an accounting point of view, to return to a normal return on investments, but this has no effect on the price and quantity of commodities. As soon as we abandon the assumptions of a rational maximization of profit under perfect competition, however, the situation changes to a certain extent. It is then more easy to agree on maintaining, by an administered price policy, the return on the old capital; and state interference and other types of authority, moreover, will rather tend in the direction of making it possible to get neither more nor less than a normal return on the values invested in the past.

Where the firms are very dissimilar, it will often be the case that some obtain more and others obtain less than a normal return on the capital invested in the past. Further, different productive services will be used. Since it is the condition of the whole market that determines which firms —if any at all—will obtain a normal return, there is no basis for attributing a special influence to the "representative firm". In those cases where we have different types of investments, *e.g.*, of factories, agricultural buildings or houses, the new investments taking place will exercise a regulating influence. After a war, however, such influence may be weak and without much effect on the formation of price as a whole, but in other quiet periods may have created such a degree of equilibrium that it may be said to be price-determining. The income from the old, cheaper or more expensive investments, as well as their capital value, may then be said to be preponderantly price-determined.

As said above, the total supply of a commodity is increased in the short run by utilizing formerly idle plants, and in the long run by new investments. If all plants are not completely similar, or if new investments do not take place immediately, supply is increased by expansion of production on the basis of the marginal cost curves of all the plants that are already in operation. Consequently, it is meaningless to designate some of the plants as marginal plants, *i.e.*, the plants in which an expansion of production actually takes place. The expansion takes place everywhere, provided that either the marginal cost curves do not end with a sharp increase or expansion of production is absolutely impossible. It is a fact, however, that the plants that are on the borderline between producing a certain minimum or not producing at all may sometimes

K

exercise a relatively great influence. The usual supply curve for a number of competing firms begins as a horizontal line to the minimum cost point of the most efficient firm, continues along its marginal curve to the minimum price of the next firm in order of efficiency. After that it has again a horizontal slope, corresponding to the firm's production at minimum price. The curve now continues with a slope which corresponds to a horizontal addition of the marginal curves for the two firms. This is illustrated by the thick line in Fig. 13. When it is a short-run problem of using an existing plant, the first horizontal part of the curve goes to minimum of AVC; when it is a long-run problem concerning the opening of a new plant it goes to minimum of ATC.

In a market with few plants and a limited competition, the first decreasing part of the cost curves, together with the demand curve, in some cases becomes a determining factor in the formation of price. In this case no independent supply curve exists. Under such market conditions plants greater than the lowest cost size may also be involved. As to the number and size of plants in such markets, the reader is referred to Part IV, Chapter 51.

CHAPTER 21

SUPPLY OF PRODUCTIVE SERVICES

A LARGE amount of reliable information is to be found on production and costs and a considerable amount of work has also been done in order to get empirical material on the conditions of demand; but we are still at a disadvantage with regard to the third kind of economic reaction: the way in which the quantity of productive services supplied is influenced by its own prices and by other economic factors. The information on this subject is so scattered that we may speak with justice about "empty boxes". In the short run there is not so much of a problem. The amount of the productive service previously supplied can at any rate be taken as a starting-point. The problem arises when a certain time is allowed for adaptation, and the solution will then be different for the different kinds of services.

We have an important starting-point in the inventories of the productive resources of different countries. As to the material means of production, it may be said that when they actually exist the supply of services is also given thereby. For farm land of different qualities and for other natural resources there are only original quantities which to a very limited extent can be increased or decreased. The different kinds of real capital, on the other hand, may in the long run be greatly changed.

Here the only limitation is the original means of production employed: workers, natural resources and stocks of materials and equipment, as well as the amount of money capital at the disposal of production as a whole. It is with regard to workers and abstract capital, the money capital, that we find a real supply problem, especially in the long run. As to the different kinds of real capital, on the other hand, we have the same conditions as with regard to other produced commodities.

The quantity of labor of a certain quality supplied is a product of the number of persons at work, multiplied by working hours, multiplied by speed of work. Since conditions with regard to each of these factors change constantly, the supply reaction can most easily be studied by considering each of the factors separately. But the interplay between hours worked and speed of work is also important.

According to the "iron law of wages" and the corresponding classical theories, the number of workers adapts itself in the long run fully to demand at unchanged real wages, equal to the absolute minimum of subsistence for a family. The reaction of population changes towards real wages and the standard of living is now less elastic in Western countries and conditions other than economic are also of great importance. Instead of an absolute and unchangeable standard of living, a customary and changeable standard exists. This does not have a controlling influence and only tends to slow down movements in the level of wages. This is due rather to its influence on the efficiency of labor and the psychological attitude adopted in wage negotiations than to its influence on the rate of increase in the population. A quicker way of influencing the number of workers supplied than by changing the size of the population, is to change the conditions of employment of married women, young people, old people, or those with limited working capacity. The decrease in real wages during wars (in connection with compulsory and voluntary mobilization) of course entails a sharp increase in supply, which disappears again with the post-war increase in real wages and as a result of war fatigue, etc. The supply for the individual industrial enterprises must in the long run be assumed to be very elastic, but adaptation will often be slow.

Both working hours and working speed are greatly influenced by organizational, political and psychological conditions; but at the same time one must take account of considerable reactions towards changes in real wages. A higher payment per unit of work generally increases working capacity, though to a varying extent depending on the peculiar social and working conditions which prevail, and depending on the time elapsed after the increase in wages. It seems reasonable to assume that through changes in working capacity as well as in the propensity to work, there is an interplay between wages, hours and working speed (and what economically means the same thing, the quality of work). A free adjustment of the latter three or four factors is as a rule impossible, however, on account of the influence of organized groups and the habits of business firms. Whereas experience tends rather definitely in the direction of increased real wages involving considerably increased working capacity in the long run, the connection between wages and propensity to work is far more doubtful, and the results here seem to point both in the direction of increase and decrease. The psychological problem of separation between working capacity and working propensity will here be only briefly mentioned.

The question of the way in which earnings influence the propensity to work may be clearly examined in small businesses, where the individual himself chooses his working hours. If the trade unions are taking part in the regulation of the conditions of work, similar motives may be presumed to assert themselves when negotiation takes place, but also other motives, as for instance considerations of wage policy, will play a part in this case. In any case, a great resistance against changes and differentiation between workers exists in organized labor markets. The sacrifice involved in work consists in exertion, loss of leisure hours, and increased fatigue in the free hours. A great many theoretical analyses have been carried out both according to the marginal utility method and by means of indifference curves, and the results have been somewhat contradictory.[1] There is every reason to believe that a supply curve constructed solely with a view to the willingness to work, will be decreasing within important ranges of wages, *i.e.*, that supply will rise with decreasing wages, and conversely.

Since a system of indifference curves requires an implicit assumption about the marginal utility of income, the discussion may just as well be conducted explicitly in terms of utility. In order that an increase in wages per hour for the whole day shall make people willing to work a little more, it is necessary to compensate for the higher marginal disutility of labor by paying a correspondingly higher amount, measured in utility, for the additional time; *i.e.*, payment per unit of time must increase more than the decrease in the marginal utility of income. This means that the elasticity of the marginal utility of income, with variation in money income, must be smaller than unity. If, conversely, this elasticity is greater than unity, the increase in wages will lead to a desire for shorter working hours. How the elasticity of the marginal utility of income actually changes with the level of income is a subject about which very little is known. It is presumably most likely that we have a preponderantly declining supply of labor with rising rates of wages, when only the effect on the willingness to work of the individual person is taken into consideration. The effect on the number of persons working, after the experiences of the last few years, also had a corresponding effect, *i.e.*, that lower real wages resulted in a greater number of workers. The somewhat doubtful and heterogeneous influences mentioned here are decisively counteracted, however, by a far stronger effect in the opposite direction, that of increased working capacity

---

[1] Ragnar Frisch, *New Methods of Measuring Marginal Utility*, Mohr, Tübingen, 1932, Chapter 11; and Kenneth Boulding, *Economic Analysis*, New York, 1941, edit. 1948, Fig. 104, page 743, cf. about saving, Fig. 117, page 777.

at higher rates of wages. In any case when the time required for adjustment is taken into consideration, an increased supply of labor at higher wages seems to be the result. In the short run, changes in supply are probably irregular and generally small.

The total quantity of capital dealt with in Chapter 18.4 being a fund (rather than a flow) quantity, the supply function cannot be of the same type as for the productive services; but a special function may be set up as a condition for static equilibrium. The level of the rate of interest and income are here of special importance. A higher rate of interest gives a greater ability to save out of incomes and of not consuming saved-up capital, especially among those parts of the population which may be assumed to save or who are owners of capital. The effect of the rate of interest on the propensity to save is more problematic, for reasons which are similar to those mentioned above in connection with the rate of wages. The appearance of maxima for the income which people find it important to secure for themselves—relatively fixed saving aims—means a weakened propensity to save when the aim has been fulfilled, as a consequence of increased income from interest.

If we take into consideration the effect both on the ability and the willingness to own capital no general rule could be laid down. At an especially high rate of interest, capital will possibly increase with the rate of interest, but at lower rates the result is open to question. In a partial approach where the amount of capital (in the sense of the static fund in existence) and the level of the rate of interest are considered as the only variables, we have intersection between demand and supply curves, and no more than one point of intersection, since the supply curve can scarcely be assumed to be declining more rapidly in any interval than the demand curve. A very small income does not allow of any saving; with higher incomes, savings increase, probably progressively, cf. the figures in Chapter 42. Small wonder that the supply of new capital which one has occasion to observe in daily life—generally as a supply of credit—reacts quite differently to changes in the rate of interest than the total quantity of capital in existence, for with regard to the supply of new capital, such things as expectations, changes in interest, prices, and monetary policy, as well as the effects of economic development on the nonconsumed income must play an absolutely decisive part. (Cf. the important dynamic factors dealt with in Chapters 43 and 44.)

CHAPTER 22

THE SETTING OF THE PROBLEM OF DISTRIBUTION

THE subject of distribution is broken down into two parts: functional distribution, *i.e.*, the formation of price for the productive services, and personal distribution. The former is already included in the theory of total economic interdependence, the subject of the first half of this part. Derivation of the demand functions for the productive services are dealt with in Chapter 17 and supply functions in Chapter 21. With regard to personal distribution, the means of production at the disposal of the individual persons (or groups of persons) are also of importance. Both functional and personal distribution are of course influenced to a great extent by economic movements, organization and state interference. These important subjects will be dealt with at several points in Parts III and IV.

The distribution of income, like economic conditions as a whole, must be explained by a network of partial interdependences of the nature described above. When, despite this, a comparatively large part of older doctrine still remains in this sphere, it may to a certain extent be due to the fact that the questions involved are sometimes of an emotional character, which has contributed to giving luster to the old theories. Whereas according to modern theory, the position of different kinds of productive services is quite the same with regard to demand, and existing differences depend on differences in long-run supply conditions, classical theory has a more fundamental distinction between three or four categories.

In the theory of functional distribution it is still customary to attach decisive importance to the classical distinction between wages, rent, interest and entrepreneurial gain or net profit. Of these the three former comprise large categories of services within which there are highly similar supply conditions, whereas the latter, as we are going to see in Chapter 38, is either of a dynamic or of a monopolistic character.

From an economic point of view there is no decisive difference between land and the other means of production. The question of the origin of the different means of production is only of economic interest in so far as there is possibility of a future change in quantity. This possibility is at times practically nonexistent with regard to certain very durable forms of real capital. These may be very nearly indestructible. We are not going here to enter any further into the discussion of the original and indestructible qualities of land. The decisive thing here is not the point of view of natural science, but the question whether there is a possibility of variation in the quantity of the different categories of economically valuable land, taken by themselves. Even if the total area of the earth cannot be increased, an area may be transferred to a more valuable class by improvement, as, for instance, by draining or reclamation. It is, by the way, a matter of indifference from an economic point of view, whether we say that new "land" is created by reclamation, or that a special kind of real capital is created which fully replaces the natural and original land and thus affects its income in the same way as an additional amount of original land. Means of transportation extended on to or in the neighborhood of a piece of land increase its earning capacity—just as they increase the value of the services of buildings and workers in the area. Even the physical properties of land are destructible to a large extent and to an extent that is very difficult to determine. And in so far as upkeep is necessary, the expense may be expected to yield interest just as an investment in real capital.

For all kinds of productive services that are not to be found in superfluous supply, there must be a positive price in order to bring about equilibrium between supply and demand. To this must be added the consideration that price to a greater or smaller extent—sometimes in an increasing, sometimes in a decreasing direction—influences the quantity supplied of the different kinds of productive services. The great amount of emphasis that used to be laid on the distinctive aspects of supply conditions is due to the fact that according to the classical real cost theory the payment for labor and capital was looked upon as necessary costs because they were payment for personal sacrifices and exertions, whereas no such costs were attached to the original and indestructible land. The claim that there is a general equilibrium between payment and sacrifices cannot be maintained, however, even by means of the strangest assumptions and exceptional laws. Especially when strict assumptions of competition and free mobility are not made, there is no possibility of a balance between payment and sacrifice for labor and capital. When, therefore, we cease to consider the income of labor and capital as "earned" by means of proportionate sacrifices, it should not give offence to anybody that as far as the question of price formation is concerned, we put it on a par with "unearned" rent.

Adherents of a special theory of rent maintain that the price-determining equilibrium with costs, exclusive of rent, is to be found on the extensive as well as on the intensive margin of cultivation. As a result of discontinuity in the qualities of land and in the methods of cultivation (or regulations, *e.g.*, regarding limitation in the height of buildings), it is possible, however, that these margins do not exist at all in real life. It is possible, moreover, that cultivation at the margin is of very little consequence and is comparatively inelastic. What happens here then, can only bring a comparatively minor modification in the formation of price for a scarce service of production—with otherwise the same kind of price formation as in other scarce services. Once a price has been established owing to the scarce quantity of good land, the addition of a little bad land results in only a small decrease in the income of good land. It is quite another thing that in a general equilibrium there must also be equilibrium between the income of good and bad land, and between the income under intensive and extensive cultivation. In the foregoing treatment of total equilibrium, including the problem of substitution, as dealt with in the theory of production, land and other means of production have the same status, however.

It is true, of course, that the size of a piece of landed property cannot at any moment be varied; but the adjustment of its size to the working ability and other means of production of a man takes place at long intervals when the farmer chooses how large a piece of land he wants to buy, in many cases only once in his life. Moreover, the quantity of land used for different crops is varied, in quite the same way as labor is distributed among different types of production. Land does not, as opposed to other means of production, have a single product, such as grain. The possibility of using the land for something else, irrespective of whether this product is considered to be "higher" or "lower", is a reason why land like other means of production is considered as a cost element for the individual product. But even if there were only a single product, competition between buyers would act in the same way, the possibility of selling to all the other buyers would have the effect of a cost in case of the individual buyer—that is when cost is understood as the price of the services employed, and not as a morally or psychologically founded "real cost" Also urban rent may be considered as a cost when space becomes scarce goods that may be replaced by others and enters into the price of the commodities—in many cases, though, only in very small degree.

That rent is exactly equal to the value of the product less the payment for other productive services at the margin of cultivation, where rent is zero, is a simple consequence of the assumed cost-price equilibrium by which the actual no-rent margin is determined.

Thus, even if there is no reason to give rent a special position in economic theory as being price-determined and not price-determining, *i.e.*, as a residual income, not entering into price-determining cost, there may, of course, be good reason to emphasize all real differences with regard to the conditions of supply, which for instance are of great importance with regard to the effects of taxation. The rent tax is not shifted, but neither are taxes on houses built at cheap pre-war prices. Moreover, the fact that the individual piece of landed property as a rule consists of sections of land of different quality, which is difficult to determine, each part getting its special individual value depending on its nature and location, means that the valuation of the individual piece of property is largely residual, the costs for labor and other relatively easily measurable productive services, which have a known market price, being subtracted from the total revenue of the property. It is largely because of the many types of land, which are so hard to determine, as opposed to the greater homogeneity and the greater possibilities of evaluation of other means of production, which have made it possible to maintain a special theory of rent so long. If, as above, we apply an exact approach to the formation of price, so that each type is taken by itself, there will be a different rent for each type of land—and the special consideration of surplus above zero loses all interest. The old theory of rent contains certain practical realities, but has no miraculous properties.

With regard to the labor theory of value, which measures things according to the input of labor, it is worth noting that it is not impossible, of course, to apply a corresponding definition of the word "value", but that neither in real life—apart from imaginable prehistoric societies where labor was the only scarce productive service and where the whole problem, therefore, did not exist—nor under the assumption of complete mobility, etc., do we ever see an exchange of commodities according to input of labor. Neither would it be realized in a socialist society with free choice of employment and of consumption. And there is little reason to believe that any useful purpose would be served by such a valuation under other political assumptions where this standard of exchange might be enforced. Where there is a scarcity of other productive services than labor, a substantial degree of importance must be attached to them in the arrangement of production and consumption.

In the above discussion we have seen how the different kinds of productive services are similar to one another, both when we consider their cooperation in production from a purely technical point of view, and when we consider their position in the total economic process. The so-called marginal productivity theory, however, has sometimes been formulated in such a way that it gives an exaggerated impression of the total economy and particularly the distribution of income being technically determined and thus assuming a character of inevitability. However, if more of a certain factor of production is added, *e.g.*, labor, adjustment takes place both by technical substitution, *i.e.*, by changing to more labor-using methods in the production of the same kinds of commodities, and by qualitative substitution in consumption, *i.e.*, by changing to more labor-requiring kinds of commodities. The same holds true with regard to the individual qualities of labor, etc., taken separately. That technical substitution should dominate economic adaptation cannot be maintained with any justice.

An essential part of the theory of marginal productivity is, however, capable of being transferred to the mixed technical and qualitative adaptation that, as a matter of fact, takes place by variation in the quantity of different services in a society as a whole. Here, too, one must reckon with decreasing returns with an increase in an individual kind of service, either because the law of proportion will prevail in the production of the individual commodities, or because the decreasing demand curves for the commodities of which more or less is being produced.

The possibility of giving technical conditions a conspicuous place in an explanation of distribution does not, of course, imply a mechanistic necessity. We may here add that the marginal productivity theory, just like other theories of static equilibrium, was constructed under a series of assumptions which are far from being fully realistic. As will be shown in Parts III and IV, distribution is to a great extent affected by dynamic considerations, monopolies, and influences of power.

Wicksell,[1] among others, mentions by way of example as one of the infinite number of possible formulae representing the law of proportion, $P = a^\alpha \cdot b^{1-\alpha}$, where the quantity P is produced by means of the services a and b, and α is a constant. On the basis of comprehensive statistical investigations comprising long periods both in the U.S.A. and in some other countries and for certain industries separately, Paul H. Douglas[2] thinks that a formula of this nature applies with great validity to variations in the quantity of labor, capital and total product.

Part of the agreement between statistical data and the formula given above, namely the constant proportion of approximately 3:1 or 2:1 between total wage income and capital income, may be due to the effect of common causes affecting the two categories of income. The variation of total product with changes in the composition of the factors of production in rather close agreement with the formula is astonishing, however. A simple technical law is out of the question, in any case, since technical knowledge was changing rapidly in the periods investigated. In modern society, moreover, considerable changes take place in the relative magnitudes of labor and capital income as a result of the policies of labor and business organizations and the state. The conclusion of the formula, that we have an elasticity of demand of -3 or -4 for labor, also seems questionable when transferred from the context of a joint change in the various factors to an assumed one-sided change in wages (cf. the footnote)—quite apart from the very limited importance that may be attached to the static elasticity of the demand for labor. The existence of a high degree of correlation between labor and total national income is not astonishing, since wages taken in the widest sense are an overwhelming part of total income, and since there are tendencies for wages to follow prices and production, and for prices to follow wages. Finally, in the long run, saving and investment, and consequently also income from capital, have a tendency to follow wage incomes. When all details are taken into consideration, changes in the direction and size of production as well as in the mechanism of distribution may, however, change the wage percentage of total income and, what is more conspicuous, the corresponding smaller percentage of non-wage incomes.

---

[1] *Vorlesungen über Nationalökonomie*, I, Fischer, Jena, 1913, page 188.

[2] *E.g.*, in the *American Economic Review*, March, 1948. Douglas uses both the formula $P = b \cdot L^k \cdot C^{1-k}$ (where L and C are quantities of labor and capital, and b and k constants) and a formula $P = b \cdot L^k \cdot C^j$, which are to allow room for increasing and decreasing returns of scale. For criticism of Douglas see Tinbergen, *Econometrics*, §34. See also Leontief in *Survey of Contemporary Economics*, Vol. I, 1948, page 409, and Mendershausen's article in *Econometrica*, 1938, in which the weak basis for multi-correlation analysis is stressed. All observations are too close to a straight line to permit the determination of the effects of separate movements in L and C.

More useful than speculations about this "macro-economic" distribution, which is only a result of very heterogeneous components, is a study of the different kinds of non-wage incomes as well as the proportion between the different kinds of wage incomes, taken in the widest sense. In this special field the question arises as to the relative importance of natural facilities, education and training, and the problem of the mobility between the social classes dealt with in wage theory and sociology respectively.

An explanation of the prices of productive services leads only half way towards an explanation of the distribution of income between persons and families. Another fact besides the prices of the services is the distribution of the services as source of income, *i.e.*, the distribution of ownership and ability to work, etc. The distribution of property and its origin, therefore, has to be considered as well as the distribution of personal faculties, admission to education and to more or less favorable jobs. The primary distribution of incomes among individuals is modified, however, by different kinds of transfers. The degree of family solidarity is here important, as well as transfers through taxation and public benefits.[3] A little more about the questions mentioned here is to be found in the two last chapters of the book.

As a result of the fact that the final personal distribution of income in a society is dependent on a multitude of heterogeneous conditions, some of which may involve large changes in the incomes of individual groups, it cannot be expected, as suggested above, that a simple formula or law (Pareto's law),[4] should be valid for the total personal distribution of income with any greater degree of exactness. What we can do is, as a purely statistical simplification, to try to find expressions for some main properties about the curve of distribution in different societies or to use definite kinds of curves for purposes of interpolation. In a well-founded statistical comparison of the distribution of income in different periods or in different countries, we therefore cannot avoid a number of details. A convenient comparison may for instance be obtained by calculating the average income of, say, the top percentile, the next percentile, and so forth, in proportion to the average income of society.[5] On account of the importance of income in kind to the agricultural population and the importance of free public goods, only a limited significance may of course be attached to the statistics of income in money terms. The statistics of income must in any case be supplemented by more complete information concerning the conditions of life within the different groups of the population.

---

[3] Alan T. Peacock, *Income Redistribution and Social Policy*, London, 1954; Ragnar Bentzel, *Inkomstfördelningen i Sverige*, Stockholm, 1952 (with summary in English).
[4] Vilfredo Pareto, *Cours d'Économie Politique*, Vol. I, Book III, Chapter 1, Lausanne, 1897.
[5] S. N. Procopovich, "The Distribution of National Income", *Economic Journal*, 1926.

PART THREE

DYNAMICS

CHAPTER 23

STATICS AND DYNAMICS

IN Part II we generally used a static approach, that is, we disregarded the fact that the economic interdependence which exists is concerned with conditions at different points of time. For the most part, we did not take into account growth, the process of adjustment, subsequent effects or time-consuming processes on the whole. In so doing, we also disregarded uncertain and mistaken expectations concerning the future as well as profits and losses. The subjects now to be included fall into two main groups: the movement itself; and the uncertainty with regard to the future, when change is possible. The task in Part III is to examine how the inclusion of these conditions influences the theoretical picture and, thus, the method to be employed.

Following Ragnar Frisch[1] we speak of dynamic and static methods of approach, according as the interdependence between quantities at various times is included in the analysis, or only quantities referring to the same point of time or the same period. As opposed to the static and dynamic methods of approach, we speak of stationary conditions or conditions in motion or development. A stationary state may be treated exhaustively by means of static theory, but may also be treated by means of the more general dynamic theory. We have here the marginal case that all increases in time are zero and all nonsimultaneous values of the same variable are

---

[1] "Statikk og Dynamikk", *Nationaløkonomisk Tidsskrift*, 1929, cf. Frisch's note to an article by Tinbergen in *Econometrica*, January, 1934, page 27, according to which we may speak of dynamics when an equation connects quantities belonging to different points of time. According to Frisch, a relation is dynamic when it "contains at least one of the variables as related to *different points of time*. This may be either in the form that the equation involves both a certain variable and its rate of change with respect to time (possibly also higher derivatives), or by the fact that it contains this variable and its integral over time (possibly a weighted integral), or that it contains both lagged and unlagged values of the variable." According to Lindahl (*Studies*, pp. 31–32), all economic theory fulfilling its purpose may in a certain sense be designated as dynamic, since it concerns "economic developments taking place in time". Accordingly, he characterizes such concepts and theories formulated in so general a way that they can be applied both to changeable and unchangeable societies as "general dynamic theory". Among theories which only make use of more limiting assumptions, he distinguishes between static theory, which deals with events which constantly repeat themselves in the same way, and the special dynamic theory, which deals with societies in motion. See also Paul Samuelson, *Foundations of Economic Analysis*, 1948, *inter alia*, pp. 284 and 314, and "Dynamic Process Theory", in *A Survey of Contemporary Economics*, Vol. I, 1948, particularly p. 354; Streller, *Statik und Dynamik in der theoretischen Nationalökonomie*, Leipzig, 1926; finally, Chapter 7 and Chapter 18, above.

equal. The "simultaneous successive"[2] method of considering a process of production in a stationary community is static in so far as we consider the simultaneous presence of the necessary quantities at all stages of production instead of the time-consuming movement through the system of production. A system in motion can be submitted to an incomplete treatment by means of static theory, in which case we abstract from certain aspects of the problem, but to a complete one only by means of dynamic theory.

Static theory deals with a series of alternative observations or possibilities, irrespective of sequence and distance in time. In dynamic theory sequence and distance in time are of central importance. Frisch, for instance, imagines observations concerning price and quantity for a commodity at different points of time noted down on cards. If we arrange the cards according to the height of price in order to get a demand curve, the treatment is static, since we assume that the two quantities can appear in alternative combinations under the same economic conditions. If, on the other hand, we examine them in historic sequence, the treatment becomes dynamic. It is also possible, however, to speak of alternative or comparative dynamics. In that case we examine the way in which a movement is changed by a change in conditions or alternative movements arise under alternative assumptions. The change may concern the initial conditions, it may be a change in an external influence or a change in the internal structure of the system.[3]

We may imagine the course of price and quantity for a commodity in a certain period illustrated by a three-dimensional figure as Fig. 14, where p indicates price, x quantity and t time. The projection of the spherical curve on the time-price plane and the time-quantity plane gives the historical price and quantity curves, which are dynamic. The projection on the price-quantity plane gives a curve which, if we assume an unchanged demand function in the period, must be conceived of as a static demand curve, cf. the treatment of empirical demand curves, p. 107. Owing to changes in other conditions, *e.g.*, cost or income, the price-quantity curve may have a course as indicated in the small figure at the upper right, regardless of the fact that demand curves, *ceteris paribus*, are usually declining curves. The main direction may also be a rising one.

If we want to undertake a more concrete dynamic analysis, it would be natural to begin by a description of the causes of the changes, the impulses, and next to explain why, owing to economic society's reaction process (slow adaptation, etc.), these give rise to conditions which fall outside the sphere of static theory. Since our aim here is not to solve concrete problems on the basis of special experience, we shall deal mainly with the other aspect of the matter: the reaction process, *i.e.*, the reactions of the

[2] L. V. Birck, *Den økonomiske Virksomhed*, Gad, Copenhagen, cf. the similar method of approach used by Cassel.

[3] Paul Samuelson, *Foundations of Economic Analysis*, Harvard University Press, 1948, pp. 351–52.

system to changes in data. At the end of this chapter, however, we shall mention some of the more important forms of economic movement, but without attempting to weigh their importance in real life. Further, as a realistic background for what follows, we shall shortly recall some of the

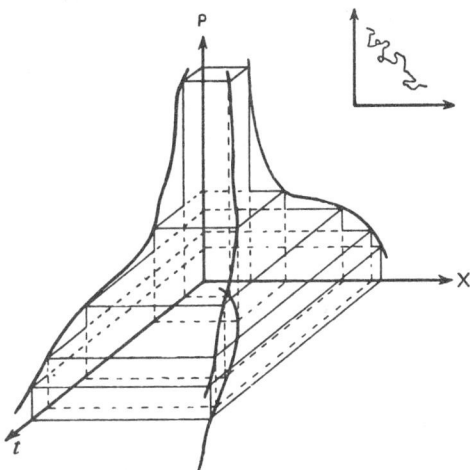

Fig. 14. A Price-Quantity-Time Diagram

most active impulses of economic change and development, some of the main forms of economic movement, and finally discuss briefly the question of the importance of economic movement.

J. B. Clark[4] mentions five main causes of economic movement: (1) growth of population; (2) growth of capital; (3) changes in methods of production; (4) changes in organization; and (5) changes in demand. To these long-run causes may be added variations in the output of crops and other changes in natural conditions, as well as changes in expectations without any objective basis. Under the heading "changes in organization" may also be included changes in the structure of individual firms, in the relations between them through the forms of organization of the market and changes in the economic policy of the state. Changes in the internal organization of the firms—but not in their purposes—may economically be regarded rather as a change in technique, even if the material arrangements and methods of production are not changed.

The policy of the state, especially in time of war, gives impulse to some of the greatest economic movements. In other cases governments and central banks exercise a decisive influence on the course of the movements. The most important forms of movement are an ordinary, relatively persistent movement (trend) comprising one or several countries or industries,

[4] *Essentials of Economic Theory*, Macmillan, New York, 1922; Moses Abramovitz, "Economic Growth" and Joseph J. Spengler, "Population Theory", in *A Survey of Contemporary Economics*, Vol. II, Richard D. Irwin, 1952.

L

business cycles (for which, of course, other impulses than the above-mentioned may be imagined), and seasonal fluctuations. Further, we have more special and limited movements of many kinds for particular trades, firms or areas.

It is impossible to give a total numerical expression to the extent to which actual economic conditions deviate from stationary conditions. The percentage changes per year can be given for prices, quantities sold, and other economic quantities, and we may possibly take an average of such percentages. Thus we may get an expression of the relative importance of the movements during different periods. It will be apparent that price movements were much greater in the decade after the outbreak of the First World War than before. The average price movement of the last two periods has been moderate, especially because of government control during and after the War. Movements in quantities and as far as the first period is concerned in employment were enormous, however, Less apparent symptoms of disequilibrium were public or private rationing, "gaps" and other tensions. Cf. Part III, Chapter 42 and Part IV, Chapter 64.

The average percentage movement per year in England, for example, was:

TABLE 3

	Wholesale Prices	Living Costs	Money Wages	Iron Prices
1871/72–1913/14	3·3	2·5	1·9	10·0
1914/15–1923/24	19·2	13·3	15·9	25·4
1924/25–1938/39	5.3a	2·4	2·0	9·6
1939/40–1946/48	8·5	3·5	6·6	7·4b

a Not including 1933–34 and 1934–35.   b Not including 1946–47.
Averages independent of sign.

CHAPTER 24

LIMITED APPLICABILITY OF STATIC THEORY

THE applicability of static theory to real life depends on the extent to which changes take place and further on the way in which they take place. If the situation is approximately stationary, prices and quantities, etc., must be assumed to correspond rather closely to static conditions of equilibrium, either the conditions of free competition or others in accordance with the organization of the market.

If the stationary condition is due to limited mobility, so that, for instance, a comparatively vigorous impulse is required to change a price, the static method of approach is not sufficient. The limitations in mobility and the conditions which prevailed in preceding periods must here enter into a dynamic explanation. A high degree of mobility and small movement, on the other hand, are favorable conditions for the application of a purely static explanation. Consequently, the static theory was not so very misleading before the First World War.

Static theory, which disregards the course of time, can only provide a limited treatment, however, of the problems of real life. In some cases this treatment will be satisfactory, in others quite unsatisfactory. This is partly dependent on the subject of the analysis, and partly on the purpose of the latter, and thereby the degree of exactness demanded. The static description is like a map without any indications of altitude. If we are concerned with a flat region, such a map will be satisfactory for almost all practical purposes. If, on the other hand, we wish to know something of the Alps or the Himalayas, the practical value of the map is very limited. But here, too, it may be used as a starting-point, because all points and the connections between them will be found on it. It may be made fully applicable for the calculation of transportation distances, estimates as to climatic conditions, and much else, if the missing indications of altitude are added.

When investigating adaptation in the short run, the quantities of labor and real capital which are used in definite ways have to be taken as data. Considering equilibrium in the long run, we assume mobility between different uses and, in a still longer run, the possibility of adapting total quantities in correspondence with certain supply functions. If in accordance with short- or long-run equilibrium theory we only ask about the effect on price and quantity of a change in taste or cost conditions, after adaptation during a shorter or longer period, there is in both cases a possibility of contenting one's self with a static analysis. If, however, we want to know how the process of adaptation takes place, from the moment when conditions are altered until we reach the equilibrium of the short or more or less long run, which, with our simplified approach means until certain conditions are fully adapted while others are still quite unchanged, we must apply a dynamic method of approach. Thus, the equilibrium of the short run and that of the long run are both static simplifications. The explanation of the process before these equilibria are reached—consequently also between the "short" and the "long"—must, on the contrary, be dynamic.

The more comprehensive a process of adaptation becomes, *i.e.*, the more one must move from a partial to a total analysis, the greater is the necessity of a dynamic method of approach. This is partly because the different speeds for different effects may be of importance for the final result, and partly because the more comprehensive movement is more protracted and important and more difficult to analyze, for which reason it is of greater interest to have an explicit statement of what occurs while adaptation takes place.

In conclusion, we should emphasize that static theory has an introductory, pedagogical value. If one wants to study the propeller of an airplane, it is practical also to examine it thoroughly before it starts moving.

CHAPTER 25

IS THERE A TENDENCY TOWARDS
A DEFINITE STATIC EQUILIBRIUM?

As an explanation of the situation in modern society, static theory is very deficient because it excludes the movements which are taking place. However, static theory is often used in another way, *i.e.*, to find the stationary situation which would result if the economic adaptations were allowed to continue without any new influences from outside. The situation which may be imagined to result from this, the "virtual" equilibrium (what Swedish writers call "det styrande jämnviktsläge") is nevertheless of only limited interest. In the first place, a great number of strong new influences, of a nature not yet known, may be expected. This does not only involve alterations when the changes actually occur, but as a result of the expectation that something will or may happen, there will immediately be important effects. In the second place, owing to the changes in conditions resulting from the movement itself, the final stationary situation, if it should ever occur, will not correspond to a static equilibrium with the "data" which one took into account at the initial stage. What happens in the course of the process of adaptation will change the "data". Temporary increases or reductions in wages will change the efficiency of the workers, the profit or loss for the enterprises, and thus the subsequent supply of real capital. A temporary forced change in consumption will change the wants of the future, and temporary claims on production will change the technical knowledge of the future. In answer to this, it may justly be asserted that the conditions which are thus being influenced by the process of adaptation, take on the appearance of variables, and not really the unchangeable data of the system. In describing sequence analysis in Chapter 35, we shall discuss the way in which, as a result of the development in an initial period, we arrive at a certain change in the "data", which, in turn, constitute the starting-point for the ensuing period, and so on.

The unequal speed of adaptation in different directions, *e.g.*, as to change in price, the spending of income for consumption, changes in the efficiency of labor as a result of changed income, etc., will influence the development and its possible final outcome. The result, therefore, differs from what would be achieved in any imaginable, infinitely quick adjustment, or an adjustment with the same velocity in all directions. Consequently it is impossible to find the unknown quantities by considering static alternatives.

The above-mentioned limitation to the applicability of static theory, that "data" can be assumed to change on the way towards equilibrium, and that therefore a dynamic analysis is needed of what takes place on the way is one of the three objections raised by Kaldor against the static system of equilibrium.[1] The other two are: that several solutions are possible (cf. Part II, Chapter 12); and that the movement may be assumed not to lead towards a definite point, but that the result may be a series of constant, increasing or decreasing fluctuations (as will be illustrated by the cobweb theorem in Chapter 36). Or the results of certain sets of data may be a more or less permanent trend, for instance an increase in population or in the magnitude of capital. Also for the "indeterminate" case a dynamic explanation will no doubt be necessary as a rule. "Indeterminate", then, only means: not determined so long as one confines one's self to the methods of static theory. Why, nevertheless, one actually reaches a

---

[1] In "a classificatory note on the determinateness of equilibrium", *Review of Economic Studies*, February, 1939, Kaldor on page 126 indicates the following possibilities of obtaining static equilibrium: (a) equilibrium is attained at once (1) either in the market form of Walras, when different prices are "called up", but sales only are made when prices are obtained that give equilibrium everywhere between supply and demand, (2) in the market form of Edgeworth, where only preliminary contracts are made, which are constantly revised until no one has any interest in further revision. In a simultaneous total adjustment for all goods and productive services, these paths to equilibrium are certainly extremely improbable in real life; (b) equilibrium may also be imagined to be reached by degrees, so long as the final result is not influenced by the way one has gone. One of the conditions is that none of the persons involved becomes richer or poorer by the sales first concluded. The remaining stocks must be of the same size from day to day. (Cf. Marshall's Appendix on "Barter".) In practice, we may imagine this to be realized, with a reasonable degree of approximation, in the case of a commodity of limited value in relation to total income, especially when we are not far from perfect foresight and perfect knowledge, but not in an adjustment of production and sales for the community as a whole. Cf. J. R. Hicks, *Value and Capital*, The Clarendon Press, 1939, pp. 127-29.

definite solution out of a group of possible ones, may be explained by taking account of other factors. This will often be accomplished by tracing through the path of the changes which take place.

CHAPTER 26

STABILITY OF EQUILIBRIUM

IN the preceding chapter we dealt with the question as to whether it is possible to find a tendency towards a static equilibrium. Further along these lines we shall deal briefly with the conditions necessary for the maintenance of an equilibrium once obtained.

An egg standing on one end and a market where demand and supply curves intersect the "wrong" way, *i.e.*, where supply is greater than demand at a price just below the intersection of the curves (and vice versa above this) are in unstable equilibrium. Such a state is only tenable if nothing at all happens. Where the curves, as mentioned above, intersect the wrong way, there will, at prices below the intersection, be an inducement to extend supply and restrict demand, which gives a tendency to movement away from the equilibrium price. A price above the equilibrium price will correspondingly give a further upward tendency.

An equilibrium may be "stable in the small", *i.e.*, it may be restored after small shocks, while great temporary influences lead permanently away from the starting-point. It may be continuously neutral within a certain range, or it may be reached alternatively at several separate points, which have their own "equilibrium in the small". Under "perfect stability of the first kind", there is a tendency back to equilibrium from any initial deviation. A frictionless pendulum swinging round its point of equilibrium is, conversely, said to have "stability of the second kind".[1]

From the case of static equilibrium, this way of thinking may be transferred, for instance, to the case where we have a definite trend. The quantities may constantly approach the trend line or fluctuate round it in a definite way, the connection may be assumed to be broken off, or the trend may be altered by temporary influences.

The attempts at maximization on the part of the economic subjects and the possibilities of mutual barter give a strong tendency towards definite forms of equilibrium, but, owing to limited knowledge and mobility, the tendency has only a limited possibility of prevailing. Decreasing costs in the long run with increases in the size of firms may, however, cause some difficulties. These are associated with those forms of

---

[1] Paul Samuelson, *Foundations of Economic Analysis*, 1948, Chapters IX and X, and the articles in *Econometrica*, 1941 and 1942.

instability which are caused by lack of competition. With competition among many firms, however, a declining demand curve and an increasing supply curve guarantee the right direction of the curves. Instability may, nevertheless, appear to a great extent as a result of a limited and unequal speed of adjustment. The great extent to which economic life seems to be "stamped by the events of the past" is an indication of a certain stability against temporary influences.

CHAPTER 27

MOVEMENT IN TIME. INCREASE. ACCELERATION

THE change in prices or sales or other economic quantity may, as in the top row of Fig. 15, be expressed by a change in the ordinates of the time curve. If the movement is continuous, a curve indicating the increase may be deduced from the movement of the original curve (second row of the figure); and by once more examining the increase in this curve, an acceleration curve may be drawn (third row of the figure). How often we

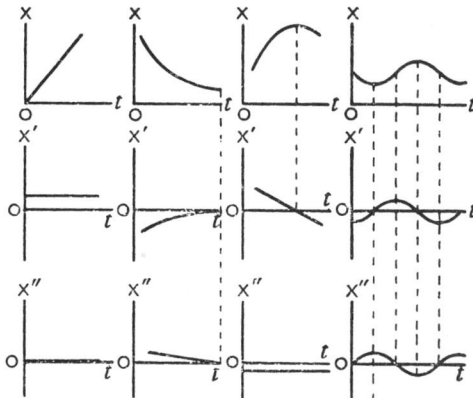

Fig. 15. Derivation of Increase and Acceleration Curves

have to continue this process before we get increases equal to zero, depends on the degree of the curve. For actual real time curves, which do not follow any simple formula, the investigation may be stopped at a certain point only if we are satisfied with an approximation and increases of a higher order can be disregarded.

Increase and acceleration have great economic importance. The number of existing plants, buildings, commodities in stock, etc., may be found as the number at any previous time, plus increase, minus decrease during the period elapsed. Conversely, the net change in the course of time can be deduced from the quantities existing at different points of time. The demand for new shipyards and machinery for them is determined, not by the increase in tonnage, but by the acceleration.

In such cases where growth or decrease and the corresponding acceleration take place through a gradual and time-consuming economic process, such as production or consumption, we may have continuous curves. If, on the other hand, we are dealing with changes in valuation or plans, jumps may take place (and consequently increases or accelerations $+\infty$ or $-\infty$ calculated for an infinitely small period). Such discontinuities will necessarily appear because human plans are not changed continuously. If we do not consider infinitely small periods, but weeks, months, or years, this discontinuity is completely or partially effaced.

The changes enter as important variables in the economic partial inter-dependences or equations. An equation in which there is an increase in one or more of the variables becomes dynamic[1] because the increase indicates a connection between different points of time. Where the velocity of growth is the dependent variable, one may speak of a velocity of reaction to certain influences.

The demand function, for instance, becomes dynamic when one regards the quantity demanded as determined not only by the actual price, but also by the price movement of the present or immediately preceding period, this movement being taken as an expression of the expected future price movement. As we shall see later, this question of expectations is a problem by itself. But as a preliminary approximation, we may regard the most recent increase as decisive. If we include the velocities of increase and the possible velocities of a higher order, we may set down a "momentary dynamic equilibrium" in the form of a number of equations for each point of time, forming a determinate system with the same number of unknowns and equations. In other words, it is possible in this way, on the basis of a set of assumptions, to give a complete and consistent explanation of why the situation is as it is at a given moment. From such a system of equations, plus knowledge of the initial conditions, we may further deduce what will happen in the ensuing periods, if new conditions do not arise.

It may be seen even at this stage how the concept of equilibrium may be united with that of movement. Frisch speaks about a "total dynamic equilibrium", or, as it might also be expressed, an equilibrium in time, where the unknowns are not simultaneous quantities (or increases), but the time curves for a series of quantities. These time curves are also known when we have a corresponding number of equations, *i.e.*, an equation between each of the quantities and time. (That there are two variables in these equations is, of course, no problem, since the points of time always come in a certain succession, and since by substituting an arbitrary point

---

[1] With regard to a great part of what follows, we may refer to the detailed statement in Ragnar Frisch's "Statikk og Dynamikk", *Nationaløkonomisk Tidsskrift*, 1929.

of time, we can always find the other variable!) Whereas the equilibrium concept used here is purely formal, only indicating completeness and correspondence from a logical point of view, we shall later deal with the *real*, dynamic equilibrium concept, which a number of economists prefer to deal with exclusively: the correspondence between expectation and result.

We shall here give Frisch's example of the demand for coke. A higher price, according to static theory, means smaller purchases, whereas an increased price, when it gives rise to an expectation of further increases, leads to increased purchases, in correspondence with dynamic theory. A person's "velocity of purchase" (*i.e.*, demand), when the quantity demanded per unit of time is called x, the price p, the increase in this p and the stocks w, is $x = f_1(p,\dot{p},w)$. In addition, he has a velocity of consumption, $z = f_2(p,\dot{p},w)$. The nature of these functions will be illustrated by the following table, indicating the "velocity of purchase" per week.

TABLE 4

VELOCITY OF PURCHASE $x = f_1(p,\dot{p},w)$ (TONS OF COKE PER WEEK)

Stock	w = 0 Tons					w = 10 Tons		
Rate of Change in Price	$\dot{p} =$					$\dot{p} =$		
Price	− $0.50 Per Week	− $0.25 Per Week	0	+ $0.25 Per Week	+ $0.50 Per Week	− $0.25 Per Week	0	+ $0.25 Per Week
$1.00	—	—	7	9	20	—	6	8
$2.00	—	—	6	7	12	—	5	6
$3.00	3	4	5	6	12	3	4	5
$5.00	2	3	4	5	6	2	3	4

The two columns in the table with $\dot{p} = 0$ correspond to the static demand series. At the same p and $\dot{p}$ demand is greatest when stocks are small. The lines of the table show the greatest demand with the greatest increase in price.

If we know the break-down of purchases and consumption as well as stocks at the initial point of time, and if we assume, for instance, that expectations correspond to the latest price movement, it is possible to construct the corresponding time curves for the purchases, consumption and stocks of the persons in question from a given price curve in the market through a kind of sequence analysis (cf. Chapter 35). The stocks at the end of a period are found by deducting consumption from initial stocks plus purchases.

If the movement can be considered to be continuous, we can set down the following equation with regard to the stocks:

$$w_t - w_0 = \int_0^t (x - z)dt$$

saying that the increase in stocks is equal to the difference between purchases and consumption summed up for all the infinitely small periods from 0 to t. The increase in stocks from t_0 to t_1 is illustrated by the difference between the two hatched areas in Fig. 16 below. If stocks are known at the initial stage, we can use this figure to obtain a curve of stocks with the top where the x and z curves intersect each other.

We are here touching on the fact that some economic quantities are obtained as increases to certain others, and that some are calculated as

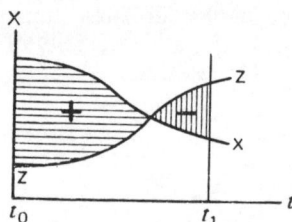

Fig. 16. Movements in Stocks

an accumulation of others in the course of time (integral). The building of houses and plants, the determination of profit and loss, belong in the category of increases. Consumption, income and production, forming the important middle group, are all calculated per period, and are the quantities used in static theory. Both increases and accumulations of these quantities are of interest to us. Property, stocks, as well as the existing amount of the means of production, which are all calculated per point of time, may be regarded as accumulated quantities, *i.e.*, "funds" quantities.[2] The quantitative connection between the first and second and between the second and third groups is of the same sort. The same economic quantity may very well be in different positions in relation to various economic quantities at one and the same time; profit, for instance, resulting from an enhanced valuation of property and, consequently, equal to the difference between two property values, may be used for consumption. Since the individual quantities have a different position to each other in different relations, it is impossible to divide them into three or more fixed classes. We may also have quantities of different nature acting together. For instance shipping, shipbuilding, and the construction of shipyards combined create a demand for labor and materials and thereby provide a source of purchasing power.

[2] Tinbergen, "Annual Survey", *Econometrica*, July, 1935, pp. 277–79, and January, 1934, page 28.

It will be obvious that the methods of population statistics are very largely applicable to such economic quantities as cattle, forests, machinery and buildings, where both increase, decrease and stocks are of importance as well as distribution in age. The same is true of raw materials in the process of production and in stocks. At the same time as there must be agreement between input, output, and change in stocks, we have the laws applying to the duration of the time-consuming processes, which will be mentioned in the next chapter. In these spheres, too, we can use the concepts of accounting: business accounts and balance sheet. This is very clear if we use the circulation approach, according to which the funds are accumulations that are unchanged under stationary conditions, and the flows, like quantities in double-entry bookkeeping, correspond to a decrease in one place in the system and an equal increase somewhere else.

CHAPTER 28

TIME-CONSUMING PROCESSES. LAGS

WHERE there is a real distance in time (lag) between two phenomena, we have a dynamic relationship. The distance in time may depend on many things and may be more or less variable. Important examples are production requiring time for technical or organic reasons, the transportation of goods, and the movement through the sales channels or the movement of income from person to person, as described by the multiplier theory. It may also be a distance in time between two phenomena which follow from the same cause with unequal velocity.

Hicks[1] mentions as an example of lag the slow introduction of the combustion engine. Technically it was completed about 1910. But before the market could be satisfied, it was necessary not only to produce millions of motors and motorcars, but also factories, roads, garages, etc.; and new oil wells had to be opened, new rubber plantations had to grow up, etc. Also economically it was necessary to tie up many years' investment, just as had been the case earlier when the railways were built. As is well known, according to the principle of acceleration, such waves of new investments have great influence on the course of business cycles.

In the so-called "pig cycles", as well as in the corresponding cycles for perennial plants (coffee and rubber), natural conditions play a decisive

---

[1] J. R. Hicks, *Social Framework*, Oxford University Press, 1942; cf. Hicks and A. G. Hart, *The Social Framework of the American Economy*, 1945. A fine numerical illustration of the acceleration principle with motorcar production in the twenties as background has been given by Gustaf Åkerman in "Om Konjunkturväxlingarnas Nödvändighet och Grundorsak", *Ekonomisk Tidskrift*, 1932, p. 14.

part. In many cases, human conditions, organizational and psychological, are of great importance. It takes time before either public or private enterprises make decisions as to new construction, expansion or restriction, or as to changes in price. Further, labor and cartel agreements as well as current contracts for delivery entail a distance in time between the cause of the change and its completion. Where a change in price is involved, it not only takes time to be realized, but where round amounts are used, the conditions of a continuous movement are lacking, and therefore an accumulation of impulses to the change must take place before the change can be realized. The time which elapses may here be partly constant, partly dependent on the strength of the impulse, and partly dependent on other conditions, such as, for instance, increases in price in other spheres or changes in the political situation. We also have tendencies to fixed prices, especially in markets with a few large firms. (Cf. Part IV, Chapter 58.)

In many cases expectations cause the lag in certain interrelationships to be substantially smaller than it would be if the effect were to go through the ordinary chain of partial interdependences. The prices and production of raw materials may, for instance, rise before the effect of increased demand for manufactured articles makes itself felt through normal sales channels. Where valuation is involved, the delay is due to the time taken for deliberation and decision.

For fixed real capital we have a special series of time intervals between investment and the appearance of the product, because the duration of the capital must be extended over a longer period, the length of which does not exclusively depend on the technical durability of the capital, but also on utilization of capacity as well as on the speed of production. The total time elapsing between the investment of the productive services and the appearance of the products may be divided into the production period of the real capital and its time of utilization.

It is a very important theoretical consequence of the consideration paid by dynamic theory to the time-consuming processes, that it is only possible in a certain sense to maintain the interdependence approach, which in the equilibrium conditions of static theory meant that all variables were to an equal extent regarded as cause and effect. We are now, in a way, returning to a causal approach, according to which the quantities which appear later must be conceived of as effects of the preceding ones. This causal explanation is, however, far more complicated than the old one. Price, for instance, is not a unique result of costs. This year's quantity of finished products is necessarily result of the quantity of raw materials on hand last year. But in determining the quantity for last year, there has been a causal reaction from commodity to raw material, *i.e.*, against the time sequence. This may be regarded as a more or less modified edition of the static interdependence theory. What, according to static theory, is an interdependence relationship between quantities I and II in Fig. 1, p. 35 appears *e.g.*, as the influence of I on II with a lag of one year, and the influence of II on I with a lag of three years. Thus the interdependence still exists between the different time series of quantities and prices, whereas for a quantity at a definite point of time, the causes may be said to lie in the past while the effects lie in the future. As will appear from the following discussion, an essential part of the dynamic adjustment takes place, however, through planning built on expectations, and is determined through the establishment of equilibrium in the intertemporal calculations of enterprises and persons. In the last chapter of this Part we shall revert to the question of causation.

CHAPTER 29

DYNAMIC SYSTEMS OF EQUATIONS

IN dynamic theory, in order to understand the whole economic inter-dependence, it is necessary, just as in static theory, to consider the demonstrable partial interdependences through a limited number of links: demand, cost conditions, etc. By following the partial interdependences as connecting links, we may arrive at an understanding of the more comprehensive interdependence. This is also to be found through one or more intermediary links between quantities that are not directly connected and to a certain extent even between all quantities in a community. Since what we have here is a quantitative connection between economic categories, it is desirable to express partial interdependences in equations, and the total interdependence by a system of equations.

The economic interdependences or equations will be of different and in many cases mixed types with regard to their relation to time. Some will, as in static theory, be exclusively related to simultaneous quantities per period of time (flows). In others, quantities from several periods will enter, or, deduced therefrom, increases or accelerations, or what in some respects amounts to the same thing, expectations regarding future points of time. Quantities from a series of past points of time will enter into the calculation of actual costs or the calculation of stocks. An equation may be of mixed content, as, *e.g.*, when demand is satisfied simultaneously by new production and by consumption of stocks, or when current production and new constructions compete for labor.

Just as in population statistics and accounting[1] we may, from the data of a past period, deduce equations which state that funds at any point of time are equal to funds at any previous point of time plus increments, minus decrements over the intervening period. It must be remembered

---

[1] Erich Schneider, "Einführung in die Wirtschaftstheorie", I Teil, *Theorie des Wirtschaftskreislaufs*, Mohr, Tübingen, 1947.

that, even if all the variables are functions of time, these functions, such as in many cases price movements, are not necessarily continuous. A sequence analysis made step by step with a division into periods may then be more applicable than equations for an assumed continuous evolution.

In order that a system of equations shall be dynamic, at least one of them must be so. If all are static, the system, as Frisch[2] says, is locked up; the solution can not be shaken out. The system of simultaneous equations in Part I, therefore, cannot be directly applied to a world in movement. If, however, only one of the unknowns varies in time, it becomes possible, through the dependence of the others on this unknown, to obtain corresponding time-determined solutions for all of them. In the solution of a dynamic system of equations, the point is to eliminate the unknown, until we have one equation (the final equation)[3] with the same unknown at various points of time. As mentioned above, in a system of dynamic equations, the unknown is not a series of quantities, but a series of time curves.

One may take as data, besides constants or definite functions, a series of irregular ("non-systematic") quantities, which set in at different points of time (for instance, public works or fluctuations in crops in definite years). These irregular events may either be regarded as foreseen and will then enter into the *ex ante* equations, or they may be unexpected shocks.[4] The variables for the periods after such an extraordinary event will in any case be influenced by the latter. The result will be either monotonic, cumulatively strengthened or damped fluctuations.

A system in movement can be expressed by an equation for every time series, to which must be added the initial values for the variables, for the system to be determinate. Where it is practical to apply a discontinuous approach, we obtain, as in Chapter 35 in the treatment of the sequence analysis, a system of difference equations. If the system is exposed to external influences or structural changes, it is practical to apply an approximate determination on the basis of values for the variables that are not too old. By taking probabilities and dispersions into consideration, the

---

[2] "Konjunkturbevegelsen som statistisk-teoretisk problem", *Förhandlingar vid Nordiska Nationalekonomiska Mötet*, Stockholm, 1931, p. 140, cf. 141.

[3] Tinbergen, *Review of Economic Studies*, 1940, p. 78, reprinted in *Readings in Business Cycle Theory*, 1944, p. 68.

[4] Tinbergen, p. 76 (in *Readings*, p. 65). He says furthermore, cf. 76–77 (p. 66): In order to be able to find the movements of the variables from a system of equations, we must know:
(a) the "structure" of the model, represented by the coefficients, the lags, and the trends in the equations;
(b) the values of the "external variables" for all time units;
(c) the "disturbances" represented by the residuals for all time units; and
(d) the "initial values" of one or more of the variables of the problem. Exactly what initial values must be given can only be indicated in each particular case.
(b) concerns quantities which are taken into consideration as determining, but themselves fall outside the sphere under examination, *i.e.*, changing data. (c) concerns all other "accidental" influences.

whole system may be made stochastic, but then it becomes rather unhandy for most economists.[5]

Where it is a question of estimating the future and forecasting laws for possible future movements, it depends on the accessible information whether one will take one's starting-point in the data of the moment (*i.e.*, of the immediate past) or allow data from a more distant past to enter into the equations.

A factual question, to which we make only a brief reference here, is that of the special position of interest in dynamic theory, especially in the theory of business cycles. Since the interest factor $(1 + r)^n$ is an expression of the relation in exchange of purchasing power at different points of time, the rate of interest will be influenced by expectations as to general price movements. The gross rate of interest is, moreover, influenced by the conditions of risk. At the same time the height of the rate of interest influences the intertemporal distribution of real goods.

CHAPTER 30

DYNAMIZATION OF WALRAS' EQUATIONS

In the following discussion we do not intend to set up a system of equations corresponding to the static system of equations in Part II, nor will we even attempt a detailed treatment of the form of the equations. Any picture that is to be even fairly satisfactory must, as will appear from the following, be immensely complicated. We shall therefore confine ourselves to indicating the most important attributes of a system of quantitative interdependences, or equations which must be considered as determining conditions under dynamic assumptions. What we attempt to provide is a preliminary theoretical orientation concerning all the interdependences which may be assumed to be important with regard to the individual quantities. In a realistic treatment of concrete cases, the next step will be to find approximate expressions for the interdependence between totals and aggregates.

30.1, DEMAND EQUATIONS

The quantity of a commodity demanded within a short period of time will be a function of past conditions and of expectations as to the future, besides being, as in static theory, a function of all commodity prices and all incomes. Conditions, especially those which prevailed in the immediate past, determine the habits of people, their attitude and the supply of

[5] Trygve Haavelmo, "The Probability Approach in Econometrics", *Econometrica*, Supplement, July, 1944. Arne Jensen, *A Distribution Model, Applicable to Economics*, Copenhagen, 1954.

goods, but at the same time they also form an important part of the data which determine expectations. Expectations may to a certain extent be expressed by the increase and acceleration in variables up to the moment at which the demand is being considered. Any point of time will have a special demand function influenced by the immediate past.

For any point of time we may, however, imagine different demand functions, both actual and expected, according to the length of the period of adjustment under investigation. Thus we may choose to examine how great the quantity demanded will be one day, one week, or one year after a definite change in the price of a commodity. If we confine ourselves to the interdependence between the quantity demanded and the price of the commodity itself, we may, starting from a definite initial situation, imagine a surface which for all immediate changes in price indicates how those magnitudes will develop in the following period. A question still further in the direction of dynamization of the demand function, to which it will only be possible to give a very imperfect answer, is what will happen to the quantity demanded, certain data having moved in definite ways in a definite period.

If we want to give a fairly convenient, statistical expression for the demand function for a commodity, we may regard the dependence of the quantity demanded on the price of the commodity and, possibly, one or a few other commodity prices and total income, as well as the time elapsed since the change in the commodity price itself and (in such cases where the demand function may be supposed to have a steady trend) the place in the real scale of time where we find ourselves (the calendar year). We may for instance set down the simplified demand equation

$$x_a = f(p_a, p_b, y, t, T)$$

where y is total income, t is the time elapsed after a definite change in price, and T the actual point of time (the year). Initial stocks may also be included as one of the determining factors.

30.2, COST EQUATIONS

The question of cost is comparatively simple in static theory. Costs are the sum of prices of the services used in producing the commodity. Since change is disregarded, it is of no importance that the services have been put in at different times before the appearance of the product. The payment of cost is a condition for the situation being kept up unchanged. If we assume free competition, price will be equal to costs, *i.e.*, we have the simple cost equation given in Part II, Chapter 11. Besides, under free competition, this equation may be supposed to apply to certain forms of public price policy, the actual aim of which is to follow the cost principle. With monopolistic price policy under static assumptions, the cost equation does not apply, or we may say that it is modified by the addition to costs of the profit which one is trying to maximize. The static cost concept, however, still applies and is of interest in connection with the calculation of profit.

If we use a dynamic approach, the cost equilibrium is disturbed even under free competition. The services necessary for the production of a commodity have been rendered in different periods at different prices, possibly with different technical knowledge and different supply of productive services, etc. Especially where fixed capital is employed, the joint production of units of the commodity appearing in different periods will disturb the simple imputation, *i.e.*, the payment of definite services as a necessary condition for the production of the individual unit of the commodity. At this point we encounter the problem of depreciation, which cannot be solved in a purely technical way unless we wish to be arbitrary. Dynamic assumptions, in any case, require that the relation between expenses which are given for productive services at any one point of time and the price which can actually be obtained for the commodity, is interrupted.

If we consider periods of changing conditions, a distinction must be made between plan and calculation on one hand (*ex ante* analysis) and result and accounting on the other (*ex post* analysis). (Cf. Chapter 34.) Under perfect competition we have, even with dynamic assumptions, an equilibrium between price and costs in the calculation (*ex ante*), but the appearance of profit and loss in the accounts (*ex post*) as a result of unforeseen events.

At each stage the payment for the sacrifices necessary for the production of the commodity must be considered as costs. At the time of investment this is true with regard to the payment for the services necessary for the construction and for the purchase of means of production which is expected to be made at a later date. In the subsequent periods, the supplementary necessary payments, plus the revenue one forgoes by using the plant or other means of production for the given production, plus the calculated reduction of future net revenue resulting from wear and tear are all costs. Thus under perfect competition we have at each moment an equilibrium between the price or the expected price of the commodity and the current price of the productive services which are in use. If, on the other hand, we take into account the prices previously paid for the services, there will be a profit or a loss.

30.3, QUANTITY EQUATIONS OF PRODUCTIVE SERVICES

If we consider the relation between the quantities of productive services and the quantities of goods produced therefrom, we may establish a separate equation for each year's productive services. The total quantity of services employed during the current year is equal to the sum of quantities used for the various kinds of commodities consumed this year and in future years. The relation between quantities of services and of finished products, consequently, is not one between simultaneous quantities, but is shifted in time by a series of lags, which are partly determined technically, but also are determined economically to a considerable extent.

M

Besides the quantity equations of productive services, which take account of the simultaneous employment of productive services used for a series of commodities to appear in different subsequent years, it may be interesting to consider the equations for the quantity and age distribution of existing stocks of means of production and consumption, which are derived from the production and consumption of the past. The employment of productive services to increase stocks competes with their employment for current consumption; but at the same time delivery from stocks competes with direct delivery from production to consumption.

30.4, SUPPLY EQUATIONS OF PRODUCTIVE SERVICES

When the supply of productive services is considered to be variable, *i.e.*, as a function of the price of the service, and the prices of all other services and commodities, it is also necessary to consider the possible influence of conditions at other times and expectations concerning the future. The equations obtained from static theory and founded on the will and ability of individuals to work and save can be elaborated accordingly. Additional equations for the growth of capital or population may be set up as in interest and in population theory. As illustrated in the figure on p. 35, the relationships between economic quantities refer to a great extent to nonsimultaneous magnitudes belonging to the different categories. Since in static theory all magnitudes are kept constant, it is possible here to replace these really intertemporal relations by relations between simultaneous magnitudes. A complete picture of dynamics, however, requires consideration of the change through time. A momentary cross-section through all the time curves (or including a period short enough to be considered homogeneous) also gives a useful picture, if we add to the dependent variables of the system (prices and quantities) increases in the variables as well as stocks. In this case we have a system of simultaneous equations which is dynamic. This system explains the momentary value of the dependent variables and determines their value as long as no new and unknown data appear.

CHAPTER 31

INDEX-EQUATIONS ("MACRO-DYNAMICS")

IF we want to draw conclusions which go beyond the forms of a general system of equations or a small sector of the community, it is necessary to replace the great number of equations applying to homogeneous commodities and services by equations in which large groups, *e.g.*, all consumption goods, all labor, or all kinds of real capital, are the variables, measured by indices, expressing total quantity and average price. In so doing errors are committed, because a uniform distribution of weights for the quantities, *e.g.*, by price at a definite point of time, cannot reflect adequately the importance of the different parts at all times and under all circumstances. Summation of the money value of a number of magnitudes, on the other hand, does have an exact meaning.

For the index quantities, appropriate equations may be set up just as for the homogeneous quantities. Total demand for food is, among other things, a function of the price index for food and for clothes. The cost of an average unit of consumption goods in general may be seen as an average of the prices of the productive services used for all the different consumption goods added up according to their respective weights in total consumption. The total quantity of labor available of each kind is equal to the sum of all uses of all the individual kinds of labor plus any unused remainders.[1]

As soon as we proceed to a statistical determination of the indices, arbitrariness is unavoidable, and this may well be important when the analysis is concerned with highly changeable economic conditions. The index equations, besides being determined by an immense mass of data of this kind, are also determined by weight relations fixed between the items which are not constant in real life. It is only in exceptional cases that considerable error is caused thereby. But a commodity, *e.g.*, with comparatively great elasticity of demand, influences an aggregate demand function more than in proportion to its initial quantity.[2] The determination of the form and the constants of the index-equations must take place by statistical observations, which are often incomplete, and the weight distribution must be fixed by decisions which may be rather arbitrary. The difficulty of procuring information will in many cases force one to make short cuts and include empirically demonstrable relations between categories, *e.g.*, between prices and the corresponding quantities, which are not concerned with exactly the same subjects. It being impossible, for instance, to include all consumption goods, one takes only a certain representative number. If we have not the figures for the movement in total income, we may possibly have to use figures which move in the same direction. In other words, owing to deficient data, we may have to put up with "symptomatic" equations the internal structure of which does not represent causal relationships.

Among the multitude of index equations which can be set up, some are only definition equations, indicating the selected combination of sub-groups

---

[1] For statistical investigations based on Walras' equations see Wassily Leontief, "Econometrics", in *A Survey of Contemporary Economics*, Vol. I, 1948, pp. 407–08 and literature mentioned, p. 407; A. Chabert, "Le Système d' Input-Output, *Économie Appliquée*, 1950; later Leontief, *The Structure of American Economy*, 2nd. Edn., 1951. A basic assumption for this system and the "Linear Programming" is constant technical coefficients and abstraction from demand and other reaction equations, what again assumes a certain stability. See the more detailed treatment at the end of Chapter 39.

[2] Tinbergen, *Econometrics*, § 10.

into main groups (agricultural products equal to grain, meat, etc.). Others are approximate or average expressions of attributes obtained by the aggregation of a series of equations in the complete system of equations for all items (wages = 25 per cent of certain costs); or dynamic examples: certain lags with regard to production or the spending of income are fixed as a certain number of months or, maybe, a simple approximate function of a few index numbers. The setting up of a closed system, with an equal number of equations and unknowns, is likely to be of a more arbitrary character than the system of "blank-equations" for all imaginable homogeneous variables of abstract theory. This follows from the fact that it is difficult, in a statistically measurable system of dynamic index equations, to include all the relations between the quantities which are actually assumed to be present; and it may also be difficult to make sure that every equation fully expresses something new. Such completeness and security against repetitions must, of course, be the aim of any explanation. The conception of the complete, exact system must, then, serve as a guide for us with regard to the structure that we give to our incomplete, approximate and more or less "symptomatic" statistical models.

When we refer above to equations, we do not mean to imply that we shall always force reality to fit our assumptions in such an exact, quantitative form. In many cases it is more important to preserve the multitude of the assumptions and the uncertainty of their nature, even if in so doing we prevent exact analytical deduction and expose ourselves to those false conclusions which easily steal into verbal reasoning as a result of indefinite and easily changing ideas as to quantities and the nature of their interrelationships. If we undertake a simplification in the form of equations, or in the form of some other model, by temporarily disregarding some of our assumptions as to reality, it is necessary, of course, afterwards to compare the result of the analysis under the limited assumptions with the circumstances which were not yet included. On this basis, we would make a correction, if necessary by a rough estimate. In most actual investigations there seems only to be a certain possibility of a partially exact, quantitative analysis, whether numerical or abstract. We use guiding models, the behavior of which can only partially, or experimentally, be transferred to reality. A complementary and corrective estimate is then a necessary supplement. Unconditional belief in three or four macroeconomic equations as the image of economic god seems in any case to be foolish.

In the face of all the difficulties resulting from the manifold variety of real life and our limited knowledge, it is constantly necessary to stress that the exact quantitative description is in no way complete, but only gives us models which have their main features in common with the actual, far more differentiated mass of real observations. Our theoretical description can therefore explain some aspects of the real problem and only with considerable uncertainty.

When we have spoken so much about the difficulties and necessary inexactitudes in aggregation,[3] *i.e.*, on the way from the homogeneous magnitudes connected with individual economic subjects to total categories (on the way from "micro" to "macro"), our purpose has not been to deter from but to stimulate the important work to be done. The explanation of the relations between total categories such as national savings and investment must essentially be references to the actions of individual households and firms and the interaction between them. The processes on the markets for the individual commodities are also essential to the explanation of "macro" economic processes. Regularities in the behavior of total categories, however, may also be observed directly, and definitional equations between them may be set down. But a "macro" analysis not going down to the "micro" phenomena will generally be very incomplete. Due to the interaction between the firms or households included in a macro group, a simple summation of plans or expectations will often be misleading. As a consequence of the general interdependence the two kinds of analysis are generally inseparable.

The methods to be used for carrying out aggregations and other statistical work belongs to the theory of statistics, which has been changing greatly during the last few years. To the same extent as our knowledge of all relevant conditions is limited, the element of chance enters in, and our knowledge consequently becomes of a stochastic character. Therefore it becomes important to determine the outside limit of the effects which the uninvestigated, "accidental" causes may have.

CHAPTER 32

UNCERTAINTY, EXPECTATION, AND PROBABILITY

UNCERTAINTY with regard to the future is partly due to the fact that external data (crops, political events, foreign prices) may be changed, partly to the fact that we do not know how other persons in the market will act. The latter kind of uncertainty disappears in a large society with perfect competition, and also in a society with central planning, in so far as one sector of the management of the economy really has full knowledge of the plans of the other sectors. We have, however a special, important kind of uncertainty where a few firms as duopolists, oligopolists,

---

[3] In *Ekonomisk Tidskrift*, No. 4, 1953, and Nos. 1–2, 1954, there has been a rather complicated discussion, Johan Åkerman versus Ragnar Bentzel and Bent Hansen. Under the catchword "aggregation" in the Index a number of cases are referred to. See also the discussion about interdependence versus one-way relations at the end of Chapter 44.

or bilateral monopolists, each pursue their own policy, and are interested in obtaining advantages at the cost of the others by tactical manoeuvres (as described in Part IV). Uncertainty for the individual firms is due to the constant appearance of surprises. These may in some cases be a result of an inability to calculate the consequences of current economic changes on the basis of facts already in existence. The appearance of new data, however, is of greater importance.

It is impossible, without being arbitrary, to decide what are internal and what are external data of economic life. This is partly a question of how we want to limit our analysis. Inventions and political events are influenced by economic conditions; but this influence, passing through personal and organizational links, cannot be predicted (at any rate, according to economic law) and is, on the whole, very uncertain. Sometimes it is possible with some degree of certainty to estimate the probability, *e.g.*, of war or other political events before they begin to have a direct effect on the economic development. In so far as a person (or a firm) succeeds in making a complete adjustment during the period before the event has direct economic consequences, the effect of surprise disappears in his case. If many try at the same time to adapt themselves in advance, they may often make adjustment difficult for each other through competing demand. We then have social effects even at the time when the expectation arises. Corresponding effects appear every time there is a change in expectations. This appears most clearly as fluctuations in the stock and commodity exchanges. For those who are interested in short-run price differences, the decisive factor is not the expectations themselves, but the changes in these. A small business group buying only a small part of the total supply of raw materials, will, in many cases be better able to adapt itself than larger economic groups which by their adjustment influence prices against themselves. The ordinary distinction between fixed and variable costs, prices, etc., indicates that the possibility of adjustment is very different.

Both expectations and plans must often be supposed to be limited in time by a certain horizon, the position of which partly depends on the greater uncertainty which exists with regard to a more remote future, and partly on the smaller degree of interest which people have in the latter. From the fact that the interests of the individual person and those of his immediate successors do not extend beyond a limited period into the future, it is impossible, however, to draw the conclusion that he does not attach any value to an asset after, say, fifty or one hundred years. The fact is that the asset can be sold or consumed before the horizon is reached, possibly in the form of a life annuity. Besides, the discounted value of an asset after so many years is so small a part of the total capital value that it is scarcely worth while to substitute a doubtful calculation for the simple capitalization for an infinite number of years. This simple form of calculation is actually applied in spite of all possibilities of deterioration in money value and transformation of the form of society.

Even if the conditions of economic life remain unchanged in a given period, it is still possible that, owing to misconceptions within certain groups, there should be a discrepancy between average expectations and the results achieved, and that this discrepancy does not show any tendency to disappear. An example of this is the constant influx to certain categories of small independent jobs in spite of constantly disappointed expectations. (Cf. below, p. 268.)

As mentioned previously, the expectations of individuals and enterprises cannot be supposed to be rational in the sense that they correspond to a complete and consistent utilization of all the facts available at the moment of action. It is, therefore, of great interest to study the actual nature and origin[1] of these expectations. They are determined by the course of events up to the present, but also to a great extent by psychological and institutional factors. A certain number of new events must occur before people realize that a change has set in. Expectations depend partly on a certain repetition of experience, partly on comprehension.[2] The conditions for prediction, therefore, are relatively favorable, even if the economic situation is not constant, if only it has some kind of regular character, *e.g.*, a long-continued trend or a comparatively regular wave movement.

Keynes,[3] who no doubt had great practical knowledge in this sphere, assumed it to be generally true that people either assume the present situation to remain unchanged in spite of past experiences as to the inconstancy of things, or that the individual takes the existing prices as a correct result of speculation concerning the future, or, finally, that the individual only takes the opinion of the majority or an average of the different prevailing opinions as the right one. In the latter case, where all support themselves on the opinion of the others, sudden changes of attitude may set in. As simple types of expectations after a certain change has occurred, *e.g.*, a rise in price, Lindahl[4] mentions (1) an unchanged continuation of the movement which is in progress, (2) unchanged continuation of the new situation, and (3) return to the old state of affairs. Hicks denotes the relation between the percentage change in the price expected by a person and the change that has actually taken place, the "elasticity of expectation".[5] According to Hicks' conception, we have in equilibrium the expected change in price equal to the actual change.

Where firms or persons make decisions on the basis of uncertain expectations as to the future, the problem is to what extent they actually make

---

[1] Hayek, "Economics and Knowledge", *Economica*, February, 1937.

[2] George Katona, "Psychological Analysis of Business Decisions", *The American Economic Review*, 1946; later: *Psychological Analysis of Economic Behaviour*, McGraw-Hill, 1951.

[3] "The General Theory of Employment", *Quarterly Journal of Economics*, February, 1937, pp. 213–15.

[4] *Studies*, p. 49.

[5] Hicks, *Value and Capital*, 1939, pp. 205, 250–51, and with regard to equilibrium p. 132.

use of probabilities, *i.e.*, is it significant to speak about probability without having a statistical basis? And do statistics suffice? The whole problem is closely connected with the question of risk, which is dealt with in Chapter 37. In some cases the different possibilities imaginable are weighted in accordance with an *a priori* conception of probability.[6] By the probability of results of a certain nature, we here understand the number of possible results divided by the total number of possibilities, in so far as the latter can be considered to have equal weight, for instance, the six possibilities in a throw of dice. Where the possibilities or the groups of possibilities under consideration cannot be presumed in advance to have equal weight, it may in certain cases be possible to give them a definite weight in proportion to their "measurable magnitudes" (cf. the probability of hitting equally near, but unequally large, areas on a target).

Whereas in the case of chance games it is possible with great certainty to use the *a priori* concept of probability, it is extremely difficult with regard to economic phenomena, where we lack corresponding uniformity. The question, then, is whether it is possible to put a concrete case on a par with experiences from a number of previous cases, to such an extent that the statistical (*a posteriori*) probabilities deduced therefrom can be transferred to the case being considered. This is made extremely difficult, partly by the fact that it is a problem of the future, and partly because most cases are of a strongly individualistic character.

It seems impossible, however, to draw any sharply defined limits between pure cases, where *a priori* probability considerations are permissible, and cases where the estimate falls outside any rational judgment. There are intermediate cases where there is room for a reasonable estimate, *i.e.*, where rational rules can be applied analogously, when corrected and supplemented in a discretionary manner.

In real life it will, as a rule, hardly be possible to get more than an approximate estimate, *e.g.*, as to the probabilities of crops, as to output with a changed method of production, as to the height of a price peak in a boom movement, which is not quite like the previous ones, as to the solvency of debtors, new inventions in the trade, establishment of competitive firms, or political events. But even in such cases, quantitative statements will have a rational meaning. One partly builds on experience and partly engages in reasoning as to differences and similarities in relation to the case under consideration. It is possible, for instance, to reason as to the placing of a case among different groups of experiences, and as to the size of the "masses" exposed. The deliberations about betting show clearly that people use *a priori* probabilities. If you meet an extreme empiricist, who asserts that the laws for a game of dice can only be found empirically, you might suggest playing a game in which he is totally

---

[6] Harald Bohr, "Om det matematiske Grundlag for Sandsynlighedsregningen", *Matematisk Tidsskrift*, A No. 1–2, 1940; Ingvar Svennilson, *Ekonomisk Planering*, Almqvist & Wiksell, Uppsala, 1938, Chap. 4; the quotation below from p. 41; H. Engberg Pedersen, "Risikofaenomenet", *Nationaløkonomisk Tidsskrift*, 1942.

inexperienced. For example, you may find that he knows very well how much he is willing to pay for 1,200 throws with a regular dodecahedron, when he can get one dollar each time a certain face turns up.

When the objection is raised against the application of the probability concept in individual cases, that in the particular case the event will either occur or not occur, and that, consequently, we cannot speak of any relative frequency, the answer must be that by indication of a probability we either refer the case to a known group of actual cases, or think of the frequency among a complete collection of equal possibilities, or possibilities with a certain relative weight. Whether we compare the case with a group of real cases or refer it to a certain collection of equal possibilities, it has only certain characteristics or symptoms in common with the whole group, since a knowledge of probability is only a partial knowledge. According to Svennilson, the practical "probability statement involves that, apart from certain attributes of the individual event, the latter is referred to a group of otherwise equal events, to which a certain theoretical probability scheme is said to be approximatively applicable. Certain data are available for our judgment. The probability statement indicates the frequency of an event with certain characteristics in the hypothetical group arising if the same data were present at the time of judging in a series of cases."

Against the application of an objective probability approach to economic events, which are often of a highly individualistic nature, it has been objected that the concept is mystic, verification being impossible, since the event, as mentioned above, either occurs or does not occur. The answer may be that there is a possibility of verification by application of the probability method in many different cases. The test may consist in the fact that business men and insurance companies with diversified risks, reckoning with probabilities and a certain dispersion of possibilities, survive in the struggle for existence. The subjective and nonverifiable probability estimates in individual cases thereby get a greater or smaller degree of verification in all cases taken together.[7]

It may be doubtful how far persons and firms actually reckon with subjective probabilities. Presumably, they often make their calculations with several different possibilities and attach a certain weight to them, which partly depends on conditions determined by a rational and neutral probability calculation, but partly also on a special valuation of security or the chance of great profit. The fact that in insurance, just as in speculation and betting, uncertain profits are reckoned at a certain discount, *i.e.,* one calculates within a certain fraction of the full amount, seems to show that probabilities are reckoned with in real life. A certain degree of equalization, in the case of great speculators and gamblers, only takes place on account of the size of their business; but probably, in the case of competition, and taken as an average, the wisest, *i.e.,* those who best understand how to reckon with probabilities, are those who earn most.

---

[7] Points of view along these lines have been set forth by Sv. Stubbe Østergaard.

Of course, in cases where knowledge of the individual circumstances is possible, this is still more profitable than reasoning about probabilities. The distinction between actual knowledge and good guesses as to probability is difficult, however.

The regularity to be found in the quantity of existing reserves, both technical and economic, seems to indicate that one has quantitatively determined ideas as to the magnitude of risk, and at the same time there is also a certain valuation of the disadvantages involved in possible losses. On the whole, we find with regard to the actual behavior, that desires for security, or other considerations, characterized by the valuation of risk-taking, already enter as determining factors, so that the actual behavior is not a pure expression of the probability estimate which, for instance, does not find a pure expression in one's willingness to bet.[8]

Where a question of an economic estimate is involved, it is possible that several people concentrate their interest, not on the mathematical expectation, nor even on the most probable case, but on one definite possibility, on which one ventures to base one's action. Further, it is possible that, instead of reckoning with the probability of bad luck, one only considers the greatest deviation in an unfavorable direction on which it is fairly reasonable to count.[9] But actually this only appears to be the first small preliminary step away from the belief in a single possibility, and in the direction of transferring the concept of dispersion from spheres in which one knows something about it to other spheres where there is reason to suppose that it also occurs.

To what extent firms actually make use of one or more possibilities and, in the latter case, how they weight them, is the great problem of actual experience, which it is difficult to solve. Whereas it is wrong to assert that complicated rational calculations are applied if the experience cannot reach further than to the "trained instincts" of business men, it is on the other hand also insufficient to content one's self with these instincts, if there may be assumed to be an essential similarity between the results of the said "instinct" and of the scientifically comprehensible, rational calculations. In this connection we may refer to the similarity which seems to exist between the actual price policy, based on estimates, and the rational price policy. (See Part IV, Chapter 61.) The belief in or the estimate of

[8] Karl Menger, "Das Unsicherheitsmoment in der Wertlehre", *Zeitschrift für Nationalökonomie*, 1934, p. 484.

[9] G. L. S. Shackle, "The Nature of the Inducement to Invest", in *Review of Economic Studies*, Oct., 1940, sets forth some rather one-sided conjectures concerning people's expectations as to business results. He imagines that one will be astonished if the results are below or above certain limits, but that within these one does not make a difference with regard to the probability. In the same number, A. G. Hart (cf. footnote 10) argues against this point of view. In his *Expectation in Economics*, (Cambridge University Press, 1949), Shackle has given a later and more detailed exposition, cf. discussion by Ralph Turvey, J. de V. Graaf, W. J. Baumol and Shackle in *Economica*, November, 1949. Cf. also the above-mentioned treatise by Engberg Pedersen on the phenomenon of risk. As to the risk concept, see further below, Chapter 37.

the dispersion of possibilities does, of course, vary greatly according to the more or less rationalist or schizofrenic nature of the individuals and the environment.

Following F. H. Knight, some authors distinguish between risk and uncertainty. Gerhard Tintner says, "Subjective risk deals with the case in which there exists a *probability distribution* of anticipations which, however, is itself known with certainty (probability one). Subjective uncertainty assumes there is an *a priori probability of the probability distributions* themselves, *i.e.*, a distribution of probability distributions."[10]

It is not only the persons and firms making economic decisions who must be presumed, to a certain extent, to make use of probabilities. In theoretical analysis, too, one has to be content with stochastic knowledge, probability knowledge, in all such cases where only part of the relevant data is known. This will often be the case owing to the heterogeneous nature of economic data and the possibility of personal influences, etc.[11]

CHAPTER 33

PLANS

ALL production which takes time, especially the employment of durable fixed plant, requires plans reaching far into an uncertain future. Expectations regarding the technical results of production, selling possibilities, prices, costs of raw materials, wages and interest are consequently important. When an enterprise is started, an investment calculation regarding expected future revenue and outlays is made, more or less conscious, and more or less detailed. Here, as in other spheres, it must be presumed that maximization of profit gives us some guidance in understanding the actual dispositions that are made by the entrepreneurs. In order to enable us to compare revenue and outlays at different times, they must be referred to the same point of time in the investment calculation, the starting-point.

---

[10] "The Theory of Choice under Subjective Risk and Uncertainty", *Econometrica*, 1941, p. 298. See also A. G. Hart, "Risk, Uncertainty, and the Unprofitability of Compound Probabilities", *Studies in Mathematical Economics in Memory of Henry Schultz*, 1942, reprinted in *Readings in The Theory of Income Distribution* (Allen & Unwin, 1950).

[11] Cf. quotation above, p. 12, Note 2, from Schams; Alexander Bilimovič, "Zur Verteidigung der Gleichgewichtsidee", *Zeitschrift für Nationalökonomie*, 1937; F. C. Mills, "On Measurements in Economics", in *The Trends of Economics*, 1924; and Trygve Haavelmo, "The Probability Approach in Econometrics", *Econometrica*, July, 1944.

This is done by discounting, using the subjective rate of interest, *i.e.*, the rate which the firm, with small marginal variations, must make use of when obtaining a loan or investing its own money. Furthermore, future amounts are calculated according to their probability and possibly corrected according to a factor of risk valuation. The estimate as to the future must be made as a sum of the estimates regarding the different possibilities that may be imagined to occur. The further one looks into the future, the more possibilities appear. It will often be impossible to consider the possibilities separately, and one may instead look at the possibility of, say, profit or volume of production falling within certain limits.[1] In a rational calculation, the sum of probabilities concerning all possibilities must be one. If the future is very uncertain, one will, when planning a plant, give it such a form that several applications or transfer of means of production to other applications are made possible. In so doing, however, some of the possible advantages of specializing are lost.[2]

At later times in the life of firms there will be occasion for constantly making new calculations paying due regard to the new conditions and the new experience with which one is faced. Then one is committed more than at the time of investment, as one has a fixed plant, an enterprise in full swing, and a series of contracts and business connections. This does not, however, preclude the possibility that temporary or permanent stoppage, expansion, restriction or change in production may appear to be profitable.[3] Just as at the time of starting the enterprise, the expected future revenue and outlays may be recalculated so as to find the momentary capital value which firms pursuing purely business aims must be assumed to maximize more or less consciously and consistently.

The aim of the firms may, however, be more complicated. Svennilson[4] points out that capitalistic firms have liquidity as a separate aim quite apart from profit. This may be taken into consideration by multiplying the neutral mathematical expectation by a valuation factor,[5] paying due regard to the degree of security involved. This is of special importance where it is not a single will that determines the dispositions of the firm, but where, for instance, managers and creditors, who are especially interested in security, exercise an influence dictated by their own personal interests. Conversely, speculative interests may tend in the direction of an increased profit at once, when it is expected that it will cause possible buyers of shares to have exaggerated expectations as to the future. Not

---

[1] With regard to details, see Ingvar Svennilson, *Ekonomisk Planering*, 1938. See Erich Schneider, "Die wirtschaftliche Lebensdauer industrieller Anlagen", *Weltwirtschaftliches Archiv*, January, 1942, and *Investering og Rente*, Nyt Nordisk Forlag, Copenhagen, 1944.

[2] Myrdal, *Prisbildningsproblemet och Föränderligheten*, Almqvist & Wiksell, Stockholm, 1927, Part III.

[3] Cf. J. M. Clark, *The Economics of Overhead Costs*, 1923, Chapter IX.

[4] Chapters 8–10.

[5] The situation is complicated if there is a different valuation of risk-taking at different times. Svennilson finds it possible that there is a relatively great interest in security at remote points of time.

only firms make plans and try to carry them through, but so, to a lesser extent do the other economical units: consumers and people who have labor, free capital, and other means of production to offer.

Just as it is important empirically to study expectations, it is also of great interest to study plans and actual dispositions. The question is to which extent a rational maximization of profit actually takes place. (Cf. Part IV, Chapters 59 and 61.) In so far as one ventures to make this assumption, it will be much easier in advance to figure out what the action of the firms will be. Otherwise it is necessary to undertake behaviorist studies of the actions of the firms. Without entering here into the problem of motives and the more or less rational realization of them, we may preliminarily take it for granted that there are plans of a certain law-directed character, and that with more or less accuracy it is possible to know what plans will result from certain given data.[6]

CHAPTER 34

EX ANTE—EX POST[1]

THUS we may expect a certain consistency in economic plans. Accordingly one speaks of considerations and calculations *ex ante* (*i.e.*, before the economic process takes place). As mentioned above, it is not only the owners of firms who have plans, but also other persons involved in economic activity, owners of means of production and consumers. Since the plans are to be found in the consciousness of human beings, it is possible for an observer to get an intuitive understanding of the plans. *Ex ante* considerations may be imagined to be divided into two stages: the expectations which are subjective, and the actual making of plans, which are capable of objective ascertainment, and which may be summed up for a number of individuals.[2] *Ex ante* analysis, as a rule, assumes simple norms of action, particularly that the firms aim at a rational maximization of profit.

The plans made *ex ante* must build on experience of actual past events and conditions and, consequently, on considerations *ex post*. These are concerned with external conditions, a sequence of events that have actually

---

[6] Cf. the discussion of this problem in Svennilson's book, pp. 16–18.
[1] Besides Myrdal (cf. Chapter 37 below) and Lindahl, *Studies in the Theory of Money and Capital*, 1939, Ohlin in *Economic Journal*, March, 1937, pp. 57–59 (cf. reprint in *Readings in Business Cycle Theories*) and Lundberg, *Studies in the Theory of Economic Expansion*, 1937.
[2] Kjeld Philip, "Betragtninger over Kvantitetsligningen", in *Nationaløkonomisk Tidsskrift*, 1943, p. 102.

occurred, and not human deliberations. Here it is a question of quantities, whereas *ex ante*, at any rate in certain cases, it is a question of schedules, *i.e.*, a mental functional relationship between, *e.g.*, price and sales. When the *ex ante* consideration is applied in the schedule sense, there is no question of saving and investment being equal or being unequal[3] unless at the same time we assume a definite rate of interest. At the second stage, when definite plans are set up a statistical summation is possible. Probably, however, the aggregated realized result will not correspond to a summation of the plans.

A consistent and within a certain sphere complete *ex post* analysis, just like a corresponding *ex ante* analysis, indicates an equilibrium in our theoretical analysis. Correct accounts are always in balance. The balance, consisting of the difference between revenue and expenditure, is entered as profit or loss. The difference between expectation and the actual sequence of events causes the unexpected profit and loss (windfall profits and losses). We may speak of a real equilibrium[4] when this difference does not appear and expectations are thus fulfilled. Thus we have equilibrium when *ex ante* is equal to *ex post*.

Plans made on the basis of expectations of the future help the individual firm (or an economic unit) to reach its goal. There is a question, however, as to what effect the anticipations and plans of several people have on the course of events, whether adjustment is not made difficult by the fact that one does not get time to take the plans of the others into consideration. If several people have simultaneously planned to carry through a certain expansion of production assuming that the others do not increase their sales, it will be impossible to realize all the plans and at the same time obtain the expected price. It may be said that a summation of the *ex ante* magnitudes, whether these be taken as quantities sold or sales curves, *i.e.*, schedules, cannot be realized.

The effect of business cycle forecasting on economic development is a problem in itself. A general confidence in the forecasting and knowledge of business cycle tendencies will change the underlying conditions which determine the course of economic development. In favorable cases the result may be a smoothing down of business cycles, in unfavorable cases less regular and less foreseeable fluctuations. Morgenstern, who has dealt with the effect of the forecast on its own underlying elements, also mentions the impossibility of a complete forecast without a revolutionary change taking place. If we knew, for instance, that a certain invention would be made in twenty years, it would already be made at the present moment. Insurance and many other provisions for security would disappear. The

---

[3] Tinbergen (in accordance with the above-mentioned article by Ohlin, p. 423), "Some Problems in Explanation of Interest Rates", *Quarterly Journal of Economics*, May, 1947, p. 406; Lawrence Klein, *The Keynesian Revolution*, New York, 1947.
[4] As mentioned above, Hicks, among others, speaks of an equilibrium when expectations are fulfilled, *Value*, p. 132. Cf. Svend Laursen in *Nationaløkonomisk Tidsskrift*, 1938, pp. 385-86.

situation in bilateral monopoly would be quite different if the parties had full knowledge of each others' condition.

Where the action of individuals or firms is mutually dependent on one another, they will only obtain knowledge of the reactions and assumptions of the others by a gradual adjustment, but the path of adjustment will have permanent consequences for the later development. Moreover, such a high degree of forecasting as required by Morgenstern is not necessary in order to bring about a real economic equilibrium. It is enough that the individuals consider their anticipations of the future as certain and that the actions carried through on the basis of the anticipations lead to realization of the expectations.[5]

Besides examining the *ex ante* and *ex post* considerations of economic units, the economists themselves apply corresponding considerations. By alternatively investigating the plans, on the basis of given data, and the result of their realization in a certain period, including the effect of this result on data at the beginning of the next period, we arrive at a deductive sequence analysis, which will be dealt with in the next chapter. It may apply to individual firms as well as to whole communities. If the analysis is concerned with an actual current development, there will be the possibility of an empirical renewal of data, gradually as new experiences occur. These apply to current research in economic development, which at the same time forms new pictures of reality and revises its basic theory.

CHAPTER 35

SEQUENCE ANALYSIS

IF we take the course of time into consideration, it may be appropriate to follow the events in their chronological sequence and see how the events in the first period form the basis for those in the following.

In accordance with the aim of the investigation, different distances in time and, consequently, also different possible divisions into periods, become most practical. In some cases it is possible to use a continuous analysis without any fixed division into periods. We may, for instance, if we look at the way in which a stock of goods is constantly determined by

---

[5] Oskar Morgenstern, "Vollkommene Voraussicht und wirtschaftliches Gleichgewicht", *Zeitschrift für Nationalökonomie*, 1935. Regarding Morgenstern's later treatment of such problems in collaboration with Neumann, see Chapter 57; Klas Böök, "Om ekonomiska Prognoser", *Ekonomisk Tidskrift*, 1936; Lindahl, *Studies*, p. 285 below, "The real import of the assumption in question is, therefore, that individuals' ideas concerning the future are such that their actions bring about exactly the conditions which they anticipated"; Alfred Cowles 3rd, "Can Stock Market Forecasters Forecast?" *Econometrica*, July, 1933.

an initial stock and the current increase and decrease (the integral of the difference between increase and decrease), refer to the figure on p. 150. In many cases, however, a practical simplification occurs if we reckon with periods given in advance with a certain uniformity within each of them, which may be suddenly changed by the transition to a new period. We shall here consider a corresponding deductive sequence analysis.

A sequence analysis with division into periods can be applied to many subjects, as *e.g.*, in the theory of business cycles, in capital theory, in the theory of duopoly, and the theory of bilateral monopoly, where we consider how the steps taken by one party affect the other party, and finally in the science of population. In those cases where the changes are really taking place discontinuously in sharply divided stages, the method used may be an exact one, but in cases where the changes are really continuous, it must be regarded as merely an illustration of a movement which can be described more completely and exactly by continuous formulae or time curves. By making the periods very small, there is, moreover, the possibility of reverting to the exact continuous approach. In economic analysis, however, the use of a fixed period corresponding to an important time-consuming process will often be practical. The most usual thing is, then, to base a division into periods, for the individual firm or for all firms and economic units, on the settling up of accounts and the consequent revision of plans, assuming that this periodic settlement and new orientation takes place at the same time for all.

The assumption made for the division into periods: that the plans and the fixing of prices and other decisions resulting therefrom are not changed continuously is not only a simplification, but is to a very large extent in harmony with real life. For one thing, this is due to the fact that the results of one's own business enterprise and partly also the observation of the surrounding world through business accounts, statistics and other published material as well as the formation of plans only takes place at certain intervals. From the moment of observation, a certain time must elapse as a rule before new plans are ready and can be put into operation. To this it must be added that the trouble, expense, and disruption of the market or disturbance of the internal organization of the firm will in many cases make the firm postpone the carrying through of a changed sales or production policy until the motive becomes strong enough or perhaps until a certain time has passed since the last change. Within a certain short period: a day, a week, a month, or perhaps a year, one may, therefore, as a first approximation, assume that firms will continue their old plans, even if certain shifts in external conditions take place within the period.

The theory of the interplay between *ex ante–ex post* calculations has of late years been developed especially by Swedish economists. Bertil Ohlin[1]

[1] "Some Notes on the Stockholm Theory of Savings and Investment", *Economic Journal*, March, 1937, reprinted in *Readings in Business Cycle Theory*, 1944. Tord Palander, "On the Concepts and Methods of the Stockholm School", *International Economic Papers*, 1953.

gives the following characteristics of the "Stockholm Theory of Processes of Contraction and Expansion", meaning thereby the analysis of changes in employment, output and prices. Firstly, in the discussion of special partial processes, attention is concentrated on the reaction of the economic system as a whole, *i.e.*, possible influences on the total volume of output and monetary demand. Monetary theory is, therefore, made a part of the general price theory. Secondly, care is taken to state clearly when concepts like income and savings refer to plans and expectations for the future and when they are concerned with a period that is already finished. Thirdly, a period method of analysis is used. Fourthly, as in Hawtrey's and Keynes' theories, attention is concentrated on the action of the individual entrepreneurs or consumers, and not much is said about what this involves with regard to the movements of the currency units. Fifthly, it has been found that the reasoning to be precise enough must be casuistic. Wide use is, therefore, made of "type models" like Wicksell's cumulative process. For the construction of such models, simplifying assumptions are necessary. Hence each of them throws light on only one aspect of the processes of expansion or concentration.

On the basis of experience of earlier periods, the firms and persons make plans for the next period within which they accordingly pursue a certain policy, keeping certain prices unchanged, for instance, or continuing the present rate of production or consumption to a certain extent. Plans and external data together bring about definite results which can be determined *ex post*, *i.e.*, at the end of the period. These results, *e.g.*, profits obtained or stocks accumulated, now enter as data in the determination of plans (*ex ante*) for the following period, etc. The costs of production paid during a certain period, for instance, are considered as income in the ensuing period. The individual persons have at the beginning of the period a definite program with regard to the use of the income, a program which they are supposed to pursue in the period without revision because of the results of other people's actions or external events. What the individual may achieve, however, does not depend on himself alone. His plan may be, for instance, to sell at a certain price or buy for a definite amount. The quantity in these cases must depend on the condition of the market.

The whole development through a series of periods may be obtained by deduction when we know: (1) the plans in the initial stage; (2) the way in which the economic units will change their plans under different conditions; and (3) the external data which are important for the results obtained as well as for future changes in the plans.[2] Lindahl speaks about "the disequilibrium method".

We shall here mention two examples explaining ordinary business cycle movements on the basis of a few simplified assumptions. With regard to the formation of price in the case of a single commodity, readers are referred to Frisch's example in Chapter 27, concerning the effect

[2] Lindahl, *Studies*, p. 51; cf. pp. 49 and 50 with regard to the length of periods, and the disequilibrium method, p. 60.

N

of expectations on the demand for coke, as well as to the "cobweb case" in Chapter 36. The price policy interplay between several firms is dealt with in Part IV, Chapter 50. In the coke example we proceeded from week to week, the demand of each week being determined by stocks which again were a result of the previous week's purchases in relation to the price of the week.

TABLE 5[3]

	Previous period's expenditure for consumption	New expenditure for consumption thus created	Demand for consumption created by public investment	Total expenditure for consumption
Initial stage 0	(1,000)	(720)	(280)	1,000
Period No. 1	1,000	720	350	1,070
„ „ 2	1,070	770	350	1,120
„ „ 3	1,120	806	350	1,156
„ „ 4	1,156	832	350	1,182
„ „ 5	1,182	851	350	1,201
„ „ 6	1,201	865	350	1,215
„ „ 7	1,215	875	350	1,225
Final Stage	1,250	900	350	1,250

Table 5 gives the first of Lundberg's sequence models[3] in a simplified form. Our preliminary starting-point is an amount of 1,000 from period 0, which is used for consumption in period 1. We assume that 72 per cent of the previous period's expenditure for consumption will be the consumption during the ensuing period, whereas 28 per cent are either costs which do not create fresh consumption for the time being, or income which one desires to save during the period. In addition, in period No. 1 and the ensuing periods, public investment takes place, creating fresh demand of 350 units for producers. This is assumed, though, not to influence the future conditions of production, *e.g.*, certain unproductive public works. In the initial period, the condition for static equilibrium was a public investment of 280. We shall not here comment on the very abstract economic assumptions and the results of the table. What is of most interest to us in this connection is to see how the total expenditure for consumption created in one period forms the basis of the expenditure of the next period. The last column of the table is a result (*ex post*) of the action of many persons as well as external conditions in the period.

[3] Erik Lundberg, *Studies in the Theory of Economic Expansion*, Norstedt & Søner, 1937, Table 1 ,p. 194. The initial equilibrium has been added.

If the figures of the last column are denoted by C, this means that C_n, *i.e.*, total expenditure in period No. n, enters into an equation which determines the corresponding consumption in the ensuing period, C_{n+1}. Demand for consumption created by public investment was 350, as indicated in the table above.

$$C_{n+1} = C_n \frac{72}{100} + 350 \qquad C_{n+1} = C_n + (350 - \frac{28}{100} C_n)$$

This equation, which is dynamic since it concerns conditions at various points of time, explains why we get a movement rising with decreasing velocity. In each period 350 is added, at the same time as the nonconsumed part of income increases as a result of a rising C until it becomes equal to 350, where a stationary equilibrium is reached, so that C_n becomes equal to C_{n+1}.[4]

Even in the simple case dealt with here the assumptions may be changed in many ways, *e.g.*, by varying investment, possibly quite irregularly, or, instead of having constantly 72 per cent and 350 by using functions of time or of C or, *e.g.*, letting C_n be partly dependent on C_{n-2}. In real life it is probable that movements in expenditures, prices or employment entail changed constants.

Lundberg has other examples where the rising movement is followed by a declining movement, and where, consequently, we have an explanation of a wave movement. Thus it is possible to set up other models applying to investment in stocks of consumers' goods, the quantity of which is influenced by investment and change in consumption, or models for investment in fixed capital used in the production of consumers' goods and, therefore, influenced by the future rate of consumption. In the production for stocks of goods, speculation occurs. In the production of means of production (*e.g.*, houses), a rise in consumption, in accordance with the acceleration principle, involves a multiple expansion of investment. A stop in the increase, on the other hand, leads to a complete stop in investment, apart from upkeep, at the same time as a large planned saving is left from the previous period of investment. Highly varying forms of movement may appear by the combination of the multiplier and the acceleration principles. As a consequence of different constants, the same simple system of formulae might result in an asymtotic movement, damped, constant, or explosive cycles, or an infinitely increasing movement.[5]

---

[4] The final stationary equilibrium (which is reached in accordance with the multiplier theory, cf. Lundberg, p. 195) is found from the equation by putting $C_n = C_{n+1}$ and considering this quantity as unknown. The stationary equilibrium, corresponding to the initial consumption of 1,000, is to be found by putting $C_n = C_{n+1} = 1,000$, and here taking the investment as unknown instead of constantly being 350.

[5] Paul Samuelson, "Interaction between Multiplier and Acceleration Principles", *Readings in Business Cycle Theory* (and *Review of Economics and Statistics*, 1939).

Tinbergen[6] has an example where, in a very understandable way, we get a cyclical movement. It is assumed that the income of the period is determined in the following way by the income of the two preceding periods. Income is assumed to be equal to total expenditure, equal to consumption plus investment.

$$Y_t = 1 \cdot 6 \cdot Y_{t-1} - Y_{t-2} + 4.$$

The negative term may be explained by the rise in income $(Y_{t-1} - Y_{t-2})$ being partially determining for the income of the period, since it is possible to write

$$Y_t = 0 \cdot 6 Y_{t-1} + 4 + (Y_{t-1} - Y_{t-2}),$$

i.e., the income of the period is partially dependent on the income of the previous period, partially constant. To this result must be added, however, the increase in income from the previous period, or the decrease deducted. The constant term in the formula, in connection with Y_{t-1} and Y_{t-2} together having a weight of less than 1, indicates that part of the purchasing power is constant and independent of the income of previous years. The

TABLE 6

	Income 2 periods before (Y_{t-2})	Income 1 period before (Y_{t-1})	Constant (K)	Income in period (Y_t)	Deviation from initial equilibrium
Stationary equilibrium	10	10	4	10	0
Period 1	10	10	5	11	$+1 \cdot 0$
,, 2	10	11	4	11·6	$+1 \cdot 6$
,, 3	11	11·6	4	11·56	$+1 \cdot 56$
,, 4	11·6	11·56	4	10·9	$+0 \cdot 9$
,, 5	11·56	10·9	4	9·9	$-0 \cdot 1$
,, 6	10·9	9·9	4	8·9	$-1 \cdot 1$
,, 7	9·9	8·9	4	8·4	$-1 \cdot 6$
,, 8	8·9	8·4	4	8·5	$-1 \cdot 5$
,, 9	8·4	8·5	4	9·2	$-0 \cdot 8$
,, 10	8·5	9·2	4	10·2	$+0 \cdot 2$
,, 11	9·2	10·2	4	11·1	$+1 \cdot 1$

$$Y_t = 1 \cdot 6 Y_{t-1} - Y_{t-2} + K; \quad K = 4 \text{ except in period } 1 = 5$$

[6] *The Review of Economic Studies*, February, 1940, pp. 83–84, reprinted in *Readings in Business Cycle Theory*. A more detailed explanation and motivation of a similar example is to be found in Tinbergen's *Statistical Testing of Business-cycle Theories, II, Business Cycles in U.S.A., 1919–32*, League of Nations, 1939, pp. 15–18. A theoretical discussion of similar cases is to be found in Tinbergen, *Econometrics*, § 41, cf. § 12.

first line of the table indicates a stationary equilibrium. What now happens is that in a single period, No. 1 in the table, an extra purchasing power of 1 is added, *i.e.*, 10 per cent of the income in the stationary initial equilibrium.[7] Hereby a rising movement is started, since an increase in Y_{t-1} precedes the increase in Y_{t-2} and, moreover, according to the formula, has a greater weight. The rise, however, is decreasing since the fact that the increase gradually reaches Y_{t-2} has a negative effect, and the constant term at the same time prevents a great change in the level. By allowing Y_{t-2} to approach Y_{t-1} closely, $(Y_{t-1} - Y_{t-2})$ is diminished greatly. Consequently, the whole quantity diminishes so that a decrease sets in. This is intensified later on by a rising negative value for $(Y_{t-1} - Y_{t-2})$. But this, too, is stopped, for reasons similar to those that prevailed in the rise.

Besides the theoretical examples mentioned here, we refer readers to the use of a sequence analysis when, according to the multiplier theory, one traces through payments from one group of persons to another group of persons, and when, according to the acceleration principle, one follows the stages in the chain of production.[8]

As may be seen from the above discussion, sequence analyses are of many different types and are applicable to many different problems. In many cases, *ex ante–ex post* calculations will play a decisive part, because the plans at the beginning of each stage depend on accounts of the results from the previous stage, etc. In other cases, plans and action are unchanged through all periods, and it is only stocks or other external phenomena which we account for periodically, by the theoretical analysis.

By sequence analyses it is possible, by means of a series of static analyses taken together, to obtain a dynamic analysis. The method is applicable when certain phenomena move so much more slowly than others, that a complete adjustment of the latter is imaginable without a change in the former. The slowly moving phenomena are preliminarily taken as data. The method is also applicable, when one assumes a discontinuous alternating reaction from two economic units. To maintain that sequence analysis is static, is just as wrong as saying that a staircase is horizontal, because all the steps are so. The use of a number of static analyses makes the work simpler, but in principle, there is nothing to prevent one from

---

[7] Constant 4 of the formula is temporarily increased to 5 in this period. K in the stationary initial equilibrium was found by putting $Y_t = Y_{t-1} = Y_{t-2} = 10$.

[8] As a good example of the influence of increases in accordance with the acceleration principle in the theory of business cycles, readers may be referred to Gustav Åkerman's numerical example of the development of the motorcar industry in the U.S.A. in the twenties. The example shows how a reduction in costs leads to a comparatively short-lived period of development for durable commodities like motorcars. Something similar applies to plants for the production of nondurable consumers' goods, *e.g.*, plants for the manufacture of artificial silk. The stop in expansion entails a decrease in production. The expansion is distributed over a number of years, however, because it does not pay to defray the cost of the fixed plant (much too great in the long run) that would be required if the market was to be satisfied quickly, in accordance with the new and cheaper methods of production. The result is a more limited overcapacity after the expansion of production in the period of transition. "Om konjunkturväkslingarnas nödvändighet" in *Ekonomisk Tidskrift*, 1932.

using a continuous dynamic method, such as a solution of equations where the distances in time are also considered to be continuously variable.

An important problem is to what extent it is possible to use sequence analysis or whether the economic quantities must be treated as inter-dependent and simultaneous. In statistical demand analysis this is a problem of using the ordinary method of regression or a system of equations *à la* Haavelmo. In most cases the behavior of an individual or a firm in each moment—and consequently the development over time—can be explained by dynamic sequence analysis, taking the behavior of other subjects as given. In explanation of a static equilibrium the interplay between several subjects has to be explained, however, as simultaneous and interdependent. This applies also to a certain extent to statistical time series and similar observations if periods of some length or the aggregates of the behavior of several individuals is considered; cf. the end of Chapter 44.[9]

CHAPTER 36

THE COBWEB CASE

IN a partial static analysis, it is assumed that with free competition there is a supply curve and a demand curve for a commodity, and that at each moment price and quantity are determined by intersection of these curves. Supply and demand may, however, in real life react with unequal speed and in different ways.[1] We now assume, what is probably true, that demand in any period corresponds to the current price, while the quantity offered reacts more slowly and is dependent on the price of the previous period.

The figure opposite illustrates the much-discussed "cobweb case",[2] which requires rather special assumptions. The original demand curve (D) (D) is imagined to be suddenly replaced by the new DD. This means that the buyers now have to pay the price p_2 for the unchanged quantity produced, x_1. For the time being, the new demand curve does not cause an increase in the quantity sold, since the quantity supplied is not increased until the

[9] Ragnar Bentzel and Bent Hansen, "Om Simultanitet", *Ekonomisk Tidskrift*. June 1953 and their essentially favorable review of Herman Wold's *Demand Analysis*, *ibid*.
    [1] Rosenstein-Rodan, "The Role of Time in Economic Theory", *Economica*, February, 1934, p. 89; cf. what Lindahl says about the offer of a price and the other party's later acceptance of it as separate actions, *Studies*, p. 60.
    [2] Kaldor, *Review of Economic Studies*, 1934, pp. 133–36; Tinbergen, *Econometrica*, January, 1934, pp. 31–34.

new higher price has been a reality for some time and has created a belief in the mind of the seller that it will also prevail in the future. In accordance with this belief, production is expanded up to x_3, corresponding to

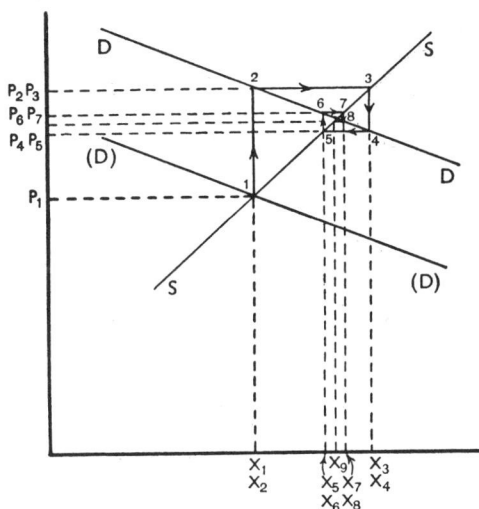

Fig. 17. The Cobweb Case

$p_3 = p_2$ on the supply curve. The quantity x_3, which will now be produced for some time, cannot be sold at a higher price than p_4, however, and apart from a few purchases on the part of the most eager demanders, sales only take place at this price. The sellers now adapt themselves to this low price, p_4, and in accordance with the supply curve, restrict production to x_5, which, owing to competition between buyers, according to the demand curve, is sold at a price of p_6, etc.

As will be seen, demand price in the present case is immediately adjusted to the quantity supplied. Supply, on the other hand, undergoes a discontinuous adjustment, starting when a price has been in force so long that a belief in its continuation has been created. The explanation may also be that time is required for a change in production. So long as one has a given production, no adjustment of the supply price takes place, but one takes the price corresponding to demand at the given quantity. The most characteristic feature of the case is the slow, discontinuous reaction of supply.

The pure case, however, is not probable in a market with many buyers and sellers. If the path from point 1 of the figure, for instance, to point 2 takes a certain time, supply will begin to react. Even if sellers are willing to produce x_3 at the price p_2, it may as a rule be improbable that they immediately should be willing and able to expand so greatly. It also appears improbable that they should really believe they could sell the large production at the same high price as the quantity x_1. Similarly, even limited foresight will prevent them from reducing the quantity to x_5, even if actually the price has temporarily fallen to p_4. If the assumption of discontinuous and alternating reaction is abandoned, smaller fluctuations may be expected, as well as a turning of the perpendicular and horizontal directions of movement towards the point of equilibrium, *i.e.*, a more rounded spiral movement with a more rapid tendency towards final equilibrium.

If, however, we confine ourselves to the pure cobweb case with alternating reactions of demand and supply, in accordance with the figure, the movement will have a different course according to the slope of the curves. If the supply curve as in the figure has the steeper slope (*i.e.*, is least elastic in the point of intersection) we get a spiral movement towards the point of equilibrium. In the opposite case, the spiral will have a movement away from its own center. And if they are equally steep, we have a constant circling round the point.

Time curves for price and quantity will have decreasing, increasing, and constant fluctuations respectively, and opposite direction of movement for price and quantity. The situation will be modified when the curves are not rectilinear, as in the figure. If the supply curve is first comparatively flat and later on steeper than the demand curve, a small initial shock will cause a movement away from the center, first with increasing and later with decreasing rapidity. The movement stops, however, when we reach a rectangular frame where the slope of the line connecting the two corners of the cobweb on the supply curve is equal to the slope of the corresponding part of the demand curve. In other words, one ends in a kind of cyclical movement with constant amplitude. If the initial shock leads beyond the frame, the movement will tend back towards this.[3]

Finally, one may consider the different speed with which the adjustment takes place. A greater speed of adjustment for demand has the same effect as if the demand curve were flatter (*i.e.*, a greater change in quantity per unit of time) and facilitates the movement towards the point of equilibrium.

If the result, as mentioned above, is that we have constantly increasing fluctuations, an "explosion"[4] of the system must occur in the end. (Otherwise price or quantity will end by becoming negative.) This means that changes in accordance with the chosen assumptions cannot continue but that the assumptions regarding the structure of the society or market in question, must be changed in some way or other. In real life, it must always be expected that such a change will take place as soon as increasing fluctuations reach a certain size. The necessity of some definite kind of transformation, *e.g.*, a social revolution, cannot of course be proved by

---

[3] Paul Samuelson, "Dynamic Process Analysis", pp. 368 ff., in *Survey of Contemporary Economics*, Vol. I, 1948.

[4] Emil Lederer, "Hindringerne for en Konjunkturopgang", *Nationaløkonomisk Tidsskrift*, 1933, p. 42.

means of the cobweb theory. Long before that the curves will have changed. *Ceteris paribus* assumptions, which are a necessary condition of every simple analysis, will as a rule only be tenable within rather narrow limits.

In real life there are a number of markets with fluctuations like those of the cobweb case and with a spiral direction as in the figure. We are dealing here with those types of products which have a comparatively long period of production. Therefore, the effect on quantity of a change in price does not appear until after a time, and extremely violent changes in the volume of production must be the result if all producers, when starting new production, expect to obtain the prices of the moment. In this connection, we may refer to the "corn-hog cycles" and the corresponding fluctuations for perennial plants like rubber and coffee and, to a certain extent, to the annual crops and to fluctuations in house building. If commodities which form a considerable part of the total national income are involved, the general state of economic activity is influenced. Information about new production already started as well as about earlier market and demand conditions may contribute to creating the correct expectations and thus tend to dampen the fluctuations.

CHAPTER 37

RISK, GAIN AND LOSS

WE shall here deal further with the problem of how uncertainty affects both planning and the results obtained, and after a discussion of the risk problem based on Myrdal's exposition[1] we shall consider the close connection between the conditions of risk at planning on one hand, and the gains and losses obtained on the other hand.

In Chapters 32–34 above we spoke of expectations. In this connection there are two problems: (1) the magnitude of the mathematical expectation = the individual possibilities, multiplied by their probability—and (2) the question of the dispersion of the possibilities over the range of more or less favorable cases. No doubt people, in using the term "risk",

---

[1] *Prisbildningsproblemet och Föränderligheten*, Almqvist & Wicksell, Stockholm, 1927. With regard to objective risk, see p. 98, cf. p. 103, market vacua, pp. 121–22, cf. p. 46, special ability to invest, pp. 127–28, favorable credit conditions or own capital, pp. 129 ff., the subjective conception, pp. 94 ff., and pp. 183 ff., valuation, pp. 146 ff., and the influence of these conditions on entrepreneurial profits, pp. 181 ff., removal loss, etc., pp. 74–75 and 86–91. For criticism of Myrdal, see H. Engberg Pedersen, "Risikofaenomenet", *Nationaløkonomisk Tidsskrift*, 1942.

generally think of the magnitude of the danger of an unfavorable result; but it is uncertain whether one wants to measure the risk in terms of the magnitude or probability of the potential damage, or the product of two such quantities, or more complicated expressions of dispersion over various sizes of potential damage. The risk of the effects of a definite unfavorable outcome may thus, *inter alia*, be expressed in the same way as an expectation. If the damage can only have one magnitude, the expectation is n.p, where n is the magnitude of the damage, and p the probability of its occurrence. If there are several possibilities, it will be a sum of such quantities. When Myrdal speaks of risk, he consequently thinks of the expectation of an unfavorable result, or the whole expectation as to the result, whatever it may turn out to be, *i.e.*, the chance of success with the opposite sign. Risk calculated in this way is expressed in dollars and cents. If we are concerned with giving a general measure of the dispersion, especially the probable or expected size of the unfavorable deviations, it is reasonable, where the rules of the probability calculus can be applied, to look at the standard deviation ($\sqrt{npq}$, where q $= 1 - $ p), or, to consider for instance three times the standard deviation, if one is interested in practically complete security against unfavorable deviations. There is scarcely any chance of a more unfavorable result.

In investment calculations and other plans made by firms or other economic units, we have, according to Myrdal:

(1) External risk-determining conditions, "the objective risk", to which corresponds the objectively correct expectation;

(2) the subjective estimate;

(3) the valuation of disadvantages or advantages of insecurity itself.

Each of these will be discussed below.

(1) The possibilities of gain and loss are not equal for all. This is due to the unequal situation of the firms with regard to location and type of industry, their unequal size and need of entrepreneurial capital and abilities in relation to the limited number of persons who have them. A person who has such combinations of capital and abilities as are most in demand, and who is "in the know", *i.e.*, who has knowledge of conditions at the decisive time and has a possibility of entering the industry, is in a favorable position. The difference in chances of success do not only appear in the case of possible new investments, but also for the owners of firms with respect to possibilities of doing business at a later date. Something similar applies to a certain extent to persons who dispose of their own labor or loanable capital, or who as consumers possess more or less favorable opportunities of purchasing the goods or services. If we are concerned with the entrepreneur's decisions, Myrdal speaks of "market vacua" ("Prisbildningsvacuer"), which yield a profit in the investment calculation. This provides a basis for an issue of shares at a price above the costs paid by the founders. Besides a greatly differentiated demand for entrepreneurs of different types, other factors are of importance, such as a limitation in the opportunities of education, lack of correspondence between the need

of capital for investment and the distribution of private fortunes, as well as personal connections, which often increase these *ex ante* chances for favorably located entrepreneurs. The special opportunities which are dependent on the demand for entrepreneurs can scarcely be separated from conditions on the supply side.

It may be said that persons who have special abilities for favorable investment (*i.e.*, at a small risk and with great chance of success) obtain a special investment profit. It may also be asserted that a certain wage is earned by the investment. What is one thing and what is the other may be extremely difficult to decide in the "mixed game of skill and chance" of real life.

As a third circumstance, Myrdal mentions the unequal ability to obtain credit, since there is no free mobility of capital, but the lenders try to find the safest investments and in the case of individual borrowers generally assume decreasing security according as the loans rise in proportion to the firm's own assets. Further, the mobility of capital is limited locally, or depending on the industry; often, too, by requirements of a certain amount of personal knowledge, and by the possibility of controlling the debtor. Thus people living in localities with large amounts of capital to be loaned, who know the lenders personally or have a specially confidence-inspiring appearance, will have an advantage. It is advantageous to give the lenders the impression that the risk is small. Uncertainty regarding the debtor's energy and honesty make creditors charge a certain compensation for the personal risk, which is especially unsatisfactory for those having more than the average amount of honesty and conscientiousness—especially if they squint, stutter, or have other qualities likely to weaken people's confidence in them. The person who has possibilities of investing his own capital in his own firm thus has an advantage corresponding to the compensation for the personal risk of lending. The circumstances here dealt with may be without importance in well-organized markets.

(2) Neutral observers of a great number of cases often agree that there may be an exaggerated optimism in a boom period, an exaggerated pessimism in a period of depression, or a permanent tendency to an exaggerated optimism concerning the entry into certain lines of business. It seems reasonable here to speak of a discrepancy between objective risk and the subjective estimate of risk of the entrepreneurs in question.

We have referred to expectations above. The expectations of the individual person must, of course, be characterized by his limited knowledge and often limited ability to draw conclusions. As a rule, estimates are made which cannot be made according to simple rational rules.[2] Thus feelings may often exercise a disturbing influence on perception itself and give it an optimistic or a pessimistic color. An emotional self-confidence

---

[2] Myrdal (p. 109), as opposed to Knight's treatment of business risks as non-measurable, emphasizes the difference between a more or less approximate and a more or less rational estimate.

is often evident. It is especially probable that exaggerated optimism is preponderant, because the most optimistic persons take the initiative and are especially active in their most optimistic moments. In boom periods optimism becomes a mass movement, which vents itself in activity. The pessimists, however, are not completely excluded; but they only step in where the chances of success are particularly good. Their favorable results, as compared with expectations, will probably bring them into possession of means which they will later on be forced to invest, and so they will scarcely be worse off than the optimists in the struggle for existence.

Later experience, of course, helps to correct wrong estimates. This correction must, however, be assumed to have a very imperfect effect, partly owing to the constant changes and the complexity of the markets, and partly owing to the inclination of the firms to conceal the results obtained. The firms have opposing interests in this case on the one hand towards possible competitors, their own workers and shareholders, customers and suppliers, as well as taxing and regulating public authorities, and on the other hand towards creditors, who will in many instances also be suppliers. A constant entry from outside over long periods to trades with abnormally low profits, *e.g.*, small retail business, may very well take place, in spite of unfavorable experiences and frequent bankruptcies.

Even if the estimate is correct, the result may in the individual case very well be both greater and smaller than the estimated expectation, which is concerned with the probability of certain events happening or not happening, *i.e.*, the average result in a number of imaginary or real cases.

(3) Whereas the "estimate" concerns the contents of one's belief with regard to the prospects (measured in dollars), the valuation (in the special sense which Myrdal gives to the word) concerns the greater or smaller subjective value which one attaches to an uncertain expectation of gain or loss. The rule is that the discomfort of the uncertainty itself and the lower valuation of a marginal amount of a larger income, according to the marginal utility theory as applied in favor of insurance and against gambling, leads to uncertain chances of profit being valued according to a factor of valuation below 1, and risk of loss being valued (negatively) according to a factor above 1. The indirect losses resulting from a stoppage give further motivation for fairly stable conditions of production and income. On the other hand, the pleasures of gambling and dreams founded on the possibility of great gain, have effects in the opposite direction. In the case of a lottery, the lack of ability to understand how small the chance of profit is, in view of the publicity and the detailed description of winners in the press, is no doubt decisive. (Cf. Part II, Chapter 19.) As a mere exception, especially when it is a case of "everything or nothing", a discontinuity in wants or in the possibilities of trade may cause a large amount to have a disproportionately high subjective value. If the

valuation does not lead to a correction of the probability, such as it is conceived, we speak of a neutral valuation.[3]

It is possible that in many cases one does not form a more precise idea, independent of the valuation, but immediately proceeds to a calculation in which one reckons with having certain desirable claims of security covered. One calculates with a "sufficient" margin of security. The determination of the sacrifice one is willing to make in return for security must, however, consciously or unconsciously, contain a valuation of risk and some idea of the order of magnitude of the probability. Even if one does not take account of a series of possibilities with the corresponding estimated probabilities, the calculation still assumes a number of alternatives in so far as one takes account of the possibility that things may go wrong.

We shall now see how the above-mentioned conditions with regard to the expectations and risk of planning affect the gains and losses obtained. If a person finds a particularly favorable opportunity for new investment or, in general, of doing business (market vacuum), gain will appear in the calculations. Something similar applies to the person who has a special opportunity for obtaining credit, or on account of his own capital can save the addition to the rate of interest which must be paid for personal risk, as well as to the person who has a special ability to invest at a low risk, if we do not prefer to call this kind of profit a wage obtained for work of a special kind.

These things, as already mentioned, enter into the calculations as gain and the same is the case with the addition or reduction which people are willing to accept because they value insecurity in an unneutral way. In the usual case where people dislike risk, it is one of the conditions of doing business that the disadvantage involved is expected to be covered and, consequently, it is covered in the calculations. These circumstances (Nos. 1 and 3 above) have a cumulative effect. The advantage of investing in a "market vacuum" may thus, completely or partially, neutralize the effect of an unfavorable valuation of risk.

The question of the correctness of the estimate (No. 2) is on quite a different level, because the calculation is determined by the estimate, and so cannot contain any correction of a possible mistaken judgment. The correction, however, comes afterwards in the comparison of the calculations and the "average result", the element of chance being disregarded.

[3] Karl Menger, "Das Unsicherheitsmoment in der Wertlehre", *Zeitschrift für Nationalökonomie*, 1934, points 8–10, an interesting statement of the valuation of risk is to be found. This varies greatly, among other things, according to the wants of the individual persons. Besides income and wealth, an independent importance is attached to the magnitude of the probability, very small probabilities of profit being undervalued, whereas certain intermediate probabilities are overvalued (cf. the tendency to lottery playing). Very large probabilities, again, according to the marginal utility consideration, are undervalued (*i.e.*, the corresponding risk of loss is overvalued). It is a question of psychological regularities which cannot be expressed in simple, uniform formulae. A closer study must be made empirically, by asking a number of persons how much they will give for a chance, while probability and amounts are varied.

This is, by the way, extremely difficult in real life, because it is impossible to decide whether it is the average that has been misjudged, or whether the individual case is a non-foreseeable deviation therefrom.

Finally, no doubt very considerable gains and losses come to the individual persons from causes that cannot be foreseen and which correspond to the deviation between their actual result and the result that should have been reached, if it had been in correspondence with the "correct" estimate of the average results. These "chance" gains and losses must be equally great for a sufficiently large group of uniform cases.

Gains and losses depend on differences between *ex ante* calculations and *ex post* results. They may have the character of income gains or losses, *i.e.*, unexpected changes in payment to productive services, or capital gains or losses. The latter are changes in the value of wealth which must usually be assumed to take place or at any rate to be established suddenly at certain points of time (cf. below, p. 198).

Myrdal mentions that, among other things, changes in the prices of the products of a firm give rise to gains and losses because, when the change takes place, the means of production are tied up in a definite form and in a definite firm, so that influx and egress cannot take place without a certain cost. When there are too many and too large firms in an industry, which is less remunerative after the change takes place, and when the opportunity of leaving the industry is limited, we shall have "losses in case of egress". In the same way we have "profit in case of influx" in trades where revenue is rising because there is difficulty in quick expansion and the entry of new competitors. As Myrdal says, "The very fact that the undertakings are constructed on the assumption of definite relations between the prices of the different means of production and between these prices and the rate of interest, is in itself a cause of loss to the entrepreneur with each change in price. It is only in exceptional cases that the undertakings will have an optimum composition or localization from the point of view of the new price conditions (inoptimum loss). Technical progress has a similar result. Every technical improvement, except with certain unusual assumptions, has the effect that the old undertakings have an inoptimum composition (losses due to obsolescence)."[4]

CHAPTER 38

THE POSITION OF THE ENTREPRENEUR

WHEREAS labor and other productive services bought by the firms are generally paid according to a previously determined price, the income of the entrepreneur is the residual which is left, out of the gross revenue of the firm after the others have received their payment. The income of

[4] pp. 88–89.

the entrepreneur thus arises in a special way. Formally and from an accounting point of view, it is a residual, which in the short run, at any rate, and under unforeseen occurrences, is very much of a reality.

The total income of the entrepreneur from the firm is very largely dependent on the amount of work and other means of production he places at the disposal of the undertaking. The income therefrom can with more or less accuracy be imputed as his special wage and interest payment. But because both the nature of the services and the firm's need of them are as a rule of a specific character, no single definite price can be established as in the case of standardized services. In determining the owner's imputed wage in the firm, it is necessary, for instance, to take as a maximum what he must pay to someone else for the same work, and as a minimum what he could earn in another firm. The situation is complicated, however, by the fact that the firm would probably be managed in quite a different way by another manager, and that his work too would be different if he went into the service of somebody else. Provided that it was really possible to indicate the price of the productive services offered by the entrepreneur himself, one might, by subtracting these prices from the revenue of the firm, find the special (possibly negative) difference between the incomes of entrepreneurs and other people.

A characteristic aspect of the position of the entrepreneur, which further complicates the question of imputation, is that he always contributes some work at the same time as he has an income as owner of capital. The work may be confined to the choice of a manager, and his capital income as owner may be negative in so far as the liabilities may be greater than the assets. Still it is he who is most deeply concerned with changing conditions so long as the creditors allow him to keep the firm. The heavily indebted owner's relatively great interest in changes in gross revenue may also be mentioned in passing. As is well known, the activity of shareholders is often extremely limited. (Cf. also Chapter 60.)

The cause of the difference between the income of entrepreneurs and other people is mainly to be found in the limitation of competition. Thus an increase of the current income is obtained. This difference in income is no doubt of great importance in real life, but not something quite unique. Other groups of persons may also be imagined to obtain a relatively great or small excess payment for their work and capital, owing to limitations in competition and mobility. And a group of entrepreneurs may, on the other hand, be imagined to be in a relatively poor position, as, *e.g.*, the farmers during the agricultural crises between the two wars.

A permanent difference between money income from those means of production which are used by an entrepreneur himself as opposed to those put at the disposal of an entrepreneur, may appear because the nonmonetary advantages of the entrepreneurs are taken into consideration, especially the pleasure of having a business or a farm of one's own, or the opportunity of being fully employed, irrespective of the organization of the labor market. This may apply to small farmers. Furthermore, there may,

as mentioned above, be such a constant and great influx of new enterprises in part of the retail trade on account of people's exaggerated belief
in their own opportunities, that incomes may be particularly low for a
long period.

In all these cases it is a question of a special (possibly negative) income
that may be calculated for the entrepreneurs by imputing to them the
ordinary wage and interest. Entrepreneurial gains and losses are quite
another matter; they are of a dynamic character and dependent on unexpected changes during the time between the fixing of the payments for
the other cooperating productive services and the selling of the products.

Whether means of production placed in an entrepreneurial position,
taken as a whole, have greater earnings, including gains and losses, than
the same means of production in another position, is difficult to decide.
The limitation in the opportunities of entering where there is one of the
market vacua, mentioned in the previous chapter, seems to indicate that
there is such an advantage just as there is the claim for payment on account
of risk. The preponderant optimism which was mentioned earlier seems,
on the other hand, to point in the other direction. A statistical solution[1]
is almost excluded, partly on account of the difficulty and arbitrariness of
the problem of imputation, and partly because it seems impossible to get
a sufficiently long and at the same time homogeneous period. If the long-
term fluctuations in prices are smoothed, the material becomes very heterogeneous. The economic and technical changes, as well as the preponderant
tendency in the direction of a rise in the price level which is not fully foreseen, have undoubtedly created great opportunities for the entrepreneurial
class. Owing to limitations in mobility and the necessary combination of
capital and ability, to the splitting of the market and the advantageous
position of those who have come first, the opportunities of the latter have
not been distributed evenly over all capital holdings and all working
persons who have entrepreneurial ability.

The object of this chapter has been to clear up the question of the relation between the component parts of entrepreneurial income. Apart from
unexpected capital gain and loss, which cannot be considered as income
from an economic point of view, entrepreneurial income is not a special
category of income, but the strategic position of the entrepreneur, just as
a more or less monopolistic or risky position of a firm, influences the
income obtained from the labor power and the other means of production
of the entrepreneur. Further, it is characteristic that the revenue from
these means of production appears as a total entrepreneurial income,
which can only be broken down by type of income by a process of imputation which is usually of a questionable nature.

---

[1] An attempt has been made in my book, *Den økonomiske Fordeling*, Nyt Nordisk
Forlag, Copenhagen, 1928, pp. 439–40.

CHAPTER 39

THE CIRCULAR FLOW

IN Part II, Chapter 14, we presented a picture of economic circulation under static assumptions. We saw there the flow of real goods arising from the productive services to the production of goods, and further to the individuals who, again, as workers or owners of material means of production yielded productive services; and the flow of payments going in the opposite direction from the individuals as consumers to the firms, thereby paying for the productive services, payments which went to the individuals as workers and to the owners of material means of production. Whereas the flow of real goods was measured in many different ways, there was one common standard for the flow of payments, which made it possible in this case to set down a clear and simple equilibrium system, or a system of equations with the same sum of payments per unit of time in all stages of circulation. Thus the values are maintained constant within the circular flow of payments, whereas in the circular flow of goods, measured according to their nature, *i.e.*, as horsepower or material quantity, influx from outside (from the sun and the coal mines) took place to a great extent as well as egress in the form of wastage.

The static picture of circulation cannot be applied in an unchanged form to a changing society. Besides changes in the width of the flows, there will be increases or decreases of funds, which now that their size is variable are of consequence also for the width of the flows. Since the circulation approach is of practical interest when statics are abandoned, and at the same time changing conditions make the problem far more complicated, it is now necessary, instead of considering each type of goods and services by itself, to group them in a few total economic categories. Here, however, we shall start with the model already described under statics in Chapter 14, with many types of goods and without express mention of the various funds.

The impulse to the change may come either from the real goods or from the circulation of payments by increase or decrease of the flow at some point or other, possibly a change in the velocity of the flow. The quantity of labor or other productive services may be altered either by changing the quantity of the means of production themselves or the degree of utilization. The quantity of output for a given input of productive services may be changed. And the direction of consumption may be changed. A change in investment may have the same effect as a change in the direction of consumption, but with the further consequence that the quantity of means of production, and the possible quantity of productive services in ensuing periods, are also changed.

The impulse may also come from changes in the width of the flow of

o

payments, due to the creation or destruction of purchasing power by the banking and monetary system or the state or due to a change in the velocity of circulation of payments between individuals and firms. Saving by some individuals without simultaneous investment, *i.e.*, increase in idle cash balances somewhere or other in the circular flow, means destruction of purchasing power.

Changes originating in one part of the circular flow must be accompanied by corresponding changes in the other. Greater quantities of services or goods need not lead to a greater total amount of payments, because adjustment is possible through a fall in the prices of services or goods. This will hardly take place, however, without a shifting in price relations and a consequent change in the distribution of revenue and expenditure, *i.e.*, a change in the flows of payment. Proportionate increases or decreases of all payments may very well be in accordance with the same. circular flow of real goods. But since changes in the flows of payment cannot be imagined to take place simultaneously and to the same extent at all points, the change when it does occur will probably manifest itself in changes either directly in the quantities of goods or in the relation between their prices, which will involve a change in the flows of real goods.

An important question, which we shall not discuss here any further, however, but which we shall leave to the theory of money and business cycles, is the elasticity which the system has in different directions, especially whether adjustment most easily takes place on the side of money or on the side of goods. What is important here is the organization of the circular flow of payments, *i.e.*, especially the monetary system and public finance. Furthermore, the nature of the circulation of real goods, the elasticity of demand, technic and the organization of the markets (rigid prices and wages) are of importance. Will it be difficult for an impulse from the side of goods or payments to prevail as a consequence of resistance to the necessary adjustment in the other circular flow? Along which channels—partly in one circular flow and partly in the other—and how quickly will a given effect spread? For instance, will an increase in purchasing power, resulting from outlays for public works or reductions in taxes, lead to rising prices or the utilization of hitherto idle means of production? The multiplier theory deals with the way in which the effects of increased payments continue to spread from link to link several times round in the circular flow, until the growth stops due to the complete disappearance of the increase in the flows of payment as a consequence of increased saving and payments to foreign countries. But both in this case and as a result of other changes, it is necessary to reckon with a highly unequal velocity for the different flows, so that, *e.g.*, part of the multiplier effect reaches two or three times round the circular flow, while another effect has only gone round once. This of course involves changes in price and quantity relations.

Figure 18 opposite illustrates in broad features economic circulation in a modern community. We shall not deal further with the facts underlying

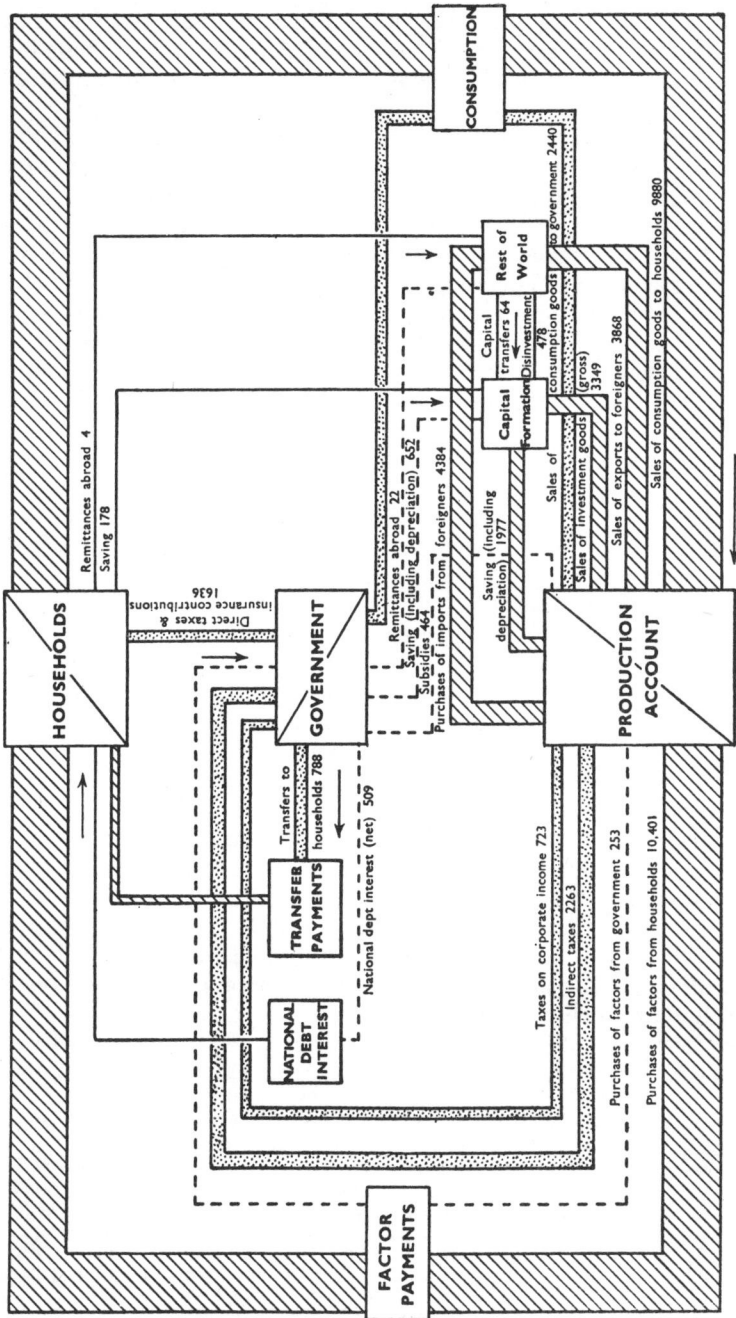

Fig. 18. Diagrammatic Representation of Social Accounts for U.K. 1951

the figures, which apply to the United Kingdom 1951, and which have been made by H. C. Edey and A. T. Peacock,[1] and as an adaptation of the "photograph" of the Swedish income in 1947 constructed by Professor T. Palander.

All money flows are drawn clockwise as in Fig. 3, p. 60, and flows of government expenditure and income are distinguished by dotted "streams". The "volume" of payments is indicated roughly by drawing the "streams" to a scale where £1,000m. = ·03 in. Indirect tax payments are attributed to those who are responsible for them irrespective of the final incidence of the tax. Payments of interest, dividends and rents by firms to households are net. Thus inter-firm payments of these items are not shown.

The thick flow illustrated by the frame of the figure from Household via Consumption to Production Account and back to Households via Factor Payments correspond to the simplified picture in Fig. 3. Capital Formation and the Rest of the World have been added, each of them connected with several other accounts, but still with some tendency towards a circular connection with Production Account, cf. the two small hatched frames. The government account's connections with the other main accounts—partly through National Debt Interest and Transfer Payments—are more differentiated, but here, too, the heaviest payments are to and from Production Account. Since Production Account for instance includes a number of firms making transactions with each other, the diagram does not include all actual payments.

A far more detailed illustration of the economic circulation has been given by the University Institute of Economics, Oslo.[2] We reproduce it here in Fig. 19 with British figures in pounds for 1938, calculated by Mr. R. G. Tress. The graph is from Mr. Tress's article mentioned in footnote 1, with his kind permission.

Associated with this is a general theory of such an accounting system and the graphic illustration of it. For each junction point, corresponding to the summations in the figure and table on pp. 60/1, input and output must be equal. This is true both when one considers payments as well as the real flows. The total national account may be built statistically on the basis either of information as to payments or valuation of the real services, according to which is most easily accessible.

The above-mentioned Norwegian accounting system has eighty variables, *i.e.*, connections between the accounts (junction points). If we

---

[1] H. C. Edey and A. T. Peacock, "Alternative Presentations of the Social Accounts", *Accounting Research*, January, 1951, with reference to Palander's unpublished lectures. The figures in the article for 1949 are substituted by figures for 1951. See also Central Planning Bureau of the Netherlands, *First Memorandum on the Central Plan*, 1946; J. B. D. Derksen, *A System of National Bookkeeping*, 1946. In R. G. Tress, "The Diagrammatic Representation of National Income Flows", *Economica*, Nov., 1948, there are graphs of the Dutch and Norwegian type (the latter reproduced in Fig. 19 opposite).

[2] Odd Aukrust, Petter Bjerve and Ragnar Frisch, *A System of Concepts Describing the Economic Circulation and Production Process*, Oslo, 1948.

subtract from this the forty-seven equations corresponding to the summations at the junction points, *i.e.*, the summations according to the scheme

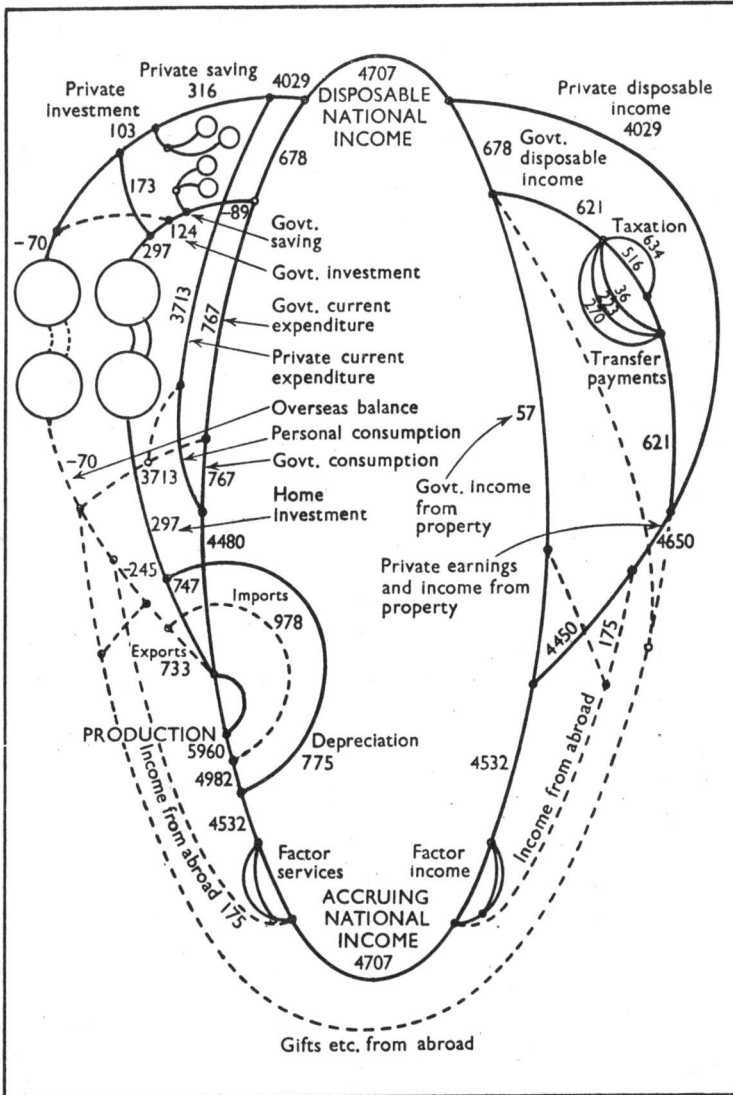

Fig. 19. The Ecocirc Graph for U.K., 1938

described above, and two definitional equations, and when one (corresponding to the absolute level of prices) is added, we obtain in all thirty-two "degrees of freedom". This means that if there were no other determining equations, one might arbitrarily choose thirty-two variables without getting any contradiction. In real life a corresponding freedom does not exist. We have reactions of demand, supply of services and technical conditions enough to give a definite solution also without the interference of the state except for the determination of the price level. But there is a problem as to the extent to which it is possible to replace the thirty-two economic reaction functions by planning, and what the resulting consequences will be, cf. the last Chapter.

As[3] mentioned above an accounting system can be constructed showing the flows between the various industries of a country. Such systems— elucidating the interdependence between industries—have in fact attracted much interest in recent years. The approach has been termed the "input-output analysis" and was originally presented by Wassily Leontief in the thirties.[4] In a number of studies this analysis has later on been extended by Leontief and others.[5]

The model generally used today is "the open static model", the framework of which may be given as follows:

Let the economic activities of a country be divided into m industries in such a way that the output of each industry may be regarded as a homogeneous commodity. For the sake of simplicity we may abstract from the foreign trade. Let X_i denote the total output in sector no. i and let x_{ij} denote the flow of raw materials from sector no. i to sector no. j. Let further x_{ia} denote the sales from sector no. i to the so-called "autonomous sectors", *i.e.*, in the case of a closed economy the consumption of

---

[3] The remaining part of this Chapter is written by Professor P. Nørregaard Rasmussen, University of Copenhagen. Cf. his *Studies in Intersectoral Relations*, North Holland Publishing Co., 1956.

[4] "Quantitative Input and Output Relations in the Economic System of the United States", *Review of Economic Statistics*, Vol. XVIII, No. 3, 1936, and "Interrelation of Prices, Savings and Investment", *Review of Economic Statistics*, Vol. XIX, No. 3, 1937.

It ought to be noted, that Ragnar Frisch had in 1934 already written an article which contains almost the same model; see "Circulation Planning: Proposal for a National Organization of a Commodity and Service Exchange", and "Circulation Planning: Mathematical Appendix", both published in *Econometrica*, Vol. II, 1934.

[5] The literature on the input-output analysis has been growing at an increasing rate during the post-war years and occupies at present a very prominent place in the leading journals. The subject has been developed not only by private research workers but also by a number of governmental and semi-governmental institutions as well as many private research institutes. Among the already vast literature on the subject the following may be mentioned: W. W. Leontief, *The Structure of American Economy*, 1919–1939, 2nd Edition (revised), Oxford University Press, New York, 1951. W. W. Leontief and Others, *Studies in the Structure of the American Economy*, Oxford University Press, New York 1953. W. Duane Evans and Marvin Hoffenberg, "The Interindustry-Relations Study for 1947", *Review of Economics and Statistics*, Vol. XXXIV, No. 2, 1952. *Input-Output Relations*, edited by the Netherlands Economic Institute, H. E. Stenfert Kroese, Leiden, 1953.

A short and clear presentation of the approach is given by Alexandre Chabert, "Le système d'input-output de W. Leontief et l'analyse économique quantitative", *Économie Appliquée*, 1950. Reference should also be made to a number of articles in *Econometrica* during the last few years, as well as a series of (unpublished, though mimeographed) memoranda—partly in English—from the University Institute of Economics, Oslo. Further a number of references can be found in the book edited by Koopmans referred to below.

households or government and the investment. X_i, x_{ij} and x_{ia} may—in case m is sufficiently large—be measured in physical units. In practice, however, it is impossible to operate with a number of industries corresponding to the number of commodities actually produced. Thus X_i, x_{ij} and x_{ia} will be measured in units of money and refer usually to a period of one year. The quantities of the output which can be purchased for one unit of money—say, 1 million dollars—may be used as a physical unit. Thus, the flows might be interpreted as physical flows. It follows that

$$X_1 = x_{1a} + x_{11} + x_{12} + \ldots + x_{1m}$$

and similar for the other sectors. In general:

$$X_i = x_{ia} + \sum_{j=1}^{m} x_{ij}, \qquad (i = 1, 2 \ldots m) \qquad (1)$$

i.e., total output in each sector equals the output used for direct consumption and investment plus the sales to other sectors.

(1) is a pure "bookkeeping" relation. The structural relations of the model consist of a set of production functions. It is assumed that the flow from sector no. i to sector no. j depends on the output in sector no. j only and this relation is further assumed to be one of proportionality. Thus, it is assumed that $x_{11} = a_{11}X_1$, $x_{12} = a_{12}X_2$, etc., *i.e.*, in general:

$$x_{ij} = a_{ij}X_j \qquad (i = 1, 2 \ldots m \text{ and } j = 1, 2 \ldots m) \qquad (2)$$

where, of course, $0 \leq a_{ij} < 1$. (Elsewhere in this book, cf. p. 45, inverse subscripts are used in accordance with Cassel.)

Substituting (2) in (1) the following m linear relations are obtained:

$$X_i = x_{ia} + \sum_{j=1}^{m} a_{ij}X_j \qquad (i = 1, 2 \ldots m) \qquad (3)$$

In this system of m equations the total output (X_i, i = 1, 2 . . . m) in the various industries may be regarded as the unknown (endogenous) variables, while the flows to the autonomous sectors (x_{ia}, i = 1, 2 . . . m) are assumed known from outside. As a_{ij} (i and j = 1, 2 . . . m) are treated as parameters (fixed coefficients of production) of the model it follows that (3) may be solved. Under the assumptions made it can actually be proved that there will exist a system of positive solutions to (3). The solution will give the unknowns X_i's in terms of the x_{ia}'s, *i.e.*

$$X_1 = A_{11}x_{1a} + A_{12}x_{2a} + \ldots + A_{1m}x_{ma}$$

and similar for the other sectors. In general we get:

$$X_i = \sum_{j=1}^{m} A_{ij}x_{ja} \qquad (i = 1, 2 \ldots m) \qquad (4)$$

It follows that this model determines the total output (in the various industries) which is necessary for supplying a given bill of goods to "the final demands": the consumption in households and government and the investment.

This is in no way a trivial answer to get. Because of the general inter-dependency between industries it is in fact a very complicated question. Thus in case the demand for the consumption of agricultural products increases by a certain amount it is generally not possible to meet this increase by a similar increase in agricultural output, because this output can only increase in case input from other sectors increases, cf. (2). This involves, however, the necessity of a higher output in other sectors and this presupposes in turn a higher input, including an increase in the input originating in the agricultural sector. The effects might be traced further back but it appears already that the total output from the agricultural sector must increase more than the increase in the final demand for agricultural products. This is a typical simultaneous problem and it is precisely these "feed-back" effects which are elucidated by the input-output model.

It appears from the foregoing that the model assumes a complete tabulation of the relevant flows between industries—the so-called input-output table. A great deal of the work on these problems has been devoted to the construction of such "Tableaux économiques", and it needs mentioning that quite apart from the validity of the input-output models these tables represent a concentrated presentation of a number of relevant data and have for that reason alone been very useful. In fact the input output table can be regarded as an extension of the systems of national accounting.

It remains still an unsettled question whether the assumptions behind the model (cf. (2)) are too far from reality to make the model a useful instrument. This is a question for empirical analysis—not to be settled by argument. The present extensive use of the model is likely to make it possible to make a judgment on this important problem in a not too distant future.

The model presented above has lately been extended in different directions. It will be seen that the model concentrates on the current flows between industries and thus does not attempt to explain the final demand (the x_{ia}'s). The latter is assumed to be given "from outside", cf. the application of demand equations in the model in Chapter 13 which of course may be assumed linear if preferred. Thus the model draws heavily on other sections of economic theory, such as the theory of consumption or the theory of investment. Lately the discussion on the possibilities of explaining these variables "inside the model" has started[6] and this is undoubtedly one of the ways in which the input-output analysis will proceed in the future. In so far as investment can be explained within the framework of the model, the analysis becomes dynamic. This follows from the fact that the investment (being a variable in the model) is the first derivative of the stock of capital—in turn also being a variable in the model—with respect to time. Another fruitful extension of the model consists in the construction of regional tables and models, which appears a fascinating approach not only for the theory of interregional trade but also for the economic geography.

[6] Cf. Leontief (1953).

It needs finally to be mentioned that the input-output models lately have been shown to be special cases of the more general theory of linear programming[7] which in the broadest sense covers a wide range of problems involving linear systems. In this field the general problem may be interpreted to be: In which way can a certain goal be reached in the cheapest way? In the theory of linear programming this question— well-known as one of the first very general problems appearing in text-books on economic theory—has been analyzed under the condition of linearity in a broad context and applied to a number of problems outside the field of economics. Typical problems for the theory of linear programming are "the diet problem": to find the cheapest combination of different foods when the diet shall contain a given minimum of certain nutrients (vitamins, calories, etc.), and "the transportation problem": a certain commodity, say steel, is produced at k different places and consumed at h different places; to find the cheapest routes of transporting the total output of steel from the producing plants to the consuming plants.

In general these problems consist in the operation of a linear model of production or the determination of the maximum (or the minimum) value of a certain linear combination of factors subject to certain linear side relations (equations or inequalities).

To go into details on these theories would take us too far. They have attracted the interest of several sciences besides economics and may thus be used as an example of another field where economists can obtain valuable results from research on the border to other sciences.

CHAPTER 40

INCOME, SAVING AND INVESTMENT

THE summations in the national accounts, illustrated in Fig. 19, contribute largely to the determination of the total economic categories and form them into a harmonious conceptual system.[1] If we consider the way in

---

[7] A brief survey of the problems in linear programming has been given by David Gale and Sven Danø, "Linear Programming: An Introduction to the Problems and Methods", *Nordisk Tidsskrift for Teknisk Økonomi*, 1954. See also A. Charnes, W. W. Cooper and A. Henderson, *An Introduction to Linear Programming*, John Wiley and Sons, Inc., New York, 1953, Robert Dorfman, "Mathematical, or Linear Programming: A Non-mathematical Exposition", *American Economic Review*, Vol. XLIII, December 1953, and John Chipman, "Linear Programming", *Review of Economics and Statistics*, Vol. XXXV, No. 2, 1953. A number of studies in this field has been published in Tjalling C. Koopmans, *Activity Analysis of Production and Allocation*, Cowles Commission for Research in Economics, Monograph No. 13, John Wiley and Sons, Inc., New York, 1951.

[1] Something similar has been done in the section, "Algebraic Discussion of the Relations between Some Fundamental Concepts", in Lindahl's *Studies in the Theory of Money and Capital*, 1939.

which the flows in the economic circulation divide and meet again, still maintaining the character of one single, though at times divided, flow, we understand that in choosing a concept of national income we decide where to cut the circular flow by a radial line. "Accruing National Income", which, according to the Norwegian statement, consists of payment for labor and other productive services, thus corresponds very nearly but not exactly to "Disposable National Income". If we add together a number of flows (or deduct parts of the total flow running backwards as a little separate circulation), it is possible in a static system to obtain the same sum for the whole of the circulation by considering a number of different stages. If, on the other hand, there are changes in the flow during the period, the income will differ according to the stage at which it is measured. We may here also mention the general equilibrium condition: value of consumption plus investment plus export plus money creation equal to value of consumption plus saving plus import plus hoarding.

We shall not here deal further with the concept of income. The difficulties depend on the changes taking place in wealth during the period. Gains may be invested or consumed in the period in which they arise. And losses may have the opposite effects. How is one to keep separate increases in wealth and income? What is the net payment to the factors of production, and what is the correct amount to be written off as depreciation? As is well known, the latter point cannot be decided without some degree of arbitrariness. Lindahl[2] mentions among other possibilities, the method of first estimating the capital value of the firms or persons, according to their capitalized expected revenue over all future time, and afterwards calculating the interest on this capital value as income in a period. The same approach may be applied to the income of labor, which in that case is considered as interest on a capital value. Deterioration in the future earning power either on account of age or loss of efficiency is by this calculation deducted from the amount earned in the period. Capital gains are ascertained by new valuations of capital value. And the difference between prospective and retrospective income in a period, calculated as interest on the capital value at the beginning and end of the period respectively, is the "income-gains". This method of calculation assumes that the distinction between the two kinds of gains depends on the length of the periods chosen.

Under static assumptions it is a simple consequence of the constancy of the total circulation that the accrued income from production for consumption and for investment (if we disregard relations with foreign

[2] *Studies*, and the discussion with Ohlin in *Ekonomisk Tidsskrift*, 1941; "The Concept of Income", in *Economic Essays in Honour of Gustav Cassel*, London, 1933. In the 1933 article, Lindahl mentions four possible concepts of income:

(1) income as consumption (Irving Fisher's concept), (2) the *ex ante* concept, income "as interest", *i.e.*, expected revenue, (3) income as a sum of consumption and increase in capital value (just as No. 4 *ex post*), (4) income as net payment to the factors of production. The calculation of a net value is, of course, arbitrary, since it requires a definition of *status quo* under changing conditions. Lindahl here finds No. 2 applicable *ex ante*, and No. 4 *ex post*.

countries) is equal to the income used for consumption and saving. Investment is, therefore, equal to saving. If we proceed to dynamic assumptions, the relation is more complicated. If we do not want to enter into calculations distinguishing investment proper (intended) and saving proper from changes in the value of capital goods, it is necessary to define both concepts so that they include the change in value during the period. We then have equilibrium *ex post* between investment and saving taken in the more comprehensive sense. In other words, investment here includes increases in value (gains) and part of the saving becomes unintended saving. This equilibrium is also a consequence of the necessary equality between the increase in assets and liabilities: somebody must own the increase in value.

Ex ante, the question of equality between investment and saving is meaningless if we think of schedules (functions of income and rate of interest), and this is generally the case. If, however, we think of definite planned amounts, *e.g.*, corresponding to a definite rate of interest, equilibrium *ex ante* may be obtained, but only by a mere accident.

Besides the theoretical concepts of income, which must be generally considered as ideals, it is of course of great importance to study actual statistics, whether they originate in the tax assessments or the statistics of production. The meaning of these figures, however, can best be brought out by a comparison with the ideal concepts and a possible correction with these as the norm. It may also be the aim of a statistical study, however, to take the observed figures as they are, and investigate the laws for their relation with other observed numerical series.

In many cases there may no doubt be reason to attach importance to what people, especially the firms and their owners, *consider*, and in their decisions take account of, as income, both because there is thus a greater possibility of getting information, and because what is important is to explain human action.

CHAPTER 41

TRADE IN CAPITAL VALUES[1]

IN static theory the problem was mainly to explain the prices and quantities of goods and services. It was here possible to conceive of quantities, also of goods, in terms of flows, sold, produced, and consumed per unit of time. The individual unit of commodity, *e.g.* a motorcar, may however be regarded as a capital good. If after being used for a time it is resold to a new consumer or possibly as a speculation to a series of owners, one

---

[1] Cf. my article in *Metroeconomica*, "A Note about Capital Values", 1949.

after another, we have gone beyond the normal economic circulation of goods, where the quantity sold is firmly connected with the production and consumption of the period. For land, which is neither produced nor consumed, conditions are especially peculiar. In this case, it is not production and consumption as a flow at all which determine supply and demand. The usual static supply curves are not found here.

In spite of the great differences in quality which actually exist with regard to land, we assume a uniform market price for a large number of uniform properties or units of land area. We may first, as in Fig. 20, draw a curve for the subjective valuation among all existing and possible owners of land at a given moment. The height and shape of the curve are determined by the capitalized expectations of revenue of all actual and possible owners by their own use of the land (including the discounted value of later possibilities of sale), modified by personal inclination or disinclination for the possession of land. The lower part of this curve is almost horizontal and based on the possibilities of sale a shorter or longer time after the valuation. Especially when the possibilities of revenue are fairly fixed, the curve of valuation, aside from the early part, is likely to be very elastic.

The price is now determined, as in Fig. 20A, by the intersection of the valuation curve, VV, and a perpendicular line corresponding to the existing number of building sites, farms, etc. (or units of area), Q. To the left of this line we have the valuation of the actual owners and to the right of the possible owners.

The demand curve of the moment, D_1D_1 may therefore be drawn, as in Fig. 20B, by shifting the part of the valuation curve situated to the right of Q in Fig. A and thus representing the valuation of nonowners, to the ordinate axis. The supply curve, S_1S_1, is obtained by taking the valuation curve for the actual owners in the converse direction, *i.e.*, plotting the piece from Q to O in Fig. A starting from the ordinate axis in Fig. B. These curves, drawn as thick lines in Fig. B, do not intersect, but they start from a point on the ordinate axis corresponding to the actual price. In an infinitely small period no sales take place. The same is the case even in a period as long as a year if all valuations are unchanged. Sales depend on changes in valuation during the period.

If we consider a certain period, say a year, it must be expected, however, that the valuation falls in case of some actual owners, owing to age, deaths, desire to change occupation or changed expectation with regard to the revenue of the property, whereas conversely, the valuation rises in the case of some possible owners, or quite different persons appear on the scene. This means a raising of the first part of the demand curve, D_1D_1, to the dashed line D_2D_2, and a lowering of the beginning of the supply curve, S_1S_1, to S_2S_2, whereby sales, X, become possible during the period, and price will be changed to p_2. The individual valuations must at any time be arranged in a falling and rising succession respectively, and the curves therefore continue to keep their generally falling and rising slopes.

Personal reasons for buying and selling arising within the period cause the first part of the demand curve, at any rate, to be situated above the first part of the supply curve.

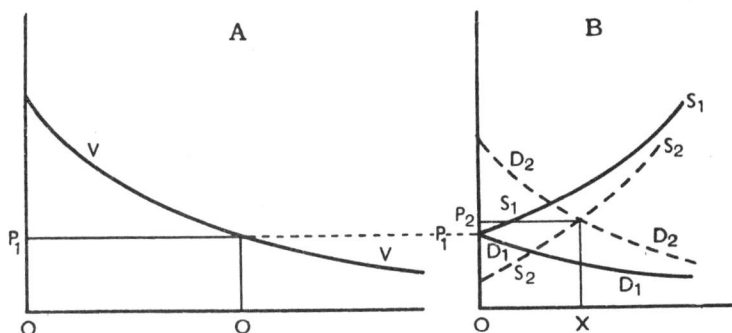

Fig. 20 A, B. Momentary Valuation and Sales of Capital Values

Aside from ordinary change of ownership, which also takes place in a stationary society, demand and supply curves, and consequently price and quantity sold, are influenced in a changing society by changed expectations of revenue, which make themselves felt in varying degrees for buyers and sellers and for different subgroups.

As will be seen, it is not, as in the case of consumption goods, different kinds of valuation that lie behind supply and demand; here they are the result of two parts of the same valuation curve. And the quantity of sales is not a stable phenomenon and has no connection with permanent qualities of demand and supply as functions of price and quantity, but depends exclusively on changes during the period. A certain part of these may, however, repeat themselves as a result of shifts of population.

In the present case, therefore, it will be meaningless to try, statistically, to find a demand curve or an elasticity of demand of just as constant a nature and with the same meaning as the demand for commodities. The magnitude of sales does not depend on production, consumption, or other regularly repeated phenomena, but on the marginal changes in the valuations of owners and nonowners during the period. Sales increase with the difference between the changes in the valuations of the two groups, and increase more, the more elastic the curves. The high degree of elasticity at the decisive part of the valuation curve round Q is counteracted, however, by greatly varying impulses to purchases and sales occurring in the course of the period and resulting rearrangements of the sequence of property holders (actual and potential) on the curve.

The above considerations, which are fully applicable to valuations of the "original and indestructible powers of the soil", may also to a certain extent be applied to more or less durable and irreproducible goods, which are objects of sale outside the normal channels from producer to consumer. Higher prices may here, however, to a greater or smaller extent and more or less quickly, stimulate supply, and the object itself may possibly be consumed at a quicker rate when the demand is great. In the next chapter we shall, among other things, deal with a related phenomenon: the magnitude of the total capital value and the more permanent level of interest, on one hand, and the loan transactions and the changes in interest on the other. Here, however, a further modifying element is of importance: the effect of changes in the amount of money.

CHAPTER 42

EMPLOYMENT, INTEREST AND MONEY

THE purpose of this chapter is not, of course, to give a satisfactory treatment of the three important subjects listed in the chapter heading in so short a space, and still less to give an account of all the discussion raised by Keynes' *General Theory of Employment, Interest and Money*. Our aim is solely to indicate how the theory of these subjects can be related to the idea that is maintained elsewhere in this book, and in this connection to outline a treatment of these special subjects. In Chapter 18, we have already mentioned how money and interest can be fitted into the static theory of free competition. We shall now endeavour to bring the explanation closer to real life by including variations in employment and, consequently, in total income.

There are different types of theory which apply to a greater or smaller extent to different types of reality: (1) what Keynes calls "classical" theory, *i.e.*, a static theory of competition. How far actual conditions from the middle of the last century and up to 1914 have corresponded thereto, is open to discussion. (2) The Keynesian theory, the background of which was England in the period between the two wars, with great unemployment and rigidity in the movements of wages, prices and interest. (When we are here speaking of Keynes, we are thinking of Keynes' *General Theory* from 1936 and the school formed on the basis of this book.) (3) A theory applying to a society with nearly full employment and with inflationary tendencies. Such a theory seems to be developing with an actual background in the conditions prevailing after the Second World War. It is a question, however, whether much the same type of theory does not hold good in the long run for a society with fairly constant degree of unemployment as for a society with full employment.

Common to (2) and (3) is the assumption of slowness of adjustment. Increased total income, provided money wages and interest on loans are fixed, leads to increased employment until nearly full employment is reached. With further increases, the money wage now becomes mobile in an upward direction, and wages and prices both rise with nearly unchanged degree of employment. Broadly stated: increase in total income entails first a movement to the right along the employment axis, and next a perpendicular rise in the price direction. In real life, as has been emphasized by Joan Robinson, the transition is not so abrupt because, with the modern organization of trade unions, wages begin to rise a good distance before full employment is reached. And moreover, full employment is not reached simultaneously for all kinds of labor and other means of production. Since the relative importance of individual industries is changing, it will be the usual phenomenon to have bottlenecks and unemployment at the same time. The rise in prices also begins before full employment, for one thing, because the marginal workers and machinery are less productive. This zone of transition before full employment will no doubt often extend far below 90 per cent employment, and its breadth changes according to conditions. In the study of concrete cases, the result will probably differ a good deal according to special conditions, and as we shall see at the end of this chapter, the solution will vary according to the preceding changes. One result of this is that a few total categories do not suffice. It is necessary here to go into detail as to differences between industries, etc.

In dealing with more general problems, a considerable simplification is, of course, reached by confining one's self to what appears to be most essential. One must, however, be very suspicious of all over-simplification, both because conditions are changing, and because we scarcely ever have a society where all the conditions mentioned in the above discussion and dominating in various periods make themselves felt at one time or other. The questions asked by economic theory in advance must therefore be really general, *i.e.*, include all the variables that may be imagined to have a determining influence.

It will be observed that in the present discussion some total economic categories are often used with all the inaccuracy attached to them. Labor and goods are taken as homogeneous masses; we consider exclusively the productivity and degree of employment of labor; the effect of changes in price relations and in distribution of income is disregarded.[1]

According to Hicks[2] we can set down the following schedule showing

---

[1] E. Schneider, "A Note on the Consumption Function", *Nordisk Tidsskrift for Teknisk Økonomi*, 1948. Cf. also Duesenberry, *Income, Saving and the Theory of Consumer Behavior*, 1949.

[2] J. R. Hicks, "Mr. Keynes and the 'Classics', A Suggested Interpretation", *Econometrica*, 1937. Similar points of view are to be found in Oskar Lange, "The Rate of Interest and the Optimum Propensity to Consume", *Economica*, February, 1938; Tinbergen, "Some Problems in the Explanation of the Interest Rates", *Quarterly Journal of Economics*, May, 1947; and Tord Palander, "Keynes' Almänna Teori och dess Tillämpning inom Ränte-, Multiplikator- och Pristeorien", *Ekonomisk Tidskrift* 2, 1942. In the latter article there is, for different cases, a three-dimensional illustration of the determination of interest and the magnitude of capital and incomes by intersection between surfaces in a coordinate system with the three quantities mentioned above as axes.

TABLE 7

	$M =$	$I =$	$S =$
Classics	kY	f(i)	F(i,Y)
Keynes' begins with	L(i)	f(i)	F(Y)
Keynes' "General"	L(Y,i)	f(i)	F(Y)
Hicks' suggested really general ..	L(Y,i)	f(Y,i)	F(Y,i)

M, Money; I Investment; S, Saving; Y, Total Income; i, interest rate; k, a constant; L ( ), f ( ), and F ( ), functions; total income is assumed to vary in accordance with employment.

the quantities which are taken into consideration by the different theories. If M is considered as given (or determined by a special equation), we have when I = S, four equations with the four unknowns, I, S, Y and i.

An essential weakness of the "classical" concept is that it assumes full employment, and thus cuts itself off from explaining fluctuations in employment and total income. The explanation also becomes very incomplete, as far as the short run is concerned, when we disregard the effect of total income (and the level of employment) on the demand for capital for investment. Also, the quantity theory is a too greatly simplified theory of money. But also Keynes is one-sided, even in his "general" theory. His disregard of the fact that changes in the rate of interest may have an effect through changed propensity and ability to save, seems at any rate in many cases to be contrary to experience, especially in the long run. His explanation that a reduction of consumption by reducing employment and total income will reduce investment correspondingly, does not apply to a community with full or constant employment at any rate. And a fairly constant level of employment in the long run seems to be a reasonable assumption. The theory can therefore at the most mean a decline in employment in the short run, when the inclination to save sets in before the propensity to invest, or possibly a limited degree of permanent unemployment. When employment has gone down sufficiently, one must expect an adjustment by means of changes in the rate of interest, in the price level, or in the rate of money wages. Thus employment is once more increased, or at least it ceases to decrease. An institutional maximum for unemployment in the long run is enough to stop the Keynesian effect of increases in saving. If the State, by means of budget policy and other measures, really stops unemployment at a certain point, short-run tendencies cannot influence long-run development.

In a society with full employment and pressure of inflation, employment and total real income will not go down either, when the tendency to save increases. The "inflationary gap"[3] and the lack of means of production will normally be an indication of an unsatisfied demand for means for investment, which will be satisfied to the extent that a reduction in consumption makes room for it. Investment may take place by means of increased employment as long as this is possible. And there is good reason for the Keynesian objection to pursuing a policy of limiting in consumption in such a case. But when there is full employment, or when otherwise employment is fixed (in the short or more often in the long run), investment must take place by means of saving, and it must then be expected that an increased propensity to save leads to increased investment.

The actual deviations from the "classical" full employment theory, and consequently also from the abstract statement regarding money and the rate of interest in Chapter 18, with its assumptions of statics and perfect competition, must either be explained *dynamically*, *i.e.*, by speculation and changes in expectation or by means of friction and slowness in changes in the rate of wages (cf. Keynes' "involuntary unemployment") and the rate of interest on loans, or *monopolistically*, the immobilities being then conceived as intended to serve a certain aim, especially determined by the wage policy of the trade unions.[4]

Increased total income gives possibilities either of greater sales or of higher prices, or possibly of both. If now we fix the rate of wages and the rate of interest, we shall have the increase in employment mentioned above, as long as there are idle means of production. After that we get an increase in prices, especially when it appears that wages can then increase with the increase in prices. No doubt Modigliani[5] is right in maintaining that "the low level of investment and employment are both the effects of the same cause, namely, a basic maladjustment between the quantity of money and the wage rates".

Conditions are complicated by purely monetary phenomena: hoarding and dishoarding of private speculative funds in view of expected movements in the rate of interest and prices. Under conditions like those in England in the thirties, for instance, fear of an increase in the rate of interest and the consequent fall in bonds may lead to the Keynesian liquidity preference's acquiring a dominating and paralyzing influence. For movements in the comparatively short run, *i.e.*, business cycles, such conditions may be of quite decisive importance. But since speculative funds can scarcely be imagined to be constantly increasing over longer periods, it is hard to imagine that this condition can have a controlling effect on employment and the rate of interest in the long run.

---

[3] Cf. Fig. 21B.

[4] A special explanation is necessary when we have simultaneously unemployment and wages above zero or the minimum of subsistence, instead of the condition that a service must either have the price zero or full employment.

[5] Franco Modigliani, "Liquidity Preference and the Theory of Interest and Money", *Econometrica*, January, 1944, pp. 76–77.

P

In a primitive barter economy and in a socialist society, we are also faced with the problems of capital and interest, although there is no question of payment for the transfer of credit. The value of future advantages is weighed against limitations in current consumption. In a rational economy, the economic planner must in these cases use a uniform internal rate of interest in his calculations, and the same applies to firms and individuals in communities with a credit economy, in so far as limitations in the mobility of credit entail a difference between the internal rate of interest and the market rate of interest. The decisive factor, however, in the society of our own times, is the uniform price formation which takes place in the credit markets, and which, through competition, has a regulating influence on the internal rate of interest of the individual persons and firms, as well as on all investment and saving.[6]

Just as in the case of wages, we are here dealing with price formation for a series of economically closely connected items, in this case, credits of varying duration and with varying risk. To these markets, or to an imaginary weighted average of them, it is possible to apply a partial equilibrium approach with intersection between curves for the supply and the demand of credit. The supply here comes from the saved part of current income, the amounts written off by firms, decrease of cash amounts, and new credit from the central bank, whereas the demand consists in credit for investment, the granting of loans for consumption, increase in private funds, and payments to the central bank.

Tinbergen's[7] very illuminating explanation corresponds closely to this. His expression for this approach to the problem is in the equilibrium condition:

$$S_t(Y_t,Y_{t-1},m_t) + M_t^n(m_t) + {}^2M_t = I_t(Y_{t-1},m_t) + {}^2M_{t+1}(Y_t,m_t)$$

where S is active saving, m interest, M^n new credits, ^2M cash holdings of the firms determined by liquidity preference, I investment, and Y total income. This equilibrium applies to any length of period. If we consider periods of short duration, the purely monetary quantities, *i.e.*, the changes in cash holdings of the firms and in the credits granted by the central bank, become quite dominating, whereas the real economic quantities have the decisive weight in the long run. The real economic and the monetary theories are thus put in their right places, side by side, and due

---

[6] Ohlin's so-called "common-sense theory", cf. "Some Notes on the Stockholm Theory of Savings and Investment", II, *Economic Journal*, June, 1937 (reprint in *Readings in Business Theory*); P. Nyboe Andersen, *Laanerenten*, Copenhagen, 1947, pp. 57–58. There may here be reason to call to mind Wicksell's combination of a real economic determination of normal interest, and the deviations therefrom as a result of disagreement between the interest on loans and normal interest (*Geldzins und Güterpreise*, Jena, 1898, and *Interest and Prices*, London, 1936).

[7] "Some Problems in the Explanation of Interest Rates", *Quarterly Journal of Economics*, May, 1947, p. 422. The equation is designated as "classical", and appears together with the income equation, $Y_t = C_t(Y_t, Y_{t-1}) + I_t(Y_{t-1}, m_t)$. C indicates consumption.

consideration is given the relations of both income (employment) and interest with S, I and M.[8]

The effect on the rate of interest of a certain increase in the quantity of money must be limited in the long run, because both real capital and its fruits rise in price. The prospect of a continued rise in the quantity of money and in prices must on the other hand gradually raise the rate of interest on loans, without a corresponding increase in real interest *ex post*, when a recalculation is made in accordance with changes in a price index.

An important objection which has been raised against the theory described above is that it does not provide an equilibrium which will be automatically realized through the mechanism of the market without public interference.[9] If the central bank, in spite of changes in real economic conditions, maintains an unchanged quantity of money and an unchanged rate of interest; if, moreover, the rate of wages is also fixed; and if the state does not interfere through the use of compensating measures, the result of increased saving must be unemployment. Conversely, the bank, by constantly increasing the quantity of money, may very well bring about a protracted inflation with the resulting effects on the rate of interest. In these cases, of course, the rate of interest does not correspond to the equilibrium which the real economic conditions would bring about if unrestricted adjustment prevailed.

When unemployment, or the rise or fall in prices goes beyond a certain limit, it is, however, highly probable that the state and the central bank will try to reduce these evils. The experiences of the thirties seem to show, though, that this political adjustment may be very inefficient and that for a long time one can very well have a large amount of unemployment which it would be possible to reduce greatly by monetary policy and other kinds of economic policy.

These considerations are of great importance in connection with fluctuations in employment, the rate of interest, and the price level in the short run, but can scarcely be imagined to mean much with respect to the level of the rate of interest in the long run, because it seems very improbable that the state will put up with increasing unemployment or a strongly rising price level indefinitely, nor that in the long run it can and will carry

[8] Another harmonious combination of short- and long-run interest theory, in a very clear and simple way, is to be found in Harold M. Somers, "Monetary Policy and the Theory of Interest", *Quarterly Journal of Economics*, May, 1941 (reprinted in *The Theory of Income Distribution*, 1946), and Fellner and Somers, "Alternative Monetary Approach to Interest Theory", *Review of Economics and Statistics*, 1941, pp. 43–48, and 1949, pp. 45–48. In the first of these articles the equality between all four marginal rates of return is mentioned: time preference, productivity, liquidity and return on securities.

[9] Thus Jørgen Pedersen, with whom I have had a long discussion by letter, in the chapter on the rate of interest in his book, *Pengeteori og Pengepolitik*, Nyt Nordisk Forlag, Copenhagen (2nd ed., 1948), is strongly in favor of this point of view. But he admits that serious disequilibrium of the kind dealt with by the classical theory may arise if the right economic policy is not pursued. See also Jørgen Pedersen's article in *Nordisk Tidsskrift for Teknisk Økonomi*, 1948, and his articles in *Weltwirtschaftliches Archiv*, 1954.

through a policy of regulation putting an end to these fluctuations in such a way that the result must be increasing disequilibrium in the price system.

If only the level of unemployment is kept constant in the long run by state and monetary policy, an increase in intended saving must lead to consumption being replaced by investment, *i.e.*, by an increased supply of capital. It is surely intolerable to allow an increase in intended saving to cause a corresponding increase in unemployment for an indefinitely long period of time. Consequently, there must be an institutional and political limit to unemployment, especially in the long run. This limit may in the future be drawn at a much lower level of unemployment than, *e.g.*, the one prevailing in England in the thirties. When the limit is reached, an increase in intended saving will result in increased investment. In any case, the limit is determined by the institutional and political structure of society, and it will be quite a different one in a capitalistic society with perfect competition and in a socialist society from what it was in Europe and the United States in the thirties.

In an economy where there is no inflationary pressure, a fresh inclination to save will entail a decrease in employment, if the terms of borrowing for investments are not relaxed. But even if it cannot be expected that a single further dollar, or a million dollars, or in the United States perhaps some billions of dollars, saved will lead to a change in the terms of borrowing, it must nevertheless be presumed that a considerable increase in saving will result in great changes in the conditions of interest and loans as time goes on.

Economic policy and economic theory cannot be separated in modern society where the public sector forms a great part of the whole and, among other things, controls the monetary system. Scientific laws as to what the public authorities will do must be treated, though, with still greater caution than principles concerned with what private persons will do. Also with regard to the latter, automatic adjustment often fails to take place as a result of the influence of large organizations and enterprises or public opinion. One then has to build on conjectures based on the discouraging experiences with the extent of unemployment and inflation with which the public authority has hitherto had to contend. The safest method is, of course, to content one's self with conjectures as to how bad things may conceivably become, but we shall reach one step further if we try to conjecture what will be done. From this point, then, there is only a short step to the more practical way of thinking, according to which one tries to find out how certain aims may conceivably be realized, *i.e.*, to economic policy. The paradox excluding full objectivity is that the more or less wise explanations and proposals of the economists may influence what actually happens.

State and central bank are important parts of the economic mechanism as a whole, and it is the task of economists both to treat them theoretically, *i.e.*, from the outside as objects of study, and from a theoretic-political point of view, to guide those in position of authority as to how they may reach their aims. Here, as in certain other spheres, it is true that if we only study short-run effects and pursue short-run policy, we shall all be more or less dead after a not very long run.

Whereas the more enduring propensity to engage in saving and investment are of decisive importance in explaining not only the existence of interest, but also its approximate level, monetary and institutional conditions are of predominant importance in explaining fluctuations in the rate of interest, employment and the level of prices, as well as in investment and saving. These movements, which are treated in the theory of business cycles, belong to the special subjects that we do not deal with in this book, apart from the quite abstract theory of tendencies to fluctuation as a consequence of the social structure. What will be the fate of the comparatively regular wave movement of the past under the probably more active business cycle policy of the future, is highly problematic.

To say that the Keynesian theory is applicable in the short run and the classical theory in the long run is too broad a statement. The aim must be a dynamizing of the theory, so that one follows the effects of exogenous interferences in the course of time from the very short run to the very long run. The aim is not to get separate static theories about short and long runs, but to get a general dynamic theory.

Let us, even at the risk of some repetition, try to examine more thoroughly the relation between short-run theory and long-run adjustment. In Paul Samuelson's[10] very clear statement of Keynesian theory, for instance, we have a static determination of national income (and consequently, employment) by means of curves indicating the propensity to invest and the propensity to save, with national incomes of varying magnitudes. Fig. 21A illustrates conditions in a society with unemployment. National income, Y, is plotted along the horizontal axis, and saving, S, and investment, I, along the vertical axis. The investment curve rises as a straight line from zero at a comparatively small national income. The same is true of the saving curve, which becomes positive at a later stage, but in return increases more rapidly and intersects the investment curve some distance before full employment. The abscissa for the point of intersection where saving and investment are equal indicates national income, Y_1. A raising of the saving curve S_1S_1 to S_2S_2 in this instance gives smaller national income, Y_2, and smaller saving, equal to investment. An upward shift in the investment curve has the opposite effect. The "deflationary gap" is the vertical distance between saving and investment, corresponding to 100 per cent employment. The corresponding Fig. 21B for a society with inflation shows the famous "inflationary gap".

In accordance with the above-mentioned static theory, unchanged curves are assumed for a period of time after a parallel raising or lowering of

[10] Paul A. Samuelson, *Economics, An Introductory Analysis*, 1948, Chapters 12–13, especially Fig. 7, p. 272. On p. 366 it appears that the author (dealing with the long run and without mentioning the assumption of full employment) is of the opinion that saving may further the prosperity of a country.

one of the curves as the result of some outside influence. When ten or twenty years have elapsed after a large displacement of one of the curves, it must be expected, however, that a substantial part of the effect has been in the form of changed prices, wages, etc., and that employment has been changed correspondingly. The reduced level of employment as a result of the higher saving curve will thus tend in the direction of a fall in wages and the payment of other means of production, as well as in the rate of

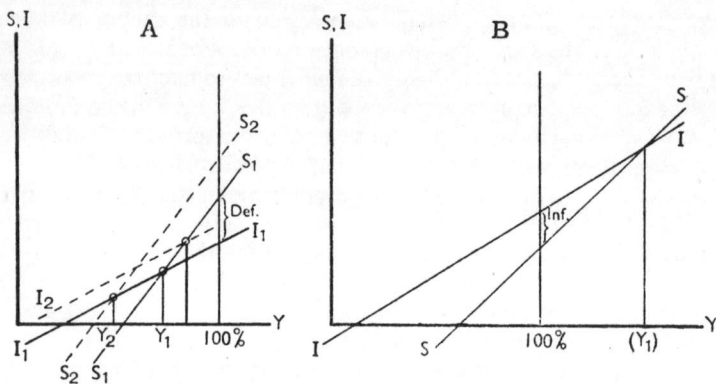

Fig. 21. Deflationary and Inflationary Dis-equilibria

interest. After the lapse of some time we may, in other words, expect that the degree of employment adjusts itself to the changed relations between price and income, as well as to more permanent institutional conditions. The latter may, however, be imagined to be of such a nature that the price system reacts only slightly, for instance when the level of unemployment, even for a long period, is above 10 per cent. But there is a limit. If a society permanently puts up with an unemployment of, say, 20 to 25 per cent, and if the state and private organizations prevent adjustment of the price system, it does not seem unnatural to say that this situation is a result of institutional conditions.

To the immediate (monetary) effects of saving and investment on employment, interest, etc., must be added the corresponding effects of the income and expenditure of public authorities and of exports and imports. Since in a small country like Denmark, with a limited capital formation, these items are greater than private saving and investment, it is easy to understand that they have a decisive place in any Danish explanation[11] of fluctuations in interest and employment, and that it is possible in this case to draw up a political, institutional or external-economic short-run theory of interest. But here, too, the short-run effects through money income are only the first of the effects on the levels of employment and interest.

[11] P. Nyboe Andersen and others, *Laanerenten*, 1947; Carsten Welinder, "Utkast til en institutionalistisk ränteteori", *Ekonomisk Tidskrift*, 1942, 1.

There is reason with Erik Lundberg[12] to warn against rash conclusions made on the basis of hypotheses of the Keynesian kind, comprising a few total economic categories, such as saving, investment and consumption, and assumptions of simple (linear) and constant relations between them. In business cycle prognoses or in evaluating definite cases of state interference, it is necessary to go into greater detail and to examine the individual components of production and consumption and, among other things, the effects of bottlenecks, which must be presumed to play a considerable part within a broad range between variations in employment with unchanged prices and variations in price at full employment. One thing that must be examined is the extent to which fluctuations in the rate of wages are determined by changes in employment or in prices.

Instead of assuming constant and given coefficients, it is necessary, through partial analyses in the individual case, to determine how the individual firms and private persons must be presumed to react to greater or smaller changes in data, immediately as well as ultimately. A static analysis by making a comparison between different states of equilibrium, reached solely by means of short-run reactions, gives us an insufficient answer. No doubt the change in the first period is of great interest, but the preliminary result here is not a new, stable static equilibrium, but a condition of tension, *i.e.*, a dynamic equilibrium, into which the velocities of change also enter. The next question is concerned with any further changes until the slower reactions also have a chance to show their effects. In some cases one may describe the changes in such a way that the quicker and slower reactions are both taken into consideration during the course of the changes for some time into the future.

As explained by Lindahl[13] it is not possible to solve the dynamic problems of existing trends by means of a system of static equations. Neither does a system of static short-run equations determine a final equilibrium. Lindahl, therefore, first transforms the Keynesian equations into a pure system of static long-run equations. After the elimination of money, the system has one unknown more than equations, which means that either wages, employment or interest is given—or politically determined. Further he indicates a dynamization involving the use of *ex ante* as well as *ex post* quantities.

At the same time as we consider total income and other aggregates, we must examine the relations between the most important subgroups, *i.e.*, price and income relations and cost relations.[14] The important intermediary cases of bottlenecks and unemployment will be among the relations

[12] Erik Lundberg, "Inflationsanalys och ekonomisk Teori", *Ekonomisk Tidskrift*, 1948, No. 3.

[13] "Om Keynes' ekonomiska System", *Ekonomisk Tidskrift*, 1953, and "On Keynes' Economic System", *Economic Record*, 1954. The article also in a very interesting way expresses Lindahl's idea about equilibrium and the conceptions static and dynamic. The indeterminateness of Lindahl's equations (without money) disappears if an equation for saving is added. Cf. Chapter 18.4.

[14] William Fellner, "Employment Theory and Business Cycles", in *A Survey of Contemporary Economics*, Vol. I, 1948, pp. 49, 75, 78, 86, and 96.

which are of decisive importance. The result, of course, largely depends on where the bottlenecks are in the actual cases considered.

Studies about the effects of autonomous wage changes have to comprise the reactions of state and the monetary system. The effects of an increase in wage rates (and consequently a movement upwards of the aggregate supply curve for commodities) will be a decrease in production and employment, *if* the total money outlay (or the aggregate demand curve for commodities) is kept constant. *If*, however, an increase in total outlay is allowed (or the aggregate demand curve for commodities is shifted upwards), the result may be either a smaller decrease or constant, or in favorable cases increased, production and employment.[15]

CHAPTER 43

TYPES OF ECONOMIC VARIATION

EXPERIENCE shows that there are many different kinds of economic variation, differing both with regard to the course of the variation and with regard to the number and importance of the quantities involved.

An upward or a downward variation may continue for long periods of time. The "geometrical progression" which applies to a population constantly increasing, or to a fund of capital increasing with accumulated interest at a constant rate, is a particularly simple form of growth. A weaker growth will occur in many cases, however, where the variation meets with opposition, *e.g.*, in the form of the law of decreasing returns. It is not very likely that the result will be exactly an equal change for each unit of time (arithmetical progression) for a quantity or a price. A growth curve which, like the total production curve of the law of proportion, begins by rising with increasing rapidity and ends by rising with decreasing rapidity, has been found, *e.g.*, for the number of telephone clients per cent of a certain group of population.[1] Protracted movements connected with changes in the structure of society are to be dealt with in the following chapter, which deals with the problem of economic laws of development.

[15] My *Arbejdsløn og Arbejdsmængde*, Chapter VI and Appendix by Sven Danø, Universitetets Økonomisk-statistiske Laboratorium, Copenhagen, 1953; a somewhat similar treatment in J. Marschak, *Income Employment and the Price Level*. Lectures 19–20 and I–IV; Sven Danø, "Pengeløn og Realløn", *Nationaløkonomisk Tidsskrift*, 1953; Bent Hansen, *A Study in the Theory of Inflation*, George Allen & Unwin, 1951.
[1] The two articles by H. C. Plessing, in *Nordisk Tidsskrift for Teknisk Økonomi*, 1942.

Cyclical variations may be ordinary economic fluctuations, special business fluctuations as, *e.g.*, the hog cycles, and seasonal fluctuations. We have previously given a few models illustrating the cyclical fluctuations, a cyclical fluctuation in income, and the fluctuations in the price and quantity of a particular commodity. Without entering into the question of the mathematical possibilities of the appearance of fluctuations in an economic quantity, and, more particularly, without entering into the decisive actual conditions and the weighing of the relevant facts, all of which belongs to the theory of business cycles, we shall venture a few observations.[2]

As appears both from Tinbergen's model, p. 176, and the cobweb case, Chapter 36, it is imaginable that a certain combination of lags, or differences in velocity of change, may bring about fluctuations when a stationary equilibrium is disturbed. In these cases, and in other comparable models, the fluctuations are fully explainable by existing conditions, and there is no need for different theories to explain the upswing, the downswing, and the turning points. The entire cycle is explained by all the existing conditions (including the original impulse) and not by a series of alternately active causes. "Change in relative strength is itself a consequence of the laws governing—in our example—expenditure. It seems to be difficult, if not idle, to attribute it to some special cause. One may construct other examples where reversal does come in owing to some specific reason, some 'ceiling' in credits or employment or still other things. But it does not follow that turning points can only be explained that way. I think this is a rather widespread misunderstanding among non-mathematical theorists."[3] Just as in physics, we may here distinguish between free and forced oscillations.[4] In the former case the system, according to its structure, reacts with a definite kind of fluctuation, when it is exposed to external (exogenous) influences, pushes or shocks. The classical examples are the pendulum or Wicksell's rocking-horse receiving a blow with a hammer. The structure of the system determines the wavelength and the possible interplay between the different variables. The strength of the impulses determines the size of the swing (the amplitude).

---

[2] William Fellner in the article, "Employment Theory and Business Cycles", in *A Survey of Contemporary Economics*, Vol. II, speaks of a modern tendency in the direction of reduced emphasis on fluctuations and a more intensive treatment of the processes going on at any moment.

[3] Tinbergen in *Review of Economic Studies*, 1940, p. 85, reprinted in *Readings in Business Cycle Theory*. The quotation refers to the example mentioned above on p. 176, Concerning turning points, see further Tinbergen's article, "Ligevaegtstyper og konjunkturbevaegelse", *Nordisk Tidsskrift for Teknisk Økonomi*, 1943 (2–4). Criticism of Tinbergen is to be found in Gottfried Haberler, *Prosperity and Depression*, League of Nations, Geneva, 3rd ed., 1941, p. 479. Tinbergen, in his *Econometrics*, § 12, also mentions types of movements. As principal types are mentioned: fluctuations, one-sided convergent movements, and movements leading constantly farther away from the starting point.

[4] Ragnar Frisch's lecture at the Scandinavian Economic Meeting at Stockholm, 1931, as well as his article in *Economic Essays in Honour of Gustav Cassel*, 1933, p. 171. With regard to the "almost periodic fluctuations" mentioned below, see Frisch's and Nybølle's speeches at the meeting.

A series of shocks can keep the fluctuations going, even if they are damped. With regard to damped, explosive and constant fluctuations, readers are referred to Chapter 36. In forced oscillations the magnitude considered follows the fluctuations of the impulse. Thus economic seasonal fluctuations are forced oscillations determined by climatic conditions. An intoxicated man, zigzagging down the road, performs free fluctuations, the swings of which are determined by his condition. If he is lying in the police car, kept down by two policemen, he will be subject to forced oscillations during the drive.

If the system is exposed to vigorous shocks, the regularity of the movement may be disturbed and we get "almost periodical fluctuations". With the many strong political impulses in the period between the two wars, it is no wonder that economic fluctuations have not been regular and wave-shaped, but irregular and alternating, because, according to their strength and direction, the impulses will now intensify and lengthen and now stop or hamper and shorten an upswing or downswing, at the same time as there is constantly a certain regularity in the way of reaction of the system and in its tendency to continue its fluctuations undisturbed. With the enormous change that has taken place in the last century, both in technology and political organization, it seems to be highly fantastic to search for long waves of a fairly constant length by means of complicated statistical studies.

Intermediate forms between a continued wave movement and an unchanged trend is a variation which changes its direction once or one which leads from one stationary state of equilibrium to another, which it may possibly approach asymptotically. The explanation may be that one element acts with increasing strength and another with decreasing, or, owing to a lag, does not become active until later (cf. in this connection the numerical example on p. 174, and the multiplier theory). Different forms of movement may be combined, such as fluctuations round a rectilinear or curving trend line, and long and short waves.

We have seen how several different tendencies of variation may act together. In statistics one will often be faced with the opposite task, that of dissolving (decomposing) an observed composite movement into its component parts. There are then difficulties regarding assumptions: whether we can say how one variation would have appeared if it had not acted in connection with another. Seasonal and business cycles in the employment in the building trades, for instance, are not independent; in bad years employment is largely stopped in the poor season.

In many cases the variations will not be continuous, either for technical or institutional reasons. Many types of expansion can only take place discontinuously. Fluctuations in prices, wages, and the rate of interest will often be staircase-shaped.

Fluctuations in one economic variable alone are hard to imagine. In special cases, where the elasticity of demand is in the neighborhood of 1, and we are dealing with a commodity that is unimportant in the total production and consumption of the country, we may imagine an approximately independent movement in the price and quantity of this commodity alone. In such cases, side effects on other economic quantities are of comparatively slight interest. We may then make a fairly exact, partial examination of the commodity itself, applying the *ceteris paribus* assumption. Under other circumstances, the fluctuation will spread through competition, substitution in consumption or changes in cost or income conditions.

As mentioned above (p. 173), the Stockholm School stresses the importance of the effect on income. This is very considerable, for instance, both in the case of fluctuations in crops (owing to inelastic demand) and in the case of changes in the building trades (owing to an elastic supply). Income, flowing in from all branches of production in order to be redistributed among them or be turned into saving, more than anything else forms the connecting link between industries and commodities and contributes to the fact that an influence at one point spreads out and affects economic activity as a whole.

Where several magnitudes are affected, it may be said that a greater or smaller part of the economic system is put into motion. If a price is increased, the prices of competing goods, of the productive services, and the raw materials used and the prices of the finished goods in which they enter will have a generally smaller and retarded movement in the same direction. The prices of supplementary goods or goods in joint supply or the quantities of goods competing for the same income or productive service, will have a tendency to move in the opposite direction, generally with different lags. We may speak of the path and the velocity with which the economic effect or the "business cycle spreads".[5]

The economy which progresses at an even rate within all sectors of which Cassel speaks cannot be imagined in real life. This is partly because we cannot have a constant increase in exploitation of natural resources without rising costs and changed price relations. Regardless of this element of unreality, it may be said, however, that the picture of the evenly progressive community has a certain value as an illustration of the effects of an increase in output, *ceteris paribus*; it shows more particularly how it becomes necessary, contrary to what was the case under stationary conditions, to use part of the productive forces for expansion, and how we arrive at a certain ratio between the percentage of progression and the percentage of saving, directly determined by the relation between the value of income and the value of capital. Income multiplied by percentage of saving = capital multiplied by percentage of investment.[6]

If we want to apply the concept, "moving equilibrium", the assumption of the same increase in all parts of the economy must enter into the explanation. In a movement consisting of a series of static equilibria, the

[5] Dag Hammarskjöld, "Konjunkturspridningen", *Arbetsutredningens Betänkande*, II Bilagor, Band I, *Statens offentliga Utredningar*, Stockholm, 1939:29, Kap. I.
[6] *The Theory of Social Economy*, Fisher Unwin, London, 1923, §8.

reason why the change took place and why it occurred with the same velocity everywhere would, however, remain unexplained.[7]

The situation is complicated where a small number of decision-making bodies, but more than one, influence the course of events, *e.g.*, through price policy. In that case, but in many other cases, too, it must be assumed that the individual persons, firms, or institutions have mutually inconsistent expectations. Further assumptions must be deficient knowledge and unequal horizons of interest and action. The horizon indicates how far into the future one goes in making one's plans. All this leads to surprises, economic fights, profits and losses. The individual persons and firms try to adapt themselves on the basis of different, possibly contrary, assumptions (cf. Part IV).

In real life most people do not try to adapt themselves to an imaginary final static equilibrium, which would be the result in the end if from now on everything was allowed to adjust itself without further change of data. But they are guided by a certain idea of the continuation of the changes in so far as they are interested in them, and they consider themselves able to see into the future to a certain extent. Besides the static theory of the equilibrium of a ship at the dock or on the calm surface of the sea on a bright summer day, it is important in real life to understand the effects of direction turnings, velocity, slope and readiness for further manoeuvres amidst other shipping in whirlwind, downpour and semi-darkness on a sea troubled by storm, swells and changing currents, and full of icebergs and submerged rocks. Dynamic theory can only try to explain and facilitate such navigation in a modest way by describing the phenomena of change, one by one or in small, clear groups of models; and, as in the case of physics, this is done with the decisive starting-point of static theory.

It will be obvious that in a society so unstable as our present one, there is no basis for considering an imaginary static equilibrium as normal. It is possible, however, more or less arbitrarily, to consider an average of ten years with a possible correction for trend or, in time of war, the conditions of the immediately preceding years of peace, as a kind of relative normal. But this concept does not acquire any precise meaning without a more or less arbitrary definition. Nor can it be considered correct to regard conditions in a definite phase of business cycles as normal because the different economic quantities will presumably reach their average for the whole of the wave at different points of time. The velocity of the pendulum is greatest when it passes the bottom position. What is considered as normal will no doubt in many cases be connected with the choice of political aims. A situation without business cycles indicates an equilibrium or a "normal" in one definite way. The normal activity of the building trades, the civil engineers and the law-makers illustrates the impossibility of dealing with a normal as something unchangeably

---

[7] The system would be "locked up", as is the "moving equilibrium" in H. L. Moore's *Synthetic Economics* (Macmillan), 1929. See further, Hicks, *Value and Capital*, p. 127, and Samuelson, *Foundations of Economic Analysis*, 1948, p. 321 ff.

permanent. In spite of everything that may thus be said against ascribing an absolute and unconditional validity to normals and simple trend lines, analyses of this kind, when used with caution, may in some cases be a useful guide.

CHAPTER 44

DEVELOPMENT, STRUCTURE AND CAUSATION

It is a highly interesting and important task to explain the economic development that has taken place and particularly, if possible, to say something about its expected further course. It is questionable, however, how far we can get by narrow economic observation and thought[1] and whether, on the whole, it is possible to establish any principles of behavior and thereby provide some possibility of explaining and forecasting.

In certain cases relatively exact conclusions may be possible, *e.g.*, with regard to the effect of increased population or increased quantity of capital combined with the assumption of an unchanged structure of society. Sometimes it may be shown that it is necessary either to make certain changes in the economic quantities with the given structure of society, or that the latter must be changed, and that this will most likely take place in a certain direction. The question of explaining and forecasting the structural changes themselves is, however, more problematic. Forecasting is only possible to a small extent; and a subsequent explanation must very largely take other than economic conditions into consideration.

A great increase in the demand for a commodity or a violent crisis will probably influence technical knowledge and the organization of society, respectively; but the possible effects will also be dependent on the position of a few leading individuals and political and other conditions, which are not subject to economic laws, but are essentially influenced by other factors. A development involving technical and organizational changes must be explained on a broader basis than a merely economic one. A similar basis must be applied with regard to prognoses concerning changes in the structure as a whole. Also where public authorities, central banks, or other large organizations interfere in economic development, a complete explanation must include the personal, political and organizational elements. It may, however, be said as a general observation that in the course of the last decades a higher degree of state intervention has been observed in slump than in boom periods[2] and good explanatory reasons may be given. But it is impossible on this basis to deduce any law

---

[1] Walter Eucken, *Die Grundlagen der Nationalökonomie*, Gustav Fischer, Jena, 1940, p. 217; Joseph Schumpeter, *Business Cycles*, New York & London, 1939, p. 13.

[2] Johan Åkerman, *Ekonomisk Kausalitet* (Gleerup, Lund), 1936.

of general application. In many cases exact, purely economic reasoning may be of importance, among other things for the understanding of the motivation for the partly personally or partly politically determined interferences; but much else is needed besides.

This is particularly true of structural changes, but it might be said almost in any instance where economic theory will contribute the solution of practical questions, that the deductive analyses are models with a very limited content, and that they must always be compared with a broader but often rather disorganized mass of ideas concerning reality. With regard to structural changes, the scope of economic deduction is particularly modest, since on the decisive points it is necessary partly to take personal, political, and similar factors into consideration, and partly, in explaining the past, to break off the line of reasoning to a large extent and accept new unexplained facts.

Wherever the actual course of events in a definite period of time is involved, the interdependence approach of static theory corresponding to a system of simultaneous equations must be replaced by a causal explanation in time.[3] Conditions in the later period must be explained by conditions in the earlier. Only by perfect anticipation can expectations counterbalance the one-sided direction of time-consuming processes. Such a causal explanation, *i.e.*, an explanation of later phenomena by earlier ones, will not be monocausal, however, like many of the explanations of earlier economic theory. It may very well depend on a functional relationship between several nonsimultaneous quantities, a relationship, however, which, owing to the unchangeableness of earlier events will have a one-sided character on decisive points.

In partial accordance with Johan Åkerman's contrast between alternative analysis and causal analysis we may, on one hand, speak of closed

[3] With regard to Johan Åkerman's special theory about alternative analysis and causal analysis, we may refer to *Ekonomisk Kausalitet*, 1936, *inter alia*, pp. 19 and 44; further, *Das Problem der sozialwissenschaftlichen Synthese* (Gleerup, Lund), 1938, especially pp. 87, 120, 145, 168, 192, 247–48 and 306; *Ekonomisk Teori* I, *De ekonomiska Kalkylerna* (Gleerup, Lund), 1939, pp. 16, 36 and especially p. 74, where he says, "The calculus models, logically and timelessly, describe the forms of thinking of the economic subjects, the causal analysis explains the total actual events by means of an investigation, attached to the time-scale, of the motives and decisions of the active groups of persons, and the interplay between these determining economic forces. The calculus models as well as the causal analysis lead to rationalizations, to theoretical models. The schemata of the calculations, however, are principles of a definitional character, always valid within a given structure; the causal analysis, on the other hand, provides a reconstruction on an empirical basis of what happens within a certain frame as to time and place.

"The calculus model forms a closed system, in which the concepts in a hypothetical situation cover the contents of the calculations, without anything being left out. The causal analysis leads to an open system in which the concepts are only instruments for the detection of acting forces in certain cumulative developments and critical turning points and with the best possible reconstruction as to the scientific goal."

Paul Samuelson in his *Foundations* (1948) has, pp. 314–15, a definition of "causal" which is different from that of Åkerman and applies the word to a closed system. "A system is said to be causal if from an initial configuration it determines its own behaviour over time." In contrast to this he speaks of "historic" systems.

spheres of deduction, which may be both static and dynamic, partial and total (abstractly), individual calculations and national-economic sums, purely economic or including psychological and other noneconomic elements. And on the other hand there may be open investigations which follow up the explanation of different phenomena, constantly "deeper" and wider in different directions by including fresh experience and assumptions in specially relevant spheres and applying as tools, whenever needed, a series of separate, closed models of the former type. A great scientific analysis will, so far, always be of this composite character. In the special case where the goal of the analysis is to explain events that have already occurred, *i.e.*, historically, we have the causal analysis described by Johan Åkerman, which is open, retrospective, attached to the actual time scale (calendar time, as opposed to the abstract and shiftable time scale, *e.g.*, of compound interest), and so dependent on changing structural conditions. If the goal is an historical explanation, it must, besides observations, include a number of deductions, the assumptions of which are simplified pictures of the often vague and manifold observations.

Whereas an abstract, conceptual deduction can say definitely what will be the result of a certain combination of assumptions, it is only possible in actual cases to give uncertain conjectures as to the future. This is partly because only some of the existing conditions are known, and partly because new surprising conditions may emerge. Especially with regard to changes in the forms of the economic functions, *i.e.*, structural changes, the prognosis will be uncertain, and the basis of economic laws of development, therefore, still more uncertain. The problem in this chapter is, by the way, closely connected with the structural problems of organizations and institutions which we deal with in Part IV.

The problem[4] *interdependence versus one-way relations* (*causation*) is very important for abstract economic theory and also for econometric research. As an introduction to the following is given a short account of some problems discussed on the European meetings of the Econometric Society in 1953 and 1954, written by P. Nørregaard Rasmussen.

> For years economists have realized that the very object of economics implies that the theory must rely on a great number of relations all of which are to be considered as interdependent. In so far as such systems were going beyond the level of pure abstract theory, the problem of estimation of the parameters (to find the numerical value of certain coefficients) involved was raised. For years the estimation was done by way of a direct correlation analysis performed for each of the relations considered.

[4] Trygve Haavelmo, "The Statistical Implications of a System of Simultaneous Equations", *Econometrica*, January 1943, and "The Probability Approach in Econometrics", *Econometrica*, Supplement, July 1944; Herman Wold, "Causality and Econometrics", *Econometrica*, April 1954, and his *Demand Analysis*, Stockholm and New York, 1952; Ragnar Bentzel and Bent Hansen, "Om Simultanitet i Ekonomiska Modeller", *Ekonomisk Tidsskrift*, 1953 (several of my arguments are taken from this very instructive article); report of the Uppsala meeting, 1954, in *Econometrica*, 1955, 2, p. 200, and "On Recursiveness and Interdependency in Economic Models", *Review of Economic Studies*, 1954–5.

Though several doubts as to the validity of this approach were raised, notably in the works of Ragnar Frisch from the 1930's, it was not before the work of Haavelmo that the problem was attacked in a really satisfactory way. Haavelmo showed that the simultaneous approach was likewise necessary in the process of estimation; *i.e.*, unbiased estimate of the parameters could not be derived unless the system of relations was considered in its entirety.

As shown by Wold there are, however, certain cases where the old classical correlation analysis might still give unbiased estimates of the parameters. This is the case where appropriate lags make it possible to consider each relation in sequence of others.

In so far as the economists have to formulate the problems of estimation put before the statisticians it is important from the point of view of theoretical analysis to be aware of these questions. As just mentioned a simple correlation analysis might still be possible if the theoretical model consists of a system of "one-way" or "causal" relations following in sequence of one another. For instance, consumption is considered as a function of the income of a previous period, investment is likewise considered as a function of the income of a previous period while in turn the income of a certain period is defined as the sum of consumption and investment of the same period. The "behaviour-equations" of this model apparently are "one-way relations" as against, *e.g.*, a model where consumption in a certain period was considered a function of income in the same period. In this latter model the consumption function apparently is one of interdependence as against a "one-way relation". The question now is whether it might be possible, with a reasonable margin of error, as advocated by Wold, to work with models without any interdependence. Clearly this would be "preferable" in the sense that—as mentioned—the estimation of the parameters involved would be much less laborious than the one required for obtaining unbiased estimates in interdependent systems.

As different names in the discussions have been used for the same concepts especially as there is danger of mixing different concepts, I should like to begin with a tabulation of a collection of simple Tinbergen-arrow-schemes (cf. Fig. 1, p. 35 above) given by Svennilson at the econometric meeting in Uppsala, 1954, and apply his terms. t_1 and t_2 are periods.

		Static		Dynamic		
		$M1:$		$M2:$		
		t_1	t_2	t_1	t_2	t_3
"One-way	a	.	.	a	.	.
dependence"		↓	↓		↘	↘
	b	.	.	b	.	.

		$M3:$		$M4:$	and	$M5:$	
		t_1	t_2	t_1	t_2	t_1	t_2
Interdependence	a	.	.	a	.	a	.
		↑↓	↑↓	↘ ↑		↓↑↘↓↑	
	b	.	.	b	.	b	.

Only the interdependent, dynamic models $M4$ and $M5$ give rise to self-contained process. "It is certainly true that a model of the type $a_t \to b_{t+1}$ $\to c_{t+2} \to d_{t+3}$, etc., *ad infinitum*, which is dynamic and built on "one-way dependence" can be regarded as self-contained. But it lacks repetition (the causal chain will never lead back to any variable that earlier has entered it, *e.g.*, b_{t+3}), and is therefore not suited for statistical testing."[5]

The behaviour of economic subjects within a short period seems generally to be autonomous in the sense that each unit takes the action of other units as a datum and does not try to influence it. What happens within a period may then be described as the joint result of the aggregate actions of all economic units. Consequently it seems possible to base economic analysis on one-way relations, with some difficulties still, *e.g.*, in the case of bilateral monopoly.

In an abstract model one may assume very short periods in which all subjects act autonomously according to exterior conditions and according to their plans at the beginning of the period, and all simultaneously make new plans "between the periods". In real periods for instance the year or other periods used in statistics it is most likely that some groups (or units within a group) will influence some other group and this again will influence the first. Further we often have information only about aggregates, and some individuals within aggregate A will (independently of the length of the period) influence some within aggregate B and the other way round.

When we leave the analysis by means of a step by step sequence analysis and consider equilibrium conditions or tendencies given by static theory or a corresponding theory about trends, clear interdependences, definitional equations and equilibrium conditions, come in besides the individual behaviour equations and the rules for their summation or aggregation. The "simultaneity" or rather interdependence in Walras' system of equations "is caused by the system being a static system of equilibrium. Such a system only expresses the conditions for the equilibrium of a certain dynamic system, *i.e.*, reproducing itself continuously." If we have one way influences of A on B with certain lags and in certain periods and corresponding influences of B on A with other lags we have interdependence between the undated variables A and B.[6]

The choice of method must depend on the nature of individual cases and what kind of questions are asked. But probably one will quite soon arrive at a point, where the interdependence between not only undated or different dated variables, but also between variables comprised within a period of a certain length, is of some importance. But that does not, however, exclude the abstraction from the interdependence as the best simplification in some cases.

---

[5] Table and quotation with kind permission of the author from his contribution to the Uppsala meeting.

[6] Cf. Ragnar Bentzel's and Bent Hansen's article, pp. 92 and 98.

Q

PART FOUR

FORMS OF MARKET AND STRUCTURE OF SOCIETY

CHAPTER 45

INTRODUCTION

ECONOMIC theory would be much simpler if the analysis, as is generally done in Part II, could be limited to a stationary society or a society with quick and frictionless adjustment. That is impossible, and the resulting problems have been dealt with in Part III. Another group of simplifications made generally in Part II, the special assumptions as to the type of markets and society dealt with, is now abandoned in order that we may proceed with the investigation of several other types. These simplifications had two characteristics: prices of commodities were assumed to be equal to the sum of the prices of the productive services employed, and it was assumed that productive services could not at the same time have a positive price and an unemployed remainder. Further, all the variables were prices and quantities, and phenomena from other, not "purely economic" spheres, such as personal feelings and ignorance, were only allowed to act through given formulae and fixed coefficients.

As fundamental assumptions, leading to these simple types of markets and societies, were mentioned free mobility and unlimited divisibility. If we wish to have an illustration from real life of a society approaching the assumptions, we may think of a society with a high degree of competition and without any great impulses to change. Perfect competition, however, is not the only possible way of realizing this form of economic equilibrium. Conditions of the same economic character might also be realized, wholly or partly, in a family household or in a Socialist society where the citizens had a free choice of consumption and employment, and the production and sales managers aimed at the formation of an equilibrium price for all goods and productive services in the same way as in a competitive society, only with the difference that the income from the material means of production did not go to private owners.

In Part II, Chapter 18, it was mentioned briefly that other assumptions with regard to the state of the market and of society involved modifications of and additions to the first schematic description. The purpose of this Part is to examine some of the most important forms of market and society, and to see what influence they have on the relation between the various economic groups and on economic development as a whole. We do not intend to give an exhaustive description of all the more important existing forms. Our theoretic treatment of the subject must be supplemented by concrete descriptive material. Reflections on the existence of the phenomena in real life will, therefore, be comparatively scattered and incomplete, and will in no case afford sufficient basis for a treatment of the problems of the real world, where the market forms are continually changing over time and place. Theory must in this case merely establish a set of alternative possibilities rather than a direct description of economic conditions as they are, but a number of viewpoints and models to be used in studying the varying and extremely complicated actual market forms and specific cases. Where such factors as monopoly, public authority or human motives are to be considered, it is important to emphasize the connection between the purely economic phenomena like 'price and quantity and psychological and other aspects of the matter. Our part of the work, however, is principally to deal with the economic aspects and the economic consequences.

As starting-point for the discussion we assume a rational maximization of profit. But in several places, especially in Chapters 59 and 61, we introduce other assumptions and discuss problems of the actual behavior of firms. Present conditions are different in the United States and in European countries. And internal and external events may change the situation completely in either place. Our rather modest task in the distribution of labor between economists is to present some theoretic viewpoints and models, which might inspire practical investigation in different types of markets, including possible future types which are unknown at present.

Rational maximization of profit seems to be a useful hypothesis to start with in any case. In cases like bilateral monopoly and duopoly the problems are more complicated, and theory here obtains a result only by means of complicated alternative hypotheses, probably containing only a certain fraction of the truth. These theories, which it has been a fine sport for some of us to elaborate and discuss in the course of the last twenty-five years,[1] are now again being attacked with some vigor by empiricists. Most of the antagonists, and probably several of the protagonists, however, look upon those theories in too literal and serious a way. The correct standpoint seems to be that they afford a useful exercise before the actual work is to be started, but if then applied without great modification, they are not less ridiculous than gymnastics used by the soldier on the battlefield. It is necessary—but often almost impossible—to procure reliable facts about the behavior and motives of the entrepreneur. But just because it is so difficult—or perhaps impossible—it is often necessary to fish for facts with a theory.

Whereas the various forms of market are dealt with in detail, the treatment of the forms of society is very brief. A more detailed treatment of this problem, more particularly of the influence of the State on economic conditions, can best be undertaken in connection with the discussion of economic policy and its special branches. The treatment of State power and forms of society in this book can therefore most suitably be considered as a short theoretical introduction to economic policy. The society of our days is highly characterized by political interference. If *e.g.*, some change or other occurs in the quantity of production or its direction, the

[1] Cf. the special number of *Économie Appliquée* about Oligopoly, 1955.

economic consequences will depend on the reactions of the State, and these again will be very much dependent on the particular conditions of the moment and the place. If one group of the population is involved in difficulties, the State in our days, for instance, will very often resort to relief measures which have an inflationist tendency. But the present author does not venture to give simple laws applying to such cases.

CHAPTER 46

MONOPOLY AND COMPETITION

IN Part II we considered the whole system of economic relations as a network of partial interdependences. In so doing we considered the production and consumption of each commodity separately without discussing the definition of "a commodity", and without further investigation of possible local and other differences within the total production and consumption of a commodity. What is to be considered a commodity, must depend on a more or less arbitrary definition, since we can imagine a series of differences in quality, from two almost identical units up to two widely different means of satisfying kindred wants. Moreover, distance and costs of transportation involve more or less important elements of heterogeneity and division of the market; and here, too, it becomes a question of definition whether we speak of separate markets or one heterogeneous market.

We use the concept of market in speaking of a group of purchases and sales, or possible purchases and sales, of at least partly homogeneous commodities or productive services, when they are related to each other in such a way that it may be considered practical to investigate them together. If we should confine ourselves strictly to the older concept of markets as "one-price-markets",[1] we should rarely find more comprehensive markets. When we consider the individual market by itself and take everything else as given and independent of the results of adjustment in the market, we speak of a partial analysis. It is here that we first come across different forms of markets. But since the total economic interdependence is established through a chain of sales, the predominant forms of markets will also decisively influence the total interdependence, *i.e.*, the economic structure of society.

The principal types of market organization are monopoly and competition, or if we consider the situation for buyers and sellers respectively:

[1] Bertil Ohlin, *International and Interregional Trade*, Harvard University Press, 1932, p. 5; Carl Iversen, *International Capital Movements*, Copenhagen and London, 1935, p. 2.

competition, sellers' monopoly, buyers' monopoly (also called "monopsony") and bilateral monopoly. As will be explained more fully in Chapter 49, conditions are complicated by a series of other dissimilarities, *e.g.*, with regard to the homogeneity of markets and the behavior of the parties. The question of market-forms mainly concerns sellers, because we can generally assume competition among a great number of buyers. Hence we are mainly concerned with the situation of the sellers. With regard to buyers, analogous conditions apply to a great extent; for the treatment of this problem readers are referred to Chapter 55.

We have an absolute sellers' monopoly when we consider the products of a seller as a separate commodity. As Chamberlin says: "The term monopoly is meaningless without reference to the thing monopolized." Whether a firm is to be considered a monopolist thus becomes a question of definition, *i.e.*, it will depend on whether other firms with, as a rule, a slightly different quality of product or place of business are considered as belonging to the market under consideration. But actual conditions can make the concept of monopoly more or less applicable in individual cases. Thus the actual situation is different for a legal national sugar trust and for the producer of a certain type of textile which is only slightly different from the products of other firms within a country. The textile manufacturer may very well be considered a monopolist, but his sales curve will be very elastic, *i.e.*, his monopoly position is very weak. However, it will not as a rule be practical to consider a case as representing a monopoly if the buyers are very nearly indifferent to the products of various sellers, these forming a group which at the same time differs essentially from the products of other sellers in competition for the purchasing power of the citizens. In case of monopoly we must investigate the economy of the monopolistic firm and its place in the surrounding world. As appears from Fig. 23A, p. 232, this approach is also applicable to a competitive firm, but in that case no explanation of the price is involved. In cases where price depends on an interplay between several firms, the explanation will be incomplete if the decisions of all the firms concerned are not taken into consideration.

The concept "monopoly" is a convenient abstraction. When speaking about monopoly in actual cases, we assume such a degree of isolation for the market considered that commodities produced by other sellers, owing to difference in quality or location, are provisionally assumed to fall outside the market sphere under consideration. If, on the other hand, we proceed to consider the relation of a monopolistic seller within a certain defined sphere to sellers outside the sphere we shall find a more or less close competition, according to the degree of difference in quality and the importance of the respective qualities of the goods, to the buyers. Where the differences *vis-à-vis* the other sellers are of less importance, we speak of monopolistic competition, but there are smooth transitions between the degrees of monopoly and competition. Without discarding the theoretical concept of monopoly, it may often be practical in discussions with persons who are not economic theorists, to speak of price policy instead of monopoly, since for historical reasons the idea of "monopoly" implies something very extraordinary and monstrous.

With the usage which has actually developed it is reasonable to speak of competition where several firms try to sell in the market under consideration, and an expansion of the sales of one firm, consequently, will reduce the selling possibilities of the others. Whether the competitors realize their relationship to one another, will not be decisive in this respect. Where there are few competitors, the resulting relations between them will be of great interest, but even here the most important thing for the individual seller is that his own selling possibilities decrease. Where the number is very large, the individual seller may not at all be interested in his competitors as such, but only in the objective effects of all market conditions, including also the effects of the existence of competitors.[2]

CHAPTER 47

MONOPOLY PRICE

WE assume that a seller has a monopoly and that he tries to maximize his profit. If demand and cost conditions are assumed to be known, it will be possible to find price and quantity sold by a consideration of either total, average or marginal values for gross income and costs. The reader is referred to Fig. 22A–C, p. 230, showing the simplest possible forms of demand and cost conditions, *i.e.*, a straight, sloping demand curve and a straight, horizontal average cost curve, which at the same time is the marginal cost curve. The demand curve *ex ante* in a monopolist's market is also called his sales curve.

In the first figure the maximum net income—the greatest perpendicular distance between income and costs—is to be found by drawing a tangent to the total income curve parallel to the total cost curve. In Fig. B and C, AF is the demand curve, and BC the average and marginal cost curve. The second figure, where the net income, *i.e.*, the monopoly profit, is measured in terms of an area, shows clearly the two determining factors: price in excess of costs and quantity sold.

Instead of price we can, irrespective of the shape of the cost curve, plot the price in excess of costs, *i.e.*, the price obtainable above average costs, along the vertical axis. The elasticity of price in excess of costs, but not

---

[2] Theodor Geiger, the sociologist, in *Konkurrence, en sociologisk Analyse*, Universitetsforlaget Aarhus, Aarhus 1941, gives an interesting description of the conception of competitors of the competitive relationship and competitors' behavior to each other. He only speaks of competition where the individual competitor takes the others into consideration. He emphasizes the subjective element in competition, the side-long glance at the others, individually or as a group.

the elasticity of demand, will then be -1 at the monopoly point. This may be considered as the point where the curve for price in excess of costs is tangent to the most extreme of Marshall's "constant revenue curves", which form a system of equilateral hyperbolae converging towards the axes.

In the third figure the monopoly point is to be found by intersection between the marginal revenue AP_I and the marginal cost curve. When the demand curve is a straight line, the slope of the marginal revenue curve will be twice as great as that of the demand curve. The demand curve may also be considered as the average revenue curve of the sellers. If it is not a straight line as in this figure, the straight lines which are tangents

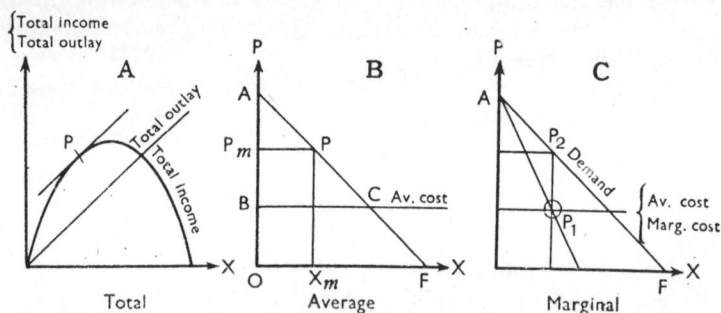

Fig. 22. Total Average and Marginal Determination of Monopoly Point

to the demand curve may be used in a similar way to find the ordinate of the marginal revenue curve at each point.

The three methods say the same thing in different ways. The marginal method has the apparent advantage that in a figure the monopoly point can easily be found at the point of intersection of the two curves. But in reality the trouble has only been shifted on to the construction of the marginal curves, which the theoretical descriptions generally take as a starting-point. This method is convenient, however, in such practical cases where only a certain minor change in the decisions is contemplated, and only the cost of the change itself is known. If, on the other hand, a few alternative calculations are compared with each other, e.g., in regard to a plant not yet built, the total method is employed rather than the marginal method. In theoretical investigations, finally, the average method has the advantage that the effects of altered sales and altered price are seen clearly by themselves.

In most real cases, knowledge of demand is strictly limited, and there may also exist calculations of cost only for a limited number of outputs. If continuity is assumed, we may still, on the basis of calculations for individual points, interpolate or extrapolate. In most cases the curves must be considered as an approximate and rationalized illustration of estimates. Price policy, by the way, is not undertaken on the basis of "real demand curves", but on the basis of the expectation of sellers as to the reactions of demand. If these expectations are not fulfilled, the seller is at a loss for the reason that he does not know whether his estimate was wrong or the curve has been displaced.[1] Particularly in cases where curves in theory would show several maxima, uncertainty in decisions may be expected and there is some chance that, owing to deficient knowledge and the fear of incurring unknown risks, the firm will remain at a relative maximum and not move to the highest monopoly point.

Firms selling under free competition will, as in the case of monopoly, try to maximize their net revenue and will continue sales until marginal revenue is equal to marginal cost. But here we have the special condition that the sales curve of the individual seller, *i.e.*, his average revenue curve, is horizontal, thus at the same time becoming his marginal revenue curve. The seller in the competitive market can only determine his quantity at the given price. The monopolist, on the other hand, can determine either price or quantity and then let demand determine the other. Since he often deals with many buyers, he may, however, be supposed to determine price deliberately. Which party first mentions the price in a market will depend on forms of organization and prevailing custom as well as on the number of participants.

Under monopoly the demand curves of all buyers form the basis of the monopolist's sales curve *ex ante* as well as *ex post*. This curve has a certain slope. Under competition, however, we obtain a special, practically horizontal sales curve for each seller, but by horizontal addition of these curves for numerous sellers, the declining demand curve of the market is formed. (It seems practical to use the term "sales curve" instead of the "seller's individual demand curve", since we are not dealing with demand on the seller's part.) Opposed to this is the total supply curve of the market, cf. Chapter 20. In the case of monopoly there is a cost curve, but no supply curve independent of demand.

Fig. 23A–B[2] for an enterprise under free competition and monopoly respectively, illustrate total, average, and marginal curves. As will be understood from the discussion of cost curves, p. 120, the average and marginal long-run cost curve will probably very seldom have this deep U-shape, but we use it here as the conventional illustration of curves probably beginning with a small decline and ending with a sharp rise. Quantities are plotted along the horizontal axes, total amounts for the whole of the enterprise along the vertical axes in the upper sections of the figures, and amounts per unit in the lower sections. In Fig. 23A the solid lines illustrate the situation for a firm under free competition among many firms with similar cost conditions. The upper part of Fig. 23A illustrates total revenue, total cost, and total net loss at various outputs corresponding to price I in the lower part of the figure. Balance is reached

[1] R. Triffin, *Monopolistic Competition and General Equilibrium Theory* (Cambridge), 1940.
[2] From Lindahl's mimeographed lectures, "Grundlinjer till Föreläsninger vid Handelshögskolan i Göteborg", 1937. Price II in Fig. 23A has been added.

at sales of about 76, whereas both greater and smaller production results in a loss. The lower part of the figure illustrates the corresponding marginal

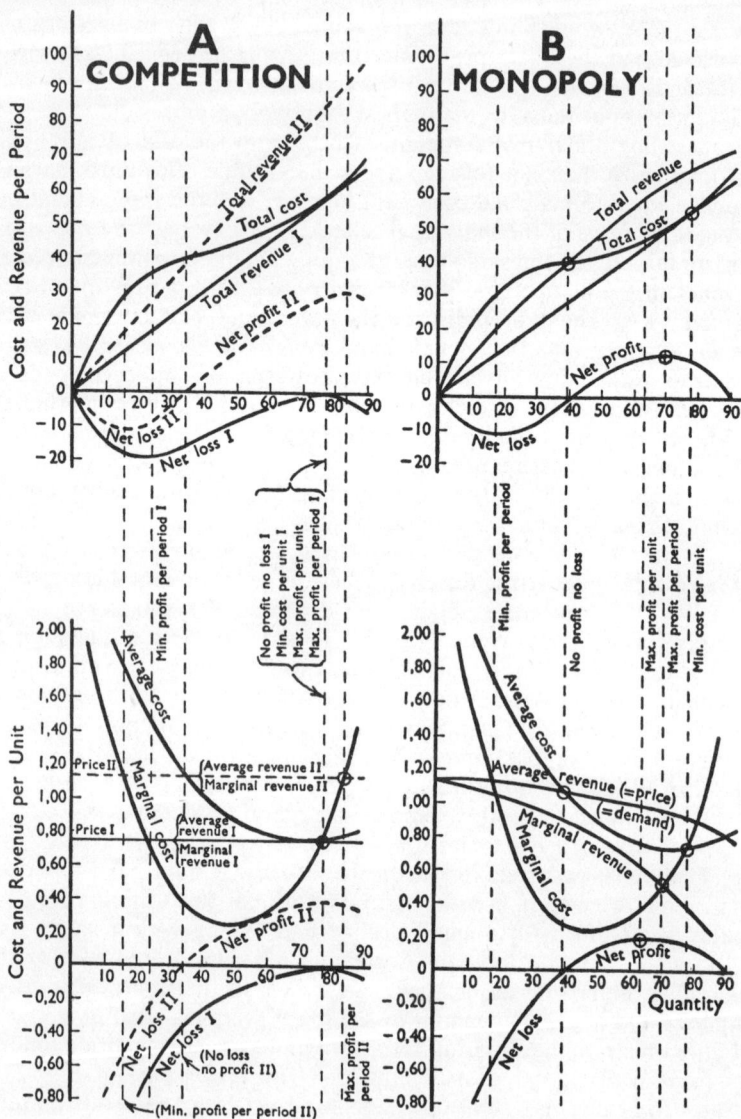

Fig. 23. Price Determination in Firms with U-shaped Cost Curves under Competition and Monopoly

and average revenues, here equal to price (price I), and marginal and average cost curves as well as the net loss per unit. Further relationships among the various curves and the economic significance of the decisive points are indicated in the explanations in the figure (cf. particularly the perpendicular lines).

In Fig. 23A the broken lines (representing case II) indicate the result when the firm has the same costs as before, but is better off than its competitors, who have cost minima corresponding to the market price, here price II. Price II may also be the short-run price of a group of absolutely similar firms, the scarcity of plant capacity determined by previous fixed costs and expectations giving a price in excess of the direct costs then considered in the figure. Whereas under free competition among firms of the same type production takes place at the lowest possible costs, one competing firm with lower costs (Fig. 23A, price II) will continue production beyond its lowest costs. But since an extra profit with perfect competitive adaptation must depend on the possession of some scarce means of production, it may also be considered as a cost. It may also happen that a monopolist, as in Fig. 23B, stops production before the point of minimum costs has been reached. If selling possibilities increase, *i.e.*, if total, average and marginal revenue curves are raised, we may on the other hand find that production is extended beyond the point of minimum costs.

As mentioned above on pp. 229/30, the elasticity of a curve indicating price in excess of average costs is equal to—1 at the monopoly point. In harmony with a form of price policy that is very common in real life, we find, moreover, that the monopoly price is: $p = c \cdot \dfrac{e}{1 + e}$, *i.e.*, equal to marginal costs multiplied by a certain factor, which is dependent on the elasticity of demand. The formula is of practical importance especially in case of constant variable costs (average costs equal marginal costs). And the proof is then very simple.[3] When monopoly is at maximum, $dp \cdot x = dx \cdot (p - c)$. Dividing by $dp \cdot x$ and inserting elasticity of demand $e = -(dx \cdot p)/(dp \cdot x)$, we obtain $1 = -e + c \cdot e/p$ and $p = -ep + ce$ and consequently $p = c \cdot e/(e + 1)$. The factor determined by elasticity of demand, $e/(1 + e)$, with which we have to multiply marginal costs in order to arrive at monopoly price, may be called the degree of monopoly. One may, however, prefer to use a term for the relative excess price, $(p-c)/c$ or $(p-c)/p$. When the elasticity of demand is -3, $p = 3/2c$; $e = -2$, $p = 2c$; $e = -1$, $p = \infty \cdot c$; $e = -\infty$, $p = c$. In case of monopoly the numerical value of e is always above 1.

We have now examined the conditions which determine the monopoly point under static assumptions and the assumption of maximization of profit. These conditions are, in the first place, modified under dynamic assumptions, cf. Chapter 58. In the second place, it is probable (cf. Chapters 59 and 61) that the well-to-do monopolist will act partly from other motives than the desire to maximize profit and, furthermore, that the monopolist's power of rational maximization is limited in real life.

[3] A more general proof is to be found in Joan Robinson, *The Economics of Imperfect Competition*, 1933, Macmillan, London, pp. 36 and 54.

If a firm undertakes a rational dynamic planning of its price policy and its general behavior, it will take account of the revenue and costs of the moment as well as all expectations of future revenue and costs, the individual amounts being determined according to their degree of security and distance in time. Even if it is only possible to carry through a rational calculation of this kind in terms of actual figures to a very limited extent, the estimates of the firms may be assumed at least to aim in this direction. The point is not to maximize revenue per year, but to maximize the capitalized value of all the future net revenue of the firm, *i.e.*, the momentary capital value of the firm itself as an asset. This means, for one thing, that a lower price may be set to begin with, if by accustoming consumers to the commodity a greater future demand may be created. The danger that new competitors may appear, or that old competitors will expand (latent competition), may also modify the price policy greatly, and this is one of the factors which make firms in real life base their price policy to such a great extent on the basis of costs, including supplementary costs, or to adopt fixed prices. The modifying influence mentioned above is, of course, dependent on whether it is possible for others to enter the market, and at what costs and how quickly this may take place. If there is no question of investing a greater amount of fixed capital, and if there is no chance of retaining even a moderate monopoly for a long period, it may be advantageous to take a high profit for a short period, *e.g.*, by cornering the market. The dynamic calculation of monopoly profit may be illustrated by a three-dimensional graph with time as the third axis together with price and quantity, future prices being discounted according to the interest rate and degree of security. Unlike the case of the static average calculation, it is a question of maximizing a volume, not an area.

Instead of considering expected selling possibilities and cost for a series of later periods, it will be possible, especially where price stability may be assumed, to act on the basis of long-run curves. The latter in this instance signify an average of future expectations, or, if it is preferred, the immediate future modified by consideration of the effects on price, sales, and costs in later periods. Possible competition from substitutes or remote competitors then means a curtailing of expected future demand, which may affect the present price policy. The fear of public interference may be conceived in the same way. Considerations of public opinion may be due to fear of a later lowering of the demand curve by means of public intervention, or to ill feeling on the part of consumers resulting in reduced profit. There may also be involved a question of a change in the aim of the monopolist away from a one-sided maximization of profit. When we speak of demand and cost curves instead of using the cumbersome three-dimensional calculation in which interest and risk are taken into consideration, these two-dimensional curves ought not to be taken as determined solely by short-run considerations, but as including expectations of the future.

CHAPTER 48

BETWEEN MONOPOLY AND COMPETITION[1]

FOR the majority of firms outside agriculture, a small increase in price is not likely to result in the total loss of sales. Thus firms will be able to carry on price policy within certain limits, and they may be said to have a monopoly in that sense. Their monopoly is limited, however. All monopolies are limited in so far as they compete with all other commodities when consumers decide how to spend their incomes. It is not possible without being arbitrary to draw a definite line between firms having a small advantage in the eyes of some buyers, as to quality, location, or personal relations, and the clear-cut monopolies recognized by everybody. As to the position of the individual firm, the elasticity of its sales curve may best indicate the limit to its monopoly power. Whether in a particular case we speak of monopoly and deduct the competitors from the sales curve of the monopolist, or we prefer to speak of competition in a more comprehensive market, including the competitors, is a question of convenience.

When there is a great difference in the valuation of the buyers between the produce of one firm and that of its competitors and when the price of one firm cannot be expected to lead to changes in the price policy of other firms, a partial analysis of the firm as a monopoly may be used, assuming *ceteris paribus* as to other firms and their commodities. The cross elasticity indicating the effect of the changes in price of one firm on the sales of another is small in this case.

Where we have clearly defined groups of qualities or markets with low costs of internal transportation, but strong protection against foreign markets, or where, as in some cities, owing to costs of transportation, there are highly isolated markets for certain commodities, we shall

---

[1] For literature on this and the following chapter, we reter to Chamberlin, *The Theory of Monopolistic Competition*, with detailed bibliography, Harvard Univ. Press, 6th ed., 1948; Joan Robinson, *Economies of Imperfect Competition*, Macmillan, 1933; D. Fritz Machlup, "Monopoly and Competition: A Classification of Market Positions", *American Economic Review*, 1937; the same later: *The Economics of Sellers Competition*, Johns Hopkins Univ., 1952; Triffin, *Monopolistic Competition and General Equilibrium Theory*, Cambridge, 1940; William Fellner, *Competition Among the Few*, New York, 1949; articles by Galbraith and Bain in *A Survey of Contemporary Economics*, Vol. I, 1948; Zeuthen, "Monopolistic Competition and the Homogeneity of the Market", *Econometrica*, 1936 and *Problems of Monopoly and Economic Warfare*, Routledge, London, 1930; Stackelberg, *Marktform und Gleichgewicht*, Julius Springer, Wien & Berlin, 1934, *inter alia* p. 2; and in this connection the classification in Walter Eucken, *Grundlagen der Nationalökonomie*, Gustav Fischer, Jena, 1940, p. 131, and Hans Möller, *Kalkulation, Absatzpolitik und Preisbildung*, Julius Springer, Wien, 1941, p. 28; Schneider, "Zur Konkurrenz und Preisbildung auf vollkommenen und unvollkommenen Märkten", *Weltwirtschaftliches Archiv*, 1938, and *Reine Theorie monopolistischer Wirtschaftformen*, Mohr, Tübingen, 1932.

generally have a practical division of markets with a great gap in the partial elasticities if competitors outside the frontier of the market are considered. One must be careful, however, in using a partial analysis, not to disregard the possibility that competitors may change their policy. A preliminary, excessively narrow limitation of markets might, however, afterwards be corrected by special analyses of the interplay between several markets. Examples of this are the treatment of the interrelation of the different domestic markets of several countries in the theory of international trade, and the relation between two kinds of raw materials used in the production of the same monopolized commodity.[2]

CHAPTER 49

TYPES OF MARKETS

IF we want to pass from provisional deductive reasoning to empirical research, it is important to distinguish between market forms according to criteria which are open to observation. Conditions in real markets, however, are generally very complicated, *vide* the American steel and motorcar industries, or the former German iron industry and its relations to the coal mines. In cases like these it is necessary, in order to understand how prices and quantities are determined, not only to know the number of firms, their size and mutual position in the market, but also the relation to byproducts, the marketing system, raw materials, and the labor market, as well as the structure of the firms and combinations, their internal organization and history, the character of the leading persons, and the attitude of the state. The present analysis, however, is of a more introductory character. The purpose is partly to prepare the way for concrete special investigations, and partly to give a more general picture of the economically decisive factors in the actually existing types of markets. For this purpose, it would be too troublesome and impractical to set up a scheme containing all imaginable forms of market by combining all essential classifications. In this chapter we shall, instead, enumerate in a schematic form some of the different properties of markets. In the next chapter we shall proceed to a more detailed discussion of price formation for a few greatly simplified combinations of these properties.

It is possible to classify markets according to the number of buyers and sellers in the field considered, and set up a schema in which we distinguish between one, two, a few, and many buyers and sellers, respectively. Thus

---

[2] Stackelberg, *Marktform und Gleichgewicht*, Chapter 3; Hick's concept "multiple exchange", Value and Capital, p. 66; cf. Ohlin's theory concerning interregional price systems.

we obtain as limiting cases bilateral monopoly and free competition, and further a number of more complicated cases, as sellers' and buyers' duopoly and oligopoly, when two, or a few, sellers or buyers are set against a great number of competing counterparts. As a special group, it is possible to insert the partial monopoly, dealt with below on p. 243, where besides one big firm carrying on price policy there is a large number of small competitors, which are unable to do so. For each of the sixteen, twenty-five, or more combinations resulting from classification according to the number of buyers and sellers, it is at the same time possible to establish a classification according to the degree of homogeneity of the market, and according to the degree of freedom of entry into the market, etc. In the first instance we shall deal with the possible classifications according to the conditions of the *sellers*, assuming a large number of competing buyers.[1]

Since the number of firms in the sphere considered will in many cases depend on a rather arbitrary estimate of what a commodity is and what a market is, the first classification will be based upon the degree of homogeneity of the markets.

49.1, HOMOGENEOUS AND HETEROGENEOUS MARKETS

In the absolutely homogeneous market all buyers have the same willingness to buy from all sellers. None of the latter is able to obtain a higher price than his fellows from any of the buyers, *i.e.*, no preference exists. It is not even possible to obtain a temporary advantage as a result of the buyers' limited knowledge of all sellers. The conditions of the homogeneous ("ideal", "atomistic", or "perfect") market can scarcely be fully realized. This does not, however, exclude the possibility that the differences in many cases are so small that it may be advantageous to treat a market as if it were homogeneous. The greater the area that is dealt with as one market, the greater will be the importance of the qualitative and local differences within the market.

Preferences for individual sellers may be due to (1) distance and costs of transportation, (2) differences in quality, (3) better knowledge and confidence, which again may be caused by previous contacts or advertising.

Whereas price in a homogeneous market must be the same for all sellers, and the individual firm therefore has no opportunity to pursue a price policy of its own, sellers in a heterogeneous market are able to carry on a price policy of their own. A small increase in price will then result in some decrease in sales. We have here the so-called *monopolistic competition*, with which we shall deal more fully in Chapter 50.3.

Finally, it is of some importance to pay attention to mixed cases where either an individual price policy may be possible temporarily, or where

---

[1] As to classification, see Hans Möller (quoted in footnote 1, page 235), and Bain in *A Survey of Contemporary Economics*, Vol. I, 1948, pp. 158–62.

R

small differences in price may appear. In such cases, just as in the homogeneous market, an approximate common price may prevail at the same time as there is an opportunity of carrying on an individual price policy to a slight extent or at least giving favors by means of rebates, delivery service, or better quality, all of which are equivalent to small reductions in price (cf. Chapter 50.4 about the special method of considering these "approximately homogeneous markets").

A classification according to the use of the commodities and the nature of the circle of buyers and sellers respectively will in many cases be an important symptom not only of the homogeneity of the market, but also of its properties in other directions. Hence the distinction between the market for industrial raw materials, machines, etc., agricultural products, day-to-day consumers' goods, quality goods and durable consumers' goods.

49.2, NUMBER AND SIZE OF FIRMS

As mentioned above, the number of sellers as well as the number of buyers are of great importance for the form of the market. More essential than the number itself, however, is the size of the individual firms in relation to the market as a whole. The partial monopoly where we have one big firm alongside a number of small competitors does not differ much from an absolute monopoly with a somewhat smaller demand (cf. p. 243). Similarly, a market with two big firms and many small ones approaches that of pure duopoly. When the individual firm has a large part of the market, it must take into consideration the fact that an increase in its own sales will require a comparatively great decrease in price.

Under monopolistic competition in a heterogeneous market, the question of number is not of the same importance as in the closed and homogeneous market and often the number is indefinite until the delimitation of the market is indicated. In the case of monopolistic competition both the number of competitors and their distance in the eyes of customers are of importance to the individual firm. In many cases the market will be a continuous chain of neighboring firms in competition (possibly with regard to quality), and the connection with the remoter links in the chain will be so weak that, without being too inaccurate, we can cut off the market to be considered almost at will, only with the result that the explanation for the firms near the frontier of the market will become most incomplete. Generally, instead of studying a market, the best thing to do will be to consider the individual firm including its relations with other firms.

Also the absolute size of firms and enterprises will often exert a certain influence on their price policy.[2] More effort may be devoted to price policy in the very large firm. On the other hand, the latter will often be

---

[2] Edward S. Mason, "Price and Production Policies of Large Scale Enterprise", Supplement to *American Economic Review*, 1939, p. 62.

exposed to private bureaucracy and have other aims than profit maximization. The financial strength and the technical possibilities for expansion will count more than the size of the firm in a fight with competitors or when pressure is exerted against them.

49.3, BEHAVIOR OF FIRMS

The behavior of firms is largely a result of the other conditions of the market mentioned above, but it also depends on quite different factors, personal and historic, and it may therefore be considered as a separate element. At any rate, such behavior is an important characteristic of the actual state of the market. If it should be preferred, it is possible to speak about market form and market behavior as two equally important properties of a market.[3] Perhaps the most important aspect of behavior is whether the firms act independently of the prospective reaction of other firms to one's own actions, *i.e.*, act "autonomously", or they take the other firms' reactions into consideration, *i.e.*, act "conjecturally". Several assumptions are possible as to the more long-term action of the firms in the market. There are also different possibilities with regard to temporary actions which change the structure of the market, as, for instance, destruction or suppression of a competitor by means of aggressive measures or boycott, combination or agreement.

Moreover, there is the question of the aim of the firms and their more or less rational action. Even in competition between many buyers and sellers, the question of behavior may be of interest. Predominant, perhaps incorrect, expectations may influence the momentary pricing and future development. But otherwise, competition will generally force the individual firm to pursue automatically a definite, comparatively simple type of action, and if there is sufficient time for adjustment, the result will be equilibrium at a price equal to cost and a fairly rational method of production. The situation is different in the case of a few competitors, where there are one or a few sellers and one or a few buyers. More or less indefinite assumptions as to the action of the others and speculations about how to influence it are here of importance. In many instances it is necessary to act according to the probability of different possible reactions on the part of the others. If for instance a definite quantity is demanded, the seller may ask a price giving profit without incurring too great a risk of a refusal from the other party.[4] In certain cases offers may be given or accepted with price as well as quantity fixed.

It is of interest to consider which magnitude or magnitudes—parameters

[3] Schneider, "Wirklichkeitsnahe Theorie der Absatzpolitik", *Weltwirtschaftliches Archiv*, July, 1942.
[4] Ragnar Frisch, "Monopole-Polypole—La Notion de Force", *Nationaløkonomisk Tidsskrift*, 1933, and the translation "Monopoly-Polypoly—The Concept of Force", in *International Economic Papers*, 1951; see also Frisch's mimeographed lectures on market mechanism under momentary production, University of Oslo, 1934.

of action—may be influenced by the individual firm. Besides price and quantity, it is possible to vary the quality of the commodity, service and advertising as described in Chapters 52 and 53. The actual forms and methods of business, as for instance quotation of fixed prices during long periods, are of importance; also the question of other aims than the maximization of profit, as dealt with in Chapter 59.

Monopoly theory, as a general rule, started with deductions from the assumptions of various given forms of behavior, without much discussion of the reality of the assumptions. This is also the easiest approach, and in the next chapter we shall generally, by way of introduction, use the same method. The primary problem, however, which will be dealt with later, is which are the actual aims of the firms and other economic agents, which behavior and which strategy are profitable for them under different external conditions, and what is their actual behavior. In markets with few sellers or buyers, their behavior is not likely often to be a given and constant factor. Rather it may be said that the decisive element is the difficult and changing choice of strategy[5] and constant conflict and negotiation between parties about the rules of games to be applied, and consequently about the structure of the market. This choice cannot be decided by the ordinary mechanism of the market, and pricing is therefore indeterminate in a theory limited in the way indicated above. Actually, however, the questions are determined in some way or other. A satisfactory theory must, therefore, also consider conditions outside the hereditary framework of economics. The difficulty is that several business units try to influence the same quantities in different directions at the same time. The same variables are simultaneously parameters of action for several firms. The problems, therefore, cannot be solved as simple problems of maximization. It is possible, to a certain extent and provisionally, to solve the problems by tricks, as for instance to assume that all firms are similar, to assume as data all the decisions made by the other parties, or to assume that the action of the other parties is determined by that of the firm itself because they react in a manner known in advance. In the latter case the quantities determined by the other firms are dependent variables in known functions, in which the parameters of action of the firm itself are independent variables.

49.4, COST FUNCTION AND DIFFERENCE IN THE COSTS OF COMPETITORS

A difference in costs does not exclude the existence of competitors with higher costs. It is likely, however, that firms with higher costs obtain the smallest sales. If the firms have similar sales curves, the marginal cost curve will intersect the marginal revenue curve at a lower quantity.

[5] John von Neumann and Oskar Morgenstern, *The Theory of Games and Economic Behavior*, Princeton, 1947 and Chapter 57 below.

49.5, CONDITIONS OF ENTRY

We deal here partly with entry of new firms, partly with expansion of existing firms. If there is no idle capacity, the possibilities of expansion will be hampered, at any rate in the short run. But also in the long run there may be obstacles, possibly institutional, as patents and franchises. Advantages of different kinds, trade marks, and goodwill among customers should also be mentioned. Further, there is a very considerable barrier to entry because of lack of divisibility. In a certain locality, for instance, there may be no room for an additional firm large enough to cover the costs or to compete. Expansion may only be possible by means of large indivisible units of machinery. The difficulty here is that the market is too small to absorb more units of production producing as cheaply as those already existing. As to the discussion of the problem of entry in connection with monopolistic competition, we refer to Chapter 51.

49.6, PRICE DISCRIMINATION

Price discrimination is not possible if mobility in the market is so great that the differences in price are removed by trade between the different parts of the market. Price discrimination is impossible under free competition. Further we refer to Chapter 54.

49.7, JOINT PRODUCTION AND COMMON PRODUCTION

While as a general rule in theoretical examples it is assumed that each enterprise only produces one commodity, which is a great simplification, the great majority of firms actually produce several commodities, and often by means of processes where several commodities are necessarily produced. The latter case may be termed "joint production" as opposed to "common production", which only indicates that the same firm actually produces several commodities, cf. Chapter 54.

49.8, COOPERATION BETWEEN FIRMS

This and the following subsection deal with decisions which are not taken by the individual firm alone. Cartels make decisions on definite points, as, for instance, price or distribution of sales, leaving it open for the firms freely to further their interests in other directions. In many cases, however, there is only silent agreement or mutual understanding, or action on the part of individual firms more or less of the same character as common action, cf. Chapter 60.

A formal arrangement of market conditions with official price quotations, market rules, conditions of sale, etc., may have been made either by the interested parties themselves or by the state and can in many cases exercise a certain influence on price and quantity.

49.9, STATE REGULATION

Besides the above-mentioned formal regulations of the market, the state (or the municipality) interferes in the individual market by taxation, subsidies, price control, social, health and technical measures, etc. To this must be added the effect of political measures of a more general character, as for instance income taxation, public investment and traffic and pensions, cf. Chapter 64.

49.10, ECONOMIC EVOLUTION AND STABILITY

During the earlier development of the automobile industry in the United States up to 1920, competition, in spite of the existence of a few, large enterprises, resulted in constantly falling prices. Since this did not bring about significantly greater sales, the firms changed their models every year, thus encouraging replacement sales. There is a widespread belief among American businessmen that aggressive price competition only pays in a period of increasing production.[6] In a period when a number of important inventions are made in an industry, keen competition may be expected, often involving a writing down of capital values and at the same time changing preference positions for the individual firms with corresponding changes in profit. This may be followed at a later stage by collective utilization or nonutilization of the inventions and expensive research institutes for large industrial combinations.

The strength of business cycles and seasonal fluctuations will also, to a great extent, influence the organization of the market, cf. Chapter 58.

49.11, ORGANIZATIONS IN ADJACENT FIELDS

Under this heading are included suppliers of raw materials, the labor market, and buyers of the finished product. The tendency to monopolistic organization often spreads. Trade unions lead to employers' associations, which again lead to cooperation also in the field of selling the products. Trade-union measures against unorganized labor may strengthen the cooperation of employers in the market of commodities. In this connection we may refer to Chapters 55 and 56, dealing with buyers' monopolies, monopoly of productive factors and bilateral monopoly. Sales of branded goods at fixed retail prices and the enforcement of the latter by means of resale price maintenance must largely influence the market conditions of the retail trade, and, conversely, buyers' monopolies in trade and the production of finished goods must influence the market conditions of the earlier stages of production.

[6] Mason, p. 70, cited *supra*, p. 238, n. 2.

CHAPTER 50

A COLLECTION OF THEORETICAL MODELS

INSTEAD of aiming at a complete and systematic filling out of the thousands of cases that may be formed by combining the above-mentioned classifications, we shall here discuss only some of the most important problems, those which presuppose a number of comparatively simple combinations of assumptions. In this chapter we confine ourselves to the differences discussed under the first five points of the last chapter (homogeneity, number, behavior, costs, and freedom of entry), and we assume preliminarily that the special conditions mentioned under the other points are of no importance. As a main classification, we employ the first criterion: the degree of homogeneity of the market.

50.1, THE HOMOGENEOUS MARKET

Even if a perfectly homogeneous market is never found, the valuation by the buyers of the commodities of the individual sellers is so similar in a great number of cases that we are able to disregard individual preferences. Even where these are not negligible, it may be useful to disregard them completely as a first approximation.

We shall first deal with *partial monopoly*,[1] *i.e.*, cases where, besides one big seller, there is in the same market a number of small sellers who individually are only of small importance in proportion to the market as a whole. Whereas the big seller may be able to carry on an individual price policy, each of the small sellers will take the price fixed by him as the given market price and adjust his quantity accordingly. The special sales curve of the big seller is then the same as the demand curve of the market less the supply of the competitors at the different prices. In Fig. 24A, D_1D_1' is the demand curve of the whole market, SS' to the right in the figure is the total supply of the small competitors at different prices; to the left in the figure this has been deducted from the demand curve of the market by horizontal subtraction, whereby we obtain the special sales curve, D_2D_2' of the large firm. The monopoly point of the latter is x_2p_2; CC' the large firm's average cost curve. Whereas if the large seller had been alone, the monopoly point would have been x_1p_1, the existence of the small competitors results in a lower price and smaller sales for the large firm, but greater total sales (x_3). Average cost here only includes direct cost when short-run adjustment is considered, but in the long run also fixed cost.

---

[1] A somewhat more detailed description will be found in my book, *Problems of Monopoly and Economic Warfare*, 1930. Part I, Chapter 3.

Figs. 24B–F show that the result depends on the conditions of demand and costs. In these cases it is assumed that a certain quantity which is independent of price becomes the share of the small competitors, and we consider a series of different quantities (cf. the dotted lines). CC′ indicates

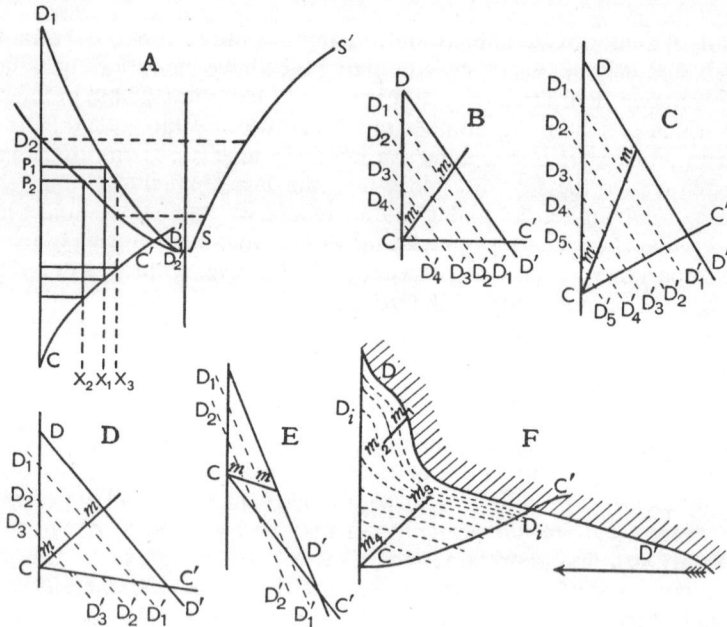

Fig. 24. Partial Monopoly

the average costs of the large firm. The line mm (the monopolist's line of retreat—or, as an exception to our general rule under the special conditions of changes in competition considered here, we may speak of a supply curve for the monopolist) indicates the way in which, under increasing competition, the monopoly point moves from the middle of DD′ towards C. If the large firm has lower costs with a small output, the fall in price is accentuated, cf. Fig. C, whereas the opposite is the case in Fig. D. As will be seen in Fig. E, it is conceivable that competition will lead to an increase in price and a consequent reduction in total sales, because the costs of the large firm rise so much that the monopoly point is situated at a higher level even with the reduced sales. The condition is that the average costs decrease more than half as much as the demand curve with increased sales. The fact that total costs rise with increased sales will, however, put a limit to this decrease, which must also be considered to be limited for other reasons, cf. p. 118. In Fig. F we have an example of a demand curve with two maxima. The monopolist's path of retreat $m_1 m_2$ and $m_3 m_4$ has been constructed in this way. The original demand curve

D_1D_1' is moved to the left. As a result, the reduced demand curves D_2D_2', D_3D_3', etc., are produced. For any of these curves we find the point that yields the largest amount of monopoly profits. The locus of all these points is m_1m_2 and m_3m_4. If the large firm is alone in the market, it will prefer a high price and small sales in this case. If competition reaches a certain intensity it is, however, advantageous to shift to another price policy with low price and large sales. When the curve D_1D_1' is reached, it jumps from the upper to the lower mm curve. This result is especially likely if the competitors have a greater supply at a higher price, as in Fig. 24A.

It is probable that the large firm in a number of cases will only allow the competitor certain sales, and if these are exceeded, will begin a price war or boycott. The firm may however be interested in the existence of the competitors, so that they may tell the state, the trade unions, or the buyers that the majority of the firms in this industry work without much profit.

The next case, dealing with a homogeneous market in which there are several large firms in the same industry, is considerably more complicated. If there are two firms we speak of *duopoly*; if there are more than two firms, but still not such a large number that the individual firm fails to notice a decrease in price when it expands sales, we speak of *oligopoly*. Also "partial duopoly" and "partial oligopoly" are conceivable in cases where two or more firms are large enough to feel the effects of their own expansion on the prevailing price, while the others behave like the small competitors under "partial monopoly".

Duopoly in a perfectly homogeneous market is hardly conceivable in real life. It may be useful, however, as an introduction to the following discussion to explain how an equilibrium—between that of monopoly and competition—may appear under certain special assumptions. The case was described by Cournot[2] in 1838 in a somewhat different form, and it revealed the fact that such a thing as competition between several firms and a price above costs was no absolute impossibility.

What happens in cases of duopoly and oligopoly depends on the expectations and behavior of the firms. We assume to begin with two firms, both of which take the previous sales of the other party as given at each

---

[2] With regard to Cournot's discussion of duopoly in a homogeneous market, 1838, cf. *Researches into the Mathematical Principles of the Theory of Wealth*, by Augustine Cournot, Macmillan, 1927 edition with notes by Irving Fisher, Chapter 7; Stackelberg, *Marktform und Gleichgewicht*, Chapter 5; Chamberlin, *Monopolistic Competition*, Chapter 3; the article by Schneider in *Weltwirtschaftliches Archiv*, 1938, Section II, and *Reine Theorie monopolistischer Wirtschaftsformen*, 1932; my own, *Problems of Monopoly and Economic Warfare*, 1930, Chapter 2; cf. the article in *Econometrica*, 1936, particularly note 6, on the result and assumptions of Cournot, in answer to A. J. Nichols' article in *Journal of Political Economy*, "A Re-appraisal of Cournot's 'Theory of Duopoly Price'", 1934. The slight change in the assumptions is mentioned here: the introduction of the "nearly homogeneous" market conditions (cf. Chapter 50.4 below) which makes it possible to reach Cournot's result approximately under assumptions which are conceivable in real life. A numero speciale about Oligopoly published by *Économie Appliquée*, 1955.

moment and thus each of them assumes that its own sales possibilities are equal to those indicated by the demand curve of the market, less the actual sales of the other party. The question can then be solved almost as in the case of partial monopoly, and the result will be the same as that of Cournot.

Fig. 25 shows a simplified case with a rectilinear demand curve for the whole of the market D_1D_1' and a common constant average and marginal cost curve for the two firms CC'. Thus the heights above the bottom line of the figure do not indicate price, but price in excess of costs. We assume preliminarily that one of the firms has chosen sales e (and for the time being we disregard the fact that quantity e in the figure corresponds to the final

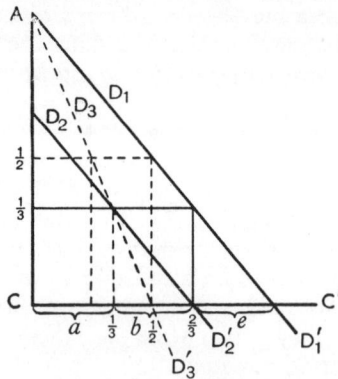

Fig. 25. The Cournot Duopoly Case

equilibrium). The sales curve for the other firm, when one firm takes e, becomes D_2D_2', and thereby its monopoly point in the special case is determined so that a = b. The position of the two firms being similar, however, the former will only be in equilibrium in so far as its sales, when the firm is considered as a monopolist, are also equal to the unsatisfied demand at price C. In the special case we consequently obtain a = b = e. Thus each of the firms, in the simple and quite special case illustrated in the figure, obtains ⅓ of the possible sales at a price equal to costs, and the price in excess of cost becomes ⅓ of AE. The movement towards equilibrium can, with the given assumptions, be illustrated if we begin by supposing e to be greater or smaller than ⅓CC', and then try to find the quantity which the other firm will want to sell. By alternative adjustment of the sales of each of the two firms to those of the other party, we shall move towards the point of equilibrium, cf. the lines of reaction in Fig. 26 below, and the zigzag lines between them.

The numerical results in the extremely special case illustrated are of course of no general validity. However, the relation between them indicates a tendency for price, sales and profit in the transition from competition to duopoly, with the assumed behavior, and from this to monopoly.

It will easily be seen how, by drawing other demand and cost curves, we shall arrive at other numerical results. Further, it will be seen how, by increasing the number of firms, we reduce the equilibrium price, increase total sales and reduce the sales of the individual firm as well as total profit. In the special case the excess price for one firm is $\frac{1}{2}$, for two firms, $\frac{1}{3}$, for three firms, $\frac{1}{4}$, and for n firms it is $\dfrac{1}{n+1}$ of the highest possible excess price (AC), and the sales of the individual firm amount to the same fraction of total sales at a price equal to costs. Total profits decrease from $(\frac{1}{2})^2 = \frac{1}{4}$ to $2 \cdot (\frac{1}{3})^2 = \frac{2}{9}$, etc. By way of comparison, the dotted lines in Fig. 25 indicate the analysis in case the firms agree to carry on a joint monopolistic policy, *e.g.*, by sharing the market equally. D_3D_3' will in that case be the demand curve for the individual firm.

Under the assumption that both firms thus assume the sales of the other party to be given and alternately try to adjust themselves to the sales of the other, the case is determinate. However, there is one drawback attaching to the Cournot assumptions, that large firms faced with many buyers cannot, as assumed, be expected to carry on the policy of quantity adjustment (output policy), but will carry on price policy; and if, in a perfectly homogeneous market, one of the firms underbids the other, be it ever so little, it will immediately take all the customers. Any alternative adjustment upwards or downwards towards the point of equilibrium is thereby excluded. When price policy is carried on in a homogeneous market, it is impossible to obtain any equilibrium without collusion between the firms —not even a competitive equilibrium with price equal to costs, because one firm, if for a time the market has been shared at a price equal to costs, will not be able to undertake a sudden great expansion (*e.g.*, from $\frac{1}{2}CC'$ in Fig. 25) and it will therefore be profitable for the other firm to increase price and reduce sales for a time (*e.g.*, to $\frac{1}{4}CC'$). The situation is complicated further if, in addition to fixed capital and the corresponding costs, we take account of the time required for expansion.

A Cournot solution may, however, be conceived in a homogeneous market in the very special cases when the few firms really carry on a quantity adjustment policy (output policy). Thus, it is imaginable that all deliver their production to the same commissioner, who fixes the price so that the exact quantity can be sold. Such cases, however, are probably very unrealistic.

A situation giving almost the same result as in the Cournot case is conceivable in certain forms of cartels (cf. below, p. 313) and similar situations may be imagined in a "nearly homogeneous market" (cf. Chapter 50.4, p. 263).

Besides the improbability of a quantity adjustment policy in the case of two or a few sellers and many buyers in a homogeneous market, it is also improbable in the long run that sellers will, as assumed, take the action of the other party as given, not trying to influence it or to change the market conditions by a combination or warfare. Profit may be increased if two firms join in a monopoly instead of carrying on a separate monopoly policy, and moreover one of them may be able to achieve a favorable position at the cost of the other, even though both continue to exist.

The question of the firms' choice of behavior[3] is especially acute in a homogeneous market. Where there are preferences for individual sellers, the latter may act as absolute monopolists within a certain price interval, before meeting the competition of the others. To a lesser extent than in the homogeneous market, they will be influenced by and will influence the others and so have less occasion to seek an advantage by influencing the behavior of their competitors. The question of choice of behavior is, however, an important problem in all cases of a small number of competitors. Only when this question has been decided, in one way or another, or when it is assumed to have been decided, do we have a determinate theory of price formation.

The situation in the homogeneous market will be illustrated by a simplified example in correspondence with Stackelberg's description. Fig. 26A indicates a rectilinear demand curve for a market with two competitors. Their costs have been fixed at zero, but might also have been given as constant, in which case the horizontal axis would have had to be drawn at a lower level. Thus the situation is the same as in the last figure.

The market being homogeneous, the firms have to pursue a quantity adjustment policy if equilibrium is to be obtained. If firm No. 1 produces the quantities indicated in column 1 of the table, it is profitable for firm No. II to produce the quantities in the second column, because II can now be considered as a monopolist in a market where the common demand curve has been reduced by the sales of No. I. With the sums of I's and II's sales thus obtained (column 3), the price corresponding to the demand curve (see Fig. A) will be as indicated in column 4, and profits for the two firms as indicated in the two last columns. The quantities in column 2 indicate the reactions of II when I as "leader" chooses the quantities given in column 1. In Fig. 26B where the sales of I and II respectively have been plotted along the axes, the *reaction curves* of the firms R_1 and R_2 indicate how much it is profitable for each of them to sell when the other party has chosen a certain quantity. The point of intersection C, indicates the equilibrium of Cournot where both take the other's sales as given. If, for instance, II starts with the quantity of 8, I will react by fixing his quantity at 1, and from this point we move by alternating reactions along the zigzag line towards Cournot's point of equilibrium where there is equilibrium if each of the firms takes the other's sales as given.

It is evident that the individual firm can obtain a greater profit if it is itself able to maintain the sales of 5 and let the other party adjust its sales accordingly. In this way we reach one of the two asymmetrical points A_1 or A_2. But which of them is first reached will depend on accident or

[3] Stackelberg, *Marktform*, and the article by Frisch mentioned on page 239, Note 4.

foresight in the present case, where the firms are otherwise quite similar. If the other party also tries to realize the favorable asymmetrical position by fixing his supply accordingly, the total quantity in the example rises to 10 and the whole of the profit disappears. If one of them is to be able to maintain the favorable position, he must resort to measures of force outside the price mechanism as for instance the threat of a price war. If one of them in advance builds a large plant, it may be most profitable for the other to adjust himself thereto. Particularly in the homogeneous

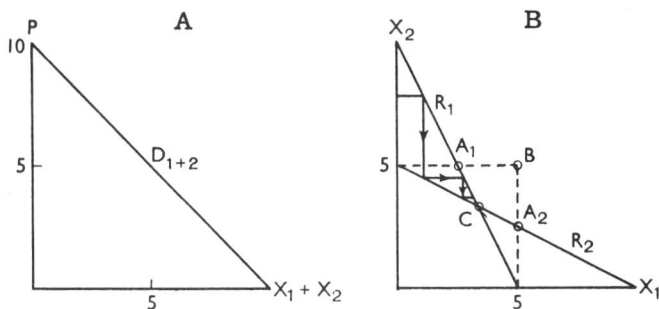

	Sale			Price	Profit	
I (Leader)	II (II's reaction curve)	I + II			I	II
1	2	3		4	5	6
0	5	5		5	0	25
1	$4\frac{1}{2}$	$5\frac{1}{2}$		$4\frac{1}{2}$	$4\frac{1}{2}$	$20\frac{1}{4}$
(Cournot's point) $3\frac{1}{3}$	$3\frac{1}{3}$	$6\frac{2}{3}$		$3\frac{1}{3}$	$11\frac{1}{9}$	$11\frac{1}{9}$
(Asymmetrical point A_2) 5	$2\frac{1}{2}$	$7\frac{1}{2}$		$2\frac{1}{2}$	$12\frac{1}{2}$	$6\frac{1}{4}$
6	2	8		2	12	4
10	0	10		0	0	0

Fig. 26. Possibilities of Behavior in the Duopoly Case

market, where the firms must be supposed to be in close touch with each other, the result will probably be that the greatest possible total profit (25 in the example) is realized by combination or by the closing down of one firm. With demand and cost curves of a different shape it is conceivable that the "position of dependence" is more favorable than the leading position and, further, when costs are different for the two firms, that they are interested in different positions, *i.e.*, the same "asymmetry" (cf. Stackelberg).[4]

In spite of the very special path of the curves in the example and the unrealistic assumption of homogeneous market conditions, we have here a good starting-point for the discussion of problems concerning the

[4] As appears from Fig. 30, page 258, corresponding lines of reaction may be drawn for firms carrying on price policy in a heterogeneous market. The lines of reaction may be constructed by means of indifference curves.

behavior of the firms, either by retaining the given number of independent firms or by reducing this number through joint action or combination, possibly after a price war or the elimination of the competitor. An equilibrium where we have several independent firms is highly improbable in the homogeneous market. Consequently, as mentioned above, the treatment of a few firms in this market is mainly of interest as a theoretical introduction.

50.2, MARKETS WHERE COSTS OF TRANSPORTATION ARE OF IMPORTANCE

The distance between buyers and sellers makes itself felt primarily as costs of transportation for the commodity. But the time it takes and the deterioration of the commodity during transportation must also be considered, as well as the smaller opportunity existing for personal contact between distant buyers and sellers, which is of decisive importance particularly in retail trade. Under changing economic conditions the time element plays an independent part. The time required for finding a new and more remote seller or buyer may also be of importance as well as difficulties in postponing buying and selling. As a rule, however, the decisive factor is the proportion of costs of transportation in the price of the commodity.

As examples of the economic importance of costs of transportation even over rather small distances, we may quote the 1938 figures supplied by an official in the Danish State Railways. For finished industrial products the costs of transportation are only a small percentage of price.

The local distribution of buyers and sellers over the market will, as a rule, influence the competitive conditions. If there are many buyers and sellers everywhere, free competition may continue to exist, but price may vary from place to place owing to the scarcity determined by local demand and supply. Between places with different prices there may exist a trade connection, and there is at the same time a difference in price corresponding to the costs of transportation (if there is no price discrimination). If all buyers and sellers, or only all within one of the groups, are gathered in one place or if they all live along a transportation route or along roads leading to a center along which price is rising or falling with costs of transportation from a definite point, we can count on one definite price for the market as a whole, with fixed additions or deductions for transportation. In other cases an average price or any other common price for the market will not be completely decisive for the quantity supplied or demanded. It is also necessary to know the price within the different parts of the field.

The number of sellers will often be limited in such a way that only a small number are situated approximately at the same distance from the buyers. In these cases discontinuity in the distribution of sellers entails a greater or smaller restriction of competition. The nearest sellers thus obtain a preferred position and a certain opportunity for carrying on price

TABLE 8

	Price per 100 Kilograms Kroner	Distance in Kilometres	Freight as Percentage of Price[5]	
			Excluding Cartage	Including Cartage
Potatoes ..	4.82	40	8·9	21·4
	—	350	26·6	39·0
Sugar Beets	2.20	15	9·1	36·4
Sugar ..	36.00	68	3·0	4·7
	—	330	5·8	7·4
Butter ..	260.00	55	0·4	0·6
	—	350	0·8	1·1
Bricks ..	about 2.00	40	21·5	51·5
	—	150	43·5	73·5
Cement ..	about 5.60	80	15·5	26·3
	—	270	27·5	38·2
Coal ..	3.30	Freight from England to Danish Harbor	15·2	—
		15 tons by rail from Mückenberg (Germ.) to Aarhus (557 Km.)	60·6	—
		Danish State Railways at home (35 Km.)	13·6	31·8
Corn ..	16.40	From La Plata to Danish Harbor	18·3	—
		Danish State Railways at home (35 Km.)	3·0	6·6

[5] Here 0.60 Kr. per 100 Kg. has been counted as cartage, corresponding to the tariffs of one of the two cartage districts of the city of Copenhagen.

policy. The more distant the areas with which they trade, the more competitors will have to be taken into consideration; and the greater the proximity of customers to competitors, the more difficult it is to overcome the competition.

In Fig. 27 we have a map of six firms, A, B, C, D, E, and F. Costs of transportation are assumed to be the same for all firms and to be proportional to distance. If all firms have the same price, the pentagon with the sides G_1, G_2, G_3, G_4, G_5 limits the sales field of A. So long as the firms maintain the same price, the perpendicular in the middle of the connecting line is the boundary. If one firm maintains a lower price, the boundary points are found as points of intersection between circles with the two firms as center and with a radius, which is as much greater for the

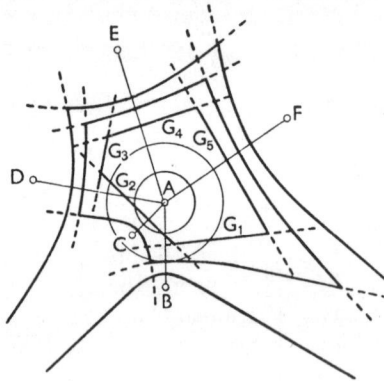

Fig. 27. Interlocal Competition

former as the distance which the reduction in price allows the commodity to be transported. These boundary lines are hyperbolae. If A reduces his price by as much as corresponds to free transportation to the periphery of the inmost circle in the figure, the boundary lines are shifted to the surrounding figure consisting of five sides curving towards A. At the next reduction in price, corresponding to the next circle, C is completely eliminated, and A's market now stretches far out between D and B and between B and F. It is now conceivable that as A's sphere is gradually extended, other firms than those mentioned may appear as competitors of A.

Both in markets where local and where qualitative differences make themselves felt, the individual seller will often have such an advantage and in the nearest part of the market such little contact with competitors that, in contrast to the homogeneous market, there will be a possibility of carrying on an individual price policy and an opportunity of disregarding the indirect effects on his own sales as a result of his own influence on the behavior of his competitors. In this case we have "monopolistic competition".

If sellers do not use price discrimination, the market will be divided in such a way that each of them sells within the area in which his price (at factory) plus costs of transportation is lowest and so that price plus costs of transportation is equally high for two competitors at the boundary between their areas. The situation may be illustrated by imagining prices (at factory) as heights above the location of the firms and local prices as craters or conic surfaces rising therefrom with a slope corresponding to costs of transportation. The projection on the map of the intersections between these conic surfaces indicates the division of the areas.[6] The situation becomes more complicated when the actual transportation routes are taken into consideration as well as costs of reloading and the variation of costs and tariffs according to distance.

Where a great part of consumption, as in the case of agricultural products, is concentrated in towns, but production is scattered over the country, it is possible in a similar way, if we know the consumption price of the towns, to find the local sales prices of the countryside by deducting costs of transportation for the various agricultural products, and so determine the most advantageous use of the soil and location of the products.[7]

While in the cases mentioned we started from the price either of the seller or of the buyer, we now proceed to the question of the choice of price,[8] taking into consideration local market conditions, among other things. We saw above that in the case of an absolute monopoly there was a definite monopoly point for the individual firm, independent of other firms, whereas, where there were two or a few firms in a homogeneous market, price formation in real life hardly led to any equilibrium until the existence of several independently acting firms had been eliminated by cooperation, combination, destruction or subjection. Where costs of transportation are of real importance owing to cost per mile or distance between firms, the effect of competition is weakened, and thus the reason why the possibility of influencing the price policy of others should react on one's own price policy. The individual firm, therefore, will no doubt

---

[6] Schneider, "Bemerkungen zu einer Theorie der Raumwirtschaft", *Econometrica*, 1935; Tord Palander, *Beiträge zur Standortstheorie*, Uppsala, 1935, Chapter IX, cf. the treatment of the question of industrial location in correspondence with Launhardt, Chapters VI and VII; W. Isard, "The General Theory of Location and Space-Economy", *Quarterly Journal*, 1949.

[7] Palander, Chapter IV, elaborating on the ideas of von Thünen. We shall not deal here with the question of the location of industry, cf., *inter alia*, Palander's critical statement of Alfred Weber's theory and the latter's shorter statement of the theory in *Grundriss der Sozialökonomik*, VI, (1914).

[8] This question of price policy has to a great extent been dealt with by means of very abstract examples, assuming, *inter alia*, an absolutely inelastic demand and an even distribution of buyers along a road or over a surface, cf. Hotelling, "Stability in Competition", *Economic Journal*, 1929; my article, "Theoretical Remarks on Price Policy, Hotelling's Case with Variations", *Quarterly Journal of Economics*, February, 1933; Schneider, "Preisbildung und Preispolitik unter Berücksichtigung der geographischen Verteilung von Erzeugern und Verbrauchern", *Schmollers Jahrbuch*, 1934; Schneider, "Bemerkungen zu einer Theorie der Raumwirtschaft", *Econometrica*, 1935; P. A. Lerner and H. W. Singer, "Some Notes on Duopoly and Spatial Competition", *Journal of Political Economy*, 1937; and Palander's book cited above.

S

in many cases act as a monopolist *vis-à-vis* an individual demand reduced by the sales of competitors. Unlike Cournot's case in the homogeneous market, there is here a real possibility of carrying on an individual price policy. If, after all, the possible influence of one's own price policy on that of the others is really taken into consideration and if competitors are distant, there will only be a question of small modifications of the demand curve, which in any case is not very well known. The interplay with the others will then only increase the uncertainty to a small extent and will rarely result in very drastic tactics.

Let us consider a firm without competitors, which is situated in a geographical area with an even density of population and the same demand everywhere as well as with costs of transportation proportional to distance.

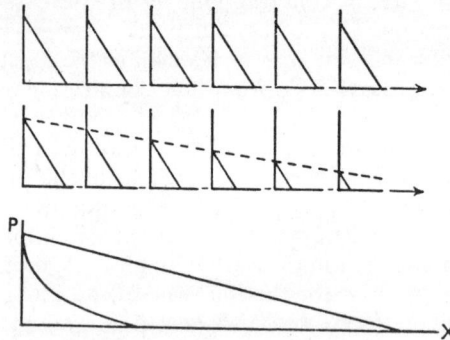

Fig. 28. Sales Curves reduced by Transportation

The upper series of small triangles from left to right in Fig. 28 indicates demand curves for a series of buyers situated along a road from the place where the seller lives. Thus the horizontal distances for each curve by itself indicate quantities, whereas the distance between the small vertical axes indicates geographical distance. The next series shows these demand curves as they appear to the seller after being reduced by costs of transportation. If buyers only live along the road mentioned above, total demand from the seller (at factory) is found by horizontal summation of these reduced demand curves. If they are evenly distributed over an area, the more distant will count relatively greatly with regard to number, but little with regard to price. At the bottom of the figure we see total demand as it appears to the seller, "foreshortened", and in comparison, the straight line shows what it would look like if all those buyers, who are not absolutely cut off by costs of transportation, had appeared with a demand not reduced by costs of transportation.[9] If population is most

---

[9] The curves for total demand have been calculated by Ole Rindung, according to the equations $X = \pi r^2 M (1 - \frac{p}{P})$ without deduction of transportation costs, and $X = \frac{1}{3} \pi r^2 M (1 - \frac{p}{P})^3$ with deduction, where M and P indicate maximum quantity and maximum price for a local demand curve.

dense around the place of production, the upper part of the curve will slope farther out.

If there are two firms, and if buyers are evenly distributed along a straight road which passes in front of the firms, Fig. 29 will show the maximum limit for the price of A when B charges a price of C. A's commodities, then, can nowhere be sold at a price exceeding C plus costs of transportation from B, *i.e.*, the line CDE, indicating the highest local price. In order to find the price obtainable by A himself, we must deduct from

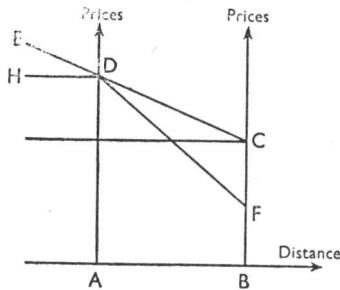

Fig. 29. Effects of Transportation on Competition

this A's costs of transportation to the individual buyers. Thus we obtain the lines DF and DH as the extreme limit. Now, competition can cut off the tops of the local demand curves, to a greater or lesser extent, depending on production costs, excess price, distance, and transportation costs of the competitor; cf. the first and second parts of Fig. 28. If the prices of the two firms in Fig. 29 are fairly equal, competition will take from A the part of the market nearest B, but the possibility of underbidding will quickly decrease, the closer A keeps to his place of business. The line FD rises with the sum of the costs of transportation for the two firms, the transportation from B becoming more expensive and from A cheaper for every step taken towards A. The main question is now how high up D would be in relation to the price that A would charge in the case of non-competition. If this price is not decreased, it is only a question of losing the intermediate market, and chiefly its most distant and least valuable part.

If we imagine the two firms to be situated on a surface with the same costs of transportation everywhere, the field will be divided by a boundary line, the situation of which is determined by the difference in price and the transportation costs. If a number of competitors are to be found more or less densely in a circle all around a firm, competition is felt more intensely because there is no untouched market behind the firm.

If the buyers are imagined to be situated in groups around the sellers, one firm for instance in every town or in separate national markets, the situation may be such that the firms, when costs of transportation are large, each utilize their market without hindrance. We then have a monopolistic multi-market situation. If costs of transportation decrease, more and more competitive situations will gradually arise. But if demand and cost conditions are fairly equal in the different places, and the firms refrain from dumping, *e.g.*, for fear of retaliation, an excess price may nevertheless appear, greater than costs of transportation from the competitor. Also when demand is distributed evenly over a surface or along a road[10] passing in front of the competitors, we can have a sort of equilibrium with prices in excess of costs, provided that each takes the price of the other firm as given. However, in this case there is a greater possibility of the instability we observed in the case of the homogeneous market.

If we imagine buyers and sellers localized at certain points, which will be the situation if we take each buyer and seller separately, a condition for static equilibrium will be that the price of a buyer can never exceed that of a seller plus costs of transportation. This will be the actual price when transportation between the two actually does take place. However, if we consider the demand of individual buyers and the costs of individual sellers as well as costs of transportation between them, not all the possible transportation routes are used. The cheaper roads will be preferred. Further, if price discrimination is not used, a number of possible routes will not be considered, as a consequence of the price policy.[11]

The question of entry into the market and of the way in which considerations of price policy react on location, will be dealt with in Chapter 51.

50.3, MARKETS WITH DIFFERENCE IN QUALITY

Regardless of limited differences in quality it will often be practical to assume that it is the same commodity that is sold within a certain market. In other cases, however, it is important to consider the difference in quality and, correspondingly, to consider a special price for each product that is differentiated as to quality. As it is the relation between the firms which interests us, we assume each firm to produce its own quality of product. Just as in the last chapter, we are here concerned with heterogeneous markets. The results as to the formation of price for the commodity itself may to a great extent be transferred analogously from the more simple case of distance to that of differences in quality. We may then consider "distance in quality" in different directions (dimensions) and a cost of transformation corresponding to costs of transportation. Where the difference

[10] Hotelling's case, cf. the literature mentioned in footnote 8.
[11] See Schneider's criticism in the article in *Schmollers Jahrbuch* of my example with two buyers and two sellers with definite mutual distances (*Nationaløkonomisk Tidsskrift*, 1933). Whereas I quite agree with Schneider's criticism and additions, I must, however, take exception to his proof (pp. 271–72) of indeterminateness in the formation of price. Each firm itself decides which routes it wants to use, but it may be forced to interrupt them by temporary measures of warfare, which fall beyond the static formation of price with which we are concerned.

between competitors depends on local distance and differences in quality, the problems are the same to such an extent that it would have been possible to deal with the two cases in one purely abstract statement. However, we prefer to give the statement a more concrete character by dealing separately with the treatment of distance and quality, even if they might to a great extent be transferred from one sphere to another. To this may be added the practical fact that differences in local prices of other commodities and services are important when local heterogeneity exists. The economy of each firm must then be seen in relation to that of its local neighborhood.

The real division of the markets is due to simultaneous differences of location and quality. There may, *e.g.*, be one baker and two grocers in a village, one automobile factory and a few steel mills in a small country. Detailed statistics for industries show how wide the distribution actually is. Circumstances like traditional trade divisions and methods of production, uniformity of consumers' demand and existing types of machinery, as well as concentration in cities and customs barriers, all these factors tend towards creating groups of comparatively similar enterprises. Technical specialization, especially in industry, trade marks and advertising for individual firms tend in the opposite direction.

Where buyers are distributed evenly over a geographical area or a scale of product qualities, every seller who is not placed together with others will be the nearest to a certain part of the buyers, but nevertheless there will be a gradual transference of customers when he changes his price, the decisive factor being distance in relation to difference in price. If, on the other hand, a certain number of customers are concentrated round each seller (placed in the same town or strongly adhering to his type of product), he will have a monopoly over them within a certain difference in price, whereas in the former case there is monopolistic competition even with the very small differences in price. With monopolistic competition the individual sales curve[12] for one seller, who alone changes his price from the equilibrium position, has a smaller slope than the individual curve which applies when his competitors change their prices at the same time and to the same extent. Where each has a monopoly, however, within a certain interval of price, the two curves mentioned above are the same within this interval. In that case it makes no difference whether the others also reduce their prices. Under free competition the curve is horizontal in the case when only one changes his price, while with a common decrease in price the sales of the individual firm correspond to a certain part of the common downward-sloping demand curve of the market.

[12] See Morris A. Copeland, "Competing Products and Monopolistic Competition", *Quarterly Journal of Economics*, November, 1940, as well Chapter 50.4 regarding the power of expansion of the individual firms in the "nearly homogeneous market", where the effect of changes in price for a single firm, however, is compared with the common demand curve of the market with the same approximate price, and not with the sales curve of the individual firm with a common change in price.

On the basis of Winding Pedersen's[13] statement, we shall now deal with the case of *monopolistic competition* between two firms, each having its special demand and cost conditions. The two sellers in the example both take the price fixed by the other as given and adapt themselves thereto by means of changes in price. Winding Pedersen calls the resulting market situation "price-competition equilibrium". This "autonomous" attitude (cf. p 239) towards the competitors corresponds to Cournot's case; but in the present instance the difference in quality makes it possible to carry

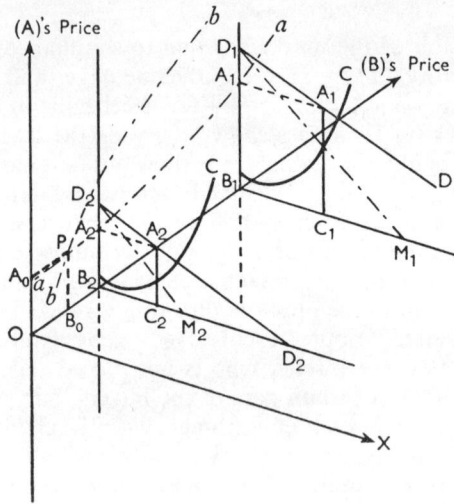

Fig. 30. Monopolistic Competition

on an individual price policy. Something similar may occur when there is some distance between the competitors. In the homogeneous market, on the other hand, adjustment must take place through variations in quantity.

The three axes in the figure indicate the prices for the two firms (A) and (B) and the quantity sold (X) for each of them taken separately. The conditions for firm (A), when (B) takes the prices B_1 and B_2 respectively,

[13] H. Winding Pedersen, "Omkring den moderne Pristeori", Saertryk af *Nationaløkonomisk Tidsskrift*, 1939, p. 11, ff. The figure has been taken from p. 12 with a single change indicated by the author. On *monopolistic competition* see further Edward Chamberlin, *The Theory of Monopolistic Competition*, 1933, 5th ed., 1946; Joan Robinson, *Economics of Imperfect Competition*, 1933; F. Zeuthen, *Problems of Monopoly and Economic Warfare*, 1930, Chapter II; Sraffa, "The Laws of Return under Competitive Conditions", *Economic Journal*, 1926; R. F. Kahn, "The Problems of Duopoly", *Economic Journal*, 1937; R. H. Coase, "Some Notes on Duopoly Price", *Review of Economic Studies*, 1937; Th. Kristensen, "A Note on Duopoly", *Review of Economic Studies*, 1938; William Fellner, *Competition Among the Few*, 1949; Hicks' *Annual Survey of Economic Theory*; "The Theory of Monopoly", *Econometrica*, 1935, see especially the three-dimensional figure in Schneider's *Reine Theorie*, p. 164; see further the works mentioned in the other footnotes and the bibliography in the fifth edition of Chamberlin's book.

are seen from the two planes $D_1B_1D_1$ and $D_2B_2D_2$, parallel to the plane (A)O(X). The prices of (A) in these planes are shown perpendicularly, and the quantities of (A) horizontally, parallel to the (X) axis. D_1D_1 and D_2D_2 are (A)'s sales curve under the assumption that (B) fixes the prices mentioned, B_1 and B_2, respectively, and that (A) takes these as given and adapts himself accordingly. Through equating the marginal cost and revenue, equilibrium is found at the intersection of the marginal revenue curves D_1M_1 and D_2M_2 and the marginal cost curve of the firm, C, which is the same in the two planes, first bending a little downwards and then upwards toward the point C. (A)'s equilibrium prices at the given prices for (B), A_1 and A_2, are carried over to the plane (A)(B) by the dotted line. If such a calculation is made for all possible (B) prices, we obtain the dot-dashed line aa as (A)'s reaction curve in the price plane (A)(B), which indicates combinations of the prices of the two firms. By means of corresponding lines in planes parallel to the (B)(X) plane, it is possible to find a corresponding reaction curve for (B) for all prices that (A) can be imagined to fix, the dot-dashed line bb, indicating how (B) would fix his price when (A) has fixed a certain price. The reaction curves correspond to those in Fig. 26B, p. 249, though there we had an adjustment of quantity, because the market was homogeneous. When, as assumed, both firms take the other's price as given and adapt themselves accordingly, equilibrium is obtained at the price combination P, indicating the point of intersection between the two reaction curves aa and bb. In order to find the quantity sold by (A) we must make use of the demand curve corresponding to D_1D_1 and D_2D_2 in a plane through P. Here, as in the market scattered over a geographical area, where the firms take each other's behavior as given, the result of the adjustment is a price in excess of costs, which the individual firm may increase when the other increases his price, though with the present assumptions there is a limit to the increases of both.

Here each firm obtained a new sales curve whenever the other changed its price. As stated in Winding Pedersen's article and elsewhere, corresponding changes of sales curves occur with other assumptions regarding the behavior of the firms. The expected selling possibilities of a firm thus become smaller if, whenever it fixes a price, it has to take into consideration the possibility that the other party may fix a corresponding competitive price, *i.e.*, the price that is now most advantageous to him. If now we do not, as before, take the other's price as given, but assume that the other party in each situation will underbid our firm by adapting his price to our new price, we obtain an *ex ante* demand curve situated at a lower level. The situation, however, is not symmetrical. As in the case on Fig. 26B, p. 249, equilibrium cannot here be reached in a symmetrical way with either firm in the position of follower. The second firm must adapt itself and, therefore, under our present assumption, we end in an asymmetrical equilibrium, corresponding to the asymmetrical equilibrium with quantity adaptation in the homogeneous market described above, where we had one firm as price leader and the other as follower.

Winding Pedersen mentions a third case. In order to avoid price competition through changes in price, the two parties may fix a price "corresponding" to the price of the competitor, *i.e.*, a price by which annoyance
to the opposite party by a reduction of his sales is avoided, at the same time
as the first firm tries as far as possible to keep its own circle of customers
and also may try to acquire completely new customers. The tendency to
carry on a non-aggressive price policy of this kind helps to explain the
stable prices which prevail to a great extent in the sphere of monopolistic
competition. The cessation of price competition, however, does not mean
the cessation of competition. Under non-price competition the methods
are advertising and improvement of quality and service, as indicated in
Chapters 52 and 53.

The price policy chosen now depends on the nature of the market and
the attitude of the firms. As mentioned above with regard to markets in
which costs of transportation are of importance, the individual seller
probably acts as a monopolist and disregards the effects of his own price
policy on the behavior of his competitors, when the latter are at some
distance, and when the contested part of the market counts comparatively
little to him. Also where there are many competitors whose action he does
not have much chance of influencing, he will act in the same way. If the
individual competitors, on the other hand, are situated closely to each
other, it is probable that they will consider the effects of their own price
policy on the others. The result may be a peaceful policy in order to avoid
exposing one's self to competition or a price-leader situation; or, the
result may be a change of the structure of the market, the number of independent competitors being reduced by agreement, fusion, or economic
warfare. Price leadership is most likely to arise if the firms are of unequal
size, have unequal costs or, what is perhaps of the greatest importance,
unequal financial strength. It is probable, by the way, that the tendency of
followers to underbid is reduced by threats of competitive wars or boycott
from the price leader. In this way the situation may be changed into one
of partial monopoly (cf. p. 243) where the smaller competitors take a
price accepted by the price leader and keep their sales within definite
limits.

On the whole, it may be expected[14] that forms between the different
types of behavior which we have described play an important part, since
it is impossible with certainty to know the behavior of one's competitors.
The *ex ante* sales curve, on the basis of which one acts, thus rests on an
estimate of the probability of different types of reaction on the part of
competitors. The actual course of price adjustment—and a change in
external conditions often requires a new adjustment—will necessarily be
full of surprises and uncertainty, when the plans of the individual firms
must rest on conjecture as to the plans of the others. We may further
refer to the fact that the aim of the plans is not a static equilibrium, but

---

[14] Winding Pedersen, Chapter III.

rather such a future course of prices, sales and costs as will give the greatest capital value in the calculation made at the moment. The very choice of behavior depends, in the first place, on the corresponding choice of the other firms. In the second place, it is influenced by other conditions than the desire for a rational maximization of profit. Price, therefore, becomes "indeterminate" if we only take the "purely economic" types of reaction into consideration. In order to make it determinate it is necessary to include other conditions in the explanation.[15]

50.4, NEARLY HOMOGENEOUS MARKETS[16]

With regard to markets with several firms whose price is not quite the same, or who have the same price, but have small advantages for their buyers, which really correspond to difference in price, it may be practical to assume a common, approximate price for the whole of the market, and at the same time allow for the possibility of the individual firm's carrying on an individual price policy. If such a possibility exists, we avoid the complications arising in homogeneous markets with few sellers.

The above-mentioned differences in advantages offered, which have the effect of small differences in price, may be differences with regard to rebates, terms of payment, service, or, perhaps, quality at a uniform price. Increased advertising may have almost the same effect as a reduction in price from the point of view of the seller and, so far as advertising gives useful information, also from that of the buyer. Either it is a question of cases where price competition can take place to a limited extent without a mass transfer of customers, or of a non-price-competition, with differences in terms that may be measured as small differences in price. The difference as compared with the usual theory of monopolistic competition is not a difference in substance, but a difference in the method of approach. The method of considering the problems here is only applicable in such real cases where the differences in price and quality are small and the firms, consequently, have to keep close together with regard to price, because they stand as an almost uniform group, separate from other markets.

The personal contact of buyers with competitors and the fear of exciting them may cause firms to prefer an expansion of sales among their old customers or the acquisition of entirely new customers, and to leave the customers of the competitors alone, or at least the total sales of the competitors. It is also a possibility that acquisition of the customers of the competitors will not occur if the latter quickly follow suit with a corresponding reduction in price.

[15] Winding Pedersen's article, Chapters IV, VI, and VII.
[16] F. Zeuthen, "Monopolistic Competition and the Homogeneity of the Market". *Econometrica*, 1936, cf. especially Figs. XIV and XVI with the ensuing text in *Problems of Monopoly and Economic Warfare*, 1930.

The sales potentialities of the individual firms are rarely of the same magnitude. A firm with two stores may, *ceteris paribus*, expand its sales twice as much with a given reduction in price as one with only one store of the same kind and size. Instead of applying the concept of elasticity, according to which the individual firm's expansion of sales is measured in terms of its previous sales, it may here be preferable to measure the expansion of sales of the individual firm in proportion to the expansion of total sales, as it would take place if the reduction in price were common to all firms. We say that the *power of expansion* is 1 when a reduction in price for this firm alone causes the same increase of its sales—probably largely at the expense of the other firms—as the increase that would take place in the sales of all firms with a corresponding common reduction in price. In other words, the power of expansion is measured by the slope

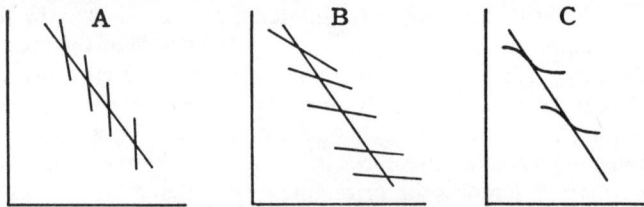

Fig. 31. Power of Expansion

of the sales curve of the indivídual firm, the unit being the slope of the common demand curve of the market.

The individual sales curve, and consequently the power of expansion, changes constantly with the prevailing situation, especially with the price, *i.e.*, the approximate price of all firms. It is only the direction and course of the curve for the short interval near the actual price that is of interest, because in the type of market here dealt with it must be assumed that with a great reduction in the price of the firm and with the "price of the market" unchanged, the firm will destroy all its competitors.

Fig. 31 illustrates how at each market price we have a certain power of expansion for an individual firm, in Fig. 31A below 1, in Fig. 31B varying and greater than 1. If the power of expansion is 1, the gradient would follow the demand curve of the market for some distance. Fig. C illustrates the likely case where competition becomes irresistible when the difference in price exceeds a certain limit, *i.e.*, that the sales curve soon becomes horizontal. We have, consequently, a "double-kinked sales curve".

Now let us first consider a case with a firm having a power of expansion of 1, *i.e.*, that a small reduction in price on its part alone results in the same expansion for its sales as an equal reduction in price on the part of all sellers in the total sales of the market, but (at any rate in the short run) does not cause any change in the sales of competitors. The entire expansion of sales is here due either to greater sales to previous customers (both those of the firm and of the competitors) or to entirely new buyers. In this case the sales curve of the individual firm follows the common demand curve of the market for a small distance. If this is the case for all firms, price will be the same as that which, in the case of Cournot, results from an adjustment of quantity, since the firms act as if the sales of the competitors were given.

In many instances the power of expansion through the kind of competitive attacks that we find in real life will probably be greater because a reduction in price will also take some customers from competitors. The

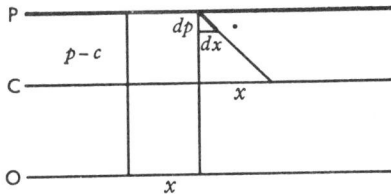

P ──────────────────────────
  $p-c$ dp
          dx
C ──────────────────────────
          x

O ──────
     x

Fig. 32. Equilibrium of a Firm in a nearly Homogeneous Market

marginal case is here that of free competition, where the power of expansion of the individual firm is infinite and where, consequently, there is no price in excess of costs. The opposite margin is the case where the market is really divided into a series of quite separate partial markets with an absolute monopoly for the individual firms. The sum of the firms' power of expansion here corresponds to the slope of the common demand curve ($\Sigma u = 1$) and the power of expansion of the individual firms towards each others' customers is zero.

In real life, however, the power of expansion of firms will no doubt in many cases be situated between the two margins indicated. It will be different for the individual firms; and here again it will be different in the case of old customers and in the acquisition of new ones from competitors, or from groups who have not previously been buyers. We shall here confine ourselves to considering a certain total power of expansion for the individual firm.

Fig. 32 illustrates the equilibrium situation for a firm. The market price is p, the (constant) costs of the firm c, its sales x, and its power of expansion (indicated by the slope of the sales curve) $u = dx/dp$, corresponds to the heavy line indicating its sales curve with a small reduction in price. Price is indicated as a heavy line allowing some deviation between individual prices. The individual price policy here dealt with is exactly the same as that of simple monopolies, mentioned in Chapter 47. At the point of equilibrium the increase in revenue as a result of an increase in price is equal to the loss as a result of the corresponding decrease in quantity, or vice versa. This means $dp \cdot x = dx \cdot (p - c)$. Since $dx/dp = u$, we have

$u = x/(p - c)$ or $x = u(p - c)$. In the figure the sales of the firm considered are found by extending the above-mentioned heavy line down to the cost line. When the market price is given, sales will consequently be determined by the power of expansion and the costs of the firm. A great power of expansion and low costs in proportion to the common price result in great sales.

In order to find the common price for several firms in a market, it is necessary to consider the power of expansion and costs of all the firms.

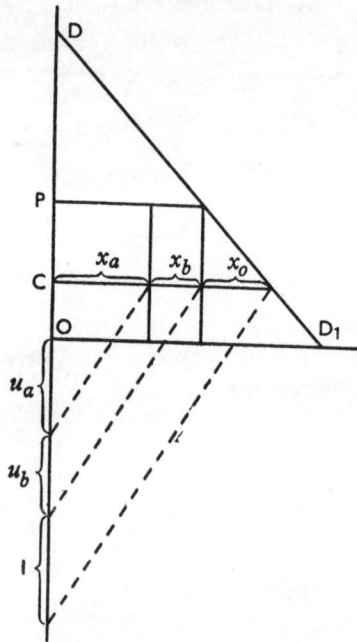

Fig. 33. Same for Two Firms

This is illustrated by the example in Fig. 33, where we have common constant costs for two firms, c, with respective powers of expansion of u_a and u_b. DD_1 is the common demand curve, which is assumed to be rectilinear within the relevant sphere. Besides an equation for the power of expansion of each firm, $x_a/(p - c) = u_a$ and $x_b/(p - c) = u_b$, we have here as an expression of the slope of the common demand curve $x_0/(p - c) = 1$. The problem may be solved graphically by drawing the rectilinear demand and horizontal cost curves, and then dividing the section of the cost curve between the y-axis and the intersection with the demand curve in the proportion u_a, u_b and u_0 ($= 1$), by means of the dashed lines below the cost line. By intersection between the demand curve, and a perpendicular through the point $x_a + x_b$, c, we find the price.

Fig. 34 illustrates how the size of the firm is determined in a case with several firms having different constant costs, different powers of expansion $(x/(p - c))$, and the same nearly uniform price (the height of which is not going to be included in the analysis).[17]

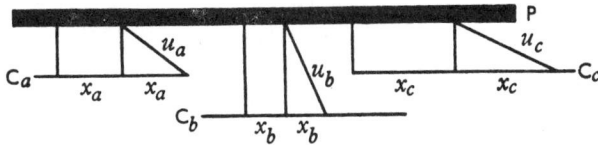

Fig. 34. Determination of Size of the Firms under same Conditions

The result is that equilibrium may be obtained at an approximately uniform price, even if the firms have different costs. Low costs or decreasing costs result in large sales for the individual firm just as does a great power of expansion. Total sales become larger and the price obtainable with the common demand curve of the market consequently becomes smaller, the greater the number of firms, the greater their power of expansion, the lower their costs, and the more steeply declining their cost curves. For a number of firms to obtain a price in excess of costs, it is a necessary condition that their power of expansion should not be infinite, as in the case of free competition.

If the firms have uniform, constant costs, we may consider the case where the triangle ABC in Fig. 35 between the cost line, the tangent to the demand curve at the equilibrium price, and the ordinate axes is drawn with the sides AC and BC equal to 1. In this case $\Sigma x + (p - c) = 1$.

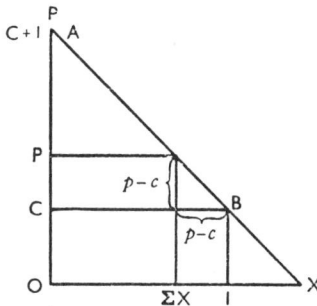

Fig. 35. Determination of Price under same Conditions

[17] With regard to more complicated cases with varying costs and simultaneous determination of the common price, readers may be referred to my article in *Econometrica*, 1936, Fig. 3, cf. the more comprehensive, but also more primitive treatment of a number of variants in *Theory of Monopoly and Economic Warfare*, Chapters II and III. Possible complications due to the sales curves having different directions for possible reductions and increases in price—"kinked demand curves"—are not taken into consideration here.

Since $\Sigma x / (p - c) = \Sigma u$ we obtain the result that the price in excess of costs $(p - c) = 1 / (\Sigma u + 1)$.[18]

If, following Cournot, we assume that each firm has a power of expansion corresponding to the common demand curve, we obtain for 1, 2 and 3 firms respectively excess prices of $\frac{1}{2}$, $\frac{1}{3}$, $\frac{1}{4}$, etc. (as fractions of AC). In cases of greater or smaller power of expansion for the individual firm, the excess prices for the individual firm are calculated in an analogous manner. If, for instance, two competitors have a power of expansion of 2 and $\frac{1}{2}$ respectively, the excess price is $1 : (2 + \frac{1}{2} + 1) = \frac{2}{7}$, and the sales of the two firms are u_a. $(p - c) = 2 \cdot \frac{2}{7} = \frac{4}{7}$, and $\frac{1}{7}$, respectively (calculated as fractions of CB).

It continues to be a necessary condition for the above-mentioned method of considering these problems, however, that the firms act autonomously, *i.e.*, irrespective of the possible effects on the price policy of the others. The case may not be realistic in a market with few firms and with the assumed nearly homogeneous quality and market price assumed above; but it is conceivable in markets with many competitors having almost the same position, *e.g.*, where many firms produce the "same commodity" with a great number of small variations. Here it is possible to carry on a more modest sort of price policy or a corresponding degree of non-price competition, and the sales and profit of the individual firms will then depend on their power of expansion and their individual cost conditions.

The possibility of a substantial excess price within a group of firms, which can at the same time be considered as a market with an almost uniform price, will exist, especially when the individual sales, as in Fig. 31A, are inelastic at certain differences in prices, or corresponding differences in quality or terms of sale.

CHAPTER 51

ENTRY AND LOCATION IN MARKETS[1]

IN order to obtain a monopoly profit, it is necessary that there should be only a limited possibility of entering the market. The principal cause of difference between a number of national or regional markets, or of more continuous differences in market conditions, is a different distribution of

[18] Putting AC = BC in the figure does not influence the result, as in any case you may multiply (p – c) and 1 with some arbitrary factor without changing the result.

[1] Especially with regard to monopolistic competition we may (in addition to the footnote on page 258) refer to Kaldor, "Market Imperfection and Excess Capacity", *Economica*, 1935; Chamberlin, "Monopolistic or Imperfect Competition", *Quarterly Journal of Economics*, 1937; discussion with Kaldor in the next volume; article by Cassel in the same volume; and articles by Machlup and Higgins in *American Economic Review*, 1939. J. S. Bain, "Conditions of Entry and Emergence of Monopoly", in *Monopoly and Competition and their Regulation*, edited by E. A. Chamberlin, 1954. Regarding total supply in a competitive market and the influence of costs thereon, see Chapter 20.3.

the means of production in relation to local demand. The difference, therefore, aside from the possibility of moving the consumers, may be limited or eliminated altogether either by transportation of commodities or by transference of labor and capital. The same is true with regard to an unequal distribution of the means of production between trades. In considering the problems of entry, it is necessary to distinguish between conditions in homogeneous and in heterogeneous markets. Further, there is reason to distinguish between entry of new firms and expansion of existing firms by influx of the means of production.

(I) Let us first consider a homogeneous market where, technically, there is room for a great number of firms of optimum size (possibly because costs are constant and all sizes, therefore, equally favorable). (1) With free influx of means of production and free opportunity of establishing new firms, we must here expect free competition, the same payment for means of production as outside the special market, and no special profit to the owners of the firms. (2) If the influx of means of production is free, but the opportunity of establishing new firms limited, the result will be: (*a*) a profit to the owners in proportion to output, in case the individual firms cannot expand beyond a certain maximum size; (*b*) if it is only the number that is limited, there will be free competition by expansion of existing firms, possibly with increasing costs; (3) if the influx of means of production is not free, but there is unlimited possibility of establishing new firms or expanding old firms, the means of production, the influx of which is limited, earn a higher revenue than outside this industry, whereas the owners of the firms do not have any profit; (4) if, finally, there is limitation both with regard to influx of means of production and expansion of the capacity of firms, the advantage of a possible increase in price will go to that factor, the scarcity of which is greatest.

(II) If in a homogeneous market there is not room for many firms with optimum production, it is readily conceivable that the existing firms make a profit without entry from outside, because the establishment of a new firm does not pay. The reasons why the establishment of new firms may be assumed to be unremunerative, may be partly the fact that the size of the market is too small for one additional firm at the existing price, partly because more competition would entail a reduction in price for the commodity or an increase in price for the productive services used. This is the case all the more if the new firms have chances of smaller sales than those already in existence.

The entry of new firms means at the same time an increase in the capacity and output of the trade and a change in the conditions of price policy, because the number is increased. This is especially apparent, of course, in the case of an increase from 1 to 2 or 3. In the long run, rising costs due to decrease in the size of firms will hamper entry into the relatively small markets. In the short run, which is here long enough to have a substantial influence, the situation is intensified by the resistance which the capacity of existing firms makes against an equal distribution of sales.

The existing firms may to a large extent see their profit in resorting to methods of warfare. If the necessary foresight is lacking among the people who are thinking of entering the market, it may possibly be advantageous for the firms already in existence to moderate their price policy in advance in order that the prospects of entering the industry shall not be too favorable.

The entry both of new firms and of means of production has been limited by the relation between the size of the market and the firms in the case dealt with here. Further institutional limitations in possible sales or entry of means of production will have similar effects to those under (I). A rigid limitation of the number may strengthen the monopolistic character of the market and may, moreover, lead to higher costs than would otherwise prevail. If the market is smaller than the optimum size for a single firm, equilibrium cannot be attained before the monopoly is established. Also if the market is only slightly larger, there is a good chance of having a single firm.

(III) If, owing to difference in quality or costs of transportation, the market is not homogeneous, the individual firm will have a sales curve which is not a horizontal straight line, but a curve which changes constantly according to the relation to neighboring firms. Whereas the formation of price, therefore, cannot be considered as an absolute monopoly based on an independent individual sales curve, a consideration of the sales curve in the position of equilibrium may yet serve to illustrate the relation between the price, profit and costs of the individual firm.

Two cases are conceivable in this connection: in the first place that a new firm, after a limited period of transition, is able to obtain the same profit as the existing firms. For instance, there is no fixed limit to the number of toothpaste brands, and a new group of customers can be created by limitation of the sales of the comparatively numerous old firms. Something similar applies to a certain extent to parts of retail trade, even if the limited number of well-situated shops is of some importance. Where entry is actually free at the same time as every firm is able to achieve a preferential position in the eyes of some of the buyers, and costs rise at the same time as the size of the firms decreases, we have the remarkable case where entry continues until a point of zero profit in excess of costs is reached because the advantage of having a preferential position in some part of the market tempts firms to enter. In spite of the fact that no profit is obtained, this form of monopolistic competition differs substantially from free competition, since costs are not forced down towards a minimum, and there is a possibility of advertising and price discrimination. Absence of profit, therefore, is no sure sign of free competition. From a political point of view, it will probably be considered a great disadvantage to have monopolistic competition which raises prices without giving profits, if one is not willing to pay a price in order to preserve a large middle class.

There is, however, another form of monopolistic competition. The possibilities of sales in this case are not distributed continuously over a geographic surface or, correspondingly, over possible variations in quality. The buyers are to a great extent gathered in towns, villages, and along transportation routes, and certain products are most in demand, either for traditional reasons or because technically their production is cheaper. Thus we see the rise, though not with marked boundaries, of favorable markets of limited size in relation to the optimum size of firms. And in the short run, which here is very long, the situation is intensified by the fact that the firms which have first established themselves in the favorable segment of the market make the entry of other firms disadvantageous to a large extent. The result is that market conditions vary greatly from place to place and from one differentiated product to another. There are consequently various possibilities of profit and of limitation in the size of the firm, usually before the least cost point, but sometimes extending even beyond this point. The favorable cases will to a great extent have the character of an absolute monopoly or oligopoly[2] within certain price margins.

Even if full equalization of profit can but rarely be expected to appear, it may be expected, nevertheless, that where monopolistic competition prevails, there will usually be a certain increase of costs beside irregularly distributed profits, when there is a great influx of firms. If long-run cost curves really have the deep U-shape of Fig. 23B, p. 232, a great increase in costs might be the consequence, and at the same time we get a permanent unused capacity if we really have U-shaped short-run cost curves as tangents to the long-run curves, as in Fig. 12, p. 119. With the more likely, rather horizontal cost curves in the long run, and also rather horizontal marginal cost curves in the short run, except near full capacity, the increase in cost might be less important. Where monopolization involves a considerable reduction in sales, the consequence, however, will also in this case be a corresponding considerable increase in average cost, fixed costs included, in the lifetime of existing plants.

In addition to the very active causes mentioned here, entrance to the heterogeneous markets may also be limited for the institutional reasons mentioned under (I). It will be of interest to investigate the extent to which the inclination to enter markets with more than normal profit is hampered by the limitation of the market and technical conditions with regard to the size of firms on one hand, and the fear of an aggressive competition on the other.

New firms are faced with the problem of the most favorable location in the market, a question that has been discussed particularly in the case of geographic location.[3] If the demand of individual buyers were quite inelastic, and if at the same time every firm took the price of the others

[2] Machlup, *American Economic Review*, 1939, pp. 231–32.
[3] Hotelling, "Stability in Competition", *Economic Journal*, 1929; Palander, *Beiträge*, pp. 248–53 and Chapter XIV; Lerner and Singer, "Some Notes on Duopoly and Spatial Competition", *Journal of Political Economy*, 1937; Copeland's previously mentioned article in *Quarterly Journal of Economics*, 1940.

T

as given, it would be advantageous to place one's self as near as possible to the competitor in order to have the greatest possible market behind one and, by giving a corresponding market to the competitor, to invite as little as possible of price competition in the market between them. If the competitors come close to each other, it is likely, however, that they will try to influence the action of each other, and the advantage of proximity may then easily disappear. With an elastic demand it will moreover be important to have a large market of one's own on all sides, and a scattered location will therefore be more favorable. If one is to be placed on a road east of the competitor, one will be the nearest to the greatest number of buyers by placing one's self immediately east of him; but the question then is, whether the distance to those living in the most eastern part does not become too great, and whether the proximity will not lead to a competitive fight, if the competitors do not prefer to carry on a joint price policy. In the latter case the reduction in costs of transportation by scattered location is also of importance.

The situation, moreover, differs if buyers are evenly distributed over the market, or they are gathered in towns or round definite types of commodities. Where many buyers are attached to a certain type of commodity which is easy to imitate, it is tempting to place one's self near the previous seller. In other cases it may be of advantage to place one's self at some distance and collect a circle of buyers by advertising one's own brand. In most cases, the location of previous buyers will have an important determining effect. With variation of quality, there is often a possibility of a changing adjustment of types of commodities without great cost; but the result might often be that the individual firms produce several types of commodities, *i.e.*, place themselves simultaneously on different points in the scale of products and at the same time work at low cost in consequence of large total production. Something similar may be attained locally to a certain extent by a system of branches.

According to Swedish experiences,[4] price discrimination, violent reductions in price, advertising and other aggressive measures against newly established competitors are not supposed to play any very large part. Agreement with suppliers, however, concerning a more favorable treatment of the existing firms with regard to credit and rebates, and in some cases exclusive agreements between industrial and mercantile organizations or with organizations of workers, seem to be of some importance. Further, it is claimed that knowing the intimate connections of the banks with Swedish industry, it may be presumed that they, too, exercise a certain regulating function with regard to the entrance of new competing firms. In Denmark, as probably in many other countries, import restrictions and other state regulations have hampered the entry of new competitors in many lines of production. The same policy has of course also favored national monopolies.

[4] "Statens Offentliga Utredningar", *Organiserad Samverkan inom Svenskt Näringsliv*, 1940. See pp. 202–205, 270 and 323.

CHAPTER 52

ADVERTISING AND OTHER NON-PRICE COMPETITION

APART from competing by means of lower prices, the firms also compete by means of better quality, service and advertising. Improvement of quality, service and advertising may to a great extent be regarded in the same way, and may result from various motives. A higher price may be obtained for a more strongly demanded commodity. Conversely, if the commodity is improved without any increase in price, it is virtually the same thing as competition by means of lower price. Where agreements or fixed prices are in force, or people are afraid of letting loose actual price reductions, competition assumes the camouflaged form of non-price competition. Finally, and not least important, the object of quality differentiation, service and advertising may be to create a favored position in the market that may be utilized by monopolistic price policy. For advertising in connection with trade marks and special equipment of the commodity, the main object is to create a characteristic stamp and thus placing competitors at a greater distance.

In real life it may be difficult to distinguish between improvements in quality which make a higher price possible in correspondence with the higher costs of production and quality differentiation on the other hand enabling the firm to charge a price in excess of costs (*i.e.*, a higher percentage of profit).

Advertising[1] influences demand by attracting the attention of buyers to the commodity and conveys to them, often by means of irrelevant influences on feeling, certain concepts true or otherwise regarding the commodity and an inducement to buy it. The limited space left in the consciousness of buyers for knowledge about the commodities makes possible a systematic and more or less forced pouring in of ideas, changing the orientation of buyers. Hotelling[2] speaks of people's attention as a scarce commodity, saying, "Expropriation of the attention of the general public and its commercial sale and exploitation constitute a lucra-

---

[1] Børge Barfod, *Reklamen i teoretisk-økonomisk Belysning*, Schönbergske Forlag, Copenhagen, 1937, and, in connection with Barfod's work, my article, "Effect and Cost of Advertisement from a Theoretic Aspect", *Nordisk Tidsskrift for Teknisk Økonomi*, 1935. Apart from the special literature, partially influenced by practical advertising experts, see Geiger, *Kritik af Reklamen*, Nyt Nordisk Forlag, Copenhagen, 1943; Erich Schneider, "Eine Theorie der Reklame", *Zeitschrift für National-ökonomie*, 1939; and Børge Barfod, "En Note om teoretisk Tolkning af Reklamen", *Nordisk Tidsskrift for Teknisk Økonomi*, 1944–45. In this article Barfod finds that the optimum advertising percentage, *i.e.*, the proportion between advertising expenses per unit and price, is equal to the proportion between advertising elasticity and price elasticity. This indicates the equilibrium between advertising policy and price policy.

[2] *Econometrica*, July, 1938, p. 257.

tive business. From some aspects this business appears to be of a similar character to that of the medieval robber barons." Karl Marx says in a footnote to *Das Kapital*: "In the bourgeois society there exists the *fictio juris* that every man as consumer has an encyclopedic knowledge of qualities", which of course is a mere fiction.

Advertising enhances the willingness to buy to the same extent as an improvement of quality, and at the same time it adds to the costs of the seller. Its value in the eyes of the buyers is due to a valuation which we shall not analyse more closely here. Reliable information as to the commodities before they are purchased may be of the same importance to buyers as information as to its use after purchase. Information in advance may be especially valuable in the case of new commodities. On the other hand, it may be said that the expensive forms of advertising have an aim other than that of giving objective and impartial information, and that buyers might obtain far more useful knowledge at a much cheaper price by impartial, critical instruction as to the quality, durability, and effects of the goods. Some advocates of advertisement claim that the buyer, when acting on the advertisement, can be said to do what he prefers at the moment, thus obtaining maximum utility, according to the definition of want and utility given by the theory of choice. But this concept of utility contains nothing about the satisfaction obtained by consumption. The consumer's valuation after the use of the commodity, is the important thing, however. It is also possible to compare from the outside the state of the consumers during and after the use of the advertised articles with their state in case of some alternative spending of their income, including the case where there exists impartial guidance.

Through advertising, the spending of consumers is shifted from other firms, other groups of commodities, or, maybe, from saving as opposed to consumption. Advertising creates an altered demand for the commodity. According to the nature of the commodity and the advertising, it is possible to imagine different types of shifting in the sales curve of the firm, cf. Figs. 36 A–E, where D_1 indicates the demand curve before advertising, and D_2 after advertising was started; M_1 and M_2 indicate the firm's most profitable combination of price and quantity (the monopoly point) before and after, respectively. Costs have been assumed to be constant (corresponding to the height of the line CC). Where this is not the case, the curve, D_1, has to be conceived as excess price curve above the average costs. As appears from the five different directions for the shifting of M in Figs. 36 A–E, advertising may be used either to obtain higher price or larger quantity, or perhaps both.

The same advertising expenditure may be given a direction which acts to a greater or smaller extent on price and quantity. Where fixed prices are the rule, advertising, in the first round, will one-sidedly aim at increasing quantity, but it also may help to keep the price, or it may make a later increase in price possible. Whereas there is no advertising with absolutely free competition (in the atomistic market) where all firms have a horizontal sales curve equal to price, it is conceivable that a firm, as illustrated in Fig. 36F, breaks out of the competitive state of indifference, and by advertising creates for itself a somewhat higher sales curve making a higher price possible.

In the maximization of profit for the individual firm, the price-quantity direction, as indicated by the arrows in Fig. 36, and the intensity of advertising, are conditions which are subject to the control of the firm.[3] It determines, moreover, price, quality and service. When a rational maximization of profit is assumed, all these adaptations take place in mutual

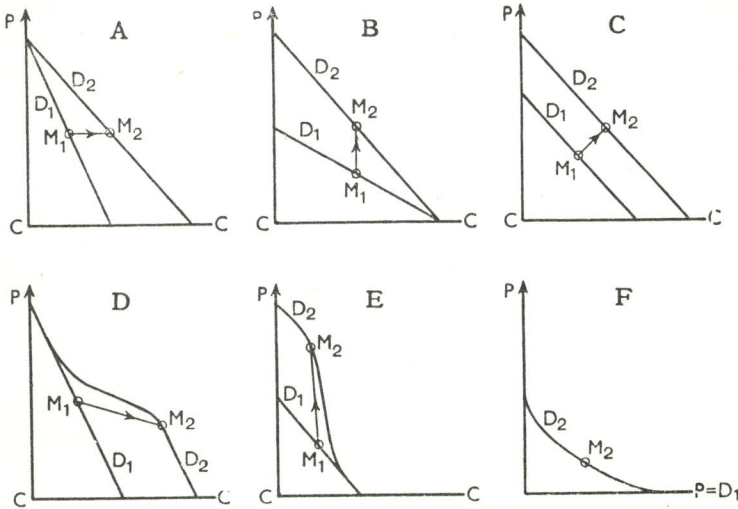

Fig. 36. Effect of Advertising on Demand

interdependence, at the same time as a partial equilibrium is aimed at for each parameter of action separately. In the maximization of profit with full knowledge of all conditions, it is possible to determine how far it is profitable to go in every direction. One will go to the intersection between a special marginal cost curve and a marginal revenue curve. After the determination of how far it is profitable to proceed with advertising, if a definite price-quantity direction of advertisement is assumed, the next object is to try to find the price-quantity direction of advertising leading to the highest monopoly point.

The situation may also be illustrated more simply, as in Fig. 37, where D_0D_0 is a sales curve without advertising, and the curves R = 50 and

[3] We have here a question of the marginal values in the shifting of the monopoly point to the right or left (as in Fig. E above) in relation to the quantity axis, cf. Figs. 4 and 5 in the above-mentioned article in *Nordisk Tidsskrift for Teknisk Økonomi*, 1935. Fig. 37 below is Fig. 6 in the same article. A statement along similar lines is to be found in Kenneth E. Boulding, *Economic Analysis*, New York, 1941, ed. 1948, Table 53, p. 710, and in George J. Stigler, *The Theory of Price*, Houghton Mifflin Co., 1947, Table 20, p. 260.

R = 90 the sales curves, which can be created by advertising expenses of 50 and 90 per period in the cheapest possible way. The hyperbolae I_1, I_2 and I_3 are points indicating equally great gross revenue (100, 196 and about 280 respectively). The perpendicular lines $C_1 = 50$, $C_2 = 80$, etc., finally indicate costs of production for different quantities. For each point in the figure, the net revenue is to be found by deducting from the gross revenue, indicated by the I curves, the costs of production, indicated

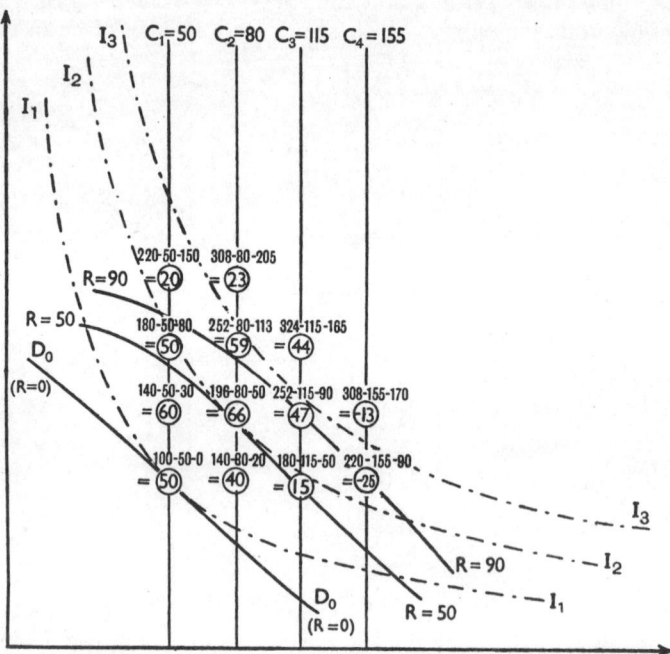

Fig. 37. Equilibrium with Advertising

by the C curves, and the costs of advertising, indicated by the R curves. Thus we find the point with the net revenue of 66 (enclosed by a circle) as the most favorable of the points for which a calculation was made. As will be seen, the figures in the graph indicate a third dimension, total amount, which may be imagined as the height above the paper.[4]

If advertising results in an expansion of sales, this may lead to reduced average costs of production in the short run owing to increased utilization of capacity or, in the long run, owing to the advantages of large-scale production. For one thing, because the extent of advertising is smaller in bad times, its effects are not, as a whole, in the direction of greater utilization of capacity, and thus of lower costs of production. The assertion, therefore, of great saving, illustrated by well-chosen numerical examples

---

[4] Since all three kinds of curves work together, the absolute maximum will probably not be situated on a point of tangency between an R-curve and an I-curve.

of better utilization of given plants, must be looked upon as typical advertising for advertising, especially because lower average costs as a result of better utilization seldom result in reduction of price. It is the much smaller decrease in costs in the long run resulting from the advantages of large-scale production, cf. Chapter 20, which is of interest for the formation of price. And precisely this is in many cases made impossible by the splitting up of the market entailed by advertising, which, moreover, strengthens the price policy possibilities of fixing a price above costs. The weighing of the effects in the directions of concentration and decentralization is, at any rate, a doubtful problem of experience, whereas the cost of advertising is an unavoidable factor, as is in many cases the price policy effect.

In cases that cannot be considered as absolute monopolies, and in which there are several firms which take account of each other's price policy, they may to a certain extent be expected also to take account of advertising and other forms of non-price competition on the part of the others, and the result may be a sort of duopolistic or oligopolistic interplay with regard to advertising as well. Experience seems to show, however, that firms are less inclined to react to this sort of action on the part of the others, and non-price competition is also regarded as less aggressive than price competition.

Since in the case of advertising, it is not only a question of obtaining, by a continuous expenditure, a continuous improvement in sales, but as greater efforts are often made temporarily, *e.g.*, when a new firm is started, the manufacture of a new commodity or an advertising campaign to create a lasting improvement in the position of the firm, a static consideration of equilibrium does not suffice. The distribution in time of expenditure and revenue, interest, risk, etc., must be taken into consideration. Advertising, moreover, is to a great extent connected with economic changes in process of development, inventions, changes in taste as well as economic and seasonal fluctuations. In this connection we may refer to the question of variation in quality, advertising and price policy for fashion goods as well as the influence of capitalistic advertising interests on the tempo and direction of economic development. Advocates of stagnation and overproduction theories may find some consolation in advertising and fashions.

CHAPTER 53

QUALITY VARIATIONS[1]

THE assumption of a limited number of homogeneous and stable commodity qualities is in many cases a practical, theoretical simplification. It precludes, however, the treatment of some important phenomena in modern industry, which are especially important where monopolistic competition and non-price competition prevail. As a substitute for or a supplement to price variations, competition by means of advertising, quality variations and services, as already mentioned, are possible.

One difficulty is the quantitative measurement of variations in quality. In some cases an objective measurement is possible, *e.g.*, weight, size, content of certain materials, etc. Further, as with regard to advertising, it is possible to apply the indirect method, *i.e.*, to consider the costs of an improvement in quality which may increase demand. The similarity between the effects of advertising upon demand and cost and the effects of quality variations makes it possible to use exactly the same' method in both cases. Nevertheless, we shall explain things in a different way in this section.

A change in quality is in some cases completely characterized by the change in a number of measurable criteria. Consequently, continuous groups of qualities are to be assumed, for which demand as well as cost are functions of price and a number of quality criteria. The general theory of profit maximization and marginal equilibrium can now be applied within such a group of qualities. Preference is given to the criteria having the most favorable relation between marginal revenue and marginal cost, and the changes in quality, according to the different criteria, are driven to a point where the marginal equilibrium is obtained. Price being also a variable, quality and price as well as quantity have to be combined in such a way that an absolute maximum net profit is obtained. Where non-price competition prevails, we have a more limited adjustment.

The determination of the optimum combination between price, quantity, and the quality criteria is complicated, and it is not possible to describe it in a two-dimensional graph, without using a trick, or to give a simple verbal explanation. The trick consists in first assuming given prices and, corresponding to each of them, indicating the costs necessary to sell varying quantities by means of increasing improvements of quality and increased advertising. We do not here as usual consider the price policy for a given quality, but the production and sales policy and the corresponding

---

[1] This is in essential a résumé of Hans Brems, "The Interdependence of Quality Variations, Selling Efforts, and Price", *Quarterly Journal of Economics*, May, 1948, and his *Product Equilibrium under Monopolistic Competition*, Harvard Univ. Press, 1951. With regard to the curves of central importance in Brems' theory, mentioned below, see the article, Fig. 1, or the book, Figs. 13–15.

costs for an article to be sold, *e.g.*, for $2.00 or $2,000 (within the production possibilities of the firm). In order to obtain maximum profit, we have to vary all the criteria of quality and advertising so as to obtain large sales and low costs. In theory we may imagine a special kind of marginal cost curve for the gradual increase in sales at the given price, but with improvement of quality and advertising efforts. This curve is the lowest possible envelope curve for all possible combinations of quality and advertising criteria. It is profitable to continue up to the point where this curve intersects a horizontal line corresponding to the given price. Similar calculations are made for other possible prices, and as a second step the most favorable price is chosen.

This is a theoretical analysis of the properties of the optimum solution, indicating how knowledge or guesses about market and cost conditions have to be combined if maximum profit is to be obtained. In actual cases a calculation of this curve in its full length is scarcely practical. Firms will probably prefer some alternative calculations of sales and total costs corresponding to certain combinations of quality criteria and price; and as a supplement and correction to that, consciously or unconsciously, make some marginal calculations about the effects of possible variations in certain criteria. Big firms know already a good deal both about costs and about the way in which demand depends on price and quality. The problem is to what extent this knowledge from very different fields is combined in a rational way or according to the relative strength of the production and sales departments within the firms.

As mentioned above, it is possible to deal with advertising criteria in the same way as quality criteria. Where criteria are too complicated or too unique to be measurable, *i.e.*, the qualities do not belong to a continuous group to which definite demand and cost functions can be applied, a direct comparison between alternatives is necessary. As in the case of advertising, investments are often involved, and multi-period planning then has to be used. The problem of quality variation and advertising is of special importance in markets with few sellers, *i.e.*, where duopolistic or oligopolistic competition prevails. The behavior as to advertising and quality may here, like price policy, be an instrument in a complicated interplay between the parties. An example is the automobile industry, with rather uniform prices within the ordinary price classes, but with violent changes in quality according to the wants and whims of consumers and fashions created by producers.

CHAPTER 54

SEVERAL PRICES AND SEVERAL PRODUCTS IN THE SAME FIRM

PRICE discrimination, *i.e.*, the situation where the same firm charges different amounts for the same service, is no doubt of far more frequent occurrence than apparent differences in the actual price would suggest. Differences in payment are often given in the form of rebates, service, absorption of transportation charges, extra credit, special guarantees, extra quality or purchase at a favorable price of the commodity that is replaced by a new one (*e.g.*, automobiles).

Price discrimination can only take place when there is some limitation in competition, since otherwise all sellers would prefer to supply the part of the market paying the best price. Further, there must be some possibility of preventing a commodity from going first to the cheaper part of the market and from there to the more expensive part at a price below the seller's own price in this part of the market. Where a seller who can be considered a monopolist is able to keep parts of his market separate, he may find it profitable to charge the price most advantageous in each part of the market, taken by itself. That the costs of production are the same for all the sales of the seller does not mean that price is the same everywhere. Marginal revenue must, however, be the same everywhere, a fact that entails a higher price in a partial market with a less elastic sales curve. This marginal revenue, which is equally great in all partial markets, must also be equal to marginal costs.[1]

It requires a high degree of theoretical simplification to consider a firm as having only a single commodity and always selling it at exactly the same price. Most firms produce a number of different qualities of goods, which can more or less utilize the same means of production. Thus it is possible for the firms to attain a size that is not too small, at the same time as the market does not become geographically too large. Besides, it is possible to get a more even degree of employment over the year by an alternating production of various products. Technical conditions, such as the production of several kinds of commodities by the same process and the successive use of the durable means of production for the manufacture of different goods are also of decisive importance.

Where a firm produces several qualities of commodities, the situation

---

[1] Joan Robinson, *The Economics of Imperfect Competition*, Book V, cf., *inter alia*, p. 182: "The monopoly output under price discrimination is determined by the intersection of the monopolist's marginal cost curve and the aggregate marginal revenue curve" (obtained by horizontal addition of the corresponding curves for partial markets); Winding Pedersen, *Omkostninger og Prispolitik*, Copenhagen, 1940, pp. 158–65; Thorkil Kristensen, "Problemer vedrørende Prisdifferentiering", *National-økonomisk Tidsskrift*, 1940.

will as a rule be partially the same as in the case of price discrimination. The profit derived from the different qualities is unequal. By joint production the same means of production are necessarily used at the same time for the manufacture of several qualities of goods either in a fixed or in a varying proportion. By multiple production the same means of production can be used alternatively, successively, or in a parallel way for the production of several qualities of goods. Price discrimination is difficult to distinguish absolutely from multiple production. Varying the type of packaging means a small difference in quality, which may make a great difference in price possible. Even where commodity and packaging are quite the same, the work of selling and transportation may often differ for the various price classes. It can be said that the commodity in its common original form is sold at a different net price when costs and special treatment are deducted therefrom.

A rational maximization of profit in the fixation of price for several qualities of goods means that, just as in price discrimination, the same marginal revenue is required of those means of production that can either be used for one commodity or the other, or which, by joint production without a fixed proportion of quantity, can increase the product on of one commodity at the cost of the other. Further, it must be assumed that production is continued until marginal revenue corresponds to marginal costs. In joint production in a fixed proportion, marginal costs must be equal to the sum of the marginal revenues of the products.

In order to maximize profit, the price of each commodity must, moreover, be fixed with some consideration of what may be expected as to the effect of its sale on the sale of the other commodities. In other words, it is the sum of the marginal revenues of all differentiated products which is to be compared with costs. In many cases increase in the sales of one product will entail a decrease in the sale of other products which it may replace, but the opposite will be the case where two groups supplement each other in consumption or help advertise each other. It is most advantageous to pay attention to the sale of another product when the sale of the latter is relatively great, when it is elastic, and when it yields a great profit.[2] In the price policy of the retail trade, for instance, both common costs and the effect of the commodities on each others' sales and possibly also sales for purposes of advertising of some commodities below marginal costs, play an important part.

---

[2] Thorkil Kristensen, "Sammensat og kollektivt Monopol", *Nationaløkonomisk Tidsskrift*, 1938. As for the results here stated, see p. 321 of the same, *Faste og variable Omkostninger*, Copenhagen, 1939, pp. 100–106; Winding Pedersen, *Omkostninger og Prispolitik*, pp. 76–83 and 122–24. Winding Pedersen has, moreover, applied Thorkil Kristensen's treatment of the composite monopoly with regard to the sale in various periods in "Omkring den moderne Pristeori", *Nationaløkonomisk Tidsskrift*, 1939; Barfod, "Forenet Produktion og Kvalitetsændring", *Nordisk Tidsskrift for Teknisk Økonomi*, 1936. As emphasized by Bjarke Fog in *Nationaløkonomisk Tidsskrift*, 1948, a single formula does not determine a quantity in these cases; it indicates only one interdependence.

CHAPTER 55

BUYERS' MONOPOLY—MONOPOLY OF PRODUCTIVE SERVICES

Up to now we have almost exclusively dealt with sellers of commodities carrying on an individual price policy. However, most of what has been said about monopolistic policy can without great change be applied to buyers of commodities and to both sellers and buyers of productive services. In these cases we shall also find the different intermediate forms: partial monopoly, duopoly, etc., and in these cases there is also a possibility of different kinds of behavior.

As an example of a buyers' monopoly, so-called monopsony,[1] we may mention the position of the sugar factories in relation to the growers of sugar beets and that of the milk companies in relation to the unorganized farmers of the surrounding district. As a matter of fact, we often have the case of raw materials bought from many small farms, forest proprietors, or small mines for manufacture in a great industrial establishment which is the only one in the region. A tradesman may also, owing to specialization and a large capital investment, be a buyers' monopolist towards such firms or towards fishermen, small artisans, and home workers. Ordinary consumers, on the other hand, owing to their great numbers and the relatively small interest they have individually with regard to a single commodity, will have great difficulty in acquiring a position which allows them to carry on an individual price policy as buyers. By a voluntary buyers' strike, a certain pressure on prices may be exercised, however. A combination of cooperative societies may carry on price policy as a large-scale buyer, and moreover it is possible for public authorities to regulate trade in a way which works in the same direction.

Organization of the sale of productive services on the side of both buyers and sellers is known especially in the labor market. We often come across more or less complete bilateral monopolies. They also occur frequently where raw materials and intermediate products are both bought and sold by big firms. There may possibly be a chain of more or less monopolistically organized stages of production, one after the other. The result here will, however, easily be integration or long-term agreement. Where a trade is monopolistically organized in a certain sphere, *e.g.*, as seller of a commodity or as employer, it will often happen that it also acquires a monopoly in other spheres.

If the monopsonist is a firm, almost the same maximization of profit may be applied as with regard to a seller's monopoly. Here, too, a stricter

---

[1] See the schematic statement of various forms of market in Chapter 49 and Joan Robinson's more detailed treatment of monopsony in *The Economics of Imperfect Competition*, Book VI.

price policy gives increased profit per unit, at the same time as quantity is reduced. If we imagine that it is the final consumers who carry on a rational price policy, it is not only a question of a cash profit at all. The subjective discomfort resulting from a reduced consumption of the commodity must here be weighed against the saving in expenditure. If sellers have large fixed costs, the monopsonist has an opportunity of temporarily making them disregard a great part of these costs; but the buyer himself thereby incurs a risk of plants not being kept in repair. This need not be decisive for him, however, if he is not dependent on the continued existence of the firm in question. If competing sellers have only current costs, and if these are constant and equally great for all, the buyer can have no interest in carrying on a monopolistic price policy. If, on the other hand, the latter has rising costs with increased purchases, it may be profitable for him to cut off the last part of the sales and bring down the price.

Figs. 38A and B illustrate price formation when the final consumers and producers respectively have a monopoly as buyers. When consumers

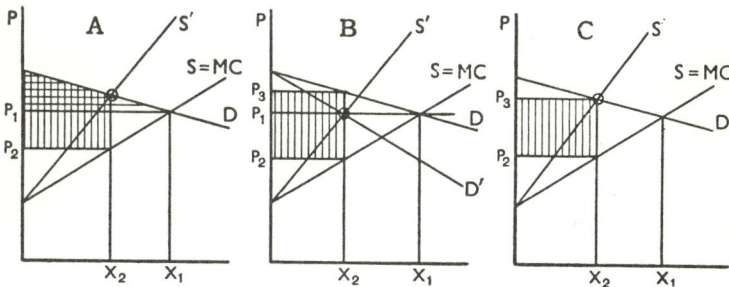

Fig. 38. Buyers' Monopoly (Monopsony)

have a monopoly ("monopsony"), Fig. 38A, they have a price policy interest in bringing down sellers' price. The quantity bought is then determined by the intersection of the demand curve and a curve, S', indicating the marginal costs for consumers when buying one unit more of the commodity, *i.e.*, the marginal curve corresponding to the sellers' supply curve, S, since increased purchases also mean an increased price for the previous units. The supply curve, by the way, is the marginal cost curve (MC) of the competing sellers. If full adaptation is assumed, it is also equal to average costs, since prices of productive services increase with the total volume of production, as explained in Chapter 20.3. Price p_2 here falls on the supply curve below the said point of intersection. The consumers' advantage in the monopolization is the difference between the area hatched only vertically and that hatched only horizontally, since p_1 and x_1 are price and quantity under free formation of price, and p_2 and x_2 under a consumers' monopoly.

In Fig. 38B, where producers have a monopsony of a raw material or some other means of production and at the same time a monopoly towards the consumers, the demand curve, D, indicates the competing consumers' demand for the product, less the producers' costs, other than for raw material (or means of production) just mentioned. We have here the same interest as in Fig. 38A in lowering the price for a group of sellers (here, sellers of the raw material), but we have, in addition, a price policy interest in raising the price for consumers, even though quantity should be reduced thereby. The marginal revenue curve, D′, therefore, is here decisive for the party which has a monopsony and a monopoly at the same time. The quantity sold is in this case determined by the intersection of S′ and D′, and price for the consumers, from which other costs have been deducted, becomes p_3, whereas the price obtained by the sellers of the productive service is p_2. While here in Fig. 38B there was no surplus under competition, the profit under the combined monopoly and monopsony becomes the hatched area. Its boundary lines indicate quantity as well as the prices of consumers and sellers of raw materials. Without monopoly and monopsony the price had been p_1.

Fig. 38C illustrates the case where the producers have a monopsony only towards the sellers of the raw produce. The hatched area here also indicates profit and its boundaries, prices and quantity. Price and quantity are here the same as in Fig. A, but the situation is less monopolistic than in Fig. B.

CHAPTER 56

BILATERAL MONOPOLY

THERE is direct bilateral monopoly when a monopoly seller is confronted by a monopoly buyer of a commodity or a productive service. We have a closely related price policy situation in the case of indirect bilateral monopoly, where two monopolists sell commodities or services entering into the same finished article, but having no direct contact, because either they are both suppliers to a group of competing firms, or there are competing firms in a stage of production between the two monopolists. As an example of the former kind of indirect bilateral monopoly may be mentioned Cournot's case, in which a monopolized copper mine and a monopolized zinc mine are sellers to a group of competing brass works.

Under direct bilateral monopoly we have, moreover, the formal difficulty that one party cannot fix the price between the parties without the cooperation or agreement of the other. If one party maintains a certain price, the other may for the time being refuse to act and thus bring pressure to bear on the former. But also under indirect bilateral monopoly there is the possibility of war or threats of war. On the other hand, it is possible that under direct bilateral monopoly one may have got over the formal difficulty, by one of the parties setting the price between the parties according to custom or by mutual agreement. We may, *e.g.*, have the following distribution of the magnitudes fixed by the parties:

			Price	Quantity
Finished article	..	..	Firm II	Consumers
Raw material	..	..	Firm I	Firm II

In the fixing of the two prices either of the parties here determines a profit per unit above costs, thereby in a similar way influencing the common output and thus the total price obtainable in excess of costs.

More important than the formal difficulty connected with direct bilateral monopoly are the real difficulties that may arise, both by direct and indirect contact between the parties when adjustment cannot take place by means of changes in quantity. But also where the demand of consumers and the supply are elastic, an unequal capacity for enduring a temporary stoppage may lead to threats and combative measures, by which means the parties try to influence each other's behavior or to enforce a decision with regard to price and, possibly, also quantity.

An important link in the determination of price, consequently, is the parties' choice of behavior. Only when this is taken as given, are prices and quantity determinate. They are determinate, in other words, if one either thinks that one is able to take a certain kind of behavior as given, or gives an explanation comprising behavior inclusive of possible influence by the opposite party, including again enforcement of an agreement by means of threats or conflict. As in the case of duopoly, uncertainty with regard to the behavior of the parties means that the application of hypothetical and subtle theories becomes important as a preliminary orientation. A more certain and detailed understanding requires, moreover, a knowledge of the way in which the parties are inclined to behave and a study of their actual behavior.

Conditions are simplest when we have relatively elastic demand and cost curves, and when, at the same time, each of the parties takes the other's excess price as given. The trade union may, for instance, be imagined to fix the rate of wages, and the employers' association the commodity price, in such a way that none of the parties tries to influence the pricing of the other. This case of bilateral monopoly where each of the parties takes certain decisions made by the other party as given, is in perfect correspondence with Cournot's duopoly case, mentioned above on p. 245. In both cases the behavior is "autonomous". Under duopoly it was the quantity of the other party, here it is his price in excess of costs, that is taken as given.

The curve DD_1 in Fig. 39 is the demand curve for a group of freely competing consumers towards the monopolist in the second stage of production, and CC_1 the sum of costs in the two stages of production. If now one party fixes his excess price at p_1—the size of which is preliminarily considered to be drawn arbitrarily—the demand curve for the other party

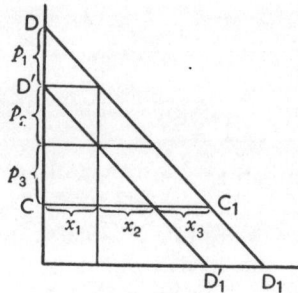

Fig. 39. Bilateral Monopoly

is reduced to $D'D_1'$, and his optimum price becomes p_3. The two monopolists being in the same position, we obtain by an adjustment of the same kind as mentioned on pp. 246 and 249 (Table) the result $p_1 = p_2 = p_3 = \frac{1}{3}DC$ and $x_1 = x_2 = x_3 = \frac{1}{3}CC_1$. The decisive part of the figure is the triangle indicating the possibilities of price in excess of costs. The curve indicating price in excess of costs will have the same form irrespective of whether the parties are dealing directly with each other or both are selling to the same third party. Whether a cost in the second stage of production is subtracted from the demand curve of consumers or added to costs is a matter of indifference.

Even if the curves have the shape indicated, the solution given above is not the only conceivable solution, nor the only possibility of a peaceful adjustment. The question is illustrated by the corresponding exposition of the case of duopoly on p. 249 with the corresponding figure and table, if only price and quantity are interchanged in Fig. 26B and the table. One of the parties may assume the position of leader, and fix his excess price in such a way that only limited room is allowed for the other party to set a corresponding excess price. But the question is whether the other party will submit to this or will resort to fighting measures, *i.e.*, as a rule a temporary discontinuation of their connection. Whereas this asymmetrical policy entails a greater decrease in sales than in the equilibrium of Cournot, it is more likely on the other hand that negotiation between the parties may lead to an expansion of production up to the same point as in case of simple monopoly, the profit being shared, equally or unequally. Such an expansion being advantageous to both, it must also be presumed to be probable.

If many parties carry on an independent price policy by themselves, as is the case, for instance, when a great number of monopolistic suppliers of raw materials, employers' organizations, and trade unions serve a group of competing housebuilders (or in the end leaseholders), price will be forced up very much and quantity reduced more than in the case of simple monopoly. This is due to the fact that the loss as a consequence of reduction in quantity partly hits the other parties and so total profit for all parties is diminished. Possibly this circumstance, more than the often mentioned technical advantages, is the principal reason why bilateral monopoly—in many cases after negotiation or fight—ends in fusion or vertical agreement by integration. It is not likely, however, that the quantity which gives the greatest total profit for the two parties together will always be realized and that only price between the parties is indeterminate until the actual behavior is decided on.[1] As in the oligopoly case, there is here a possibility of one party's dominating the other as leader.

Different numbers of firms are conceivable in different successive stages, or in complementary production. Excess price and total monopoly profit will then increase with the number of stages and decrease with the number of competing firms at each stage and with their power of expansion.[2]

A great number of market situations are obtained by combining the market positions of sellers and buyers, possibly for a series of stages in the economic chain.[3] The solution in the different cases may either be found by intersection between marginal curves or by inserting the maximum area of profit between demand curves and average cost curves. An especially important example is a labor market and the corresponding

---

[1] Cf. Fellner's article and my book quoted in footnotes 3 and 2 below. The classical "contract curve", where none of the parties has any advantage of changing his behavior by himself, is a vertical line. But adaptation by means of independent movements of the parties on their iso-profit-curves will either be very clumsy or lead to united action, *i.e.*, the disappearance of the bilateral monopoly.

[2] If we assume approximately homogeneous markets, total excess price and sales may be calculated if we know the number of firms at each stage, the power of expansion and cost conditions, cf., my *Problems of Monopoly and Economic Warfare*, Chapter III, and p. 265 above.

[3] A. Bowley, "Bilateral Monopoly", *Economic Journal*, December, 1928. William Fellner, "Prices and Wages under Bilateral Monopoly", *Quarterly Journal of Economics*, 1942, cf. the footnote p. 508, where he has Value Product (*i.e.*, demand), Marginal Value Product and Marginal Marginal Value Product. If one party can seize upon all the profit, the opponent is forced to pursue the average curves.

Bernard F. Haley on pp. 22–33 in *A Survey of Contemporary Economics*, Vol. I, 1948, deals with the case by means of a figure with 3 decreasing and 3 increasing curves, where there is otherwise a basis for a peaceful decision; the stronger of the parties may "push his advantage still further by determining the quantity to be exchanged, on an all or nothing basis, as well as price".

John T. Dunlop and Benjamin Higgins in "Bargaining Power and Market Structure", *Journal of Political Economy*, 1942, p. 19, strongly emphasize the fact that the different sections of the market must be treated together, and in a figure with a corresponding table they indicate the following sequence for the "bargaining power" of the workers (first conditions in the product market are indicated, next in the labor market): 1 Competition—Monopoly, 2 Monopsony—Monopoly, 3 Monopoly—Monopoly, 4 Bilateral Monopoly—Monopoly, 5 Competition—Competition, 6 Competition—Bilateral Monopoly, 7 Monopsony—Competition, 8 Bilateral Monopoly—Competition, 9 Monopoly—Competition, 10 Competition—Monopsony, 11 Monopsony—Monopsony, 12 Monopoly—Monopsony, to which must be added the 13th more indefinite case: Bilateral Monopoly—Bilateral Monopoly.

U

commodity market. The costs of the workers are to a great extent opportunity costs. These are for small sections of the labor market relatively
high in the long run, but probably low for all industries taken together.
Towards full employment the cost curve rises steeply. Employers pursuing a monopolistic policy as well on the labor market as on the commodity market involve a greater reduction of sales than a trade union
which is only monopolist in one of the two markets.

There is under bilateral monopoly a possibility of a series of different
modes of behavior. If the parties together try to obtain the greatest possible profit, production and employment are not limited so severely, and
profit may be shared equally or unequally according to the distribution of
power. Where one party in a bilateral commodity or labor market is tied to the
market for a shorter or longer period, the other party may be strong enough
to fix both price (wage) and quantity on an "all or nothing" basis. The
weaker party may then be forced to accept a price (or wage) situated on his
own average curve or close to it. Especially on the commodity market
under stable conditions, there must be a tendency towards the quantity
giving the greatest possible total profit. This profit, then, will be shared by
the parties in some way or other. Instability, alternative future possibilities,
love of independence, and the particularistic interest of managers counteract
this tendency, however, in a similar way as in the case of oligopoly.

The schematic exposition given here must of course be very largely
modified, not only because the parties do not act rationally but also
because separately they scarcely act as units where all members have the
same influence and where the same weight is attached to the interests of
all members. There are conflicting interests between employed, unemployed and workers who may possibly be ejected from the industry if
employment is reduced, and between employers having much capital
behind them and those who have not. Access to unemployment benefits, laws,
habits, existing agreements, etc., are all of importance, conditions that are
treated in greater detail by social policy and the practical theory of wages.
The exposition here, therefore, can only afford a theoretical starting-point
for a more detailed study elsewhere. Most important, however, is that the
peaceful adaptation by means of the market mechanism may fail completely
and we get economic warfare as described in the next chapter.

CHAPTER 57

ECONOMIC WARFARE

WE have dealt above with cases in which the formation of price, in spite
of the existence of different types of monopoly, takes place by means of
the mechanism of the market, as we know it from the theory of classical
free competition, *i.e.*, by a gradual adjustment of price and quantity,

conditions determined by the demand of consumers and the costs of production. Cases in which price and quantity cannot be determined in this way, were formerly often regarded as indeterminate, though a determination actually took place, but it is true a determination by means of forces which did not come within the traditional framework of economics. Such a limitation of the scope of economics is unsatisfactory. One may examine how the determination takes place, even if in so doing we should go beyond the methods usually employed. Also where there is a possibility of adjustment through the usual economic mechanism, other forces may modify the result. Considerations of this nature now seem to have won a certain degree of recognition and understanding.

Where a firm or group of firms may take the behavior of other economic factors as given, a simple maximization of one's own advantage may take place by so-called autonomous behavior. In other cases the behavior is conjectural, on the basis of assumptions as to the behavior of the others, and what is decisive, one tries to influence this. Several individual wills often influence the same quantities from their different motives, which excludes the possibility of applying, as is usual in economics, a simple logic of maximization. It is necessary, as emphasized by Neumann and Morgenstern to resort to the kind of logic applying to games, fighting and strategy, which will be mentioned further at the end of this chapter.

A formerly much discussed, but less realistic example of bilateral monopolies[1] is the case of isolated barter, *e.g.*, between one farmer who

---

[1] With regard to Barter, see Alfred Marshall; *Principles*, pp. 791 and 844; Knut Wicksell, *Föreläsninger i Nationalökonomi*, Lund, 1928, 1, p. 50. As to bilateral monopoly generally, see A. Cournot, *Researches into Mathematical Principles of the Theory of Wealth* (1838), Irving Fisher's edition, New York, 1927, Chap. IX; Edgeworth, *Papers Relating to Political Economy*, I, p. 111; V. Pareto, *Cours d'économie politique théorique*, Lausanne, 1897, § 141; Marshall, p. 493; A. Bowley, *The Mathematical Groundwork of Economics*, London, 1924, p. 62, and *Economic Journal*, 1928; Pigou, *The Principles of Methods of Industrial Peace*, London, 1905, Appendix A; articles by Wicksell and Schumpeter in *Archiv für Sozialwissenschaft*, 1927; F. Zeuthen, *Problems of Monopoly and Economic Warfare*, 1930, Parts III and IV; H. von Stackelberg, *Marktform und Gleichgewicht*, Berlin, 1934, in which there is also a critical survey of older literature; cf. also Hicks' survey in *Econometrica*, 1935, and E. Schneider, *Reine Theorie monopolistischer Wirtschaftsformen*, Tübingen, 1932, and his brief statement in "Zielsetzung, Verhaltensweise und Preisbildung," *Jahrbücher für Nationalökonomie*, 1943, of the classical exposition of the possible interval of negotiation and the contract curve, determined by the points of tangency between the indifference curves of the parties, and thus indicating the combinations of price and quantity where none of the parties has any interest in making changes by himself alone. A. J. Nichol, "Monopoly, Supply and Monopsony Demand", *Journal of Political Economy*, 1942, treats the same question by means of an ordinary price-quantity diagram; Gerhard Tintner, "Notes on the Problem of Bilateral Monopoly", *Journal of Political Economy*, 1939; William Fellner, "Prices and Wages under Bilateral Monopoly", *Quarterly Journal of Economics*, 1947; and *Competition Among the Few*, 1949, Chaps. IX–X. Fellner thinks that there is a great chance of the parties under bilateral monopoly in the commodity market in connection with negotiations about price, agreeing as to the quantity which will give the greatest total profit, so that it is only price that is not determinate by means of the usual mechanism of the market; J. Pen, "A General Theory of Bargaining", *Amer. Econ. Journ.*, 1952. A short explanation of the classical *contract curve* occurs in Schneider, *Pricing and Equilibrium*, 1952, pp. 266–74.

has hens and another who has geese. The difficulties are here due not only to the lack of competition, but also to the lack of divisibility of the commodities, and to the fact that the barter takes place in a natural economy, with the result that when business is being carried on, we do not have one party who is in possession of a highly divisible means of exchange, the value of which for both parties is not essentially influenced by the extent of the sales. While with full divisibility there will be a definite ratio of exchange, at which none of the parties desires to continue the exchange, it may happen that where two persons are exchanging indivisible units there may be several ratios of exchange. When there is no competition, it is very possible, however, that, irrespective of divisibility, the exchange will come to an end at a point where one party would like to continue. It is of no use, of course, that where the lack of divisibility does not prevent it, there exists a ratio of exchange at which both are interested in exchanging corresponding quantities, if one party prefers a more favorable ratio against giving up the possibility of obtaining all that he might want to receive at the given ratio, *i.e.*, he carries on an independent price policy. But which of the parties is to determine the ratio of exchange in his own favor, or how are they to agree when it is not determined by competition between several parties on both sides? As in the cases of bilateral monopoly mentioned below, the determination cannot here take place by means of the ordinary mechanism of exchange, but such things as willingness to have the exchange postponed or risk that it does not take place at all because of extreme demands, ability to estimate the position of the other party, bluff, etc., are here of decisive importance. Thus the case is only indeterminate if we disregard determining factors other than those we know from the ordinary mechanism of competitive markets.

Some of the same difficulties are apparent in a money economy when large indivisible objects are being sold, and both parties hold limited monopolistic positions *vis-à-vis* each other. When determining the salary of an older confidential employee in a firm, the employee may often be assumed to be of great value to the firm, but to have only small chances of getting a well-paid job elsewhere. Competition is here as a rule excluded within a broad interval, and an exact calculation is consequently impossible, *i.e.*, we have a case between the first and fourth of Böhm-Bawerk's four cases:

Goods which may be	Replaced	Not replaced
Employed elsewhere ..	1	3
Not employed elsewhere	2	4

Something similar applies to durable production goods that could not without a cost be transferred to other firms. A similar situation exists in markets for real estates, livestock, and antiques, etc., in which there is a limited circle of interested people with a knowledge of the often highly individual object of exchange. In this connection we may also mention the bilateral negotiations between countries in modern times.

We shall now disregard the questions of a natural economy and divisibility and consider the more usual cases of bilateral monopoly. We have a particularly practical example of bilateral monopoly, with determination by means of war or threats of war, when organizations of workers and employers both are tied to an industrial area so that the workers can only earn essentially less if they have to leave the industry, and machines and buildings, etc., also have an essentially lower earning power if they are to cooperate with other workers. Demand and the cost curve of the workers, however, need not be absolutely inelastic when a certain quantity is reached. If, for instance, we have a "kinked" demand curve as in Fig. 40, and a horizontal cost curve comprising the sum of the price determining costs of employers apart from wages and workers, alternative and other

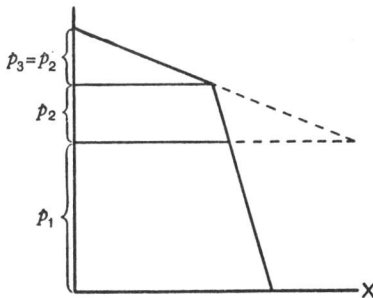

Fig. 40. Bilateral Monopoly and Kinked Demand Curve

costs, there cannot be a peaceful adjustment through variation of quantity. If one party demands a profit, p_1, per unit, the optimum profit for the other party, by peaceful adjustment, can only be p_2. But by resisting, *i.e.*, by threatening a temporary discontinuation of cooperation, there is a possibility of obtaining a greater share. Sudden increases in the cost curve, when we get beyond a certain quantity, may lead to the same result as a kinked demand curve. The decisive point is the possible excess price, *i.e.*, the difference between demand curve and average cost curve. Even where the curves are not kinked, a difference in economic power between the parties may make it advantageous for one of them to apply coercive measures. The stronger party will not allow an equal sharing of profit as in the case of the autonomous bilateral equilibrium in the last chapter.

Let us now consider a pure case where both employers and workers are absolutely tied to each other and to the trade, and both parties are organized monopolistically.[2] Employers, for instance, may find it advan-

[2] The following pages have been taken from my book, *Arbejdsløn og Arbejdsløshed*, Nyt Nordisk Forlag, Copenhagen, 1939. Earlier, more detailed expositions are to be found in *Problems of Monopoly and Economic Warfare*, 1930, Chap. IV; *Archiv für Sozialwissenschaft und Sozialpolitik*, 1929; and *Den økonomiske Fordeling*, Copenhagen, 1928.

tageous for the ensuing period of one year to pay $2.50 per hour to all workers, instead of being idle, whereas the workers will prefer a rate of wages as low as $.50 per hour instead of having no employment in the trade at all. Thus within the sphere of $.50–$2.50, any agreement will be more advantageous to both parties than having no employment at all for the ensuing year. Normally, however, there is a narrower range within which both parties prefer agreement, not to one year's stoppage, but to a conflict entailing essentially less costs and as a rule ending with a result situated at some distance both from the highest limit of the employers ($2.50) and the lowest limit of the workers ($.50). If, *e.g.*, both parties expect wages to be $1.30 after a conflict, cf. section I of Fig. 41, p. 291, and if the workers expect that the loss to them resulting from a conflict corresponds to a reduction in wages during the period of agreement of $.30, they will find it advantageous to accept any wage above $1.30 − $.30 = $1.00, instead of engaging in a strike. If in the same way the employers estimate the loss in a strike to correspond to a loss of $.40 per hour, any agreement with wages below $1.30 + $.40 = $1.70 will be to their advantage. The possibility of a conflict which is more favorable to either party than complete stoppage for the whole of the period has, consequently, reduced the "indeterminate" sphere to $1.00–$1.70.

If one party could hand over an unconditionally binding ultimatum, and the parties totally disregarded the influence of their actions on other industries and on later periods of agreement, and were not in the least interested in their own prestige, the second party would always find it advantageous to agree to any wage, be it ever so unfavorable, within the range. The only thing, then, would be to hand down one's ultimatum before the other party. The workers, for instance, would prefer a wage of $1.05 and the employers a wage of $1.65 to a strike.

The demands put forward by one of the parties may, however, be withdrawn. If one of the parties has threatened a work stoppage in case its demands were not fulfilled by a certain hour, and both parties desire to avoid the strike, the question will be whether the demand is first withdrawn by one party, accepted by the other (both, possibly, after unofficial "feelers", negotiations by intermediaries, etc.), or whether none of them does anything before the expiration of the time allowed, so that a stoppage of work occurs in spite of the fact that both parties would have preferred the agreement offered, or finally whether the time limit is postponed and they begin to negotiate about intermediary positions.

Here the whole technique of negotiation is of very great importance (illustrated, for instance, by the important "negotiations about rules of negotiations", which have taken place at short intervals between Danish organizations during the last few decades). Also psychological conditions are of great importance. It is essential for either party to convince the other party that its demand is unalterable. By exciting their own members they therefore try to cut themselves off from retreat or, if possible, to make only the opposite party believe that retreat is impossible. If then the opposite party is also firm, it may be an advantage to be able to find a way back after all, by which one does not lose too much prestige in the eyes of one's own members, of the opposite party, and of the public. The negotiating ability of individual persons will be of importance, their knowledge

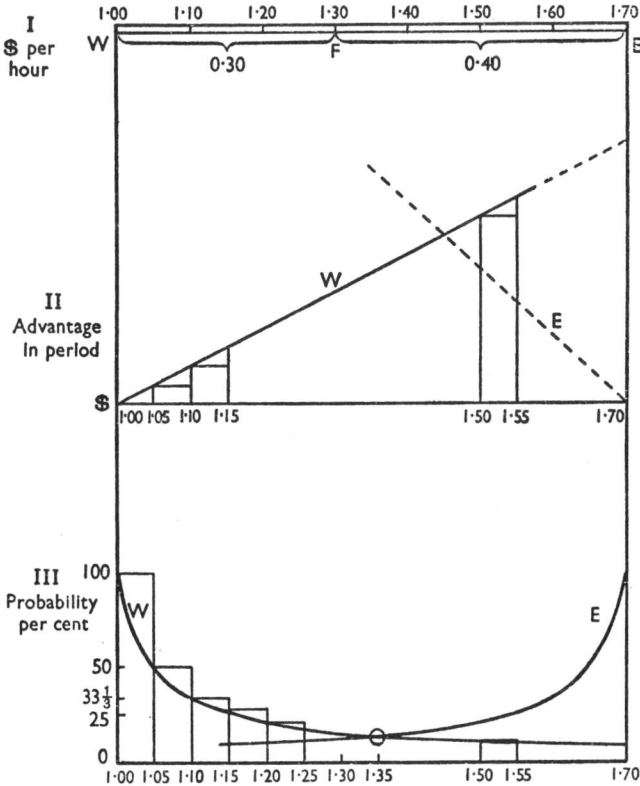

Fig. 41. Equilibrium between Workers and Employers

of the position of the opponents, their ability in certain cases of camouflaging their own, their adroitness, firmness and power of bluffing their opponents.

All these circumstances, however, may only be presumed to have a certain limited influence. The objective conditions determining the limits of the contested sphere: the result of a possible strike and the costs to the parties, seem to tend towards an agreement, which, if special conditions do not assert themselves, will be situated round the middle of the sphere or at any rate at some distance from its extreme limits. This tendency, which in the complicated circumstances of real life is combined with other tendencies, may be illustrated by parts II and III of Fig. 41.

The example, as mentioned before, is concerned with an industrial sector with fully organized workers and employers who are all unconditionally tied to the industry for the ensuing period. Both parties expect that a possible strike will result in a wage of $1.30. Since the workers think that the strike in itself will cause them a loss estimated to be equal to $.30 per hour for the ensuing period, $1.30 − $.30 = $1.00 will be their extreme point, cf. section I of the scheme. Similarly, $1.30 + $.40 = $1.70 becomes the extreme point of the employers, when the latter estimate the loss resulting from a right to be $.40.

Section II of Fig. 41 gives a survey of the advantage of the workers at any agreement above their extreme point. Since full employment, irrespective of the rate of wages, is assumed in the example, and one disregards the fact that $.05 per hour will probably mean less to them at high than at low wages, the result is that the advantage increases proportionately with the increase in wages. It would not, by the way, have involved any fundamental change in the example if we had assumed the advantage to increase in some other proportion, and had made a modification corresponding to changes in employment.

If the employers have offered a wage of $1.00, corresponding to the marginal point of the workers, and if the workers have demanded $1.05, it will unconditionally be of advantage for them to maintain this claim, assuming $.05 to be the smallest conceivable unit of negotiation. If they accept $1.00 in advance, they will not be better off than in the case of a strike. If, on the other hand, they insist on $1.05, they will gain an advantage of $.05 (the height of the small step from $1.00 to $1.05), in so far as the employers submit. If the negotiations, however, are about the interval $1.05–$1.10, the workers, as compared with the $1.05 which the employers here have offered, will lose $.05 if a strike results, and gain $.05 if the employers yield to their claims of $1.10. Consequently, it is here of advantage to the workers to insist on their demands if there is more than 50 per cent probability of the employers submitting to the $1.10. The more that can be obtained without a strike, the greater will be the loss in proportion to the profit of attempting to make further demands. If, for instance, the employers have offered $1.50, a strike will entail a loss to the workers of $.50 per hour of work, whereas insistence on a wage of $1.55 only means a further advantage of $.05. Here it will only be advantageous for the workers to display such aggressiveness during the negotiations that the risk of a strike is 1/11. At the margin there must be equilibrium between the advantage if the other party yields and the loss if he does not. Thus we obtain here, with x indicating the probability of a strike and (1 − x) the probability of the other party yielding to his demands: $(0.55 − 0.50)(1 − x) = 0.50x$; *i.e.*, $x = 1/11$.

From such calculations of the relation between profit and loss, as indicated in section II of the scheme, we may find the maximum probability of a strike, which it is profitable for the workers to risk, gradually as higher and higher intervals of wages are made the object of negotiations.

In this way we get the decreasing series of probabilities, indicated by the decreasing staircase from left to right in section III of the figure. If we assume negotiation about infinitely small intervals, we obtain the corresponding decreasing curve.

If, now, we consider the advantage to the employers of agreement at different rates of wages below $1.70, we get an increasing gradient, like the broken line in section II, from which we may calculate the curve decreasing from 100 towards the left in section III. Whereas the two gradients in section II have no connection with each other, because the advantages are felt by different groups and are not directly comparable or interchangeable, the intersection between the two curves (or corresponding staircase series) in section III is of decisive importance.

The idea of this is that at very low rates of wages where the workers will lose nothing or almost nothing by a strike, whereas the employers by making further claims may only gain little as compared with their loss in a strike, the workers will be far more eager for a strike than the employers. And conversely, the employers will have far more fighting spirit and the workers be far more cautious at rates situated near the upper limit of the range. In negotiations about each interval of wage, the party most afraid of a conflict will find it profitable to yield. Equilibrium will then be obtained at rates of wages where the parties are about equally ready to risk a strike.

As will be seen from section III of the figure, the curves decrease most rapidly near the extreme limits where an intuitive consideration also gives the same result. If there is a possibility of negotiation about a long series of wage intervals, the difference in the boldness of the parties will not be very great around the middle of the range where the fighting spirit is small, and moreover only varies little. Equilibrium is here obtained where the boldness, *i.e.*, the probability of a strike they are willing to expose themselves to, is equally great, or almost equally great. The tendency points towards the intersection of the curves, which must fall in the middle of the range (in the figure, at $1.35), so long as the curves of advantages in section II are rectilinear, as has hitherto been assumed (and the length of the step is the same for different wage intervals). Owing to the small differences in the range around the middle, the tendency, however, is here comparatively weak, so that other circumstances, such as the parties' deficient knowledge of the situation, unequal willingness to run a risk, and their actual tactics may have a comparatively great influence on the result.

The starting-point of the whole of this explanation is that negotiations take place under conditions of uncertainty, and that the parties themselves by their behavior, including excitement of their own members, can make it more or less risky for their opponents and for themselves to maintain a certain position. The fact that a strike may actually result in cases where both parties would have preferred to avoid it, as well as the great importance of public discussion and the behavior and tactics of the leaders, seems to indicate that one actually moves in such a state of uncertainty in these cases.

The quantities that are compared and which are comparable (as opposed to the profit and loss of the two parties measured in terms of money or utility), is the probability of a strike to which a party will expose itself, and the probability one believes the opponents will expose themselves to.

When each party has a correct estimate of the fighting spirit of the other,[3] the situation is comparatively simple, and equilibrium may then be obtained in accordance with the above exposition without a strike. Conditions, however, will often be complicated by the parties having wrong estimates of the seriousness of the threats of their opponents, partly because they have an insufficient knowledge of each other's economic position in case of peace and in case of conflict, and partly because it is in their interest to give their opponents an exaggerated impression of their own willingness to fight, which sometimes may induce the latter to think that it is all bluff. All this means, in the first place, that a strike may occur although both parties would have preferred its avoidance, and in the second place that the results of negotiations may be shifted in one direction or in the other. This may be illustrated by supplementing the curves at the bottom of the figure on p. 291 with curves indicating the position of the parties according to the expectations of the opponent.[4] The negotiations will probably proceed gradually, and the parties will generally approach each other. Thus, at the beginning, the negotiations are concerned with large intervals and both parties seem rather willing to fight. Through a series of intermediary stages which, perhaps, are not all officially expressed, the parties will approach each other more and more closely.

In real life the situation is further complicated when the effect of the negotiations on other labor markets are taken into consideration, when the prestige of the parties or the negotiators attains an independent importance beside the economic result itself, or when, *e.g.*, a desire of strengthening the organizations or political motives incites the parties to conflict. The internal structure of the organizations, groups with different interests, rules of voting, etc., will be of importance since it is not a single will which brings about the result. It may then be possible that the majority which the leaders may muster around a given demand dwindles if the danger of a strike becomes too great or, conversely, if the claim

---

[3] Such a certain and correct estimate of an uncertain relation requires, in order that one may arrive at a definite figure, a further definition, *e.g.*, a reference to the estimate one day or one half hour before the expiration of an ultimatum. One may, for instance, have a certain knowledge of the other party's economic conditions and psychological premises in broad outline without knowing his tactics in the particular case. In spite of all that may be said against *a priori* probabilities, it seems necessary that these or corresponding fractions must enter into a rational deliberation as to the most profitable behavior in a situation of uncertainty.

[4] Cf. Figs. 30 and 31 in *Problems of Monopoly*.

becomes too moderate. It is also probable that ideas of justice and fairness may directly impel the parties to take up a particularly determined position with regard to certain demands.

J. R. Hicks[5] mentions another way in which we may determine what the rate of wages will be within a certain range where both parties prefer agreement to conflict. A party will probably continue a stoppage of work for a longer period the closer the proposed wage rate is to the limit where the advantages of conflict and agreement are equal. Since the party which may hold out the longest time can enforce its will, the point of equilibrium will be found in the place between the two extreme limits where the parties are willing to hold out for the same period of time. In a diagram with the rate of wages plotted along the perpendicular axis, and the duration of the conflict along the horizontal axis, the point of equilibrium is obtained by intersection between a curve for the workers, declining from the highest wage they want to obtain in consideration of the possibility of employment (duration of conflict = 0), and a curve for the employers, increasing from the lowest wage they are interested in giving when efficiency is taken into consideration (also with duration of conflict = 0).

Since the duration of conflicts is variable, but not all durations are equally probable, and the outbreak of a labor conflict in all cases must be assumed to be regarded by the parties as a loss of a certain minimum size, it may be presumed that both Hicks' and my own explanation only indicate tendencies asserting themselves simultaneously[6] and which must be combined with a number of other tendencies, organizational conditions, tactics, the connection with other labor markets, etc., as well as a preference for definite rates of wages that may be defended by simple arguments, as, *e.g.*, an unchanged money rate or unchanged real wages, arguments that according to the changing conditions may be favored by one party or the other and, moreover, are likely to impress the public and the state. In a case like the one before us, the determining conditions are so multitudinous and difficult to define that there can scarcely be any advantage in including all conditions in a single formula. We must be satisfied with a cautious application of different simpler models in order to elucidate the many simultaneously active conditions. It is, for one thing, an important limitation of the above, mainly economic, theory that the organizations may often be assumed to have other aims for their members than the maximization of this income.[7]

[5] J. R. Hicks, *The Theory of Wages*, Macmillan, London, 1932, Chap. VII.

[6] Hicks agrees with me in this, cf. *Econometrica*, January 1935, p. 18.

[7] In illustration of this we may give the following quotations from A. M. Ross, "Dynamic Wage Determination under Collective Bargaining", *American Economic Review*, 1947, pp. 793–4, 800–1 and 822. "The model of the union as a monopolistic seller of labor motivated by the desire to maximize some measurable end, commonly the total wage bill, is a deeply misleading one. The union does not sell labor. It is a political agency. . . ." "When, therefore, a union behaves as though it had other ends in view than maximization of the wage bill . . . it would be imperceptive and mistaken to lay these problems to irrationality. . . ." "The proposition might be offered that 'face' and prestige are bargained more closely than money, especially

The theory of bilateral monopoly has here been presented with a number of details associated with the labor market. The same theory may also be applied to bilateral monopoly in the commodity market, but must there, no doubt, be very largely adapted to different institutional conditions. The relative power of fighting firms may to a certain extent be measured by their internal rate of interest. The analogous case of warfare between competitors is dealt with more fully in the next chapter. A general and mathematically founded theory based on actions involving certain probabilities of different results has been given in von Neumann and Morgenstern's great book, *The Theory of Games and Economic Behavior.*[8]

For Robinson Crusoe the economic problem was a simple maximum problem with given data. In a society with perfect competition, the situation is not very different. Prices are here data for the individual. Where the behavior of a few acting subjects, as in the case of duopoly or bilateral monopoly, are decisive, the process is more complicated: "... each participant attempts to maximize a function ... of which he does not control all variables. This is certainly no maximum problem, but a peculiar disconcerting mixture of several conflicting maximum problems. ..." "Those 'alien' variables cannot, from his point of view, be described by statical assumptions. This is because the others are guided just as he himself, by rational principles." Each party has what Frisch calls his parameter of action, *i.e.*, certain quantities which he is able to determine.

In some games with two participants there exists a "saddle point", *i.e.*, a situation where both parties simultaneously attain equilibrium when

---

in a period of general prosperity. After all, the officers of a union, the officials of a corporation, and the representatives of an employers' association are all dealing with other people's money. The fact that this goes on without noticeable damage indicates how loose are the ties which bind the economy together." "Greater weight is attached to changes in wages than to the sum of wages obtained. Definite fair claims are fought for with regard to equality or difference in wages." "A sixty-day strike over two cents an hour may be irrational in the economic lexicon, but viewed as a political behavior, it may have all the logic of survival." Old-established European organizations without competing unions may be nearer simple rationality, however. Carl M. Stevens, in considering the determinateness of "Union Wage Policy", *Review of Economics and Statistics*, August 1953, discusses how to get empirical knowledge about the problem.

[8] Princeton Univ. Press, 1944 (2nd edition quoted here, 1947). This work contains too much mathematics and too many details about games for ordinary economists. Essential parts of it, however, are quite easy to read separately when supplemented by one or two of the reviews, *e.g.*, p. 11, about conflicting endeavors to maximize; pp. 92–5 about maximization and saddle points; pp. 143–4 and 146 about mixed strategy with matching pennies as an example; and p. 541 about the application of threats (the quotations below are from the pages mentioned); Oscar Morgenstern, "Oligopoly, Monopolistic Competition and the Theory of Games", with discussion elucidating several of the most important economic applications, *American Economic Review*, May 1948, No. 2 (Papers and Proceedings). The most elementary review is probably that of J. R. N. Stone: "The Theory of Games", in *Economic Journal*, June 1948. A more critical one is C. Kaysen, "A Revolution in Economic Theory?" *The Review of Economic Studies*, 1946–7. A more detailed review is one by L. Hurwicz in *American Economic Journal*, 1945, and one by J. Marschak in *Journal of Political Economy*, 1946.

determining the magnitude which they are able to control (cf. above, Fig. 41, III). This situation, and the meaning of the saddle point, is most easily explained for "zero-sum, two-person games", *i.e.*, cases where the profit of one party is equal to the loss of the other party, because a given sum is to be divided between the parties. If there here exists a saddle point, it is reached in case of rational behavior. It will be a point of equilibrium for both parties when determining their magnitude in such a way that the corresponding maximization of the opposite party gives a minimum ("minimum maximorum") and consequently leave to the first party the greatest possible remainder ("maximum minimorum"). Saddle points with equilibrium for both parties in (zero or non-zero) two-person games do not always exist, however. In bilateral monopoly, a determinate equilibrium is—according to our exposition on p. 284—attained, when each party fixes his own magnitude, if the parties have to act autonomously in accordance with the rules of the game, and if demand and cost curves have some elasticity. On the other hand, if the curves have no elasticity, *i.e.*, if the capacities of the parties are absolutely tied to the special market, and the total advantage to be distributed accordingly is constant, we get a case where mixed strategy has to be resorted to, and where a saddle point is only attained by means of this more complicated strategy.

The meaning of mixed strategy and the necessity of using it in some cases is clearly illustrated by Neumann and Morgenstern with reference to the matching pennies game. "In playing Matching Pennies against an at least moderately intelligent opponent, the player will not attempt to find out the opponent's intentions, but will concentrate on avoiding having his own intentions found out, by playing irregularly 'heads' and 'tails' in successive games." "The player's strategy consists neither of playing 'tails' nor of playing 'heads', but of playing 'tails' with the probability of $\frac{1}{2}$ and 'heads' with the probability of $\frac{1}{2}$." . . . "By this device, the opponent cannot possibly find out what the player's strategy is going to be, since the player does not know it himself."

In more complicated games it is a difficult task for either party to choose optimum probabilities. But still a saddle point is attained by mixing probabilities for peace and war in different proportions.

The very pure and simple example of mixed strategy in the extremely simple game of Matching Pennies is also the essence of the strategy of the bilateral monopolies in the labor market described above. In this description as well as in real life it is further mixed up with a lot of uncertain knowledge, bluff and changes in behavior during the rather long "moves" of the game.

For other real economic games such as bilateral monopoly in the commodity market, duopoly, oligopoly, and the formation of cartels, conditions are similar. Corresponding to playing with 50 per cent probability of Matching Pennies, the strategy in the real games is the more clumsy method: by propaganda, etc., to create an atmosphere of uncertainty that gives a greater or smaller chance of conflict if the other party does not accept.

The theory of rational strategy in games is a theory of rational diplomacy (also when the other party makes blunders). But it is no theory explaining the outbreaks of conflicts involving loss to all parties or, at any rate, reducing the total sum of advantages for all parties. Conflicts, also in economic life, have to be explained, however. The "assumed complete information for all players, and a perfect interplay of threats, counterthreats, and compensations among them" is very far from real conditions. It seems, therefore, essential, as a supplement to the theory of rational behavior, to add a theory showing how other and more real assumptions in many cases lead to conflict and losses for "the totality of the players". The main causes are probably, apart from the lack of information and ability to master the mass of relevant facts with sufficient speed, the deviations from rationality due to belligerent feelings and the distortional and cumulative effects of propaganda—in many cases also on the propagandist himself and his employer. True knowledge about the other party's strength works for peace. Propaganda about one's own superiority works for war.

CHAPTER 58

DYNAMICS AND THE STRUCTURE OF THE MARKET

Even if in the following we speak of monopolistic competition, much of what is said may also be applied to conditions prevailing between monopolistic buyers and sellers. Conversely, a great part of the theory in the previous chapter, mostly written with reference to bilateral monopoly, may also be applied to monopolistic competition. We have already touched on the possibility of applying a dynamic approach to absolute monopoly and monopolistic competition. In the following we shall discuss various questions concerning the connection between dynamics and the organization of the market.[1]

Changes in the economic conditions, as, *e.g.*, changes in technique, the size of the population, and taste, contribute to counteracting a state of

[1] Winding Pedersen, "Omkring den moderne Pristeori," *Nationaløkonomisk Tidsskrift*, 1939; Schneider, "En dynamisk Teori for Prisdannelsesprocessen under Tilbudsduopol", *Nationaløkonomisk Tidsskrift*, 1942, including a report on an empirical investigation by O. Schröder, *Kostensenkung und Leistungssteigerung*, 1936, pp. 112–15; Bjarke Fog, "Dynamic Price Problems under Monopolistic Competition", *Nordisk Tidsskrift for Teknisk Økonomi*, 1946–7 (3–4). See further, Ragnar Frisch, "Monopole, Polypole, la Notion de Force dans l'Economie", *Nationaløkonomisk Tidsskrift*, 1933, p. 254 ff. (English translation in *International Economic Papers*, 1951); and Thorkil Kristensen, *Faste og variable Omkostninger*, Copenhagen, 1939, pp. 145 ff. In *Monopoly and Competition*, edited by E. H. Chamberlin, 1954, Machlup deals with stability, Lombardini with rigidities, and Hennipmann with progress.

free and equal competition. The new and improved plants will in many cases have a preferential position, and a position which is not equalized by competition because there will often be room only for one or a few new firms in the particular markets. As to the opposite case, the influence of the form of the market on the rate of progress, discussed in connection with the question of rationalization, it may be said that whereas it is usually and, perhaps, justly asserted that a monopoly weakens personal initiative, it is worth pointing out that the concentration of capital and the plentiful resources often accompanying great concentrations, have in a number of cases resulted in very large and remunerative expenditures for experiments and "induced inventions", as, *e.g.*, in the American electrical industry and the German dye and chemical industry, before the Second World War. There are the opportunity and the means to think of more than the daily fight for existence. The competitive interest in getting in front of the others disappears; but in return, progress that may at the same time benefit all members of an industry is of greater value to those that pay for experiments, etc., because the progress will have effects on the whole of the great monopolized sphere.

From static price policy, which we considered as maximization of profit per period, we proceeded to a consideration of maximization of profit for the whole of the expected future, brought back to the present by discounting for interest and risk. This means that we consider a maximization of the capitalized value of the firm. The result of the plan is not only a definite price, but a certain development of planned prices and production, etc., which branches off into alternatives in the future, alternatives that will be reconsidered for a renewed choice and revision with a view to what might later arise. Among other things, the possibilities of a future expansion of consumption at relatively low prices, the danger of future competition, and expected or possible changes in demand or cost conditions must be taken into consideration by the individual firm in the *ex ante* calculation or the estimate which determines its present behavior.

The actual development of market conditions, which one tries to elucidate by an examination *ex post*, is dependent on the plans of the individual firms, the consumers, and other economic units, as well as on the way in which the external conditions of the industry actually develop, possibly influenced by unexpected political, technical, and economic events, and of the actual rates of reaction. Among the rates and distances in time which are of importance for the development of the conditions in a market, we may mention the quickness with which competitors react to changes in a firm's price policy and, consequently, whether the movement will take the course of a series of alternating adjustments, cf. the zigzag lines between the reaction curves in Fig. 26B on p. 249, as well as the cobweb problem, Fig. 17, p. 179. It is probable that the other parties will often react before the individual firm has completely adapted itself to the long-run conditions of the market with regard to demand and costs. So in real life one must reckon with different reactions at different time distances from a change, and one must reckon with the possibility that, *e.g.*, a lead in price reduction will involve a lasting conquest of customers from a competitor, according to the mobility of the preference of individual buyers, whether, for instance, the tastes are founded only on a recently acquired habit, or whether the choice is due to the buyers' possession of supplementary technical equipment most suitable to the type of commodity in question.

It is possible to a certain extent to explain conditions by means of model constructions, *e.g.*, a sequence analysis of two firms, which simultaneously fix new prices at the beginning of each period. What is the most favorable price policy for a firm in one period must be judged on the basis of expectations as to the price policy of the other party,.which, again, is based on experiences, *e.g.*, regarding the earlier prices of the first firm. One begins with a certain structure of expectations with regard to the behavior of the other party; but it must be revised according to experience—a revision which is never finished as new data are constantly changing the old premises. The situation and the direction of movement at each moment will constantly be characterized by the previous development. The profits and losses connected with a favorable or unfavorable position in relation to competitors may have a cumulative effect. However, we shall probably not be able to go very far with models of this kind with previously assumed rules for the game. In real life, changing situations will often require a radical change of behavior: integration, cut-throat competition, or tactical manoeuvres which take account of such possibilities later on.

The more a market is controlled by a few firms, the greater is the importance of individual personal decisions. Thus, existing cartels and trusts bear the stamp of human and historical drama. In this connection we may think of the history of American trusts and of German cartels and firms, Rockefeller, Carnegie, Morgan, Stinnes, etc. In a market with many competitors, phenomena of mass psychology may sometimes have a corresponding importance, as indicated by the psychological explanations in the theory of business cycles. The danger of mistaken decisions as a consequence of disagreement in plans seems, however, to be greatest on the path between a market with many independent firms and one with the highest degree of concentration. It is here that conjectures as to the behavior of the others are of the greatest importance. It is here, too, where the power is divided between a few big competitors or opposing executives, that one may expect conflict and sudden change in the situation of the market, the "fight of the whales", as my teacher, L. V. Birck, used to say. Both in oligopoly and in bilateral monopoly, individual conditions and historically founded situations are of great importance. But at the same time an essential part of the explanation of the conflict between competitors must no doubt be sought in a theory of the same kind as the one given in the previous chapter with regard to bilateral monopoly.

In an article on Price Theory and Oligopoly,[2] K. W. Rothschild writes:

[2] *The Economic Journal*, September 1947, pp. 310 and 317.

"Price wars, while tending to occur infrequently, are a dominant feature of the oligopolistic situation. They may be caused by external or internal factors. The preparation for them, aggressive or defensive, leads to the adoption of measures which are peculiar to oligopoly. . . . The background to oligopoly . . . is . . . a struggle. But this is, of course, not a continuous struggle. On the contrary, most oligopolies will try to keep such struggles, costly as they are, at a minimum. Their normal desire will be to entrench themselves in as secure a position as possible which will enable them 'to hold what they hold' and—should an opportunity arise—to launch an offensive into rival territory. Price policy will take a pivotal place in this entrenchment policy. A price will have to be quoted that will allow the oligopolist to hold his own both *vis-à-vis* existing and potential rivals and *vis-à-vis* the consumers. This means that in 'normal' periods the price must not be so low that it provokes retaliations from the competitors, nor so high that it encourages new entrants, and it must be within the range which will maintain the good will of the customers—*i.e.*, will maintain a protection against aggressive policies of the rivals."

Oligopolistic conditions are likely to lead to an alternation between periods with stable market conditions and violent shifts when changes take place in the number of firms or in their mutual relations. New competitors arrive, or firms are defeated, often after a period of prices that are not remunerative in the long run. Possibly price discrimination is used, advertising conflict, boycott and other more violent, in some cases illegal, means. As an example of how far it is possible to lower the price during a competitive fight, two Scottish river companies[3] have been mentioned. One of them in the end carried passengers gratis, after which the other threw in a big meal in addition, with the final result that both companies had to liquidate. In many cases where competition is particularly severe, there is no doubt that points of view other than rational maximization of profit are active. The fight, however, is not always a fight for existence. The object may also be to force an otherwise independent competitor to limit his price competition or his sales.

It was mentioned in the last chapter that in the case of bilateral monopoly where quantity is inelastic, the formation of price cannot take place through a peaceful adjustment and that also in cases where adjustment is possible by changes in quantity, it may be advantageous for one party to force the other to a certain limitation in his price policy. Presumably, it will nearly always be practical where a single buyer is faced with a single seller to come to terms for a certain period. Contractual ties of this kind are of importance when the economic conditions are changed. Even if it is in the common interest to renew agreements, this may often be attended with much friction. The relations between competitors are similar. Besides, agreements, offers on the side of one party, or state interference, may lead to the parties taking up an "active" or "passive" position

---

[3] Hans Möller, *Kalkulation*, p. 192, and the article by Fuhr quoted there.

respectively, according to their ability to determine their mutual relations,[4] one party having for a period bound itself in various ways.

Both in competition between a few firms and between different monopolized stages of production, the situation is unstable because the possibility of an increase of total revenue is an incentive for obtaining a reduction in the number of independent units, either by peaceful or by warlike means. To this must be added the advantage which one party may possibly obtain at the cost of the other, and the possible economies as the result of technical concentration. On the other hand, the existence of profit will have an alluring influence on bystanders, even if the costs of production will be somewhat greater for a new and often smaller enterprise. If the co-operating firms have not permanently given up their independence, attempts to get a larger share of the profit, *e.g.*, greater sales within a cartel, may easily lead to a breaking down of cooperation between the firms.

The tendency towards monopoly is very largely dependent on external conditions. The advantages of large-scale industry and the dispersion of production are active forces in this direction, whereas cheaper costs of transportation and freedom of trade work in the opposite direction, at any rate so long as the result is not an elimination of competitors. Where there is not room for a sufficient number of firms of optimum size to bring about effective competition, we may expect a tendency in the direction of monopoly or—at least for a time—oligopoly; but the movement may possibly take place as a dramatic race between several firms as to who can reach the greatest reduction of costs by expansion of production.

Decreasing marginal and average costs have caused great difficulties for the Liberalist theory of equilibrium. Is it possible with decreasing costs to obtain a stable equilibrium without monopoly?[5] First, three negative answers may be imagined: (1) Costs do not continue to fall enough to exclude competition. Thus we have also in the long run a U-shaped cost curve. The existence of its increasing branch may, however, in many cases be problematic. (2) For long periods at least, no equilibrium is established; there are alternatively competitive fights and periods of mutual understanding. (3) The final result is monopoly.

Besides the three above-mentioned refutations of the question whether the conditions assumed may be simultaneously fulfilled, there are two attempts at a positive solution: (4) It is granted, in accordance with No. 1, that the advantage of expansion of the individual firm as a result of internal economies ceases when the firm has reached a certain size, but for the industry as a whole costs continue to fall as a consequence of

[4] Kjeld Philip, *Det Offentliges Finanspolitik og den økonomiske Aktivitet*, Munksgaard, Copenhagen, 1942, pp. 32–5.

[5] Marshall, *Principles*, p. 459, the note, and IV, IX, 7; IV, XIII, p. 367; pp. 374–5; V, VII, 1–2; V, XII with appendix H—and in continuation hereof the discussion in *Economic Journal* from the middle of the twenties, especially the Symposium by Robertson, Shove and Sraffa in March 1930; J. Schumpeter, "The Instability of Capitalism", *Economic Journal*, 1928.

external economies (common auxiliary industries, transportation plant, etc.). (5) Before the firms become very large, they will be so old that they will be less efficient because the leaders now belong to the third or fourth generations, or the management, in case of corporations, will become bureaucratic. Marshall here uses the analogy with "The trees in the forest" growing up to a certain height.

The importance of external economies[6] ought not to be exaggerated— nor under modern conditions the time it takes before a firm may become very large in proportion to the particular markets. Actually, experience shows a high degree of monopolistic conditions in markets of limited size, and at the same time a great instability where large-scale production is of importance. In local and special markets—and in a small country like Denmark, in several cases in the national market—the cost curve will not curve upwards in time to get a number of firms of optimum size with free competition. Even in the United States oligopoly is considered to be the predominant form of market in manufacturing industry.

The difference between commodities with fixed and flexible prices[7] is in a number of cases dependent on the conditions of production and demand. The fluctuating crops in connection with inelastic demand contribute to comparatively strongly fluctuating prices of agricultural products as compared with industrial products. But to this must be added the price policy causes: the difference between free prices, where there are competition and quantity adjustment for the individual firms and fixed prices where one or several firms carry on price policy and a decision consequently is necessary in order to change the price. Wherever sellers influence price, they may have an interest in preventing buyers from thinking too much about the price. Reduction of price may lead to speculative hoarding by the purchaser and possibly doubt as to the quality of the commodity; and an increase in price may entail a critical attitude, causing a switch to other commodities or claims of state interference. As to branded commodities, fixed price will often enter as an important link in the recognized and esteemed characteristics of the commodity. Furthermore, a firm having a margin of profit, will consider the trouble and costs of a change in price to a greater extent than a firm under free competition.

Where it is a question of cartel agreements, the difficulties involved in a change of the agreement, and the possible danger of a disruption of cooperation when the old terms are to be reconsidered, will in many cases

[6] Joan Robinson, *The Economics of Imperfect Competition*, Appendix: "Increasing and Diminishing Returns."

[7] F. C. Mills, *The Behavior of Prices*, New York, 1927; for statistical information as to the flexibility of price of different commodities, see Jørgen Pedersen and O. Strange Petersen, *An Analysis of Price Behavior*, Copenhagen, 1938. With regard to the explanations given here, see Paul M. Sweezy, "Demand under Conditions of Oligopoly", *Journal of Political Economy*, 1939, and as to the "kinked" demand curve generally, Bernard F. Haley in *A Survey of Contemporary Economics*, Vol. I, 1948, pp. 7–8; Winding Pedersen, "Omkring moderne Pristeori", *Nationaløkonomisk Tidsskrift*, 1939, p. 37 ff.; Burns, *The Decline of Competition*, London and New York, 1936; W. H. Hutt, "The Nature of Aggressive Selling", *Economica*, 1935.

tend to reduce the number of changes in price. Somewhat similar is the case with regard to the vertical agreements made for a certain period or terminable on notice. As has been seen in the labor market, especially in quiet times, both parties—and perhaps even to a greater extent the outsiders—will often be in favor of unchanged wages. Stability in money wages, by the way, contributes on the cost side to the relative stability in the prices of industrial goods mentioned above.

Under monopolistic competition there are, moreover, special motives for not touching price. Any change in the relation of prices between the competing goods may involve price competition among the competitors, which may be disagreeable whether one allows the other party to adapt himself by underbidding, or one enters one's self into price competition. It is probable, therefore, that even in many spheres where no agreement or tacit understanding may be demonstrated, we shall get stable prices owing to a general recognition of the danger involved in beginning to touch a price that is found fairly satisfactory to all. This price or combination of prices for related qualities may have come into existence under other economic conditions, and may thus be considered as accidental in relation to the conditions of the moment, *i.e.*, it is historically determined.

The danger of a reduction in price—the "fear of spoiling the market", as Marshall says—is greatest when the variable costs are small and there is a possibility of a great deal of idle capacity and a large amount of capital yielding no revenue in a depression. In this case it asserts itself even in spheres with comparatively many and ordinarily freely competing firms. But increases in price are also dangerous when there is idle capacity in the industry, and therefore a possibility that not everybody will follow suit. Increases are avoided, moreover, in spheres where a conscious price policy is pursued, because a temporary increase gives more chance of a later reduction that may let loose competition. Further, it has been maintained that the tendency to a decline in price in a depression is reduced by the fact that the remaining demand is more inelastic and so invites a sharper price policy.

According to Paul Sweezy, businessmen "frequently explain that they would lose their customers by raising prices, but would sell very little more by lowering their prices". This means that their "imagined demand curve" is very elastic with regard to increases in price where one does not think that competitors will follow suit, but inelastic with regard to price reductions where one believes that the others will follow suit. To this much discussed "kinked demand curve" there corresponds a great gap between marginal revenue, calculated on the basis of upward or downward moving price changes. The marginal cost may then move within this interval without making either increases or reductions in the previous price advantageous.

There are other and important causes making it natural that prices are mobile where there is free competition among a great number of sellers, but stable in monopoly or monopolistic competition. In the case of competition, the many sellers adapt their quantities, and many conditions may be imagined to make one of them change his supply. The fact that there is no monopoly profit makes them extremely sensitive to any change. Since the buyers also adjust quantity, price is allowed to adapt itself freely to any change in total demand and supply.

If a single seller is standing *vis-à-vis* a great number of buyers, it is the seller who sets the price, and it is improbable that he will change it with small changes in demand or costs; moreover, there is just a small difference in profit with a series of prices around the optimum one. Uncertainty then means that it will probably often be impossible to decide which is the optimum price within a rather wide interval.

Stabilization of the prices of a commodity means greater fluctuations in its sales when demand is changed. The effects of this from the point of view of social economy will be discussed in Chapter 62.

CHAPTER 59

AIMS AND BEHAVIOR

In the preceding chapters we have largely confined ourselves to considering the way in which firms would behave under different market conditions, provided they maximized their profit in the short or in the long run. It is presumably a justified belief, held by most economists, that such deductive investigations of the solution of the problem of profit maximization may at least offer some guidance as to actual economic behavior. Before proceeding in Chapter 61 to a discussion of the prevailing experience with regard to price policy, we shall here discuss more generally the question of motives and the ability to achieve the aims, and in the next chapter the influence of organizations on economic behavior.

The conceptions of classical economics of an economic man apply fairly well to an entrepreneur in a large and frictionless competitive market, because, if he does not constantly try to maximize his net income, he will be defeated by his competitors. Hard-pressed entrepreneurs and workers, living under the iron law of wages, besides making serious endeavors to earn as much as possible, must as consumers spend their money in a rational way for material, or at least for egoistical or family egoistical wants. According to this conception of society, it is only great landowners and people who acquire casual and temporary gains who can behave extravagantly both with regard to income and expenditure. In other cases people are so tied down by necessity that what they are bound to do may be calculated in advance, according to rational rules.

The criticism, especially raised by the German historical school[1] and later continued by the American institutionalists and behaviorists, emphasizes that the motives, in so far as it is possible to speak of them, are far more numerous, that behavior is very largely determined by habits and feelings of justice (institutions in the wider sense of the word), and that we must stress not only the isolated behavior of the individuals, but the effects of the different kinds of relationships between individuals. Attempts to attain objects other than the greatest possible income have been of great importance and are still so in many cases. At any rate, as far as the official ideologies of the social groups are concerned, the aim seems in many cases to be a customary standard of life according to social position rather than income maximization or other reckless maximization of individual advantage. Production does not always take place in the cheapest way, but in accordance with custom and the limited knowledge of the individual person, and prices are far from being always fixed according to the principles of business economics. A very great part of economic dispositions are made by joint stock companies, cooperative societies, and public institutions; and the behavior of these is determined by rules and principles, adopted by the original owners jointly, and which in their realization are more or less modified by the conceptions and motives of the administrators.

Whereas the criticism of deductive theory from historical, sociological and practical quarters has often been used as an argument for the rejection of such theory, the modern dynamic and monopolistic development of theory is opening possibilities of greater harmony. Alternative premises are assumed, each of which only claims application towards definite types of real life, changes in data, exogenous impulses, alternating speeds of reaction, the effects of organizations and interference by authority. And it is admitted that the result is in some cases indeterminate, if only the forces usually dealt with in economics are taken into consideration. By these additions room is definitely left open within the circle of economically determining factors for forces other than the purely economic ones of classical free competition. It is difficult, however, to bring such a refined and more complicated theory into agreement with the simpler explanations of entrepreneurs as to what they really think and do.

Even with a high degree of competition it is possible that the behavior of entrepreneurs may differ from the ideal of the economic man, but it is then necessary that the deviation should be almost universal. It may be a question of certain concessions to buyers, *e.g.*, with a rising level of prices, or of workers, *e.g.*, when production is decreasing or in case of accidents. The means employed in order to achieve the aim of the enterprise may be characterized by old-fashioned methods, in opposition to the best knowledge of the time, or by an emotional optimism or pessimism with regard to economic development that may entail losses. Where

[1] Hildebrand, *Die Nationalökonomie der Gegenwart und Zukunft*, Frankfurt a. M., 1848. As to the reply of the theorists, see Menger, *Untersuchung über die Methode der Sozialwissenschaft*, Leipzig, 1883. For the rejoinder of the younger historical school, see Schmoller's review of this book in *Schmoller's Jahrbücher*, Vol. I, 1884.

competition prevails comparatively unhindered, there will, nevertheless, be a tendency towards the economic-man type being victorious in the struggle for existence.

Where a firm holds a monopolistic position, the tendency towards automatic adjustment is diminished, however. With the forms which the sales and cost curves may be assumed to have, there is scarcely any great difference in revenue with variations around the optimum combination of price and quantity sold. (Cf. the figures in Chapter 47.) Even if motives other than the profit motive are comparatively weak, they may therefore easily entail a considerable deviation from optimum price and sales. In the many markets with oligopoly or bilateral monopoly, the formation of price is also so uncertain that the behavior of an individual firm and its management may happen to have a decisive influence.[2]

Probably the preponderantly "nobler" motives mentioned below will as a rule affect a monopolist in the direction of lower price and a greater quantity sold than would be the case at the long-run optimum point, which is already situated at a lower price than the short-run optimum point. Uncertainty, especially as to the nature of demand, may work in the same direction; on the other hand, it has been maintained that businessmen—perhaps because they still think as under free competition—have as a rule too little faith in the possibility of expanding sales by means of lower prices. The comparatively great revenue which monopoly in many cases gives rise to, support the "nobler" motives. The fact, as Hicks says, that "the best of all monopoly profits is a quiet life", may have effects both in the direction of higher and lower prices.

Douglas[3] mentions the following motives which assert themselves beside the profit motive:

(1) The desire to benefit humanity.

(2) The fascination, or joy, of the work itself.

(3) The desire to project one's own personality in the work at hand.

(4) The desire to be esteemed by one's fellows in the field of activity.

(5) The desire for the esteem and approval of the general public.

(6) The craving for notoriety. (This may be quite distinct from the two previous incentives.)

(7) The desire for power over men and over things.

It will be seen that as motives, besides the ordinary, more or less materialistic economic-man egoism or family egoism and pure altruism (1), a number of other motives are mentioned, which of course have a strong

---

[2] Galbraith stresses this, but probably overemphasizes it when saying in *A Survey of Contemporary Economics*, Vol. I, 1948, pp. 101–2, 112 and 127, "One certain fact about oligopoly (and its counterpart on the buyer's side of the market) is that the entire market solution can be altered unilaterally by any single participant . . . oligopoly and hence a large area of entrepreneurial discretion. . . . It is of the essence of the oligopoly solution that any individual can affect the solution."

[3] Paul H. Douglas, "The Reality of Non-Commercial Incentives in Economic Life", a contribution to the collection, *The Trend of Economics*, ed. by Tugwell, 1924; F. W. Taussig, *Inventors and Moneymakers*, 1915; Richard Lewinsohn, *Die Umschichtung der Europäischen Vermögen*, Berlin, 1926.

effect, especially when one has got above a certain minimum standard, and which moreover may be difficult to keep distinct from each other. The behavior of people, for instance, in international conflicts might seem to indicate that the deviations from the sober, rational maximization of income are not less dependent on a desire to conquer or hurt other people, on envy, revenge, etc., than to the above-mentioned, very largely noble motives. Pugnacious motives within the economic field particularly lead to stoppages, lack of cooperation or, possibly, irrationally high prices or strict terms, limitation of sales, and collaboration.

Either the "nobler" motives may affect the determination of prices, the extent of production, quality, terms of work, or the like, before the revenue of the firms or the individuals appears. The result may then be lower prices, greater production, better quality, more favorable terms, finer technique, more beautiful and better constructed plants or better conditions of work. Or the motives may assert themselves after the money has been earned in the spending of the money. The oil trust magnate, for instance, first earns money through high prices of petroleum, thereby preventing, *e.g.*, poor Chinese from getting oil for their lamps. Afterwards he gives away his money to the poor Chinese, who thus can better afford to buy, *e.g.*, petroleum. The employer with the narrow-minded, traditional attitude is illiberal with regard to wages and terms of work, but will perhaps afterwards distribute his money to charities for the benefit of very largely the same persons. The endeavor to earn money has not only become a sport, but to many people a kind of duty for which one has been trained in the hard struggle for existence under quite different conditions. It has been asserted[4] that business people are unable to see the effects of monopoly and monopolistic competition, and that they are still partly living in the Liberalist faith that, as under free competition, they serve society best by earning as much money as possible; and then they think they are doing good once more by afterwards giving away their money during their life-time or after they die. The above-mentioned belief in economic harmony and the duty to earn as much as possible, seems to be exposed to attacks of doubt, as gradually modern monopoly theory is being admitted into the teaching of schools of business. This theory has not been invented in order to teach people to earn money. The motives have been purely scientific, to explain some hitherto paradoxical problems, and, besides, contrary to those of business economics, to expose and thus fight the growth of monopoly. Empirical studies of business aims must, of course, be carried through with very great caution, since a great part of what is said by businessmen is intended to create self-satisfaction and gain the approval and confidence of others.

The question of motives, though, does not only concern entrepreneurs and firms, but also the way people dispose of income and wealth as well as their choice of work and working conditions. Where connections

---

[4] Donald H. Wallace, "Monopolistic Competition and Public Policy", *The American Economic Review*, Supplement, 1936, p. 87.

between buyer and seller, employer and worker, owner and tenant, are more stable, as under old-fashioned and rural conditions, personal acquaintance will more easily lead to deviations from maximization of revenue than in great and mobile markets where one stands *vis-à-vis* an anonymous crowd of persons on the other side of the market and where one's own action only affects the totality to a very small extent. In the former cases it will often be necessary to be more flexible in order to acquire the esteem of people in the community and a more idealistic behavior will in many cases shade off into what is most profitable in the long run. Here, for instance, contrary to the great competitive market, the employer may see his advantage in a non-momentary improvement in the efficiency of his workers and their children. In times of political, national and religious struggles, there are comparatively great possibilities of sympathy and antipathy causing deviations from the economic-man behavior.

We shall not here enter into any more profound discussion of whether it is possible at all to know anything about people's motives, and if, on the whole, people do act on motives. When as in the above we have used some terms, well known from daily speech, to indicate motives, even the most hard-boiled behaviorist will scarcely be in doubt as to which tendencies with regard to human behavior we are hinting at. And agreement as to this will be sufficient for the economist for the present. One may then, at one's own pleasure, by introspection imagine an internal mental condition, or one may in a cautious, behaviorist way be satisfied with stressing the external and visible effects.

Whatever the motives and behaviors we may very well call them "economic" in every case where they actually affect the economic process. By a more narrow definition of "economic" as distinct from "non-economic", we may have to confine ourselves to the satisfaction of the egoistic and family egoistic wants of the traditional economic man and his efforts to avoid pain and exertion. As soon as one includes a semi-noble motive, as the esteem of one's fellow human beings, into the economic-man motives, it will scarcely be possible to carry through the distinction. Even within the narrow horizon of economic man, though, there are a number of motives: besides maximization of income and wealth, security, agreeable living and working conditions, leisure, etc.

Quite different from the question of motives and aims is that of a rational choice of the means that take you toward the achievement of the aim in the best possible way.[5] To an extreme behaviorist this question does not

[5] According to Johan Åkerman, *Das Problem der Sozialökonomischen Synthese*, Gleerup, Lund, 1938, p. 35, the concept "rational behavior" implies that the individual wants to act in his own interest and that he knows what is required for doing so, and that he can act in accordance with his knowledge; Alfred Schuetz, "The Problem of Rationality in the Social World", *Economica*, 1943, including a detailed discussion of the concept "rationality"; George Katona, "Psychological Analysis of Business Decisions", *American Economic Review*, March 1946, discussing among other things the psychology of routine and expectations; George Katona, *Psychological Analysis Analysis of Economic Behavior*, McGraw-Hill, 1951; O. Lange, "The Scope and Method of Economics", Section 5, *Review of Economic Studies*, 1945-6.

exist, because one only knows the aim in so far as it has been defined by the actions. If one commits what people call mistakes, the cause might be an exceptionally high appreciation of freedom from thinking—as we might explain it behavioristically in a non-behaviorist terminology. The wishes being defined by the actual behavior, there is no possibility of examining whether it is expedient and rational. Calculations as to the future on the basis of limited and one-sided premises, miscalculations, failure to use the most profitable and cheapest methods of production, are types of behavior, though, which to a great extent may be ascertained from the outside and which must find a place in the explanation of economic events (cf. Chapter 37, as to correct and incorrect estimate of risk).

What we wish to emphasize here is that market conditions and the economic conditions of society are highly characterized by the behavior of the time and the place, which, according to the above criteria, is more or less rational, as for instance with regard to technical knowledge, economic understanding, technical training, etc. We wish to emphasize, too, that differences between individuals in these respects are also of great importance. In competition there may be a tendency to eliminate the less efficient forms if they are not generally used. In monopoly, large-scale industry and economic surplus may, or may not, offer possibilities of cultivating the most efficient methods and promoting the invention of new methods. In agriculture experimentation, technical guidance, and development of new products and methods to a large extent have been transferred from individual enterprise to public or semi-public institutions. Measures that are not remunerative for the individual person may here be advantageously performed by several together.

There is always a rational limit to how far it pays to go in the direction of rationalization. It does not pay, of course, to spend an unlimited amount of cost and thought on every one of the many small decisions of practical life. An unchanged behavior in spite of small changes in exterior conditions, conventional behavior and simple approximations might reduce administrative cost. Changes in behavior as a rule only appear when changes in conditions are not small. "Flexibility is a function of the subjective realization of new conditions." "The psychology of expectations is a part of the psychology of learning, and learning (and expectations) are explained by repetition and understanding (or both)."[6]

As a result of the multitude of motives and the often not very rational character of economic behavior, the consequences to be drawn from the convenient hypothesis of rational maximization of profit must be modified by inclusion of other assumptions into the theory. It is useful here to build on experiences from other spheres with regard to motives and human behavior generally. But more essential still is the modification and verification of theories by confronting them with the facts of the market and the opinions of people taking part in the deliberations which we shall deal with in Chapter 61.

[6] P. 51 in the article by Katona, quoted in footnote 5, p. 309.

CHAPTER 60

COLLECTIVE BEHAVIOR

WHETHER the number of competitors is great or small, there is a possibility of increasing revenue by cooperation in some form or other, leading to a uniform price policy. If competition still goes on among a few competitors, there must be some special causes, as, for instance, ignorance, love of independence, lack of confidence, instability or legal hindrance.

The theory of cartels (and less formal cooperation with the same real object) comprises two parts: the negotiations about the formation of the cartel and the behavior of the individual firm as limited in certain respects by the agreement.[1]

The agreements themselves come into existence by negotiations accompanied by possible threats or offers of special advantages to those unwilling. The relative strength determining the influence of the individual firms on the contents of the agreement, is a result of the ability of the firms to undertake a competitive fight, *i.e.*, productive capacity, low costs, capital resources, and possible connections with suppliers of raw materials, granters of credit or others who may exercise pressure on the competitors. Since all are interested in coming to an agreement and in drawing in the others, there is still no question of one-sided dictation on the part of the strongest, but a certain compromise is necessary (cf. Chapter 57). If the negotiation takes place through special organizations, the rules of the latter as to voting, etc., must be of certain importance. Thus, it is usual for members of cartels to arm themselves against the moment when the renewal of the cartel is under discussion by larger and more efficient plants. This is true with regard to quotas and other arrangements.

Let us begin our theoretical analysis of the problem by considering the simplest case: negotiation about a cartel price in a homogeneous market. In Fig. 42 overleaf, we have drawn curves indicating expected gross profit in the period of agreement under discussion corresponding to different possible cartel prices, the price corresponding to the zero point of the diagram being the competitive price in force without agreement. The dotted parts of the curves indicate negative gross profit. Curve $A + B + C$ is the sum of gross profits of the three firms.

In the present case, agreement about any price above the competitive price up to b_2 will be favorable to B, and any price up to c_2 will be favorable to C. A can only work without loss where prices between a_1 and a_2

---

[1] Thorkil Kristensen, "Sammensat og kollektivt Monopol", *Nationaløkonomisk Tidsskrift*, 1938; Ragnar Frisch, "Priskartellisk Prisdannelse", *Statsøkonomisk Tidsskrift*, 1941; G. Elmers, "Produktionslänkung und Preisbildung in der Marktform des Kollektiv-monopols", *Zeitschrift für Nationalökonomie*, 1941; Ivar Sundbom and Holger Bohlin in *Ekonomisk Tidskrift*, 1944; and Hans Brems, *Product Equilibrium under Monopolistic Competition*, Harvard University Press, 1951.

are agreed upon. None of the firms prefers a price below p_a or above p_c. If the parties are able to arrange a system of compensations—it may possibly be B and C giving compensation to A—$p_{(a+b+c)}$, giving total maximum of gross profit, will be favorable to all, and it will be some kind of equilibrium price. When a system of compensation is used, a firm may agree to prices giving it a negative gross profit, apart from the compensation.

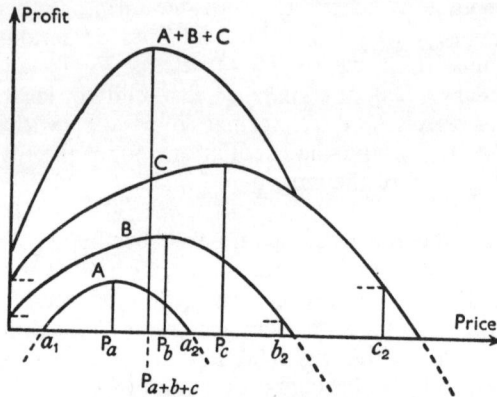

Fig. 42. Cartel Negotiations

But a more complicated game may go on. A may try to refuse any price above p_a. But if C, who has a profit in any case, and probably is financially strongest, says he will then continue with competition, A probably has to agree to a higher price. The solution will most likely be attained by the same kind of negotiations as described in Chapter 57 with reference to bilateral monopoly, *i.e.*, by threats involving a risk for all parties or in the terminology of Neumann and Morgenstern, by playing a "mixed game". In the present case we shall probably, if no compensation scheme is agreed upon, get a price a little to the left of p_c, but essentially dominated by C.

C might also begin by doing away with A, and possibly also B, after which C's curve will rise to a higher level than its curve in the figure, which assumes the existence of all three firms. What will happen depends on the cost of a price war and the likelihood of new competitors stepping in when prices rise after the extermination of A and B. If we do not, as we have done before, assume a homogeneous and ideal market, competitors may be beaten down or forced to obedience without a general reduction of C's own price, by price discrimination or by stopping the sources of raw materials or labor for A and B.

If the firms produce different, but competing commodities, the problem might be still more complicated. Only some of the firms might here agree and raise their prices somewhat, the others standing outside the agreement and increasing their sales. In the heterogeneous market it is a problem of fixing several prices, but otherwise conditions are essentially the same as in the homogeneous market, *i.e.*, that within certain limits agreement is favorable to all parties, but that there may also be threats and actual conflict.

Still more complicated cases arise when the quality of the produce is varied—with or without simultaneous variation in prices—and when rules about compensation and fines are established for production below and above certain fixed quotas, and so forth. Further multi-period analyses may be applied and security may also be taken into consideration as a separate good besides profit.[2]

In cases of competition between more than two firms, it is generally in the interest of all parties to make the coalition as comprehensive as possible, and the Neumann and Morgenstern problem[3] of obtaining advantages by the exclusion of some parties probably does not often arise in this sphere, except where boycott measures are applied simultaneously. Those three- or four-cornered problems might, for instance, arise where we have one seller and two buyers, or vice versa, or two on each side of the market, or perhaps three stages in the production (trilateral monopoly), or with regard to the various groups in the distribution of the national income. The last case might be a political "simple majority game", approximately of the "zero-sum" type in the short run. What a "player" is able to obtain by an agreement, excluding some other parties from the profit, depends on what he is able to obtain by other possible agreements. We have here the classical diplomatic alliance game.

The theory of the behavior of a firm tied in some respects by an agreement is considerably less complicated than the theory of the formation of cartels and agreements. During the period in which a price agreement is operative, a firm will be interested in expanding its sales by means of advertising and other non-price competition or, perhaps, hidden and irregular price competition in case the cartel price is above the price giving the greatest profit in view of the selling possibilities and costs of the firm. This will be profitable until the extra income is counterbalanced by the extra expenses for advertising, etc.

Now let us imagine a case in which the individual members of a price cartel, by rebates or other forms of moderate sales policy, separately and without touching the sales of the competitors, might obtain the same expansion of sales as would result if all simultaneously reduced their prices (expansion along a common demand curve). Here, a cartel price of the same height as the price in Cournot's oligopoly case, Chapter 50.1, will give equilibrium, since the inclination towards the peaceful expansion of sales will cease at this price; nor will the individual firm at this price gain any advantage from further increases in the selling expenses.

In real life, however, it is very difficult to find an equilibrium for all members at any cartel price. In the many cases where there is idle

---

[2] Cf. the book by Hans Brems quoted in footnote 1.
[3] Neumann and Morgenstern, pp. 36, 222–3, 227.

capacity and thus very low marginal costs for production itself, it is probable that the participants would like themselves, by means of advertising and other non-price competition, to expand to a net revenue that may be situated at some distance below the cartel price, which usually covers at least an essential part of the fixed costs.

The form and strength of the connection affect the formation of price in all looser forms of cooperation: tacit agreements, mutual knowledge and understanding among colleagues, price leadership, common bank or supplier, joint board of directors, mutual or one-sided ownership of capital in competing firms, as well as cooperation in commercial and industrial trade organizations, officially without any price-policy aim. Of late years the great industrial organizations in Denmark, and probably also in other countries with restrictions on imports, have had an opportunity of directing production and investment away from the fields in which there already was home production and as far as possible over to new lines. This was due to the fact that almost any starting of, or greater extension of, production, required the cooperation of the public authorities, a cooperation that is effected after negotiation with and under strong influence of the organizations.

Standardization of bookkeeping and cost calculation, common statistics within an industry, cultivation of "industrial ethics", as well as the emphasis on standard or "norm" figures, have surely often had as their real object that of limiting competition, more particularly of obtaining prices at least covering all the normal costs of the industry. If we add "normal" or "fair" profits or full covering of all costs, with a cautiously fixed "normal" degree of utilization, this really is the same as an incitement to a common price policy. In this connection readers may be referred to the treatment in the next section of average costs as a price policy norm.

Especially when we proceed from one-man firms to partnership firms, joint stock companies or cooperative societies, there is a possibility of the external behavior's being affected by the internal operation of several decision makers.[4] This is, of course, of the greater importance, the less the company is forced by competition to adopt a definite behavior, but is at liberty to carry on an independent price policy. It is the opposition between different groups of persons sharing in the management which asserts itself, the well-known conflicting interests of managers and shareholders; between the different departments of the enterprise: technicians,

---

[4] Svennilson, *Ekonomisk Planering*, Uppsala, 1938, Chapter 10; Edward Mason, "Price and Production Policies in Large-Scale Enterprise", *The American Economic Review*, Supplement, March 1939, especially p. 67. In his section of the *Survey of Contemporary Economics*, Vol. I, 1948, Galbraith reports on comprehensive American investigations as to control in corporate enterprise. At the end of the thirties "it was commonly assumed that in most large-scale corporate enterprise, the divorce of ownership from control, either in an immediate or ultimate sense, was complete". The result was "control without ownership". (P. 107.) Papandreou, "Some Basic Problems in the Theory of the Firm", *Survey of Contemporary Economics*, Vol. II, 1952.

sales and advertisement departments, bookkeeping, etc.; between different parts of capital, including borrowed capital, which acts through influential creditors. The opinions of the groups differ as to security versus the chances of great profit. Speculators, as opposed to permanent shareholders, are interested in raising or lowering the price of shares, possibly by measures that at the same time prejudice the future prosperity of the company. The technical management desires technical perfection and experiments, and the financial is interested in security or in the price of shares. Further, there is the general interest of employees in expansion, perhaps by an excessive amount of self-financing, in employment, and in the avoidance of trouble and inconveniences. Rules of taxation may, moreover, make luxurious buildings and expensive administration particularly tempting. And finally, there are interests from outside, which may have support within the enterprise: groups of shareholders and directors, representing the interests of competitors, suppliers or creditors, as well as the workers of the enterprise joined in great workers' unions and public authorities.

The greater and the older an enterprise becomes, the more it will as a rule assume the character of an institution, the power being shifted to the administration, which has the opportunity of furthering its own views and interests. But in a number of cases there will at the same time be an interest, not for the purpose of profit, in the "prosperity" of the enterprise, its usefulness and position in the society. This is intensified where the position as monopolist entails a public concession or regulation, especially when the interest of capital is only concerned with the demand for obtaining an income, limited according to fixed rules. If then at the same time the economic interest of the administration is limited, the management must aim at other objects than maximization of profit, or fall back on bureaucratic passivity. The last eventuality is scarcely common, however, in fields where experts of some kind or other are influential. Even where the interference of public authorities is not decisive, the fact that a firm only requires a small amount of equity capital, in proportion to its sales, and credit is easily obtainable, may lead to power being vested in management, and not in the owners of capital. This no doubt applies very largely to life insurance, for instance, irrespective of whether this is carried on by joint stock companies or mutual insurance companies.

The less the power in an enterprise or an institution is vested in representatives of definite interests, the greater is the possibility that consideration may be given to the general wishes of the population, the consumers, or the employed. At the same time, however, the interest of the group directly involved in cheap and efficient production disappears—an interest which may be very limited, though, where it is not a question of a permanent owner, creditor or cooperator, but where the interest concerns the price of shares or the temporary possibilities of profit.

Veblen speaks of three stages with regard to agreement between social productivity and profit: the community's interest demands that there should be a favorable difference between the material cost and the material serviceability of the output; the corporation's interest demands a favorable pecuniary difference between expenses and receipts, cost and sale price of the output; the corporation directorate's interest is that there should be a discrepancy, favorable for purchase or for sale, as the case may be, between the actual and the putative earning capacity of the corporation's capital. . . . Under the régime of the old-fashioned "money economy", with partnership methods and private ownership of industrial enterprises, the discretionary control of the industrial processes is in the hands of men whose interest in the industry is removed by one degree from the interests of the community at large. But under the régime of the more adequately developed "credit economy", with vendible corporate capital the interest of the men who hold the discretion in industrial affairs is removed by one degree from that of the concerns under their management, and by two degrees from the interests of the community at large.[5]

The latest development, however, does not seem to tend in the direction of the supremacy of speculation. Rather it is the technical and administrative management, supported by public interference, which gradually sets aside the pure maximization of profit.

CHAPTER 61

EXPERIENCE IN MARKET FORMS
AND PRICE POLICY

THE previous treatment of market problems has mainly been of a deductive character. Still, on occasion we have added scattered empirical remarks, mostly allusions to well-known conditions. Owing to the changeable and complex combinations that are found everywhere in real life, a statement of actual conditions, covering more than a limited number of cases, would have to be very comprehensive and analogous conclusions as to new cases and new situations must be very uncertain. The information as to the existence of different forms of market is comparatively certain, and on this subject we shall only make a few brief observations. But when we come to the question of actual price policy, *i.e.*, verification of the theories, everything becomes much more problematic.

Both with regard to monopolistic combinations and to markets having a single or a few sellers, we have much information from many countries. It appears therefrom that trusts, cartels, or less conspicuous forms of cooperation are to be found within a very great sphere of production and

[5] Thorstein Veblen, *The Theory of Business Enterprise*, 1904 ed., New York, 1927, pp. 158–9.

trade in Western countries. To this must be added cases with one or a few firms dominating the production of a commodity in a country. Thus we are informed by a trust commission in Sweden[1] that 30 per cent of industrial production was controlled by private monopolies. Of the monopolized markets, 12 per cent had only one seller, 17 per cent were sales cartels, 44 per cent were subject to some market agreement, and 27 per cent to price agreements. As to Denmark, a calculation shows that 56 per cent of industrial production was subject to agreement or monopolistic price policy. In 1939 60 to 80 per cent of the value of building materials in that country was regulated by national agreements or trusts, to which must be added the effects of local agreements. At the same time both workers and employers in the whole of the building trade were strongly organized. With regard to the United States,[2] investigations "suggest that pure competition, many small seller monopolistic competition, and single firm monopoly are in practice rather special cases, and that oligopoly, as the general case, may require elaboration and subdivision".

In a statistical investigation, the easiest thing is to get information about agreements or the position as sole producer within clearly defined spheres of market. Ascertainment of monopolistic competition between producers of competing types of goods, so largely discussed in economic theory, as well as of conditions of duopoly and oligopoly with different behavior of the parties, requires special investigations and an estimate with respect to which the parties involved and the neutral investigator will often disagree. The interest in avoiding an objective and impartial investigation, so common among monopolists, found a characteristic expression some years ago, when the leaders of a large and highly esteemed Danish concern declared that they would only be willing to cooperate in an "objective description fitting in with our own interests" as to the conditions within the industry in question.

Fritz Machlup,[3] who besides being very familiar with price theory took part in the management of the price policy of a large firm for ten years, states that in this work he was in constant agreement with the practical people who together with him took part in the management:

> This perfect agreement about policies, incidentally, has brought me to the belief that sensible businessmen do act as sensible economists suppose them to act, although it is true that my partners often rationalized their correct decisions in a misleading way. An investigator who would have based his findings on their answers to questionnaires or even on personal interviews,

[1] "Statens Offentliga Utredningar", *Organiserad Samverkan inom Svenskt Närings-liv*, 1940–5. A comprehensive international survey, "Monopoly and Competition in different Countries", is given in *Monopoly and Competition*, 1954.
[2] Joe S. Bain, *A Survey of Contemporary Economics*, Vol. I, p. 136.
[3] "Evaluation of and the Practical Significance of the Theory of Monopolistic Competition", *American Economic Review*, 1939, p. 234, and "Marginal Analysis and Empirical Research", *ibid.*, 1946, pp. 534–5. For criticism of the latter article see H. M. Oliver, Jr., "Marginal Theory and Business Behavior", *ibid.*, 1947. Cf. also Machlup, *The Economics of Sellers' Competition*, 1952.

Y

would have come to erroneous results. An investigator who could have seen all the actually or potentially available statistics would have come to no results at all. The only possibility for a fruitful empirical inquiry into these problems lies, I think, in the more subtle technique of analyzing a series of single business decisions through close personal contact with those responsible for the decisions. We have had a paucity of that sort of investigation, as I do not need to remind you.

Machlup's own experience tends to show that there is rarely a case of monopolistic competition in which the individual buyer is equally close to a large number of competitors. Oligopolistic conditions between few competitors are, however, of great importance, and the result is often rigid prices and increases in selling costs. Great weight must be attached to the superstition as to the importance of average costs, and to the consequences of decisions being made by definite persons (cf. the last chapter on the distribution of power within the firms).

In the later article Machlup describes the relation between the deliberations of businessmen and a theoretical analysis with a reference to the reactions of a trained driver in overtaking another car under difficult conditions on a narrow road with oncoming traffic. The driver actually, in a definite way, takes account of distances, speeds, his own acceleration and a number of other conditions, in spite of the fact that he is quite unable to put down these quantities in a rational calculation.

"The extreme difficulty of calculating, the fact that it would be utterly impractical to attempt to work out and ascertain the exact magnitudes of the variables which the theorist alleges to be significant, show merely that the explanation of an action must often include steps of reasoning which the acting individual himself does not consciously perform (because the action has become routine) and which perhaps he would never be able to perform in scientific exactness (because such exactness is not necessary in everyday life)."

The statistical institute of the University of Oxford has published the results of an empirical investigation[4] of price policy within a number of firms, of which only a few seemed to be bound by agreements. By direct questioning and conversation with leaders of 38 greater English firms, mainly within industry, the position of the firms was classified in the following way: 4 monopoly, 4 oligopoly, 11 monopolistic competition (in some cases bordering on monopoly) and 19 monopolistic competition in connection with oligopoly. The distinction was difficult, though, and in all cases it was found that the firms to a certain extent took account of competitors and the possibility of reaction on their part, if they changed their own policy with respect to price and quantity. A general result of the investigation was that no rational calculation was made on the basis

[4] R. L. Hall and C. J. Hitch, "Price Theory and Business Behaviour", with an introductory article by R. F. Harrod, in *Oxford Economic Papers*, May 1939. Investigations by Bjarke Fog and by Erich Schneider are going to be published; preliminary results are published in *Nationaløkonomisk Tidsskrift*, 1954, and *Weltwirtschaftliches Archiv*, 1954.

of the marginal cost curve and the marginal revenue curve of economic theory. As a rule there was very little understanding of the elasticity of demand, and the main rule for the fixation of price was generally said to be the covering of full average costs. When price was fixed in accordance with the principle of full average cost, it had a tendency to remain unchanged so long as no great changes took place in wages and prices of raw materials. The existing prices, therefore, would to a great extent have to be explained by the historical development.

It appeared, however, that the application of the principle of full average cost was far from consistent, and this led to interesting information as to when and why this principle of cost of more or less arbitrary character was departed from, *i.e.*, why something like the price policy of economic theory was followed after all. Of course, there was no question of maximization of profit in the short run on the basis of the cost and demand conditions of the moment, but such expressions as "taking goodwill into account", just as fear of new competitors in case of excessively high prices, were in substantial harmony with an approximate and moderate maximization of profit in the long run. Deviations, however, from such a definite tendency, were far from accidental, but strongly characterized by simultaneous tendencies in the direction of fixed prices and maintenance of certain preconceived ideas as to costs as the basis of price formation. At the same time the norm of costs acts very largely as a kind of business ethics and a belief in what in the long run is of greatest advantage to one's own interests. (The difference between the costs of different firms easily brings about the result, as in the case of the cost accounting standardized cartel, that recognized business standards are taken as the basis, instead of a consideration of the firm's own costs.)

In view of these English experiences, it may be asserted with some truth that English firms are rather more conservative in their price policy than others. In the German business economy one may, however, come across just as inelastic a conception of price policy,[5] according to which it is recommended that a certain average profit be kept in excess of costs of production for all the products of a firm together. In giving the reason why not more than "normal" profit should be taken, reference was made to the danger of influx of competitors, which seems to indicate that the real aim was maximization of profit in the long run; but in that case an investigation of the conditions for price policy would seem to be more rational than a previously fixed, arbitrary and uniform rate of profit. State regulation or fear of state interference may also act in the direction of customary and moderate rates of profit.

When, as mentioned above, the leaders of the firm know nothing of marginal cost curves and marginal revenue curves, this is not of very great importance because the intersection of these two curves is only one

---

[5] Bredt, "Preispolitik und Kostenrechnung," *Nordisk Tidsskrift for Teknisk Økonomi*, 1939. See also the statement by Rothschild quoted on p. 301, about normal profit under oligopoly.

of the signs that the maximum is being reached, and much the same result may be obtained by calculation or estimate as to total revenue and total cost in a series of roughly calculated cases. If these are supplemented by an interpolation based on an estimate, the actual result will be the same as by a conscious marginal calculation. A calculation on the basis of average revenue less average cost multiplied by quantity must, of course, give the same result as a calculation on the basis of total revenue and cost, since the average magnitudes are found by dividing by the quantity, by which it is multiplied later on. That calculation by means of total, average and marginal values is only three expressions of the same thing, has been illustrated above in Fig. 22, p. 230.

When in the Oxford investigation the firm states that price was calculated on the basis of costs, there are several reasons why this cannot be taken as an invalidation of the assertion of economic theory with regard to maximization of profit as the main principle of pricing. In the first place, it is often admitted that exceptions are made both in particularly unfavorable and favorable instances, obviously according to what is supposed to be most profitable in consideration of the elasticity of demand. The percentage of profit also differs for different firms and is not unchangeable.

Secondly, the costs that are taken into account are very largely a result of price policy. Thus calculations are made on the basis of a certain "normal" utilization of capacity, which is conservatively estimated, *i.e.*, so that price becomes sufficiently high. Furthermore, interest on fixed capital enters into the accounting of fixed costs. But capital value, among other things, is dependent on price policy possibilities, and may be written up or down when these are changed. If we find relatively stable prices on account of an oligopolistic situation, the result may be, when a price has lasted a certain time, that the costs and the interest on capital corresponding to the price are considered as normal. What from the outside is called "monopolistic price policy" may often from within appear as "sound calculation of costs". In Denmark there has been a very serious, but somewhat humorous, discussion as to how to obtain a "sound" interest on the capital of the state railways by an arbitrary writing down of their capital value.

In the third place, calculation of price on the basis of costs offers a good opportunity of taking account of selling possibilities in the fixation of the percentage added to certain costs. According to the Oxford investigation, "an overwhelming majority of the entrepreneurs thought that a price based on full average cost (including allowance for profit) was the 'right' price". "The formula used by the different firms in computing 'full cost' differ in detail . . . ; but the procedure can be not unfairly generalized as follows : prime (or 'direct') cost per unit is taken as the base, a percentage addition is made to cover overheads (or 'oncost' or 'indirect cost'), and a further conventional addition (frequently 10 per cent) is made for profit."

Both in fixing the capital values, the degree of utilization and the addition for profit, there is plenty of room for a valuation of the selling possibilities and deliberation as to the best utilization of the latter. The connection with cost conditions is especially blurred where the additional percentage includes indirect cost as well as profit.[6]

The business method of calculation: direct costs with addition of a certain percentage fixed with due regard to the elasticity of expected demand may completely correspond to the formula of monopoly price mentioned on p. 233, $p = c \cdot e/(1 + e)$. This formula is especially applicable when the direct cost per unit does not vary with the output. No doubt this is very largely the case in industry, where the U-shaped cost curves, applied by economic theory in the thirties must be supposed to give an exaggerated expression of variation in cost even with a fairly normal utilization of capacity. The slope of the cost curve must, at any rate normally, be assumed to be essentially smaller than the slope of the demand curve, so that variation in monopoly profit per unit with a change in production must chiefly depend on demand.

With price policy in the short run, *i.e.*, when certain costs are fixed, it is consistent to consider net profit and "covering of fixed costs" as one quantity, gross profit, to be maximized. With price policy in the long run fixed costs are also variable, but if the ratio between the two categories of cost is known, the sum of all costs, which here determine price, may of course be calculated as the direct costs with a percentage addition. Price may then in individual cases be fixed by the employees, as a direct cost plus a certain percentage, without consideration of demand. The same is true with regard to cartels.[7] In firms producing many and varying types of goods, or large units of custom-made commodities, the fixed percentage addition to direct cost, or certain direct costs, seems extremely practical and is also used to a great extent. For various oil products, however, different percentages of profit are applied in consideration of the elasticity of demand.

[6] Austin Robinson, in a detailed review in *Economic Journal*, September 1939, p. 538, is very sceptical of the Oxford investigation: "Several firms reckon as 'full cost' the direct cost multiplied by some factor (in several cases approximately 2)." "Would it not be at least equally legitimate to say that experience in that industry has taught that, if one accepts this empiric formula, one is more likely to survive?" In other words, that to treat elasticity of demand as about 2 gives the best results?" "Is Mr. Harrod's 'moral rule' more than a pious hope that others will refrain from cutting price and leave you under no obligation to do so?" "But if an irrational line of conduct is assumed to be normal, it can only persist so long as few diverge from it, for those who diverge in the direction of rationality are more likely to survive than those who adhere to it most rigidly." One may doubt, however, how great the results will be of this natural selection. As to the importance of average costs as an actual norm, and as to deductive and empiric price theory, readers may be referred to Winding Pedersen, *Omkring den moderne Pristeori*, VII; Hans Möller, *Kalkulation, Absatzpolitik, und Preisbildung*, 1941; *inter alia*, pp. 119, 167 and 203–4; Schneider, "Wirklichkeitsnahe Theorie der Absatzpolitik", *Weltwirtschaftliches Archiv*, 1942; the article by Bjarke Fog quoted below; Hans Brems, "A Discontinuous Cost Function", *Amer. Econ. Rev.*, September 1952.

[7] Anders Östlind, "Prisstabiliserande Egenskaper hos en Säljares Efterfrågeföreställninger, *Ekonomisk Tidskrift*, 1943; "Cost Behavior and Price Policy", Committee on Price Determination for the Conference on Price Research, 1943, p. 268; "Various Views on the Monopoly Problem", *The Review of Economics and Statistics*, May 1949, with contributions by Mason, Jastrau, Kaysen, Adelman, Nichol and Chamberlin. Jastrau speaks about the need for workable internal controls.

With different kinds of rather likely changes in conditions, a fixed percentage addition to direct costs will continue to give maximum profit. This is true if all prices and costs (and consequently the demand curve and cost curve) have decreased or increased in the same proportion, if the demanded quantity has risen or fallen in the same proportion at all imaginable prices, and if the cost level has risen or fallen. One condition, however, is that elasticity of demand continues to be the same at the prices in question (*i.e.*, the same elasticity as before in the relevant sphere of the same or a new shifted demand curve).

Kalecki[8] thinks that he is able to prove statistically that "gross margin", covering both share in fixed cost and net profit, rises with the degree of monopoly and, therefore, with the increase in the relative costs of transportation, as a consequence of a decrease in the more flexible prices of the commodities themselves. During wars and in boom periods it increases greatly.

Thus far we seem to have good possibilities of bridging the gap between the practical cost plus a certain percentage rule and orthodox monopoly theory. Exceptions to this rule are made, cost and capital values are to a certain extent calculated according to demand conditions, and finally, the determination of the percentage added to marginal cost or any other cost proportional with it opens the way for a rational monopolistic price policy, at the same time in full accordance with the marginal, the average and the total method of calculation.

Disharmony enters, however, if theorists use short-run curves in cases where the firm really is acting under the influence of long-run expectations, and if theorists deny the considerable deviations which follow from the application of a probably very slowly and incompletely adapted approximation and crude simplification. How often theorists are wrong here, and how often the disharmony arises from first- and second-hand readers disregarding their limiting assumptions and supplementary remarks, is difficult to know and without great importance.

Calculations in traditional and relatively inelastic forms, based on the rather rigid figures of the accounting department, have this notable real consequence, however, that maximization of profit can only be very approximate in the individual case and adaptation very slow. As mentioned above in connection with rigid prices, the immobility itself has price policy advantages. Changes on the whole are not so much needed in order to maximize in the long run. Though renouncement of maximum advantage is no doubt of frequent occurrence in large and well-established firms, it is well worth investigating, nevertheless, the extent to which immediate renouncement creates a chance of later advantage, and thus can be identified with a discretional endeavor to obtain maximum profit in the long run.

Without discussing whether theorists are really so very wrong, I agree with Bjarke Fog in the description of economic facts when he writes:[9]

---

[8] "Cost and Prices" in *Studies in Economic Dynamics*, 1942.

[9] Bjarke Fog, "Price Theory and Reality", *Nordisk Tidsskrift for Teknisk Økonomi*, 1948, p. 92.

The assertion by theorists that fixed costs need not be covered in the short run, but only in the long run, does not convince businessmen, for if price does not cover full cost in the short run, it never will. In cases, however, where price does not form a standard by which subsequent price announcements are judged, *e.g.*, in isolated offerings, it may prove advantageous to go down toward marginal costs. Theory has concentrated too much on complex curves, mostly interpreted as short-run curves, and has paid insufficient attention to practical cases where prices charged at different instants of time or prices charged for deliveries are interrelated. . . . Overhead, then, has to be covered, at least when dealing with regular customers. On the whole, the long-run point of view is more emphasized in real life than economists think. The gap between theory and reality is partly due to theory's concentration on the short run and reality's emphasis on the long run.

Another question has to do with the consequence of simplifications and approximations due to the great number of relevant circumstances, uncertain knowledge and limitation of human and entrepreneurial faculties. How great a margin in the determination by external facts has to be given to differences in personal ability and way of thinking? What uniformities can be apperceived by statistics and other methods of investigation?[10] What degree of collusion is realized in the important oligopolistic markets?[11]

Where it is a question of ascertaining whether a firm can really be considered to let a stated method of calculation determine its behavior, or of tracing approximately in which directions firms would have to make their calculations if they aimed at the greatest possible profit, economic theory would seem to be useful, yielding not finished results, but inspiring to a detailed factual investigation. Of course, we are not here thinking of the simple theoretical cases of the textbooks, but of a theory which reckons with heterogeneous firms in a heterogeneous market, several types of goods in the same firm, uncertain expectations of the future and other complications. Theory must not be expected to solve the concrete problems to the extent that it can predict the price policy that will be pursued in a given case, *e.g.*, with a given change in the costs of a firm. Since a reasonable economic theory has never believed that it could go so far, criticism of deductive theory shoots beyond the mark when it attacks it for not being able to predict what will happen. The object is the much more modest one of giving preliminary working hypotheses, models and

[10, 11] J. S. Bain, "Price and Production Politics", pp. 155–7 in *A Survey of Contemporary Economics*, Vol. I; J. K. Galbraith, "Monopoly and Concentration of Economic Power", *ibid.*, pp. 99–103; J. M. Clark, "Towards a Concept of Workable Competition", *Amer. Econ. Rev.*, 1940, pp. 241–56, reprinted in *Readings in the Social Control of Industry*; C. D. Edwards, *Maintaining Competition*, New York, 1949; J. S. Bain, "Workable Competition in Oligopoly", *American Economic Review* (Papers and Proceedings), 1950, pp. 35–47; J. M. Markham, "An Alternative Approach to the Concept of Workable Competition", *ibid.*, pp. 349–61; Hans Brems and Bjarke Fog in *Det Danske Marked*, 1950; H. Winding Pedersen, "Effektiv Konkurrence (Axel Nielsen til Minde)", *Nationaløkonomisk Tidsskrift*, 1954, pp. 221–43; *Monopoly and Competition and their Regulation*, 1954, includes a contribution by J. M. Clark.

tools, which must always be much less complicated than concrete cases. At the same time, work with concrete cases ought constantly to lead to revision of the assumptions on which deductive theory is based. This is also what seems to have taken place, and the resulting, more complicated theory seems to be at no great variance with observation.

Unsolved is still the important quantitative problem of measuring the extent to which simplified forms of pricing, lack of knowledge, personal arbitrariness, and aiming at other things than profit lead to deviations from the rational maximization of profit.

CHAPTER 62

THE ECONOMIC EFFECTS OF MARKET FORMS

WE shall not here enter more fully into the very comprehensive and important question of the effects of forms of organization on methods of production. Any general answer in respect to the individual forms of market cannot be given here. It will often be true that monopoly in the shape of a single large firm entails savings as a consequence of large-scale production; but at the same time there are instances where bureaucracy involves expenses and impedes development. A division of the market, carried through in a practical way, geographically or with respect to types of product, tends to save costs, whereas a quota arrangement or a price cartel enabling a firm with relatively high costs and small sales to continue, tends to raise prices. Integration leads to saving. And finally, uncertain conditions and economic warfare, where several parties simultaneously carry on an independent price policy either as competitors or against each other as buyer and seller, will lead to failure of plans, temporary stoppages and unutilized means of production. Most people will no doubt think immediately of free competition as a basis of comparison with these cases. This must not be mistaken for monopolistic competition combined with free entry to heterogeneous markets. Here the result is likely to be high costs of production as a consequence of poor utilization of capacity in the short run and inoptimal size in the long run, as well as large selling costs. Which form of organization that in a given case can produce a certain quantity products with the least use of means of production, will no doubt very largely depend on a series of conditions other than the form of organization, as for instance the qualifications and attitudes of the management and other persons involved, as well as on the technical, economic, political and cultural conditions that prevail.

Even if one knows the forms of market in the different spheres of a society, it will nevertheless be difficult to judge their importance for price formation and distribution. If we assume that free competition gives us prices in correspondence with costs, how much will then a limitation of competition increase prices in excess of costs, and to what extent is this effect counteracted or intensified by a change in costs? Very little is known about the important question of the magnitude of the profits created by monopolistic price policy. And the whole thing is complicated by the fact that the changes in organization resulting from price policy have effects not only on the technique of production, but also on the prices of productive services. If simultaneously an independent price policy is carried on with regard to several commodities or several stages of production, it is problematic to what extent the effects on the distribution between several groups of persons compensate each other, and what will be the result of the various opposing influences on relative prices.

As mentioned above in Chapter 18.2, the formal equilibrium approach for the whole of the community, possibly expressed in a system of equations will still be applicable, even if some cost equations are replaced by similar equations where profit per unit has been added to costs, provided conditions of maximization of profit are added. In the same way the quantity equations for a productive service (total quantity equal to quantity in all applications plus a possibly unutilized remainder) may be supplemented by adding a condition of maximization of the total payment for the service, instead of the supplementary condition under free competition, that either the remainder or the price of the service shall be zero. Here where price policy is used, as well as in the case of free competition, a simple transition to dynamic assumptions is possible; only it is necessary to modify the individual equations or conditions in accordance with the new assumptions. Even oligopoly or bilateral monopoly can be fitted into an ordinary equilibrium analysis without any great disturbance, so long as one assumes a behavior that can be expressed in a simple formula, *e.g.*, if in accordance with Cournot, one lets the individual firm act autonomously, *i.e.*, in such a way that the quantities or excess prices fixed by the others are taken as given. Also vaguer assumptions, *e.g.*, consideration of consumers or primitive methods of business economy, can very well be fitted into a quantitative picture of a total static or dynamic equilibrium. In a society where several wills act against each other, a more complex and casuistic explanation may be required at some crucial points, whereas the other links in the chain work in the usual way.

We shall not here go deeper into the general and abstract treatment of equilibrium conditions in a "world of monopolies" or under "universal monopoly".[1] Here, by way of introduction to the following, more concrete treatment, we have only wished to call attention to the fact that an

[1] Joan Robinson, *The Economics of Imperfect Competition*, London, 1933, Chapter 27; and Erich Schneider, *Reine Theorie monopolistischer Wirtschaftsformen*, Tübingen, 1932, Chapter III. A monopoly of each separate commodity is conceivable or perhaps of each kind of productive service, or possibly of all commodities taken together, of certain large groups of commodities or productive services, and in connection with the others, a possible monopsony.

exact explanation of the total interdependence must assume a network of the previously mentioned partial interdependences (equations), modified as they are by the new assumptions of market forms.

The effects of a monopolistic price policy for a specific commodity spread through the chain of economic links to wider circles.[2] Not least of all is the interest that attaches to changes in the spending of income. If there is a monopoly for a certain consumers' good, an increase in price may be expected if profit per unit is not fully counterbalanced by cheaper production. Increase in price is attended by decrease in production and sales as well as in the employment of the productive services involved.

In order to decide whether monopolization will lead to greater or smaller total expense for a commodity or a group of various types of commodities,

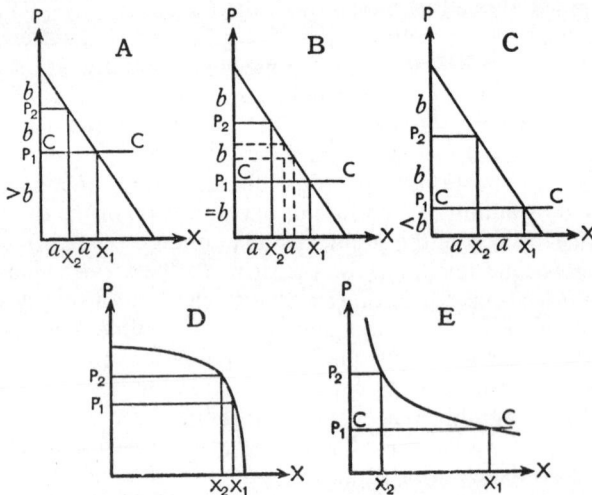

Fig. 43. Effects of Monopolies on Consumers' Outlay

it is not sufficient only to know the elasticity of the demand curve under monopoly price and under competitive price. In Fig. 43 A, B and C we have a rectilinear demand curve and a horizontal cost curve, but a varying position of costs in relation to demand. In all these cases, profit maximization involves a halving of sales and an increase in price up to midway between the intersection of the demand curve with the ordinate axis and the cost curve. At this price the (negative) elasticity of demand is greater than 1, but the elasticity of price in excess of costs is 1. In Fig. B this means a doubling of price, in A a smaller and in C a greater increase. From this it follows that, with the above-mentioned halving of sales, the expenditure for the commodity in cases A, B and C become

[2] Casper, "Monopol und Sozialprodukt in der Stattik", *Zeitschrift für Nationalökonomie*, 1935.

smaller, unchanged and greater, respectively. With the given special assumptions, the decisive fact is whether the elasticity of demand, at a price equal to costs, is greater or smaller than $\frac{1}{2}$. If in case B one did not go quite up to the pure monopoly price, there would be an increase in the consumers' expenditure for the commodity. An increase in expenditures for consumers will occur in the special cases here dealt with, if the monopoly point is shifted nearer to the center of the rectilinear demand curve.

Figure 43 D and E illustrates a couple of cases where the demand curve is not rectilinear. The former is a case with increased expenditures, the latter with diminished expenditures for the commodity under monopolization. A non-horizontal average[3] cost curve will entail a certain modification in the analysis. One would expect that, owing to the effects of the distribution of income, a situation like Fig. E would be general when large groups of goods satisfying similar wants, *e.g.*, footwear, are taken together. A slope of the kinked curve type and an elasticity in its decisive segment corresponding to Fig. D will, however, no doubt be fairly general for the products of a firm pursuing an independent price policy in keen competition with other types of products or localities, and where, consequently, competition cuts away the upper part of the demand curve. An independent price policy should here be moderate, and it would then lead to an increased turnover for the firm, and consequently greater expenditures for its products combined with a moderate increase in price and a moderate decrease in sales, at the same time as less money is left for other commodities.

Conditions are complicated by a change in the consumption of other goods, spending of the monopoly profit, and dislocation in income as a consequence of altered payment for the productive services used by the firm and altered employment of these services. If free competition and free mobility for productive services are assumed, a monopoly in some or all finished products should not entail unemployment for workers and other means of production. Under these conditions full employment is reached partly by the spending of the monopoly profit and partly by a fall in price of productive services. Simultaneously a shifting takes place in production and employment for the various commodities. The occurrence of idle capacity will appear, however, when the assumption of free adjustment of price and mobility for productive services is abandoned. It is then the changes in the transition to a new state which involve difficulties of adjustment and unemployment. The extent to which the changes may lead to unemployment or to inflation will, by the way, depend on the reaction of monetary and fiscal policy.

The question is now whether unchanged employment of means of production means unchanged total production of commodities. It does so, of course, if the total product is measured in terms of the productive services used. From the point of view of consumers, however, this measurement

---

[3] As to the justification for applying this curve to the theoretical considerations, see above, Chapter 47.

is misleading. To them the different ways of distributing means of production among the production of the individual commodities are not of equal value. The means of production do not, in a society with monopolies, give the same marginal product in all applications. The reduced real wage may be imagined to lead to either a somewhat greater or a somewhat smaller total quantity of work performed.

An important effect of the commodity monopolies is the increase in the entrepreneurial income at the cost of other incomes. Which persons receive the profit, depends on the conditions of entrance to the favored positions, cf. above Chapter 51. If entrance to an industrial sphere with preferential positions *vis-à-vis* buyers is free both legally, technically and otherwise, the profit may disappear completely, and the effect within the sphere will then only consist in an increase of costs as a consequence of overcrowding. The effect may be different for the different kinds of means of production employed. The overcrowding mentioned above may result in greater demand, especially of leaders. But otherwise, the higher price must be expected to bring about a smaller demand, at any rate of raw materials and labor.

If production is decreased within certain spheres, there will also be a decrease in the demand for the special services employed. Generally speaking, the owners of means of production, who are not themselves entrepreneurs, are hit both by the above-mentioned decrease in the value of total production, and by the fact that entrepreneurs as holders of a monopoly are receiving an increased share thereof. The possibility is not excluded, however, that some workers and other owners of productive services may obtain an increase in income as a result of shifts in consumption (luxury for the monopolists, substitute goods for others) or altered methods of production. Moreover, such means of production as are especially applicable in monopolized firms and in the monopolization itself may be imagined to have a special advantage (people with strongly mercantile capacities, corporation lawyers, and easily mobile capital in the period of transition). Since the opportunity of becoming holders of the favored enterprises is very largely dependent on mobile capital, not requiring too much security, it is possible that this capital as a whole, during the period in which monopolization takes place, receives an increased income. The profit goes to the persons who find themselves "nearest" to the opportunities and who, besides having the needed abilities, are in possession of the necessary capital, perhaps in a definite form at the given moment, cf. the treatment of entrepreneurial profit, "vacuum of price formation", etc., in Chapters 37 and 38.

Whereas monopoly profit is fairly easy to calculate, at any rate theoretically, where a transition from competition to monopoly takes place in a single sphere, and monopoly profit is an extremely appropriate theoretical concept in an abstract consideration of isolated cases, there is no possibility of numerically distinguishing any part of the total income in a community as monopoly profit. What is profit at one stage of production becomes costs at the next. In the case of a monopoly of productive services or a buyer's monopoly of them, the very prices on which the cost calculation of the goods is based are exposed to monopoly influence in an upward or downward direction. We therefore do not have monopoly profit as a special category of income, but the different kinds of income are influenced by their own market position and that of the other categories of income. So the problem may at the most be one of separating monopoly profit for the individual firms or groups of means of production by themselves, through a partial comparison between monopoly and competition in this sphere, *ceteris paribus*. With static assumptions, where profit and loss resulting from change disappear, all entrepreneurial profit is due to monopoly. However, in dealing with actual conditions it would no doubt be necessary to make very problematic, hypothetical calculations in order to separate the monopoly profit of individual persons and firms. A contributory cause is that profits and possibilities of profit are capitalized and thereby acquire the character of cost for the later producer.

Price policy, speculation in capitalized monopoly opportunities, and advertising give to the people within the sphere who are in possession of suitable abilities a special value in the eyes of the firms. Especially where the power within the firms is divided and no consistent maximization of profit takes place, there is also a possibility that those participating in the management and in closest touch with it get a share in the profit beyond their value to the firm, *e.g.*, in sinecure offices or as favored sellers of certain raw materials, a "detached profit" figuring in the accounts of the firm as a cost.

Whereas commodity monopolies in the long run only mean a shifting of means of production among several goods, a monopoly of productive services, on the other hand, causes unutilized remainders of the latter. If there is a monopoly of commodity production and of productive services at the same time, or if there is both a sellers' and a buyers' monopoly with regard to the services, the situation becomes more complicated. In the latter case it is conceivable that price and quantity of the services remain almost unchanged, but otherwise the result will be idleness or scarcity of services, according to which part is the stronger. The total result of the monopolies will be a series of shiftings in prices, quantities and distribution, determined by all the conditions together. As a rule the stronger monopolies obtain a profit. There will be an increase in price, especially when there is monopoly at several stages in the production of a commodity. In the modern, strongly organized society the unequal degree of organization has substantial effects.

Whereas monopoly entails a tendency to stair-shaped price movements, with few changes in price and generally smaller scope for fluctuations, contrary to the continuous price movements with great distance between the highest and lowest prices under free competition, there is one condition, however, which may give us a tendency in the opposite direction. In trades where the direct costs are small and the utilization of capacity fluctuates greatly, *e.g.*, tramp shipping, price under free competition will not rise substantially until later, but then greatly and rather suddenly when the limit of capacity has been reached. If, on the other hand, one has a monopoly, *e.g.*, of line shipping, a rise in demand will at an earlier stage make an increase in price advantageous and possible. (This will easily be seen from a graph showing a gradual shifting of the demand curve and the marginal revenue curve.)

The result of fixed prices is fluctuating production and employment. This effect of the price policy of the firms within individual branches of production is intensified when monopolistic organization or a limited mobility for labor or other productive services prevents the previously mentioned adjustment by means of shifts in the direction of production. To this must be added the effect on expenditure of the price policy pursued for the productive services. If workers in slump periods are able to keep up wages, the possibility of reducing the level of costs by means of curtailment of employment will be greatly reduced. Inelastic cartel prices tend in the same direction. Whether maintenance of commodity prices and wages makes the maintenance of purchasing power possible, or whether it has the opposite effect owing to reduced sales, is dependent on the elasticity of demand for the products, cost conditions, as well as on the general economic policy of the state.

Conflict and tactical manoeuvres between large competitors or bilateral monopolists may easily lead to failure of plans and losses as a result of stoppage. Preparation of members of a cartel for negotiations on the renewal of an agreement may also result in unutilized capacity. Stackelberg maintains that instability has hitherto been restrained by a lack of knowledge as to what can be achieved by a monopolistic policy as well as by considerations of justice and decency on the part of the parties concerned. When the teaching of business economics rationalizes the way of thinking, thus removing these restraints, there may be an increased danger of instability, and an increased need of regulation.[4] Presumably it is just as much the excessively stabilizing effects of monopolies and organizations, which call for intervention.

The surpluses earned as a result of monopolistic price policy may often be presumed in bureaucratic large-scale enterprises to be spent on an excessive investment in one's own firm. Especially if one assumes that there is a strong tendency within large parts of the industrial world to carry on a price policy restricting production, it is conceivable that the result may be that difficulties arise in investing the surplus. However, one way out is to take up more lines of production, possibly by vertical expansion, or the formation of firms with diversified production.

Monopoly within the individual countries has, for instance through dumping, exercised great influence on international trade, and thereby also on its regulation by the state, which again has contributed to difficulties

---

[4] Stackelberg, *Marktform und Gleichgewicht*, Chapter VI, cf. my review of it in *Nationaløkonomisk Tidsskrift*, 1935.

in foreign policy. Sometimes combines or firms in several countries agree to form international cartels. In the strictly regulated trade of modern times, the nations very largely stand *vis-à-vis* each other as economic units, at the same time buying and selling or laying down the rules for the buying and selling of private firms. Thus a very complicated, bilateral (or multilateral) monopoly policy arises. If there is no common means of exchange, relatively independent of the policy of the different countries, trade between national monopolies approaches the case of isolated barter mentioned above (p. 287).

Hitherto we have dealt only with the effect on quantities and relative prices. The organization of the market, however, may easily influence absolute prices not only on account of the above-mentioned effect on international trade, but also on account of the ways in which business cycles are influenced. Here the resistance against a fall in prices and reduction of wages is one of the important factors which strengthens the tendency towards adjustment by means of increasing absolute prices or hampers the tendency to decreasing prices.

When transition from competition to monopoly changes the form of the market to a considerable extent, this involves at the same time a change in the whole structure of society.

CHAPTER 63

PROPERTY AND POWER

THE distribution of property and other privileges, as well as the actual distribution of ability to work together with the functional distribution, *i.e.*, the prices of production services, are the most important elements determining the personal distribution of income. The personal distribution is, moreover, influenced by transfers of income through the economic solidarity of the families, voluntary redistributions among individuals, and the redistribution taking place through the state.

Economists as a rule are mainly interested in the distribution of income, particularly the functional distribution, to a smaller extent in the distribution of property which concerns quantities of funds and not the size of flows. Nevertheless, it may be reasonable to make a short reference to the origin of the given distribution of property: the saving of current income, increase in the value of land and plants, gains due to price movements, speculation and private acquisition of unused and common land, the origin of great fortunes by royal gifts still in existence, etc. In this connection, mention must also be made of the transfer, partition, and sometimes accumulation of property by inheritance, and, finally, its reduction by means of taxation. It is only in case we take the given conditions of property as data that these factors can be kept outside the economic explanation. Whereas it may be practical to leave the explanation concerning the property and privileges already in existence to history, sociology, and law, it is necessary in a dynamic treatment to include the explanation of the rise and disappearance of property in the period under consideration, on account of the direct connection existing between what occurs in the period and the size of the properties at its beginning and end. Saving and consumption of property as well as investment and consumption of stocks and supplies, together with current expenditure and revenue, affect the business accounts of the year. But also fluctuations in value and transfer of property may in many instances affect economic development.

An important institutional element besides the distribution of property is the distribution of possibilities for obtaining well-paid work. This distribution, again, is to a great extent determined by opportunities of education and training as well as by restrictions and privileges. Further, there are the differences with regard to the opportunities for obtaining the most favorable positions as entrepreneurs. (Cf. Chapters 37, 38 and 51.)

The problem of economy and power was much discussed during the first decades of this century in continuation of the discussion raised by the criticism of classical theory, which the historic school and the socialist authors started. What place is to be accorded to power as an economic cause, is, however, very largely a question of definition. If any ability to achieve a given result is not to be considered as an outcome of power, the use of the concept must be limited. It is not practical to designate any ability to acquire commodities in return for money through normal sales or to acquire payment for work performed or for the services one's property yields, as power. In other words, it will not be practical to say that it is due to power that the rich man can go into a shop and bring away expensive goods in return for putting the money down on the counter, or that the expert can earn high fees because his service is valuable. Since it is possible to give a clearer explanation of the origin of monopoly income, it is not practical here either to explain it by the more indefinite and comprehensive term of power.

It is reasonable, on the other hand, to designate incomes obtained by physical or other force, outside the normal mechanism of sales, as power incomes. Besides theft, robbery, conquest, and other forcible, gratuitous acquisition of property, possibly backed by the moral justification of one or perhaps both parties, we may mention the attainment of advantages by usury, advantages in one sphere obtained by an economic pressure in another, *e.g.*, a cheap purchase of other goods than those usually bought and sold, favoritism by appointments of business friends and their friends, and other personal admissions. The state official or the manager of a joint stock company has no personal power so long as he tries to do his duty. If, on the contrary, he uses his position to attain economic or other personal objects, it is an application of power—a misuse of power in so far as it does not take place by permission of the institution as a recognized part of his pay.

Besides the acquisition of property, there may be a question of influencing prices, methods of production, and other economic relations, by means of power. Similarly, the existing right of property and other rights, as well as, very largely, monopolistic price policy are maintained by power, in the latter case both *vis-à-vis* the latent competition and the inclination of members to break out of the agreement. The same is true in the case of trade unions and employers' associations. The use of power is, therefore, in many cases a necessary condition for a monopolistic price policy. In other cases natural conditions afford a sufficiently secure basis.

The forms of economic conflict or threats of conflict which often bring about the decision in bilateral monopoly, or in the case of a few competitors, may also be designated as power, since it is not here a question of a current exchange of goods, but of a temporary interference of quite another nature. Threats of inconveniences are issued, or at least threats of a temporary discontinuation of a connection which both parties are interested in keeping up.

Besides this kind of economic pressure, the basis of power may be physical or psychological (moral) pressure. In the latter case one makes use of something the other party himself wants to do, so that the case from his point of view may be regarded as action stemming from a non-economic-man motive.

Economic power in another sense than that here dealt with is to be found when, as in the case of expensive propaganda to achieve political and ideal aims, the path does not lead from power to money, but, conversely, from money to power. In the matter of political propaganda, the path may possibly lead back again from advancement of ideas to one's own economic interests. Class solidarity or national solidarity which finds expression in preferential business relations with employment or other methods of favoring one's own, is also an important economic factor of power. The most important agent of power is the state in connection with municipalities and other institutions to which it delegates its power.

If we bear in mind that heterogeneous forces together determine economic development and if we remember the definition of the concept of power given above, the problem is not, as it was to classical liberalists or to anti-theoretic historians, "power *or* economic law". It is really a question of how the ordinary mechanism of the market is modified by other influences or in some cases replaced by them. This interplay between heterogeneous forces is best elucidated by examining the way in which the most important factor of power, the state, influences economic life.[1]

---

[1] With regard to the problems dealt with in this and the following sections, see Böhm-Bawerk, "Macht oder ökonomisches Gesetz", *Zeitschrift für Volkswirtschaft, Sozialpolitik und Verwaltung*, 1914; Schumpeter, "Das Grundprinzip der Verteilungstheorie", *Archiv für Sozialwissenschaft und Sozialpolitik*, 1916–17; Carl Landauer, *Grundprobleme der funktionellen Verteilung*, 1923; v. Wieser, *Das Gesetz der Macht*, 1926; Wilhelm Keilhau, "Wirtschaft und Macht", *Jahrbuch für Soziologie*, 1926; L. V. Birck, *Den økonomiske Virksomhed*, Gad, Copenhagen, 1928.

z

CHAPTER 64

THE POWER OF THE STATE
AND THE STRUCTURE OF SOCIETY

THOUGH the influence of the state on economic life in a modern community is scarcely less than that of private organizations, we shall nevertheless deal with it very briefly. There are so many and varied forms of interference that general treatment of the problem does not carry us very far. Moreover, among the multitude of possible types of intervention, it is most practical preferably to examine the means employed or the means that are likely to further the most relevant political aims, or the measures actually taken within limited historical and geographical spheres. These questions, however, are best dealt with coherently in the field of economic policy and its different branches, as well as in the analysis of economic history and current developments, all of which are beyond the scope of this book. We shall here confine ourselves to scattered remarks and examples to illustrate the nature of the interplay of political and economic forces.

The simplest method of approach, which is adopted in the following examples, is to take the interference of the state as a datum and see what will be the reactions of other economic units. In some cases the state has a previously known type of reaction to economic impulses. Taxes, for instance, increase automatically with incomes, and according to law, benefits are given in case of unemployment. In such cases we do not have quantities as politically given data, but politically given equations enter into the system of economic equations. Where the reactions of the state cannot be predicted in advance, the problems cannot be solved without including political assumptions as to aims, choice of means, and the power behind the different aims. Purely economic laws, consequently, cannot be established. Since in our own time this is true with regard to important spheres, economic explanations and predictions are only possible when political elements are included, as appears clearly from current surveys of business cycles, which often deal far more with politics than with pure economics. A complete theory of employment, interest, and money, not including the expected behavior of the state and central banks, is also impossible, as indicated in Chapter 42.

Part of the state's use of economic power is connected with the markets for commodities or productive services. It may be a question of measures to promote competition, as for instance support of traffic, or prohibition of combinations or their use of coercive measures to keep others out; or the state may conversely strengthen the cooperation between competing units. The establishment of stock exchanges or market places, the publication of prices and information as to price and quality all work in favor of competition. Protection of privileges, limitation of entry to trades, and employments, patents and trade marks and, not least of all, restrictions on foreign trade, all act in the opposite direction. Of late years, the states have often, as in the case of subsidies to agriculture, helped an industry in which the great number of enterprises made it difficult to carry on a satisfactory price policy through voluntary organizations. The effect of such aid is to enable the industry to pursue a price policy which is similar to that of other trade and social groups. In many cases we have had rather far-reaching policy of price supports to meet agricultural crises.

The state also interferes more directly with the conditions of the market in many ways. We shall mention here some of the simplest examples of how state intervention in existing conditions determines economic quantities. A maximum price that is maintained acts as a horizontal beginning of the demand curve at the level of the maximum price, cf. the heavy line in Fig. 44A, where DD indicates demand, SS supply, p_m maximum price,

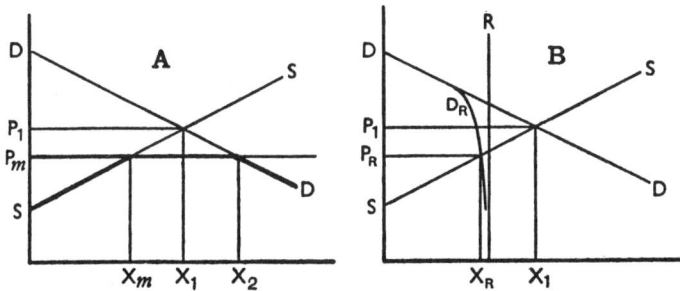

Fig. 44. Maximum Price and Rationing

p_1 and x_1 competitive price and quantity. The part of the supply curve lying above p_m and to the right of x_m has disappeared. The maximum price here causes a state of tension, the buyers wanting to have the quantity x_2 but sellers only wanting to surrender the quantity x_m at the fixed maximum price. If this price is maintained, and if rationing is not introduced at the same time, the extent to which the individual buyers get what they want will depend on chance, willingness to queue up or personal favoritism. The excluded buyers, however, are tempted to pay more, and since competition in an illegal market is probably limited, the price in individual sales may exceed not only p_m, but also p_1. Correspondingly, a minimum price above the competitive price acts as a horizontal beginning of the supply curve until intersection with the original supply curve.

When purchases are rationed, the demand curve DD in Fig. 44B is replaced by DD_R, converging towards DD and the perpendicular line RR, which corresponds to a full ration for all individual citizens. This line may possibly only be reached when price is negative. Since all the citizens do not take out their full rations, at any rate until prices are very low, the new demand curve is not continued directly from DD down RR. When

sales are rationed, the supply curve is similarly replaced by a curve converging towards SS and RR. In either case the quantity sold may be
somewhat smaller than the sum of the full rations. The party whose
quantity is directly limited by the state thereby obtains an advantage in
price at the cost of the other party. The strongly inelastic course of the
rationed demand in the last part of the curve may, nevertheless, give
sellers, who have previously competed, an impulse to carry on a cooperative price policy. Just as in the case of maximum price, rationing
creates a state of tension which tempts the individuals or firms cut off by
rationing to seek illegal channels, and also in this case there may be a
certain wide scope for individual prices. Tension and temptation are
essentially reduced when maximum prices are backed by a corresponding
rationing of purchases, which at the same time leads to a less arbitrary
distribution of the scarce supplies. If the purpose is to help sellers, a
minimum price, or a relatively high official price, may be backed by a
sellers' quota.

The effect of a maximum price on a monopoly is illustrated in Fig. 45.[1]

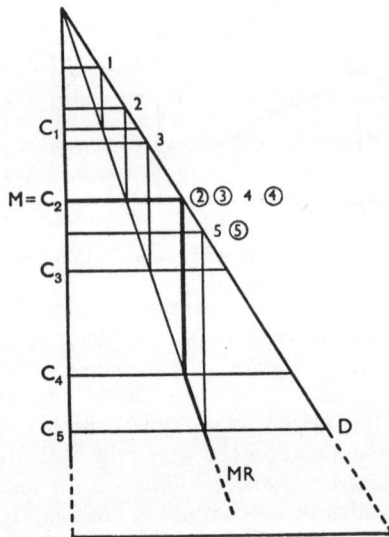

Fig. 45. Monopoly and Maximum Price

The relation between market conditions and maximum price is illustrated,
not by a multitude of maximum prices, but by alternative cost curves and
an unaltered maximum price.

The lines D and MR indicate demand and marginal revenue without
state regulation of price, M maximum price, and C_1 to C_5 different possible costs. The not encircled figures on the demand curve indicate price

[1] This illustration is due to Erik Thrane.

and quantity without maximum price for the corresponding cost curves C_1, etc. As a result of the maximum price, production disappears if costs are above $C_2 = M$. The marginal revenue curve is now the thick zigzag line. At costs situated between the maximum price ($M = C_2$) and C_4 (passing through the point on the marginal revenue curve vertically below the point of intersection of the maximum price curve and the demand curve), price will be the fixed maximum price, and sales will be at the corresponding point according to the demand curve (cf. the encircled figures on the demand curve). At costs below C_4, the monopoly price is not influenced by maximum price, being already situated below the latter, if we disregard the psychological inclination to increase price up to maximum price. The figure illustrates that production may be increased when the monopoly price is reduced by state action.

Another simple example of the adaptation of price formation to state interference is a tax per unit, which may either be illustrated as a parallel shift of the demand curve downwards or a corresponding raising of the cost and supply curves. A subsidy per unit may be treated as a shift in the opposite direction. With varying taxes or subsidies in proportion to price, distances from the original curves will vary correspondingly.

A policy of compulsion to produce and sell certain definite minimum quantities affects the market in so far as the policy can be carried through, the same as a supply without a positive supply price, until the compulsory quantity has been reached. Correspondingly, a certain compulsory consumption will cause the demand curve for a certain quantity to be raised, as far as incomes and obedience to the law permit. Orders to use certain methods of production or subsidies or imposts for certain methods of production, have the same effect as a change in the technical combinations.

Besides the fact that the rules are usually more complicated than those mentioned here (with varying treatment, for instance, of different groups, or with graduated scales regarding size, incomes, etc.), state intervention will often be associated with qualitative factors, possibly of a somewhat discretionary nature (*e.g.*, the estimate of the administration as to ability, need, worthiness, possible effectiveness of the intervention, etc.). Moreover, it may not be a question of unconditional coercive intervention, but of information as to the interests of one's self and others, moral suasion, possibly in connection with some pressure through the threat of coercive measures. Whereas in the latter case there may be a question of calculating the weight to attach to the pressure, by a rational estimate as to the probability of what gives the greatest profit, the effect in other cases will be some deviation from the narrowly egoistical calculation and behavior of the economic man.

The possibility of carrying through the orders of the state depends on the state's means of enforcement. Most people have for moral reasons a disinclination against breaking the laws, for fear of losing the respect of one's fellow citizens, or from one's own interest in other people's respect of the laws. At the back of it all are the state's economic, police and military means of coercion. In severe social and economic conflicts the physical power of the state and the social classes appears as a last and decisive force behind other means of justice and power.

Observance of rules is easiest in the case of standardized commodities and services, and when sales and the controlled action are visible to all. Especially when the party enjoying the advantage of the state's intervention supports its enforcement, the regulation may have the effect of a monopolistic organization of the interested party brought about by the state. This is true, for instance, of agricultural minimum prices, minimum wage legislation, or price control of ordinary consumption goods, supported by consumers and perhaps in some cases received with sympathy by sellers, possibly because of a strong social feeling, for instance, at the beginning of a war period. The propensity to disregard laws was probably considerably greater in most countries at the end than at the beginning of the forties. Where control is difficult, where many people on either side doubting perhaps the justification of the control, and where evasion is easy, enforcement is difficult. This is the case, for instance, with regard to the control of rent and the assessment of income for tax purposes.

The same is true regarding observance of the orders of the state as with regard to cohesion within organizations: that the obedience of most people does not have the character of a categorical imperative, but is quantitatively limited by the relation between sacrifice and punishment, including moral uneasiness at breaking the law, which, however, in an emergency is easily set aside as immoral by some individuals. Thus one sometimes observes a convenient inclination to consider the officials of the state as a gang of robbers when they infringe too heavily on one's own interests. No doubt most people have a limit of revolt, where the official administration of justice in their own case is considered as robbery and violence. As the individual citizens are law abiding to an unequal degree and do not have the same temptation to break the law, we shall have an increasing number of breaches of the law, according to how the rules are strengthened in relation to the means of enforcement. In the black market, prices are irregular and the premium on risk great.

Political measures interfering with important commodities or categories of productive services or interfering with a number of spheres in a similar way, will very largely affect other spheres too. In such cases not only the market form, but more or less the economic structure of society as a whole is changed. As examples of this we may mention the guild system, mercantilism, the ultra-liberalistic state, and the modern planned economy. Most strong acts of intervention by the state have general income effects which spread to all spheres of the economy. In some cases a general effect on the economy as a whole is the real aim, as for instance in the case of interference in the monetary system or in personal distribution by means of progressive income taxation and social services.

The planned economy of many non-Communist countries in the forties is an example of a combined, more or less coordinated state regulation on a great number of points. In connection with the Norwegian national accounting, illustrated on p. 193, the system was spoken of as having a great number of "degrees of freedom". Economic equations corresponding to summations of quantities are true according to simple logic. It was consequently the remaining interdependences, the equations of reaction, which were assumed to be changeable at will. To a certain extent it is, of course, possible to change a demand equation or a supply equation of a productive service by means of state influence in the same way as through the influence of advertising. But another thing is probably more essential. In a society with inflationary pressure incomes tend to become greater than the potential consumption plus investment. Consequently, no unemployment or idle capacity will arise even if many prices are regulated rather arbitrarily, and many branches of production restricted or increased by subsidies. Instead of unused remainders of productive services, we here get negative remainders—labor shortages and commodity shortages—less visible, however, and absolutely invisible in a system of equations which omits all negative magnitudes. The final equilibrium between supply and demand is attained by rationing, queueing up, or similar methods (at the same time as the inflationary pressure is regulated, more or less, by fiscal and monetary policy). If the inflationary pressure and the distortion of the free equilibrium system are too great, supplementary measures to increase the mobility of labor and capital are applied in order to obtain full utilization of all means of production. The valuation of this distortion (*e.g.*, in case of war, reconstruction, etc.) is, of course, a political question. Ten per cent idle capacity means ten per cent decrease in national income, if this is measured by input of productive services, but in another way considerably less, because it is the least important production that is given up first. The importance of 10 per cent excess demand depends on the difference in importance between the consumption given up and its substitutes. To this must be added changes in distribution and "good" or "bad" long-term effects of the plans. The "repressed inflation" briefly dealt with here is in any case an important state of economic affairs.

Economists have sometimes spoken about "overdetermined" systems, for instance, when a maximum or minimum price is fixed. An overdetermined system, however, agrees neither with the rules of logic nor with our conception of reality. But it may be the first step in an analysis to mention a number of influences, not all of which can be realized at the same time. If we start the discussion with an overdetermined system, it is necessary to correct our assumptions just as when we start with an indeterminate system. In case of overdetermination, we have to explain the way in which some of the rules are set aside or transformed and reduced in number, *e.g.*, by political compromise between certain groups. It may be added in this connection that dynamic conditions and not an overdetermined, *i.e.*, contradictory, static system has to be used in explaining the path of adaptation from an arbitrary initial price towards the static equilibrium price.[2] Dynamic analysis is sometimes spoken of as the "disequilibrium method", presupposing equilibria to be static.

An apparently overdetermined system may be transformed into a determined system either by reducing the number of conditions, as mentioned above, or by adding some new variable expressing tensions. A static demand curve intersecting a static supply curve is a system with two equations determining two variables. When we add a maximum price (corresponding to a horizontal line) below the intersection of the curves, we obtain, if we prefer to consider it in that way, three equations and determination of three variables: price, quantity supplied (in this case equal to the quantity realized) and the quantity demanded or, what is more appropriate in this case, the unsatisfied excess of demand at the price given.

If further we add as a fourth condition a certain quantity to be delivered independent of costs between the intersections of the price line with the supply and demand curves, we get a fourth equation fixing the quantity (corresponding to a vertical line): Four variables are here determined: actual price, actual quantity, the quantity sellers want to supply, and the quantity buyers want to buy, at the price fixed, or, instead of the two last quantities, the excess quantity sellers have to supply, and the deficit in the quantity buyers want to buy, at the price and quantity fixed. The two just-mentioned hypothetical quantities are examples of tensions considered as part of a solution which is neither over- nor underdetermined. If, however, we disregard hypothetical variables and only consider the actual magnitudes, we also have a clearly determined system. In the latter case the price and quantity lines fixed by the state replace the curves of the free market in a way corresponding to the partial replacement in Fig. 44. It is characteristic of the examples that the economic magnitudes are determined at two different levels: state decision and the reaction of buyers and sellers within the frames fixed by the state. In some cases it is the same group of persons, *e.g.*, all members of a cartel or trade union who influence the decisions on both levels, more or less (cf. the discussion about "involuntary unemployment").

In a dynamic consideration of economic development or business cycles, or, to a smaller extent, of the economic changes to which individual persons and firms are exposed, the activity of the state is of importance on many points. There may be a question of retarding an extraordinary increase in price by price control or retarding a reorganization of production by regulations and the requirement that plans have to be approved in advance, or, conversely, of promoting reorganization by subsidies or information. Important state measures either intensify or dampen busi-

---

[2] Overdeterminateness, degrees of freedom, etc., have been discussed a great deal by Frisch and Haavelmo in the memoranda from the University Institute of Economics, Oslo; in this connection, see especially, Haavelmo, "Økonomisk Likevekt og økonomisk Velferd", *Statsøkonomisk Tidsskrift*, October 1949; cf. also Chapter 39 above. J. Tinbergen, *On the Theory of Economic Policy*, 1952, and *Centralization and Decentralization in Economic Policy*, 1954, North Holland Publishing Co.

ness cycles. And, in addition, war and other political events provide a strong stimulus to economic movements.

Against the background of the experiences of the last generation, it may be said that the destructive activities of the states have been a dominating factor in economic life. On the other hand, international disputes very often have an economic motivation; but still there seems good reason to doubt the appropriateness of war as a means of realizing economic aims. The extent to which this may be explained by the use of inexpedient means for the attainment of economic aims, and the extent to which motives other than economic are involved, is outside the scope of the present investigation. In 1943–4 war expenditure in Great Britain was more than half of the gross national product. Of the total war expenses 1939–45, 40 per cent was covered by an increase in production, 20 per cent by reduction of private consumption, $1\frac{1}{2}$ per cent by reduction in state expenses for civil administration, 20 per cent by consumption of internal capital, whereas $18\frac{1}{2}$ per cent came from abroad.

The most important aspect of the problem as to the structure of society is only partly a question of the policy of the state. The nature of the economic units and the distribution of management and rights of property also are of the first importance. Production may take place in self-sufficient households, in enterprises with a proprietor as manager and receiver of a residual income, in joint stock companies, in cooperative societies, or in large collective units. Even if private enterprise is typical of modern Western society, the other forms are also found to a large extent, just as in Eastern countries we find private and cooperative units. In addition to consumption of home-grown products, especially in agriculture, one must not forget the work done in households, which is still a great and variable part of the output of society. For the very reason that these forms of family self-provision vary very much for the different classes of the population, and their importance changes with economic changes, it is impossible to disregard them as, for instance, the effects on national income of an extension of women's work in times of war or scarcity.

The cooperatives and public enterprises of modern times are intermediate types in so far as they are partly carried on according to the principles of private enterprise and partly aim at a direct satisfaction of wants. When dealing with the self-supplying enterprises and the large collective units we cannot, as in the case of private firms, consider maximization of profit as a suitable starting-point. The starting-point in this case is rather declared aims, political principles, or standards that the observer deduces from actual behavior. As an example of price formation in the case of economic aims, which deviate more or less from maximization of profit, we shall mention the price policy of public enterprises.

If, as in Fig. 46, we assume a rectilinear demand curve, DD, and a rectilinear horizontal cost curve, CC, a small decrease in price from p_1 to $p_1 - dp$ will give the public enterprise a loss of $A = x_1 \cdot dp$, due to reduction in price, and a profit of $B_1 = p_1 \cdot dx$, due to expansion of sales

(p_1 being here price in excess of CC and not the whole price). Consumers gain A. By means of a marginal consideration, the question of consumers' rent on the first units is here avoided. This method of calculation can be carried through further, not in utility units, but in money, if we start from a knowledge of the course of the cost curve and demand curve only in

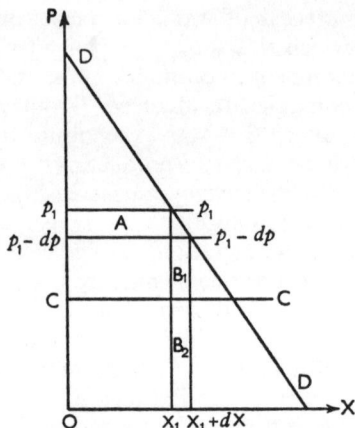

Fig. 46. Public Price Policy

the relevant interval, disregarding the possible influence of changes in the value of money.

If now the enterprise does not at all consider the welfare of the pur-chasers, it will fix the monopoly price so that $A = B_1$, *i.e.*, at a point where the elasticity of price in excess of cost becomes -1. Conversely, if the state considers the advantage of the citizens to be equal to its own, price will be $= C$, marginal profit B_1, as well as total profit, thus becoming $= 0$, but the sum of advantages to citizens and state (the triangle between the demand curve, the cost curve, and the ordinate axis), is maximized. Owing to the cost of collecting taxes and distributing benefits, it is prob-able that the state estimates the value of money in its own treasury to be somewhat higher than the value of money in the pockets of the citizens. If, therefore, the value of the citizens' money is reduced by multiplication by the politically determined factor of valuation, v, the problem is to maximize $A \cdot v - A + B_1 = B_1 - A(1 - v)$. The maximum is reached when the advantage of extension of sales and the net loss with a reduc-tion of price are equally great, *i.e.*, $B_1 = A(1 - v)$; $(1 - v)$, consequently, is equal to B_1/A, but this quantity is equal to $(-)dx \cdot p/dp \cdot x$, *i.e.*, equal to the elasticity of price in excess of costs.

By using the excess price curve instead of the demand curve, and using the tangent direction to this if it is not rectilinear, we obtain the general conditions of equilibrium which apply irrespective of the form of the curves, namely that the elasticity of excess price at the point of equilibrium is to be $(-)E = 1 - v$. For the inconsiderate public monopolist this gives in the marginal cases the elasticity of price in excess of costs -1, *i.e.*, maximization of profit just as in the case of the private monopolist. For the public enterprise, on the other hand, which values money in the public treasury and in the pockets of the citizens equally highly, elasticity becomes 0, *i.e.*, a price equal to costs. The principle here described applies to a society where public authorities only control part of the total economy. If the state controlled all prices, it would be possible to fix these more consistently in accordance with marginal costs, with a uniform supplement.

If the public authorities in the case of certain goods or classes of consumers desire to give subsidies to consumption, it can use a price below costs. Even where the "cost principle" and the "free choice of consumption" are followed as a main rule, however, free or cheap feeding of children is often provided, and the price of spirits is enhanced by taxation in consideration of the effects on others than the direct consumer. Correspondingly, education is in many cases given below costs. Since in the short run it is only the use of means requiring a sacrifice that are termed costs, we here disregard fixed costs including interest on fixed capital, just as private firms pursue a rational maximization of profit when an isolated transaction is involved. If capacity is scarce, price will still be higher than the variable costs. The conditions for the building and maintenance of plants are, however, that there is a prospect of having the costs thus incurred covered. The consequence is such a scarcity of capacity that a desired surplus will be covered, in so far as the actual situation develops in accordance with expectations. Similarly, a stable equilibrium under stationary conditions assumes interest charges and writing-off of plant as well as the covering of expenses for wages, etc., all costs being here variable. It is true here, to a still greater degree, perhaps, than in the case of the price policy of private firms, that the rational methods described above can only give us a partial and uncertain guidance to the understanding of the actual formation of price, since the political machinery often pursues several aims at the same time.[3]

If it is a self-sufficient household or a larger collective or socialistic community that is in question, the form of logic usually applied in economic theory requires that the wants shall be satisfied to the greatest possible extent in the succession desired by the management. If it requires sacrifices to apply certain means, these are used up to the limit where, according to the valuation of the management, the sacrifices reach the same magnitude as the advantages thus obtained. An attempt is made to reach a

---

[3] See Marshall's *Principles*, p. 489, on "compromise benefit", which it has here been found defensible to use in a marginal way and measured in money. My article "Public Price Policy" in *Economic Essays in Honour of Gustav Cassel*, Allen and Unwin, London, 1933; my discussion with Erik Schmidt in *Nationaløkonomisk Tidsskrift*, 1945; the discussion of Hotelling and Frisch in *Econometrica*, July 1938 and April 1939; articles by Radomysler and Coase in *Economica*, 1946; articles by Fleming and Meade in *Economic Journal*, 1944; Hicks on consumers' surplus, *e.g.*, in *Review of Economic Studies*, 1945-6

given aim by the smallest possible effort and to achieve the greatest possible advantages with a given effort, satisfying different wants in such a way that efforts and satisfactions are equalized at the margin.[4] All this is merely the result of a rational maximization. There is a question, however, as to what weight the management will attach to the different wants including those of the future.

In explaining the actual state of affairs in the societies in question, the same points of view may, by the way, be applied as mentioned above in Chapter 59 in connection with the capitalistic firms when we were dealing with motives and behavior. This is especially true in the case of societies where several exercise their influence. The form of organization has a great effect on production, distribution, and, consequently, on consumption. The result of production will vary according to time and place for the different forms of society, and distribution may differ very much both in a community consisting of isolated households (possibly with unequal distribution of property) and in great collective groups. If within the latter there is a free choice of consumption and employment, the formation of price may be approximately the same as in a competitive society. When individuals are not able to save up capital by voluntary saving, the management must, however, decide on the extent of the saving and carry it through in the form of taxation. If the individuals have no free choice, the will of the management, possibly supported by a calculation or an estimate of the wants of the members in conjunction with the weight which is attached to them by the management, will be decisive, just as in the patriarchal household. In investigating how the above-mentioned "economic" way of thinking works, "wants" and "advantages" must, on the whole, be understood as a somewhat elastic expression of the goals, towards which the persons in charge are aiming or seem to be aiming. Other goals, as the rate of progress, security, mobility, order, national expansion, etc., are hereby given a certain weight beside maximization of consumption, just as in a capitalistic society.

In many cases it will be necessary at the same time to take account of economic units of different size and rank. The members of a cartel, for instance, maintain their independence to a greater or smaller extent at the same time as the cartel acts as the superior unit with a sales office or other facilities of its own. In a combine the individual firms may have more or less preserved their own capital with partial special interests, just as management and personnel may have a preferential interest in the prosperity of their own firm or branch. National economic solidarity, both through the finances and through the more intimate connection and mutual interdependence within the frontiers of a country, leads one to a certain extent to consider the nations as "economic circles", and to deal with their economic conditions, internally and externally, in a manner similar

[4] Articles by Lange, Lerner and Dobb in *Review of Economic Studies*, 1934–7, and *Economic Journal*, 1937; Cassel, *The Theory of Social Economy*, 1923, sections 15 and 27; Abram Bergson's article in *A Survey of Contemporary Economics*, Vol. I, 1948.

to the way in which business economics deal with firms.[5] The business accounts and balance sheets for the more comprehensive "economic circles" can, irrespective of how the circles are defined, be found by a summing up of the accounts of the circles included, all the internal payments cancelling out against each other.

Some readers may perhaps wonder at the fact that we have come to the end of the book before tackling some of the more concrete problems of the actual social and economic conditions that prevail. As emphasized at the beginning, however, our aim was not to solve concrete, practical problems. For this purpose other tools are just as necessary as abstract economic theory and method, such as a comprehensive description of the changing practical conditions and the use of statistical techniques in the handling of factual information. But abstract theory, like the technician's knowledge of mathematics and physics, is one of the tools—but only one of the tools—of the economist. It is necessary for purposes of general orientation and guidance when the problems are to be posed and solved in the individual case. It is quite impossible, under the variegated and unstable conditions of modern times, as was done in the textbooks of the past, to write down the truth once and for all, ready for practical application under all circumstances.

The treatment of the "qualitative", more human subjects at the end of the book, where we deal with motives, behavior, power, etc., has, among other things, been designed to show that these human and practical factors, when it comes to an actual issue, do not displace abstract economic theory, but that, on the contrary, there is some possibility of placing the various heterogeneous elements involved in such a relation to each other, that the result is agreement and coherence.

[5] Articles by Ivar Jantzen, Ragnar Frisch and Erich Schneider, quoted in the last footnote in Chapter 7.

LITERATURE IN ENGLISH BY AUTHORS FROM NORTHERN COUNTRIES

THIS list has been prepared as the result of a suggestion made by an English friend. It has been intended to include only books and articles about the *subject dealt with in the book*. It has, however, been difficult to draw a uniform and reasonable line of division and probably a number of works have been omitted as it was not practicable to send out questionnaires to all possible authors. A great number of articles descriptive of national economic conditions and about more specific monetary, business cycle and international trade theories or about problems of economic or social policy are not included. The same applies to numerous "Summaries" in English. I am grateful to Mr. Erling Olsen of the Institute of Economics and History (Copenhagen) for cooperation in compiling this appendix.

The following abbreviations are used:

A.E.R. = *The American Economic Review.*
(D) = Denmark.
E.E.H.G.Cassel=*Economic Essays in Honour of Gustav Cassel* (London, 1933).
E.J. = *The Economic Journal.*
(F) = Finland.
(I) = Iceland.
J.A.S.A. = *The Journal of the American Statistical Association.*
J.P.E. = *The Journal of Political Economy.*
K.O.P. = *Kansallis-Osake-Pankki, Economic Review* (Helsingfors).
(N) = Norway.
N.S.J. = *The Nordic Statistical Journal* (Stockholm).
N.T.T.Ø. = *Nordisk Tidsskrift for Teknisk Økonomi* (Copenhagen).
Q.J.E. = *The Quarterly Journal of Economics.*
R.E. and Stat. = *The Review of Economics and Statistics.*
R.E. Stat. = *The Review of Economic Statistics.*
R.E. Stud. = *The Review of Economic Studies.*
(S) = Sweden.
S.A. = *Skandinavisk Aktuarietidskrift* (Uppsala).

Åkerman, Johan (S): "Quantitative Economics," *Weltwirtschaftliches Archiv,* 1932.
—— "Knut Wicksell a Pioneer of Econometrics," *Econometrica,* 1933.
—— "The Setting of the Central Problem," *Econometrica,* 1936.

Åkerman, Johan (S): "The Meaning of Induction in Social Science," *Theoria*, 1940.
—— "Political Economic Cycles," *Kyklos*, 1947.
—— "Discontinuities of Employment Cycles," *N.T.T.Ø.*, 1948.
—— "Structural Limits in Economic Development," *De Economist*, 1949.
Aukrust, Odd (N): "On the Theory of Social Accountancy," *R.E. Stud.*, 1949–50.
Barfod, Børge (D): "The Theory of Advertising," *Econometrica*, 1940.
—— "Polysony-polypoly," *N.T.T.Ø.*, 1948.
Benzel, R. (S): *vide* Wold.
—— with Bent Hansen: "On Recursiveness and Interdependency in Economics," *R.E. Studies*, 1954–5.
Birck, L. V. (D): *The Theory of Marginal Value*, London, 1922.
Bjerve, Petter Jakob (N): "Some Comments on Ragnar Frisch's Oecocirk-system," *Cowles Commission Discussion Paper, Economics*, Chicago, 1949.
Brems, Hans (D, in U.S.A.): "Some Notes on the Structure of the Duopoly Problem," *N.T.T.Ø.*, 1948.
—— "The Interdependence of Quality Variations, Selling Effort and Price," *Q.J.E.*, 1948.
—— *Product Equilibrium under Monopolistic Competition*, Cambridge, Mass., 1951.
—— "On the Theory of Price Agreements," *Q.J.E.*, 1951.
——"Employment, Prices and Monopolistic Competition," *R.E. and Stat.*, 1952.
—— "A Discontinuous Cost Function," *A.E.R.*, 1952.
—— "Foreign Exchange Rates and Monopolistic Competition," *E.J.*, 1953.
—— and Ralph Turvey: "The Factor and Goods Markets," *Economica*, 1951.
Carlsson, Gösta (S): "Sampling, Probability and Causal Inference," *Theoria*, 1952.
Carlsson, Sune (S): *A Study on the Pure Theory of Production*, London, 1939.
—— *Executive Behaviour* (A Study of the Work Load and the Working Methods of Managing Directors), Stockholm, 1951.
Cassel, Gustav (S): *The Nature and Necessity of Interest*, London, 1903.
—— "Some Considerations about Interest," *E.J.*, 1908.
—— *The Theory of Social Economy*, London, 1923.
—— *Fundamental Thought in Economics*, London, 1925.
—— *On Quantitative Thinking in Economics*, Oxford, 1935.
Dahlström, Edmund (S): "Some Aspects of Quantitative Verification in Sociology," *Theoria*, 1951.
Dahlgren, Einar (S): See Erik Lindahl (S), Einar Dahlgren (S) and Karin Kock (S).
Einarsen, Johan (N): *Reinvestment Cycles and their Manifestation in the Norwegian Shipping Industry*, Oslo, 1938.

Eiriksson, Benjamin H. (I): *Outline of an Economic Theory*, Reykjavik, 1954.

Fog, Bjarke (D): "Dynamic Price Problems under Monopolistic Competition," *N.T.T.Ø.*, 1946.
—— "Price Theory and Reality," *N.T.T.Ø.*, 1948.

Frisch, Ragnar (N): "The Interrelation between Capital Production and Consumer-Taking, *J.P.E.*, 1931—"A Rejoinder," *J.P.E.*, 1932— "A Final Word," *J.P.E.*, 1932. (Discussion with J. M. Clark.)
—— *New Methods of Measuring Marginal Utility*, Tübingen, 1932.
—— "New Orientation of Economic Theory. Economics as an Experimental Science," *N.S.J.*, 1932.
—— "Propagation Problems and Impulse Problems in Dynamic Economics," *E.E.H.G.Cassel*, London, 1933.
—— "Outline of a General Theory of Polypoly," *Econometrica*, 1933.
—— *Pitfalls in the Statistical Construction of Demand and Supply Curves*, Leipzig, 1933.
—— "More Pitfalls in Demand and Supply Curves," *Q.J.E.*, 1934.
—— "Circulation Planning," *Econometrica*, 1934.
—— "The Principle of Substitution. An Example of its Application in the Chocolate Industry," *N.T.T.Ø.*, 1935.
—— "The Problem of Index Numbers," *Econometrica*, 1936.
—— "On the Notion of Equilibrium and Disequilibrium," *R.E. Stud.*, 1936.
—— "General Choice-Field Theory, Three Lectures," *Report of the Cowles Commission Research Conference*, 1937.
—— "The Responsibility of the Econometrician," *Econometrica*, 1946.
—— "Repercussion Studies at Oslo," *A.E.R.*, 1948.
—— "Overdeterminateness and Optimum Equilibrium," *N.T.T.Ø.*, 1948.
—— "Prolegomena to a Pressure-Analysis of Economic Phenomena," *Metroeconomica*, 1949.
—— "Alfred Marshall's Theory of Value," *Q.J.E.*, 1950.
—— "Decision Models," *Econometrica*, 1950.
—— "Monopoly—Polypoly—The Concept of Force in the Economy," *International Economic Papers*, No. 1, London and New York, 1951.

Geiger, Theodor (D): "Some Reflections on Sociometry and its Limitations," *Theoria*, 1950.

Gelting, Jørgen (D): "On Redistribution of Income," *N.T.T.Ø.*, 1948.

Gloerfelt-Tarp, B. (D): "The Marginal Productivity Function and the Walras-Cassel System of Equations," *N.T.T.Ø.*, 1948.

Grøn, A. Howard (D) and Jørgensen, Frits (D): "Calculation of Sylvicultural Balance-Numbers," *N.T.T.Ø.*, 1948.

Haavelmo, Trygve (N): *A Dynamic Study of Pig Production in Denmark*, Aarhus, 1939.
—— "The Effect of the Rate of Interest on Investment," *R.E. Stat.*, 1941.
—— "The Statistical Implications of a System of Simultaneous Equations," *Econometrica*, 1943.

AA

Haavelmo, Trygve (N): "The Probability Approach in Econometrics," Supplement to *Econometrica*, 1944.

—— "Family Expenditures and the Marginal Propensity to Consume," *Econometrica*, 1947.

—— "Methods of Measuring the Marginal Propensity to Consume," *J.A.S.A.*, 1947.

—— "A Note on the Theory of Investment," *R.E. Stud.*, 1949–50.

—— "The Notion of Involuntary Economic Decisions," *Econometrica*, 1950.

—— "The Notion of Price Homogeneity," *Festskrift til Jørgen Pedersen*, Aarhus, 1951.

Haavelmo, Trygve and M. A. Girshick (N): "Statistical Analysis of the Demand for Food: Examples of Simultaneous Estimation of Structural Equations," *Econometrica*, 1947.

Hagström, K. G. (S): "Pure Economics as a Stochastical Theory," *Econometrica*, 1938.

Hansen, Bent (D, in Sweden): *A Study in the Theory of Inflation*, London, 1951.

—— "A Study in the Theory of Inflation," *International Economic Papers*.

—— with R. Bentzel: "On Recursiveness and Interdependency in Economics," *R.E. Studies*, 1954–5.

Hegeland, Hugo (S): *The Quantity Theory of Money*, Göteborg, 1951.

—— "The Multiplier Theory," *Lund Social Science Studies*, 1954.

Henriksen, E. K. (D): "Simultaneous Operation of Several Machines by one Person. Application of a Method of Probability," *N.T.T.Ø.*, 1948.

Iversen, Carl (D): *International Capital Movements*, Copenhagen and London, 1935.

Jantzen, Ivar (D): *Basic Principles of Business Economics and National Calculation*. (Including following articles: "Increasing Return in Industrial Production"—"On the Theory of Planned Economy" —"Problems of National Calculation"), Separate Volume and *N.T.T.Ø.*, 1939.

—— "Social Production Theory," *N.T.T.Ø.*, 1948.

—— "Laws of Production and Cost," *Econometrica*, 1949.

Jensen, Arne (D): "Stochastic Processes applied in a Simple Problem of Administrative Economy," *N.T.T.Ø.*, 1948.

—— *A Distribution Model applicable to Economics*, Copenhagen, 1954.

Jørgensen, Frits (D): See A. Howard Grøn and Frits Jørgensen (D).

Jørgensen, Jørgen (D): "The Development of Logical Empiricism," *Encyclopedia of United Sciences*, 1949.

Juréen, L. (S): *vide* Wold.

Kaitila, Esa (F): "On Interest as a Cost Function," *K.O.P.*, 1950.

Keilhau, Wilhelm (N): "The Equations of Payments," *E.E.G.H.Cassel*, London, 1933.

Keilhau, Wilhelm (N): *Principles of Private and Public Planning, a Study in Economic Sociology*, London, 1951.

Kock, Karin (S): See Erik Lindahl, Einar Dahlgren and Karin Koch.

—— *A Study of Interest Rates*, London, 1929.

Kragh, Börge (S): "Two Liquidity Functions and the Rate of Interest: A Simple Dynamic Model," *R.E. Stud.*, 1949–50.

Kristensen, Thorkil (D): "A Note on Duopoly," *R.E. Stud.*, 1938.

Kristensson, R. (S): "Division of Labour as an Optimum Problem in Organisation and Management, *N.T.T.Ø.*, 1948.

Kruse, Fr. Vinding (D): "The Method of Social Sciences," *Theoria*, 1947.

—— "Svend Ranulf's Argumentation," *Theoria*, 1950.

Laurila, Eino H. (F): "On the Determination of Fluctuations in the Wage and Salary Level," *K.O.P.*, 1953.

Laursen, Svend (D): "Production Functions and the Theory of International Trade," *A.E.R.*, 1952.

Lindahl, Erik (S): "The Concept of Income," *E.E.H.G.Cassel*, London, 1933.

——, Einar Dahlgren and Karin Koch: *National Income of Sweden 1861–1930*, Part One, London, 1937.

—— *Studies in the Theory of Money and Capital*, London, 1939.

—— "On the Keynesian Economic System," *Economic Record*, 1954.

Lundberg, Erik (S): *Studies in the Theory of Economic Expansion*, Stockholm and London, 1937.

Myrdal, Gunnar (S): *The Cost of Living in Sweden 1830–1930*, London, 1933.

—— *Monetary Equilibrium*, London, 1939.

—— "The Relation between Social Theory and Social Policy," *British Journal of Sociology*, 1953.

—— *The Political Element in the Development of Economic Theory*, London, 1953.

Myrvoll, Ole (N): "The Profit Motive and the Theory of Partial Equilibrium of the Firm," *N.T.T.Ø.*, 1948.

Nienstaedt, L. R. (D): "Economic Consequences of Technical Development," *Econometrica*, 1937.

—— *Economic Equilibrium and Natural Resources*, Bloomington, 1942.

Nyblén, Göran (S): *The Problem of Summation in Economic Science. A Methodological Study with Applications to Interest, Money and Cycles*, Lund, 1951.

Ohlin, Bertil (S): *Interregional and International Trade*, Cambridge, Mass., 1933.

—— "A Note on Price Theory with Special Reference to Interdependence and Time," *E.E.H.G.Cassel*, London, 1933.

—— "Some Notes on the Stockholm Theory of Savings and Investment," I and II, *E.J.*, 1937. Reprinted in *Readings in Business Cycle Theory*, Philadelphia and Toronto, 1944.

Ohlin, Bertil (S): *The Problem of Employment Stabilisation*, Columbia University Press, 1950.

Palander, Tord (S): "Concepts and Methods of the Stockholm School," *International Economic Papers*, London and New York, 1953.

Pedersen, Jørgen (D): "The Control of the Value of Money in a Free Economy," *N.T.T.Ø.*, 1948.

—— "Interest Rates, Employment and Changes in Population," *Kyklos*, 1948.

—— and O. Strange Petersen: *An Analysis of Price Behaviour*, København and London, 1938.

Petersen, O. Strange (D): See Jørgen Pedersen and O. Strange Petersen.

Petersen, Erling (N): "Some Aspects on the Equation of Exchange, especially in Relation to Replacement Rates," *Econometrica*, 1936.

—— *Macro-Dynamic Aspects of the Equation of Exchange*, Oslo, 1938.

Pfannenstill, Bertil (S): "Methods and Object in Sociology," *Theoria*, 1942.

—— "Positivism and Sociology. A Reply to Sven Ranulf," *Theoria*, 1942.

—— "Sociology and Natural Science. Reply to Svend Ranulf: Once more Positivism and Sociology," *Theoria*, 1943.

—— "Sociology, Positivism and Natural Science: A Last Reply to Svend Ranulf," *Theoria*, 1944.

Philip, Kjeld (D): "Structural Changes on the Labour Market and Mobility of the Wage Level," *International Economic Papers*, London and New York, 1952.

Pipping, Hugo E. (F): "The Concept Standard of Life," *E.E.H.G.Cassel*, London, 1933.

—— *Standard of Living. The Concept and its Place in Economics*, Helsingfors, 1953.

—— "Welfare and the State," *Unitas*, 1953.

Plessing, H. (D): "Some Examples of Growth Curves," *N.T.T.Ø.*, 1936.

Ranulf, Sven (D): "Two Types of Sociology," *Theoria*, 1940.

—— "Positivism and Sociology," *Theoria*, 1942.

—— "Once more Positivism and Sociology," *Theoria*, 1943.

—— "A Last Note on Positivism and Sociology," *Theoria*, 1944.

—— "Definitions in the Social Sciences," *Theoria*, 1947.

—— "Vinding Kruse's Philosophy," *Theoria*, 1948.

Rasmussen, Arne (D): "The Determination of Advertising Expenditure," *The Journal of Marketing*, 1952.

Rasmussen, P. Nørregaard (D): "Some Remarks on the Joint Effects of Simultaneous Relations between Economic Variables," *N.T.T.Ø.*, 1948.

—— *Studies in Intersectoral Relations*, North Holland Publishing Co., 1956.

Ross, Alf (D): "On the Logical Nature of Propositions of Value," *Theoria*, 1945.

Rübner-Petersen, K. (D): "The Error in the 'Fundamental Equations'. A New Interpretation," *A.E.R.*, 1934.

Segerstedt, Torgny T. (S): "Imperative Propositions and Judgements of Value," *Theoria*, 1945.

Sinding, Thomas (N): "Some Remarks on Objectivity and Subjectivity," *N.T.T.Ø.*, 1948.

Tegen,Einar (S): "The Basic Problem in the Theory of Value," *Theoria*, 1944.

Törnqvist, Leo (F): "On the Economic Theory of Lottery Gambles," *S.A.*, 1945.

Warming, Jens: "A Theory of Prices and Wages," *International Labour Review*, 1931.

Wicksell, Knut (S): *Lectures on Political Economy*, 1–2, London, 1935.

—— *Interest and Prices. A Study of the Causes regulating the Value of Money*, London, 1936.

—— "The Enigma of the Business Cycle," *International Economic Papers*, London and New York, 1953.

—— *Value, Capital and Rent*, London, 1954.

Wold, Herman (S): "A Synthesis of Pure Demand Analysis," *S.A.*, 1943 and 1944.

—— and R. Bentzel: "On Statistical Demand Analysis from the Viewpoint of Simultaneous Equations, *S.A.*," 1946.

—— "On Giffen's Paradox," *N.T.T.Ø.*, 1948.

—— with L. Jureen: *Demand Analysis. A Study in Econometrics*, Stockholm and New York, 1953.

—— "Ordinal Preferences or Cardinal Utility," (Additional notes by G. L. S. Shackle, L. J. Savage and H. Wold), *Econometrica*, 1952.

—— and E. Cansado: "Some Properties of Price-Consumption and Income-Consumption Curves, *Trabajos de Estadística*, 1950.

Zeuthen, F. (D): *Problems of Monopoly and Economic Warfare*, London, 1930.

—— "Public Price Policy," *E.E.H.G.Cassel*, London, 1933.

—— "Theoretical Remarks on Price Policy, Hotellings Case with Variations," *Q.J.E.*, 1933.

—— "Effect and Cost of Advertisement from a Theoretic Aspect," *N.T.T.Ø.*, 1935.

—— "Monopolistic Competition and the Homogeneity of the Market," *Econometrica*, 1936.

—— "On the Determinateness of the Utility Function," *R.E. Stud.*, 1936–7.

—— "A Note on Capital Values," *Metroeconomica*, 1949.

—— "Recent Development in Economics," *Q.J.E.*, 1954.

A survey of economic thought in northern countries is given by Hans Brems in "American Economic Review", Vol. XLVI, May 1956, 352–59.

NAME INDEX

Abramovitz, M., 141
Adelman, 321
Åkerman, J., 12, 21–2, 161, 217–19, 309
Åkerman, G., 151, 177
Allen, R. G. D., 93, 96
Alt, F., 93
Andersen, P. N., 206, 210
Armstrong, W. E., 99
Arrow, K. J., 46, 52
Aukrust, O., 192

Bain, J. S. F., 120, 235, 237, 266, 317, 323
Barfod, B., 66, 271, 279
Baumol, J. W., 166
Bentzel, R., 135, 161, 178, 219, 221
Bergson, A., 102, 344
Bernouilli, D., 99
Bilimovič, A., 13, 167
Birck, L. V., 4, 24, 35, 140, 300, 333
Bjerve, P., 192
Bohlin, H., 311
Böhm-Bawerk, E. von, 333
Bohr, H., 164
Böök, K., 171
Boulding, K. E., 102, 104, 128, 273
Bowley, A., 50, 285, 287
Bredt, 319
Brems, H., 118, 276, 311, 313, 321, 323
Burns, 303

Casper, 326
Cassel, G., 21–2, 35, 43, 49, 50, 54, 58, 70–2, 198, 215, 266, 344
Chabert, A., 159, 194
Chamberlin, E., 115–17, 228, 235, 245, 258, 266, 298, 321
Charnes, A., 197
Chenery, H. B., 112
Chipman, J., 197
Clark, J. M., 28, 93, 121, 168, 323
Clark, J. B., 141
Coase, R. H., 258, 343
Cooper, W. W., 197
Copeland, M. A., 257, 269
Cournot, A., 43, 245–8, 254, 258, 263, 266, 282–4, 287, 313, 325
Cowles, A., 171

Danø, S., 197, 212
Dean, J., 118
Debreu, G., 46, 52
Del Vecchio, G., 104

Derksen, J. B. D., 192
Dobb, M., 344
Dorfman, R., 197
Douglas, P. H., 134, 307
Dunlop, J. T., 285
Duesenberry, J. S., 93, 203

Edey, H. C., 192
Edgeworth, F. Y., 145, 287
Edwards, C. D., 323
Eitemann, W., 120
Elmers, G., 311
Epictetus, 6
Eucken, W., 217, 235
Evans, W. D., 194

Fellner, W., 207, 211, 213, 235, 258, 285, 287
Fielding, A., 14
Fisher, G., 117
Fisher, I., 134, 198, 245, 287
Fleming, 343
Fog, B., 19, 279, 298, 318, 321–3
Friedman, M., 9
Frisch, R., 17–18, 27, 29, 79, 93, 99, 104–5, 110, 128, 139–40, 148–9, 154, 173, 192, 194, 213, 220, 239, 248, 296, 298, 311, 340, 343–4

Galbraith, J. K., 235, 307, 314, 323
Gale, D., 197
Geiger, T., 15, 21, 229, 271
Gloerfelt-Tarp, B., 56, 66, 112
Gollnick, H., 108
Gorman, W. M., 102
Graaf, J. de V., 166
Grøn, A. H., 117
Guthrie, G., 120

Haavelmo, T., 108, 155, 167, 178, 219–20, 340
Haberler, G., 213
Haley, B. F., 120, 285, 303
Hall, R. L., 318
Hammarskjöld, D., 215
Hansen, B., 161, 178, 212, 219, 221
Harrod, R. F., 318, 321
Hart, A. G., 151', 166–7
Hawtrey, R. G., 173
Hayek, F. A., 163
Henderson, A., 197
Hennipmann, N. I., 298

355

SUBJECT INDEX

Abstraction, method of decreasing, 30–2, 77

Acceleration, principle of, 147–51, 175, 178

Accountancy, 151, 153, 157
see Book-keeping

Accounts
national, 39, 54, 58–63, 189–97
household, 92, 109, 191–2
and ex-post analysis, 170, 177

Advertising, 261, 268, 271–7, 301, 313, 329

Aggregates, 25–6, 29, 39, 40, 50, 54, 58–63, 72–7, 158–61, 189–99, 203, 221

Analytical statements, 7

Behaviour
autonomous, 239, 258, 266, 283, 287, 297, 325
conjectural, 239, 287
of firms, 239–40, 245, 248, 250, 259, 260–1, 283, 286, 299, 300, 305–11, 312–16, 323, 344
co-operation, 241, 247, 249, 260, 271, 305, 317
collective, 311–16
parameters of action, 239–40, 273, 296
strategy, 240
see Cartels
see Economic warfare
see Games, theory of

Behaviourism, 94–5, 169

Behaviourist school, 306, 309–10

Bilateral monopoly, *see* Monopoly

Black-markets, 338

Book-keeping, 26, 29, 39, 40, 60, 151, 195, 314

Business cycle, 80, 85, 142, 151, 173, 205–9, 213–16, 241, 300, 340
forecasting, 170

Buyers' preferences, 237, 243, 248, 268, 300

Calendar scale, 12, 219

Capital
demand equation for, 88
supply equation of, 87–8
supply function of, 129
kinds of, 86–7, 117, 126
quantity of, 85–8, 129, 134, 143–4, 152, 157, 208
investment of, 124–5

return on, 86, 124–5, 134, 328
and the rate of interest, 85–8, 129
and money, 86
and saving, 129
abstract, 127
money, 127
as a fund, 86, 129
growth of, 141
mobility of, 183, 328, 339
in static theory, 85–9
and static equilibrium, 85, 88
gains and losses, 188, 198

Capital values, trade in, 199–202
valuation curve, 200

Capitalization, *see* Revenue

Cartels, 241, 247, 297, 302–3, 311, 313, 316, 319, 321, 324, 330, 344

Causal analysis, 35, 51, 81, 98, 140, 153, 217–21
and "one-way relations", 80, 219–21
see Dynamics

Ceteris paribus, condition of, 24–5, 73–5, 92, 181, 235
see "isolation" method

Choice, theory of, 94–104

Circular flow, 50, 58–63, 151, 189–97

Classical theory, 31, 87, 130, 202–4, 209, 286, 305

Cobweb case, 178–81, 299

Commodities, nature of, 11, 25–6, 70–1, 227

Competition
free, static assumptions of, 31, 52, 96, 110, 121–3, 125, 131, 143, 156, 161, 178, 225, 231, 233, 237, 241, 250, 263, 265, 267–8, 272, 286, 296, 299, 303–4, 306–8, 317, 324–5, 229–30
latent, 234
limitation of, 186, 278, 314, 325
and monopoly, 227–9, 244
non-price, *see* Advertising
see Quality variation
see Price war
see Duopoly
see Oligopoly
see Monopolistic competition

Consumption, 44, 53, 62, 94, 133, 145, 174–5, 197–9, 205–6, 210–11, 220, 227–8, 253, 339, 344
substitution in, 50, 70, 94–9, 133
function, 91
velocity of, 149

358

DATE